MW01092796

# NOAH AND THE FLOOD IN WESTERN THOUGHT

In a world beset by climatic emergencies, the continuing resonance of the flood story is perhaps easy to understand. Whether in the tortured alpha male intensity of Russell Crowe's Noah, in Darren Aronofsky's eponymous 2014 film, or other recent derivations, the biblical narrative has become a lightning rod for gathering environmental anxieties. However, Philip C. Almond's masterful exploration of Western cultural history uncovers a far more complex Noah than is commonly recognised: not just the father of humanity but also the first shipbuilder, navigator, zookeeper, farmer, grape grower, and wine maker. Noah's pivotal significance is revealed as much in his forgotten secular as in his religious receptions, and their major impact on such disciplines as geology, geography, biology, and zoology. While Noah's many interpretations over two millennia might seem to offer a common message of hope, the author's sober conclusion is that deliverance now lies not in divine but rather in human hands.

PHILIP C. ALMOND is Emeritus Professor in the History of Religious Thought at The University of Queensland. A noted authority in the history of religion and of ideas, he has written many books on subjects as diverse as God, the Devil, the afterlife, witchcraft and witches, Adam and Eve, heaven and hell in Enlightenment England, and early modern demonic possession. His recent works include *The Buddha: Life and Afterlife Between East and West* (2024), *Mary Magdalene: A Cultural History* (2023), and *The Antichrist: A New Biography* (2020), all published by Cambridge University Press.

'Philip Almond is a world-leading authority on the history of religion and a highly versatile scholar. It is this versatility which makes him such a suitable choice for a subject as massive and multifarious as the reception history of Noachic themes in Western thought. There is nothing in the literature as broad-ranging and accessible as this book. It has the potential to become the established leader in the field, with a wide market and an enduring shelf life. There is a rich comprehensiveness in the book that is unrivalled in the scholarly literature. It ranges from the flood stories of antiquity, including the Gilgamesh legend, to the modern biblical theme park in Kentucky devoted to the Ark. Nor does Almond confine his exploration to the Christian understanding of Noah and the flood, but also includes substantial discussion of the story's exegesis in the rabbinical tradition and by Islamic interpreters. Moreover, the book broadens out beyond hermeneutics to explore the rela-tionship of the Noah story to a wider history of notionally secular disciplines – geography; proto-anthropology; demog-raphy broadly conceived, and the peopling of the world; zoology; geology; mythography; and even maritime technol-ogy. Philip Almond is a scholarly phenomenon, always arresting in the works I have read – as well as authoritative – and his latest book offers a compelling revisionist take on the conventional history of Western knowledge.'

Colin Kidd, Professor of History, University of
St Andrews, author *of The Forging of Races: Race and
Scripture in the Protestant Atlantic World, 1600–2000*

'Philip Almond's book seeks to demonstrate how a well-known biblical story – specifically the flood narrative in Genesis 6–9 with its main character Noah – has made and continues to make an impact upon Western ideas and thought, both religious and secular. It breaks new ground in charting the impact of the flood story in secular thinking. Its coverage of a wide range of literatures – in Christian, Jewish, and Islamic traditions of Noah – invites the reader to partake in the rich conversations, controversies, and debates among the many interpreters of the flood account. While there are resources available for Noah's reception history, this intriguing book goes further in arguing that the impact of the biblical narrative of the flood extends well beyond religious circles. It would make for a good sourcebook for students in religious studies and will be accessible too to readers interested in how Noah continues, in multiple contexts, to be an important figure in contemporary culture.'

Philip Yoo, Assistant Professor of Hebrew Bible and Jewish Studies, University of British Columbia, author of *Ezra and the Second Wilderness* and co-editor of *To Gaul, to Greece and into Noah's Ark*

# NOAH AND THE FLOOD IN WESTERN THOUGHT

Philip C. Almond

*The University of Queensland*

CAMBRIDGE
UNIVERSITY PRESS

Shaftesbury Road, Cambridge CB2 8EA, United Kingdom

One Liberty Plaza, 20th Floor, New York, NY 10006, USA

477 Williamstown Road, Port Melbourne, VIC 3207, Australia

314–321, 3rd Floor, Plot 3, Splendor Forum, Jasola District Centre,
New Delhi – 110025, India

103 Penang Road, #05–06/07, Visioncrest Commercial, Singapore 238467

Cambridge University Press is part of Cambridge University Press & Assessment,
a department of the University of Cambridge.

We share the University's mission to contribute to society through the pursuit of
education, learning and research at the highest international levels of excellence.

www.cambridge.org
Information on this title: www.cambridge.org/9781009557221

DOI: 10.1017/9781009557252

First published 2025

Printed in the United Kingdom by TJ Books Limited, Padstow Cornwall, 2025

*A catalogue record for this publication is available from the British Library*

*Library of Congress Cataloging-in-Publication Data*
NAMES: Almond, Philip C., author.
TITLE: Noah and the flood in Western thought / Philip C. Almond, The University
of Queensland.
DESCRIPTION: Cambridge, United Kingdom ; New York, NY, USA : Cambridge
University Press, 2025. | Includes bibliographical references and index.
IDENTIFIERS: LCCN 2024041956 (print) | LCCN 2024041957 (ebook) |
ISBN 9781009557221 (hardback) | ISBN 9781009557238 (paperback) |
ISBN 9781009557252 (epub)
SUBJECTS: LCSH: Noah (Biblical figure) | Floods–Religious aspects. |
Deluge–History of doctrines. | Bible. Genesis, VI–IX–Influence.
CLASSIFICATION: LCC BS580.N6 A64 2025 (print) | LCC BS580.N6 (ebook) |
DDC 222/.1109505–dc23/eng/20241021
LC record available at https://lccn.loc.gov/2024041956
LC ebook record available at https://lccn.loc.gov/2024041957

ISBN 978-1-009-55722-1 Hardback

To Alex

# CONTENTS

*The plates can be found between pages 210 and 211.*

# PLATES

8 *Story of Noah: Noah sending the Raven and the first Dove.* Detail of Interior Mosaics in the St. Mark's Basilica. Eleventh century. Credit: © Fine Art Images/ Heritage Images. Heritage Image Partnership Ltd/ Alamy Stock Photo.

9 *Noah's Ark, from the Nuremberg Bible.* Coloured woodcut. German School. Fifteenth century. Credit: Private Collection. The Stapleton Collection/ Bridgeman Images.

10 *Prophet Noah and the Ark.* Ottoman miniature, manuscript. Turkey. Sixteenth century. Credit: Museum of Turkish and Islamic Art, Istanbul, TurkeyG. Dagli Orti /© NPL – DeA Picture Library/Bridgeman Images.

11 *Johannes Buteo's (c.1485–c.1560) ark designs.* From Johannes Buteo, *Opera Geometrica* (1559). ECHO – Cultural Heritage Online. Detail by author.

12 *Fragments of English Shipwrightry.* Mathew Baker (c.1530–1613). (Pepys Library, PL 2820, p.1). By permission of the Pepys Library, Magdalene College, Cambridge.

13 *France: The Building of the Tower of Babel.* Folio 17v. The Bedford Hours. Paris, c. 1420. Credit: Pictures from History/Bridgeman Images.

14 *English: Jacob Bryant's Moon-ark.* William Blake (1757–1827). Credit: The Picture Art Collection/ Alamy Stock Photo.

15 *A Map of Earth and how after the Flood it was divided among the Sons of Noah.* Joseph Moxon (1627–1691). Credit: EMU history / Alamy Stock Photo.

16 *Isidore of Seville, Liber Etymologiarum, fol. 177v.* T-in-O map, with letterpress place names. Woodcut.

German School. Fifteenth century. Credit: Newberry
Library, Chicago, Illinois, USA© Newberry Library/
Bridgeman Images.

17 *The Scorn of Ham.* Bernardino Luini (c. 1480–1532).
Painted 1510–1515. Oil on board. Credit: Pinacoteca
di Brera, Milan, Italy © Pinacoteca di Brera, Milan/
With permission of the Italian Ministry of Culture/
Bridgeman Images.

18 *The Curse of Ham.* Ivan Stepanovich Ksenofontov
(1817–1875). Oil on canvas. Credit: Bridgeman
Images.

19 *Shem's Wife Ar'yel in the Kitchen of the Ark* (2017). The
Ark Encounter. Williamstown, Kentucky. Credit: Jim
West / Alamy Stock Photo.

# ACKNOWLEDGEMENTS

This book was written at the University of Queensland in Australia. I have been fortunate to have been able to call this institution my academic home for over forty years. For the last eighteen years, The Centre for the History of European Discourses and its successor, The Institute for Advanced Studies in the Humanities, have provided a congenial, stimulating, and, more often than one can hope to expect, exciting context in which to work. For me, this has been and remains the collegium of scholars at its best. For this I am indebted in particular to my friends and colleagues, Emeritus Professor Peter Harrison and Emeritus Professor Peter Cryle. We have been colleagues for the better part of forty years, and I appreciate their friendship and support. They have both given of their time to talk with me on numerous occasions.

I am also especially grateful to my long-term friend and colleague, Emeritus Professor Fred D'Agostino. He has read this work section by section as it progressed and provided many valuable comments. All my emeriti colleagues and I look with pride at the younger generation of scholars who have passed through the Centre and the Institute. We hope to have had as beneficial and lasting an influence upon them as they have had upon us.

A wide-ranging book such as this is inevitably indebted to those scholars who have previously done the hard yards in this intellectual domain. As a result, this is a genuinely collegiate and collaborative work. Without their often groundbreaking research, this book would not have been possible. There are too many to mention here, although I have expressed my debt of gratitude to many of them in the course of this study. That said, I am indebted to the groundbreaking work of Don Cameron Allen in his *The Legend of Noah* (1963). He showed the enormous richness of the tradition of Noah in the Renaissance. But I am especially grateful to Norman Cohn and his *Noah's Flood: The Genesis Story in Western Thought*. I purchased this delightful book when it was first published in 1996. Both erudite and entertaining, it awakened my interest in the story of Noah, and it sits before me as I write this. I hope that this volume is a worthy successor to it.

I take the opportunity once again to thank Alex Wright, my editor at Cambridge University Press, for his support and encouragement of this work. We have worked together on twelve books over the last thirty-seven years, leading us both to wonder where the years have gone. I am grateful for his friendship. This book is dedicated to him. I am also indebted to my partner, Patricia Lee. She has listened yet again day-by-day to this text as it progressed and has offered much helpful advice.

# ABBREVIATIONS

**ANF**

Robert, Alexander and James Donaldson (eds.), *Anti-Nicene Fathers* (Peabody, MA: Hendrickson Publishers, 2004).

**NPNF (First Series)**

Schaff, Philip (ed.), *Nicene and Post-Nicene Fathers (First Series)* (Peabody, MA: Hendrickson Publishers, 2012).

**NPNF (Second Series)**

Schaff, Philip (ed.), *Nicene and Post-Nicene Fathers (Second Series)* (Peabody, MA: Hendrickson Publishers, 2012).

**PL**

Migne, J. P. (ed.), *Patrologia cursus completus, series Latina* (Paris, 1844–1864).

# PROLOGUE

~

This book tells the story of the cultural and intellectual history of Noah in Western thought from its beginnings in the Mesopotamian, Biblical, Greek, and Latin traditions to the present. The story of Noah and the flood remains one of the best-known stories within Western culture and, next to the story of Adam and Eve in the Garden of Eden, the most popular of the stories of the beginnings of human civilisation.

In just four chapters of the first book of the Bible, the book of Genesis, we are told the story of God's decision to destroy life on earth through a cataclysmic flood due to the wickedness of humanity. Except for Noah and his family, who found refuge in a ship that Noah built, all life on earth was destroyed. Thus, after the flood, Noah became the father of all humanity – the new Adam. As such, he was to become a key figure not only in Christianity but also in Rabbinic Judaism and Islam.

The historical and spiritual meaning of Noah and the ark aside, the story itself is charming, entrancing, and more than a little frightening. At God's direction, Noah builds an ark. He assembles two of every kind of animal on the earth and cares for them on the ark. The vulnerable ship is pounded and battered for a year by a deluge that destroys all remaining life on earth. Only Noah, his family, and the animals on board survive the flood. The earth is replenished by the surviving people and animals.

The central meaning of the story of Noah and the flood was a clear one to all its Christian, Jewish, and Muslim readers – all living things were destroyed by a universal deluge caused by human wickedness. That is a story of particular relevance to the modern world as it increasingly faces climate change and its attendant cataclysmic events.

The importance of Noah as the founder of humanity after the flood within Christianity, Judaism, and Islam has been much underplayed within modern cultural and intellectual history. The overall aim of this book is to show the significance of the role that Noah played in Western thought. It demonstrates how Noah is a pivotal figure in the history of Western *religious* thought as the parent of a new humanity after the flood and as the transmitter of the ancient knowledge of nature (terrestrial and celestial) that had come down from Adam.

But it also shows how the story of Noah, the flood, and its aftermath had a highly important and much forgotten role, from the seventeenth to the twentieth centuries, in the development of *secular* thought in an array of modern scholarly disciplines – biology, geology, geography, anthropology, demography, zoology, mythography, religious studies, and even naval engineering. He was, after all, the father of all humanity, the first shipbuilder, the first navigator, the first zookeeper, and the first farmer. He was also the first grape grower and wine maker, although that, as we will see, didn't turn out quite so well.

Since the beginning of the common era, the history of the story of Noah has been the history of the attempts to create a coherent narrative from the Biblical story by adding to or subtracting from it, by ironing out its contradictions and incoherencies, and by making its story historically credible, consistent with science, culturally relevant, and theologically acceptable. Learning, piety, and imagination have all been brought to bear on the Biblical (and later the Qur'anic) text to inform or persuade its readers, from an array of religions, societies, and cultures over the past twenty centuries, of its truth, its value, and its possible relevance to their lives.

Thus, there are many meanings to the story of Noah to be found within the history of the attempts to interpret it. This book explores those many meanings chronologically, beginning with the Biblical account in the book of Genesis and continuing up to the present time. The first three chapters of the work deal with how the story of Noah was appropriated within the Christian, Jewish, and Islamic traditions up to the end of the first millennium. The remaining four chapters examine how the story of Noah and the flood played a significant role in the formation of the modern West from the late medieval period through to the present time.

Chapter 1 sets the scene for the remainder of the work with a detailed account of the flood traditions of the ancient world. It begins with the story of Noah and the flood as it occurs in the book of Genesis. It then traces the origin of the Biblical story in the Babylonian *Epic of Gilgamesh* (thirteenth–twelfth centuries BCE) and the Babylonian Noah Uta-napishti. It then outlines how these flood traditions were appropriated within the early Jewish and Christian traditions. This is followed by an account of Greek and Roman Flood stories and how they were seen within the ancient world in relation to the Biblical and Mesopotamian traditions. Consideration is also given to Noah as 'the man of righteousness' in the New

Testament, his role in the Jewish *Sybilline Oracles* (early first century BCE), and in the literature between the Old and New Testaments.

With the ancient flood stories outlined in Chapter 1, the overarching theme of Chapter 2 is an account of the elaborations of the flood story in Hellenistic Judaism with particular attention paid to the story of Noah by the Jewish writers Josephus and Philo. They were both writing for Greek-educated Jewish audiences. But where Josephus wrote 'history' for a Greek-educated Jewish audience, Philo focused on the philosophical meaning of the narrative – constructing Noah as an ancient virtuous Stoic sage who was able to overcome the passions and desires that the flood represented.

Josephus and Philo were both committed to the truth of the Biblical texts, whether as literal history in the case of Josephus or allegorical philosophy in that of Philo. But there was another group of interpreters in the second to fourth centuries CE, whom we generally gather under the broad title of 'Gnostics'. This chapter also explores the variety of ways in which the story of Noah and the flood was radically converted into various stories about the primeval Gnostic Noah's battle against the spiritual forces of evil in the highest places.

In contrast to the Gnostics who inverted or subverted the literal or historical meaning of the Biblical text, the early Christians were committed to it, despite their recognition of its inconsistencies and incoherencies. But, like the Gnostics, they gave it a radically new meaning as they sought the 'spiritual' meaning of the Noah story behind the literal or historical meaning – vertically, in terms of the heavenly realities to which the text pointed, and horizontally, in terms of the events in the life of Christ and the church that were prefigured in the text. This section of Chapter 2 explores the many allegorical and prototypical readings of the Noah story that dominated Christian readings for the first millennium.

The chapter ends with a discussion of Hugh of St. Victor's (1096–1141) *De Arca Noe Morali*. It is argued that his account of the ark is an early sign of the increasing emphasis for the next five hundred years within the Christian tradition on the literal and historical meaning of the story of Noah, as the Christian interpreters used the Biblical story to direct, fashion, and sharpen their own questions about the natural and human worlds.

Chapter 3 begins by exploring the interpretations of the story of Noah in the traditions of Rabbinic Judaism from the third century CE onwards to the end of the first millennium. It demonstrates how the rabbinic interpretations of the story of Noah took precedence over the Biblical account as the rabbis engaged with paganism, Christianity, Gnosticism, and Islam, adapting their reading of the Hebrew Scriptures to the cultures that surrounded them while they told and retold the Scriptures.

This chapter then turns to Islamic readings of the flood. As in the Christian and Judaic traditions, the story of Noah and the flood in the Islamic tradition is also the story of the Muslim interpreters of it. And just as the Christian and Judaic interpretations of Noah and the flood drew upon the story in the book of Genesis, this chapter demonstrates how the Noah story in the Qur'an, derived from the Biblical one, remained the bedrock of Islamic readings. And, like Christian and Jewish interpreters, where the Islamic commentators found gaps in the Qur'anic account, they filled them in. Where they found difficulties, they clarified them, sometimes by drawing from the details in the Genesis story and in the rabbinic tradition. And they embellished and elaborated the Qur'anic story of Noah with legends that were told on street corners and in mosques within the earliest Islamic communities.

Chapter 4 explores the turn within Western thought about the story of Noah towards its historical meaning. On the one hand, there was an increasingly clear sense within the Catholic tradition that, at the least, the literal meaning had to be discerned before any other meaning could be built upon it. On the other hand, Protestant readings from the sixteenth century onwards, in accord with the Protestant commitment to 'scripture alone', were decisively literal and historical in their orientation.

Crucially, the production of new 'knowledges' in the secular arts and sciences during the late medieval and early modern periods could not but generate critical reflection on the most important 'knowledge' of all, namely the one contained within the Bible. In so doing, the importance of the literal and historical meanings of the Bible, now read through knowledges created outside of it, not only reinforced the importance of the literal meaning but created radically new literal and historical readings.

Thus, this chapter explores late medieval and early modern discussions on the size and shape of the ark, what animals were on the ark, and how the ark could feed and house them all. It details the role of the ark in the early modern classifications of animals, the relation of the shape of the ark to contemporary shipbuilding; the problem created for the ark by the discoveries of animals in the New World; the story of the dispersal of Noah and his

descendants to Europe, Africa, and Asia; and the connection of the Indians of America to Noah and his family.

Chapter 5 focuses on the relationship between the story
of Noah and the New Science. It begins with the contemporary discussions about the date of the flood and the
calculations about the numbers of people from the time
of the flood to the present. It continues with the late
seventeenth-century debate about the universality of the
flood and the origin of the present seas, rocks, and mountains, culminating in Thomas Burnet's *The Sacred Theory
of the Earth* and William Whiston's *New Theory of the
Earth* on the role of comets in the flood of Noah.

The issue of the date of the flood leads also to the
problem of fossils and their relation to the flood of
Noah, with particular attention to John Woodward's *An
Essay Towards a Natural History of the Earth* and the debate
initiated by it. The chapter concludes with a discussion of
how the shifting time scales on the age of the earth during
the eighteenth century cast doubt upon the role in the
formation of the earth that had traditionally been ascribed
to the flood, along with attempts to harmonise the Biblical
story with the new age of the earth.

Chapter 6 deals with the question of how the story of
Noah begins to leave the world of history to enter the world
of myth and legend. It begins with a discussion of Noah and
his family within the developing field in the eighteenth
century of comparative mythography. Particular attention
is paid to the idea of Noah and his family as the origin of *all*
religions in the works of Jacob Bryant. The chapter also
continues the discussion from Chapter 5 on the populating
of the earth after the flood with an account of the role of
Noah and his sons in the development of 'race science' in

the eighteenth and nineteenth centuries, followed by a discussion of 'the curse of Ham'.

Chapter 7 begins with a consideration of the beginnings of source criticism of the first five books of the Bible and the discovery of *The Epic of Gilgamesh* that cast doubt, as a result, on the historical and literal truth of the Genesis text. This chapter also takes up the development of 'creation science' as a means of shifting the debate on evolution versus the Bible to one of evolution versus 'creation science' and the role of Noah and the story of the flood in this transition.

We will also see how the belief in Biblical inerrancy leads to the modern conservative Christian quest to find the lost ark and, in the absence of that discovery, to recreate the ark this century in the US state of Kentucky. It shows how the 'Ark Encounter' in Kentucky creates a new legend of Noah, one based on the Biblical story but reflecting creation science and incorporating a back story from a three-volume fictional account of the life of Noah before the flood – *The Remnant Trilogy*.

The narrative developed around the Kentucky Ark perfectly demonstrates how the history around the interpretation of Noah and the flood cannot but reflect the cultural context within which it is created, even though it is derived from the Biblical story. In short, the Kentucky ark perfectly exemplifies the theme of this book – that the meaning of the story of Noah from the earliest times to the present is the history of its many cultural interpretations.

Taking its lead from Darren Aronofsky's film *Noah*, the Epilogue suggests how the legend of Noah and the flood has greater relevance in the present moment than any other legend in Western thought.

# I

# Ancient Floods and Heroes

∼

## Biblical Beginnings

According to the Book of Genesis, the first book in the Bible, the earth and all living things on it were destroyed by a flood 1,656 years after its creation.[1] There was a notable exception to this universal destruction – Noah, and those that went with him into the ark. At the time of the flood, Noah was said to be 600 years old.

By the time of the flood, ten generations had passed since God had created Adam and Eve and had driven them out of the Garden of Eden for their disobedience. Noah was the direct descendant of Adam and Eve through their son Seth, third born after Cain and Abel. He was the son of Lamech who named him Noah saying, 'Out of the ground that the Lord has cursed this one shall bring us relief from our work and from the toil of our hands' (Genesis 5.29). The descendants of Adam were remembered mostly for their longevity. Lamech was 182 years of age when Noah was born. Methuselah lived the longest of all – some 969 years. Almost immortal, but not quite. He beat the next longest-lived – Jared – by

---

[1] There are variations on the length of this period between the Hebrew story and the Greek account in the Septuagint. Modern translations follow the Hebrew. The figure is calculated by adding together the ages of the patriarchs at the time of the birth of their key descendants (Genesis 5.1–32) and adding Noah's age in the year of the flood.

seven years and Noah by nineteen. No one in the Bible was ever again to live as long as Methuselah.

The shortest-lived was Jared's son Enoch. He survived on this earth only for some 365 years, 530 less than the next most short-lived. The shortness of his life was perhaps mitigated by the fact that the text suggests that, rather than dying, 'God took him' (Genesis 5.24). This was the source of the tradition in Judaism and Christianity that Enoch, like Elijah, had ascended into Heaven without dying. Life before Noah was long, and men were potent in those days. Noah was more than 500 years old when he became the father of Shem, Ham, and Japheth. As we will see, this longevity was not to last much beyond Noah.

Why did God decide to destroy that which, 1,656 years before, he had created and concluded that 'indeed, it was very good' (Genesis 1.31)? Tucked away between the story of the disobedience of Adam and Eve, their expulsion from the Garden of Eden, the story of the murder of Abel by Adam's other son Cain, and God's decision to destroy it all and start over is the strange story of the sons of God and the daughters of men. Within the century before the flood, we read, 'When people began to multiply on the face of the ground, and daughters were born to them, the sons of God saw that they were fair; and they took wives for themselves of all that they chose. Then the Lord said, "My spirit shall not abide in mortals forever, for they are flesh; their days shall be one hundred and twenty years." The Nephilim [the giants] were on the earth in those days – and also afterwards – when the sons of God went into the daughters of men, who bore children to them' (Genesis 6.1–4a).

In later Jewish and early Christian traditions, these verses were elaborated into a complex account of the origin of evil in the world as the result of the lust of God's angels for the daughters of men. Along with this went the fall of the angels from God's heavenly council and the populating of the world with demons and evil spirits. But in its original context, the story of the mating of the sons of God with the daughters of men, and the hint that the giants were their offspring, was intended as one that explained the reduction of the original longevity of human beings as a divine punishment for this commingling of the sons of God with the daughters of men.

The verses that followed the story of the sons of God mating with the daughters of men and producing offspring suggest that it was, for God, the last straw: 'The Lord saw,' we read, 'that the wickedness of humankind was great in the earth, and that every inclination of the thoughts of their hearts was only evil continually. And the Lord was sorry that he had made humankind upon the earth, and it grieved him to his heart' (Genesis 6.5–6). Where before God looked and saw that it was very good, now he saw 'that the earth was corrupt; for all flesh had corrupted its ways upon the earth' (Genesis 6.12). So, God decided, then and there, to destroy all humankind along with animals, creeping things, and the birds of the air (see Plate 1).

The humans that were to be destroyed were, for all intents and purposes, totally depraved, being made up of the descendants of Cain. With the exception of Noah and his sons, the descendants of Adam via his son Seth were already dead, Methuselah being the last of these. Methuselah died in the year 1656 after the creation, the same year as the flood. The descendants of Cain, who had murdered his brother Abel, were to be destroyed, along with the giants, the descendants of the sons of God. Later traditions held that, among the misdeeds of the Nephilim (the giants), were cannibalism, sexual promiscuity, bestiality, and the drinking of blood. But they also taught men the arts of warfare and told women about cosmetics, adornments, and astrology. The only exception to the destruction of all was Noah, his family, and the creatures that he would take into the ark. 'I have determined,' God said to Noah, 'to make an end of all flesh, for the earth is filled with violence because of them; now I am going to destroy them along with the earth' (Genesis 6.13). All in all, nothing was ever to be the same again.

Before the flood at least, Noah was a righteous man who 'walked with God' (Genesis 6.9). So, God decided to spare him and his nearest and dearest. God told him to build an ark and gave him detailed instructions how to do so. We can only assume that they were clear to Noah, for they are anything but clear to us. But we can probably say something like this. God told Noah to build an ark of 'cypress' (or planks of cypress), to make rooms in the ark (or cover the ark with reeds), and to cover it inside and out with pitch (see Plate 2). The ark was to be three hundred cubits long, fifty cubits wide, and thirty cubits high. It was to be covered by a roof finished 'to a cubit above' (or with an overhang of one cubit).[2] How big was the ark? Well,

---

[2]  For the bracketed details, see Joseph Blenkinsopp, *Creation, Un-creation, Re-creation: A Discursive Commentary on Genesis 1-11* (London: T. & T. Clark International, 2011), pp. 137–138. I am indebted to Blenkinsopp for this account.

uncertainty about the length of a cubit makes it difficult to determine. But we can probably say that a cubit was about 18 inches. In this case, the ark would be 450 feet long (137 metres), 75 feet wide (23 metres), and 37.5 feet in height (11.5 metres) – roughly half the length and two-thirds the width of a modern cruise liner.

God then announced for the first time how he was going to destroy the earth. It was to be death by drowning for everyone and everything – 'I am going to bring a flood of waters onto the earth, to destroy from under heaven all flesh in which is the breath of life; everything that is on the earth shall die' (Genesis 6.17). But Noah was to take his wife, his sons, and their wives, eight of them in all, into the ark with him. And along with his family, God instructed Noah to take two of every kind of living creature, a male and a female, animals, birds, and creeping things (see Plate 3). He was also told to take with him seven pairs of all clean animals and a pair of unclean animals, together with seven pairs of birds, male and female in each of these cases.[3] So as to keep them all alive, Noah was instructed to take sufficient food for all. The vegetarianism that was put in place at the time of creation was still the rule (Genesis 1.29–30), so no animals needed to be taken onto the ark to serve as food for others. Only after the flood was the mandatory vegetarian diet overturned (Genesis 9.2–4).

So, Noah built the ark and took his family and two of all living things into it. God shut the door behind them. The

---

[3] These two different lists of animals are the result of the Genesis story including two different sources for its story of Noah and the flood. See Chapter 7.

rains began when Noah was five hundred years old on the seventeenth day of the second month (see Plate 4).

On that day, 'all the fountains of the great deep burst forth, and the windows of the heavens were opened' (Genesis 7.11). In this case, God, as it were, reverse engineered his original process of creation. In the first chapter of Genesis, there was originally nothing but a watery chaos. In the middle of the waters God created a solid dome (a 'firmament') that separated the waters under and inside the dome from those that were above and outside of the dome. The dome was called the sky. God then gathered the waters that were under the dome in one place. These he called the seas. This allowed dry land to appear that he called the earth. Beneath the earth there remained the abyss or the deep. Now, as the flood began, the fountains from the deep beneath the earth burst upwards and the windows in the firmament above were opened. The waters poured up from below and down from above. It was a return to the chaos that was before the creation.

The deluge continued for many days:

> [A]nd the waters increased, and bore up the ark, and it rose high above the earth. The waters swelled and increased greatly on the earth; and the ark floated on the face of the waters. The waters swelled so mightily on the earth that all the high mountains under the whole heaven were covered; the waters swelled above the mountains, covering them fifteen cubits deep. And all flesh died that moved on the earth, birds, domestic animals, wild animals, all swarming creatures that swarm on the earth, and all human beings; everything on dry land in whose nostrils was the breath of life died. He blotted out every

living thing that was on the face of the ground, human beings and animals and creeping things and birds of the air; they were blotted out from the earth. Only Noah was left, and those that were with him in the ark. And the waters swelled on the earth for one hundred fifty days.

(Genesis 7.17b–24)[4]

In the middle of this turmoil, God remembered Noah and all who were with him. As a wind swept across the waters on the first day of creation (Genesis 1.2), so too here, God made a wind blow over the earth. The fountains of the deep and the windows of the heavens were closed, the rains stopped, and the waters gradually receded from the earth. On the seventeenth day of the seventh month, the ark came to rest on the mountains of Ararat. By the first day of the tenth month, the tops of the mountains had appeared.

Forty days later, Noah opened the window of the ark and sent out a raven. It flew to and fro until the waters dried up. But we can assume that it didn't return to the ark. For Noah then sent out a dove to see if the waters had subsided from the land. But the dove too found no place to rest and returned to the ark. Seven days later, Noah again sent out the dove. It came back to him that evening with a freshly plucked olive leaf in its mouth. Noah then knew that the waters had begun to subside from the earth. He waited another seven days. The dove was again sent out and, this time, did not return to him (see Plate 5). So, Noah knew that the earth was dry.

---

[4] Genesis 7.17a, a different source to 7.24, has the flood lasting for only forty days. According to this source, Noah will open the window in the ark at the end of the forty days (Genesis 8.6).

God told Noah to leave the ark with his family – his wife, his sons, and their wives – and to take out with him every living thing that had been with him in the ark 'so that they might abound on the earth, and be fruitful and multiply on the earth' (Genesis 8.17). Noah's three sons were to be the originators of a new humanity (see Plate 6).

Then Noah built an altar to God, the first altar recorded in the Bible, and took one of every clean animal and one of every clean bird and sacrificed them on the altar. God smelled the odour from the sacrifice and was appeased by it. Although he recognised the evil inherent within the hearts of humankind, he determined that he would never again curse the ground because of humankind, nor would he ever again destroy every living creature: 'As long as the earth endures, seedtime and harvest, cold and heat, summer and winter, day and night, shall not cease' (Genesis 8.22). A new world had begun.

But it was a damaged world after the flood. Noah and his descendants had a different relationship with the natural realm. Humans and animals would no longer exist in the harmony of the original creation: 'The fear and dread of you shall rest on every animal of the earth, and on every bird of the air, on everything that creeps on the ground, and on all the fish of the sea' (Genesis 9.2). The fear and dread of the animal realm was occasioned, no doubt, by the end of the vegetarianism of the first creation. Now, 'Every moving thing that lives shall be meat for you' (Genesis 9.3). The only prohibition was eating meat with the blood still within it. This taboo was also connected to murder. Both animals and humans would now be held to account for the taking of human life. To do so was to efface the image of God in man. Thus, 'Whoever sheds the blood of a human, by a human shall that person's blood be shed' (Genesis 9.6). This was an early statement of the equitable principle, 'An eye for an eye and a tooth for a tooth.' It was a new creation, but only partly so. Humanity no longer had the innocence of Adam at the time of his creation. God recognised that 'the inclination of the human heart is evil from youth' (Genesis 8.21). Nevertheless, God now established a covenant with Noah, his sons, and all living creatures that he would never again destroy all life by a flood. The rainbow became the sign of that agreement.

Noah became the first man to plant a vineyard. And the first to become drunk. Righteous he may have been but, like Adam, he was brought undone by eating (or drinking) the fruit of a plant. In both cases, nakedness is involved, and shame follows. Lying unconscious and naked in his tent, he was seen by his son Ham who told his brothers Shem and Japheth. They took a garment and, laying it on both their shoulders, walked backwards and covered their father with it. When Noah awoke, realising that his son Ham had seen him naked, he cursed Canaan, Ham's son. The curse on Canaan provided a pretext for the later conquest of the abominable Canaanites, the descendants of Canaan, by the Israelites, the descendants of Shem via Abraham. Canaan was to be the 'lowest of slaves' to his brothers (Genesis 9.25). More generally, Ham's seeing his father drunk and naked was later to provide Biblical justification for the institution of slavery, for all those who were enslaved were the sons of Ham.

After the flood, Noah lived another three hundred and fifty years. Six hundred years old at the time of the flood, he died at the age of nine hundred and fifty.

The story of the flood in the Greek version of the Old Testament, the Septuagint (third–second century BCE), has minor variations to that of the Hebrew version, mainly about the timing of events. Thus, where the Hebrew has the rain beginning on the seventeenth day of the second month, the Greek has it on the twenty-seventh day of that month. According to the Hebrew, the ark came to rest on the seventeenth day of the seventh month. The Greek has the ark coming to rest on the twenty-seventh day of that month. In the Hebrew version, the tops of the mountains are visible on the first day of the tenth month. By contrast, in the Septuagint, the mountains appear on the first day of the eleventh month.

The Christian Latin version of the Bible, the Vulgate (late fourth century CE), has slightly different dates again. The Vulgate agrees with the Hebrew version that the rain began on the seventeenth day of the second month. But it agrees with the Septuagint that the ark rested on the twenty-seventh day of the seventh month. While the Hebrew and Greek versions have the ark resting on Ararat, the Vulgate has the ark coming to rest on the mountains of Armenia. Whichever mountains it may have been, the Vulgate agrees with the Hebrew version, against the Greek, that the mountains were visible on the first day of the tenth month.

The story as outlined above follows the modern English versions, themselves translations of the original Hebrew text. There is general agreement that the Hebrew version of the book of Genesis received its current form around the year 500 BCE, sometime after the Jews had returned to their homeland from their exile in Babylon. The destruction of the world and the salvation of the virtuous Noah spoke eloquently to a generation recently returned to Judah from Babylon. For them, it was a story of new beginnings. And the Jews returning from exile saw themselves, like Noah and his family, as a righteous remnant that remained after the disaster of the conquest of Judah, the fall of Jerusalem, the destruction of the Jewish temple, and their deportation to Babylon in c.598 BCE.

We will deal in a later chapter with the possibility that two different versions of the story of the flood are combined in the Genesis text. For the moment, however, we can note that the Biblical story of Noah and the flood was not the only one. More than three hundred accounts of destructive floods can be found on every continent except Antarctica. And in many of these, as in the story of Noah, it is more than merely destructive. As Brian B. Schmidt puts it, 'In sundry traditions, the flood manifests a re-creative act, a new beginning for humanity. Where the gods seek to exterminate the existing generation by means of a flood, a miniscule remnant survive to become the founders of a new world order.'[5]

## Mesopotamian Traditions

The story of Noah was not the only flood legend to come from the Ancient Near East. The flood story most like the

---

[5] Brian B. Schmidt, 'Flood Narratives of Ancient Western Asia,' in Jack M. Sasson et al. (eds.), *Civilizations of the Ancient Near East* (Peabody, MA: Hendrickson, 1995), vol. 4, p. 2337. On non-ancient Near Eastern flood accounts, see Bernhard Lang, 'Non-Semitic Deluge Stories and the Book of Genesis: A Bibliographical and Critical Survey,' *Anthropos* 80 (1985), pp. 605–616.

Biblical account occurred in Tablet 11 of the Babylonian *The Epic of Gilgamesh* (thirteenth–twelfth century BCE). This text told the story of a mighty king of Uruk, Gilgamesh, who suffered a crisis when his friend Enkidu died: 'My friend, whom I loved, has turned to clay... [Shall] I not be like him and also lie down, never to rise again, through all eternity?'[6] He travelled to find Uta-napishti to whom the gods had given eternal life to see if he would tell him how he had found eternal life. In response to this, Uta-napishti told him the story of the flood.

The gods, said Uta-napishti, once lived in the town of Shuruppak that stands on the banks of the river Euphrates. The gods – Anu the father of the gods, Enlil the god of storms, Ninurta the god of war and farming, Ennugi the god of irrigation, and Ea the god of wisdom and magic – met in a secret council and decided to send down a great flood. In contrast to the Biblical account in which God decided to destroy everything because of human wickedness, here the divine decision to destroy the world was quite arbitrary.

The gods had been sworn to secrecy. But the god Ea betrayed their plans to Uta-napishti in a dream. The reason why Uta-napishti was to be saved is not clear, although it is probably the result of his being a worshipper of Ea. Uta-napishti was told to build a boat. Its length and breadth were to be the same. It was to be one acre square and ten rods or 110 cubits high, covered with a roof.

---

[6] *Epic of Gilgamesh*, 10.245-8, in Christopher B. Hays (ed.), *Hidden Riches: A Sourcebook for the Comparative Study of the Hebrew Bible and Ancient Near East* (Louisville, KY: Westminster John Knox Press, 2014), p. 76.

It was to have six decks divided into nine compartments. He was to take on board 'all living things' seed,'[7] together with his gold and silver, his animals, his family, 'the beasts of the field, the creatures of the wild, and members of every skill and craft'.[8] When the boat was completed, with the weather turning threatening, Uta-napishti entered the boat and sealed the hatch.

The next morning, the storm arrived. It was so violent that 'even the gods took fright at the Deluge ... and went up to the heaven of Anu, lying like dogs curled up in the open'.[9] Belet-ili the fertility goddess wept at the destruction of those she had helped create. The Anunnaki gods, wet faced in their sorrow, wept with her. For six days and seven nights, the storm continued. But on the seventh day, the wind died down, the ocean grew calm, and the deluge stopped. When Uta-napishti saw that everyone had been destroyed, 'down sat I, I knelt and I wept'.[10]

The ark eventually ran aground on the mountain of Nimush (in what is now Northern Kurdistan). On the seventh day after its grounding, Uta-napishti brought out a dove and released it. But when it found no place to land, it returned. Then he brought out a swallow and let it go. The swallow returned too, having found nowhere to land. Then Uta-napishti released a raven that found food and did not return.

Having disembarked from the boat, Uta-napishti made a sacrifice on the top of the mountain to the gods. Just as God had smelt the pleasing odour of the sacrifice of Noah, so the gods smelt the offering of Uta-napishti

[7] *Ibid.*, 11.27, p. 77.  [8] *Ibid.*, 11.86-7, p. 78.
[9] *Ibid.*, 11.114-6, p. 79.  [10] *Ibid.*, 11.138, p. 80.

and 'gathered like flies around the man making the sacrifice'.[11] The goddess Belet-ili arrived, wearing a necklace
of lapis-lazuli with beads shaped like flies. She asked her
beads to make her always remember this disaster. She
would not endorse the god Enlil coming to the sacrifice
because it was he who had brought on the flood. When
Enlil nonetheless came and saw the boat, he was filled
with rage. He demanded to know how anyone had
escaped the flood, since 'No man was meant to survive
the destruction.'[12]

After the god Ninurta told Enlil that it was Ea who had
betrayed the plan of the gods, Ea chastised Enlil for
attempting to destroy everything, arguing that it would
have been better only to have punished those who had
erred: 'On him who transgresses, inflict his crime! On him
who does wrong, inflict his wrongdoing!'[13] Wolves,
plague, or famines, he went on, would have sufficed to
punish those who deserved it rather than destroying all
with the deluge. Enlil then made Uta-napishti and his
wife kneel, touched their foreheads, and conferred
immortality upon them. 'In the past,' he declared, 'Uta-
napishti was a mortal man, but now he and his wife shall
become like us gods.'[14]

In the *Epic of Gilgamesh*, the hero of the flood received
divine blessing, as did Noah. In the case of Noah, his
descendants were to multiply and fill the earth. In the
case of Uta-napishti, he and his wife received the gift of
immortality, an option not available to Noah, since
immortality was lost when Adam and Eve disobeyed

[11] *Ibid.*, 11.163, p. 81.   [12] *Ibid.*, 11.176, p. 81.
[13] *Ibid.*, 11.185-6, p. 81.   [14] *Ibid.*, 11. 204-5, p. 82.

God in the Garden of Eden. And after the sons of God had mated with the daughters of men, God had restricted the life of all those who were to follow Noah to one hundred and twenty years (Genesis 6.3). In the case of the Biblical story, the blessing of Noah was succeeded by a covenant between God and Noah, his descendants, and every living thing never again to destroy the earth by a deluge. The flood in the *Epic of Gilgamesh* had outcomes specific only to Uta-napishti and his wife, whereas the Biblical story had consequences for all those who came after. In the *Epic of Gilgamesh*, Uta-napishti and his wife lived forever. In the Biblical story, Noah and his wife lived forever, but only through their descendants.

The parallels between the stories of Noah and Uta-napishti are reasonably clear. Without putting too fine a point on it, both accounts give a reason for the flood, both are the result of a divine decision to destroy, both give a reason for the salvation of their respective heroes, and each is commanded to build an ark and to enter it. Both Genesis and *Gilgamesh* contain parallel descriptions of the deluge, of the opening of the windows of the vessels, of the reconnaissance by the birds, and the exit from the ark. Both contain an account of the making of a sacrifice and the divine smelling of it. In each case, a promise was made to humanity: in the case of Genesis, the promise never to destroy all life again by a flood; in the case of *Gilgamesh*, the gift of immortality to Uta-napishti and his wife.

That said, the differences are also significant. Unlike the many gods battling it out for supremacy in *Gilgamesh*, only one God dominates the Genesis story, namely Yahweh. Moreover, the motives for the floods are quite different – human moral wickedness in Genesis, arbitrary divine decision-making in *Gilgamesh*. In addition, in the Genesis story, Noah's righteousness is the reason for his salvation, whereas in *Gilgamesh*, the choice of Uta-napishti is not obvious. Most importantly, the accounts differ in their overall purpose. *Gilgamesh* is focused above all on the quest for individual immortality, granted in the end only to Uta-napishti and his wife. Genesis, by contrast, is the story of a new creation and a new covenant between God and humanity, one that, within the larger history of the Bible, will be followed by the covenants made by God with Abraham, Moses, and David.

The most likely conclusion to be drawn from these parallels within the texts is that the later Biblical editor was shaping his account of the flood from a tradition of Mesopotamian or Babylonian origin, to which he added distinctive elements of Israelite theology.[15] It is perhaps not surprising that Ancient Near Eastern flood myths should arise in Babylonia (Mesopotamia). As Ed Noort notes, '[T]he area that was known as Babylonia is prone to catastrophic disasters resulting from the irregular flood waters of the Tigris and Euphrates rivers and the southern storms that blow out of the Persian Gulf.'[16] The *Epic of Gilgamesh* was the most likely direct source for the Biblical account. But it was not the only Babylonian story

[15] See Gary A. Rendsburg, 'The Biblical Flood in the Light of the Gilgamesh Flood Account,' in J. Azize and N. Weeks (eds.), *Gilgamesh and the World of Assyria: Proceedings of the Conference Held at Mandelbaum House, The University of Sydney, 21–23 July 2004* (Leuven: Peeters, 2007), pp. 115–127.

[16] Ed Noort, 'The Stories of the Great Flood: Notes on Genesis 6:5–9:17 in its Context of the Ancient Near East,' in Florentino Garcia Martinez and Gerard P. Luttikhuizen (eds.), *Interpretations of the Flood* (Leiden: Brill, 1998), p. 7.

of the flood. It was preceded by the so-called *Epic of Atrahasis* (eighteenth century BCE), named after its hero Atrahasis ('exceedingly wise').[17]

In the primeval times, we are told, humanity was created by the gods to do the labour necessary to keep the world ticking over. Humanity multiplied to such an extent and became so noisy that the chief god Enlil could not sleep. Unable to reduce the human population through drought and famine, he finally decided to destroy all humankind by a flood. The compassionate god Enki was bound by an oath, against his wishes, to keep the plan secret. Nevertheless, Enki warned King Atrahasis of Enlil's plan to destroy the world by flood. He told him to destroy his house and build a boat to escape within seven days. It was to have a roof, upper and lower decks, and to be covered with pitch to strengthen it.

Atrahasis gathered the elders together and explained to them that Enki and Enlil had argued and that, since he was a devotee of Enki, he could no longer live on the earth of Enlil. It was necessary for him to leave in his boat to live with his own god. The boat was built and loaded with Atrahasis's possessions, birds, and animals. He sent his family on board and held a banquet. But Atrahasis could not eat. Because of the impending doom, 'his heart was broken and he was vomiting gall'.[18] As he sealed the door, the deluge began. Except for those inside the boat, all humanity was destroyed. The flood 'bellowed like a bull, / [Like] a whinnying wild ass as the winds [howled]'.[19] Enki

---

[17] W. G. Lambert and A. R. Millard, *Atra-hasis: The Babylonian Story of the Flood* (Oxford: Clarendon Press, 1969).

[18] *Ibid.*, Tablet 3, 2.47, p. 93.    [19] *Ibid.*, Tablet 3, 3.15-16, p. 95.

and the rest of the gods were deeply grieved at the loss of the creation. The mother goddess bitterly blamed Enlil. 'My offspring,' she lamented, '– cut off from me – have become like flies!'[20]

After seven days, the flood ended. Unlike in *Gilgamesh* and Genesis, we have no mention of the sending out of birds to determine if the waters were subsiding. However, as in *Gilgamesh* and Genesis, upon disembarking, Atrahasis made an offering to the gods: '[The gods sniffed] the smell, / They gathered [like flies] over the offering.'[21] Enlil relented on the further destruction of humans but required Enki and the mother goddess to organise them better, no doubt to ensure for himself a better night's sleep.

## Greek and Roman Traditions

The Babylonian flood tradition became familiar to the early Hellenistic world via the *Babyloniaca*, a work intended to provide Greek readers with an introduction to Babylonian culture. It was written somewhere around 290–278 BCE by Berossus, a Babylonian priest capable of writing, if poorly, in Greek. Berossus, we can assume, was relying, like the Genesis editor, on a late Mesopotamian tradition. That the Biblical and Babylonian stories of the flood as told by Berossus were related was recognised by the Jewish historian Josephus (c.37–c.100) in his *The Antiquities of the Jews*. We can reasonably assume that he thought that they referred to the same event and that, naturally enough, the Biblical story was the original.

[20] *Ibid.*, Tablet 3, 3.44, p. 95.    [21] *Ibid.*, Tablet 3, 4.35, p. 99.

'Now all the writers of barbarian histories,' he declared, 'make mention of this flood [of Noah]; among whom is Berosus the Chaldean.'[22]

According to Berossus, the God Cronos [Ea] appeared to Xisouthros in a dream and revealed that, on the fifteenth day of the month of Daisios (May), humankind would be destroyed by a flood. He ordered Xisouthros to build a huge boat – 900 metres long by 360 metres wide – and to embark on it with his family and closest friends. He was to load it with food and drink and gather all the winged and four-footed creatures into it. On the third day after the flood had come and swiftly receded, Xisouthros released some of the birds to see if they might find land. But finding neither food nor a place on which to alight, the birds returned to the ship. A few days later, Xisouthros again released the birds. This time they returned but with their feet covered in mud. On their third release, they did not return to the ship. Xisouthros knew then that the land had reappeared.

Xisouthros saw that the boat had come aground on a mountain in Armenia. He disembarked with his wife, his daughter, and the pilot. After setting up an altar and sacrificing to the gods, he and his wife, his daughter, and the pilot disappeared. When they failed to return, those who remained in the boat disembarked and searched for Xisouthros, calling out his name. A voice from the sky told them that, because of his piety, he, his wife, and the pilot had gone to live with the gods. The voice also told

[22] William Whiston (trans.), *The Antiquities of the Jews*, bk. 1, ch. 3, para. 6, p. 34. Available at https://en.wikisource.org/wiki/The_Antiquities_of_the_Jews/Book_I.

them that they were to return to Babylon. After hearing this, they too sacrificed to the gods and returned on foot to Babylon. A portion of the ship, Berossus reported, still existed in the mountains of the Korduaians of Armenia, and some of his contemporaries scraped pieces of bitumen off the ship, brought them back, and used them as talismans.[23] The tradition of relics of the ark began early.

Berossus' account of the flood was transmitted to the Christian world by the Christian Greek historian Eusebius of Caesarea (c.260–339 CE) and the Byzantine chronicler George Syncellus (d. after 810 CE) via the Greek scholar Alexander Polyhistor (c.110–c.40 BCE). Syncellus recognised the parallels between the stories of Noah and Xisouthros but went out of his way to emphasise the differences. Thus, after his account of the flood, he declared, 'All of the above is from Alexander Polyhistor, who in turn took it from Berossus, the false prophet of the Chaldeans [Babylonians]. It is possible for those wishing to understand correctly what really happened to refer to the holy writings of Genesis to see how much they differed from the above account of the Chaldeans, full of unbelievable stories.'[24]

The Greeks themselves had stories of great floods within their own traditions. In the fifth century BCE, for

---

[23]  See Stanley Mayer Burstein, *The 'Babylonaica' of Berossus* (Malibu, CA: Undena Publications, 1978), pp. 20–21. For a comparison of Berossus' and the Biblical accounts, see John Day, *From Creation to Babel: Studies in Genesis 1-11* (London: Bloomsbury, 2013), ch. 4.

[24]  Quoted by Day, *From Creation to Babel: Studies in Genesis 1-11*, p. 76, n. 45. See also Robert Bedrosian (trans.), *Eusebius' Chronicle: Translated from Classical Armenian*, p. 8. Available at https://archive.org/details/EusebiusChroniclechronicon/page/n7/mode/2up.

example, Plato had referred in his *Timaeus* to a great deluge which Deucalion, the son of Prometheus, and his wife Pyrrha survived.[25] So it is perhaps no surprise that Deucalion and his wife were to become the heroes of a Greek version of the Babylonian tradition contained within a collection of Greco-Roman myths known as *The Library*. These were attributed to the Greek scholar Apollodorus of Alexandria, and probably written in the second century CE. In this case, the Greek Deucalion was the equivalent of the Jewish Noah.

According to the account of Apollodorus, Deucalion was the husband of Pyrrha, the daughter of the first woman Pandora, and the son of Prometheus who, on account of his theft of fire, had been kept bound for many years on Mount Caucasus and subjected to his liver being eaten every day by a visiting eagle (and regenerating every night).

The flood was brought on by the god Zeus, although his reasons for doing so were not specified. Nor was any reason given for the salvation of Deucalion and his wife. On the advice of Prometheus, Deucalion built a 'chest' ('ark') and, having stocked it with provisions, embarked in it with his wife Pyrrha. By pouring rain from heaven, Zeus flooded the greater part of Greece and, except for a few who fled to high mountains, all men were destroyed.

Deucalion floated in his boat for nine days and nights, and drifted to Parnassus. When the rain ceased, he landed and sacrificed to Zeus, the god of escape (or perhaps the

---

[25] See *Timaeus*, 22.b, Edith Hamilton and Huntington Cairns (eds.), *The Collected Dialogues of Plato* (Princeton, NJ: Princeton University Press, 1961), p. 1157.

god of very close shaves). Zeus sent Hermes to Deucalion to ask what he would like. Deucalion chose men. At the bidding of Zeus, Deucalion picked up stones, threw them over his head, and they became men. The stones that Pyrrha threw became women (see Plate 7). Thus was the world re-populated.[26]

Educated Jews and Christians knew the story of Deucalion and saw the parallels to that of Noah. Thus, for example, the Jewish Biblical exegete Philo (20 BCE– c.50 CE) noted the necessity of the Creator preserving one just man for a new creation, along with specimens of each kind of living creature, to make good the annihilation of the wicked of the first creation. 'This person,' he wrote, 'is called by the Greeks Deucalion and by the Hebrews Noah.'[27] Similarly, the Christian apologist Justin Martyr (c.100–c.165), always keen to align Christianity with the Classical tradition, remarked that the flood left no one but the one man with his family 'who is by us called Noah, and by you Deucalion, from whom again such vast numbers have sprung, some of them evil and others good'.[28] The occasional 'pagan' also seemed to have heard of the story of Noah. Thus, for example, the Greek philosopher Celsus (fl.175–177 CE) viewed the Biblical story as little more than a decadent version of the story

[26] See James George Frazer (trans.), *Apollodorus: The Library, Volume 1: Books 1-39*, 1.7.2. (Cambridge, MA: Harvard University Press, 1921), pp. 53–55.

[27] F. H. Colson (trans.), *Philo: Volume VIII*, 'On Rewards and Punishments,' 23, (Cambridge, MA: Harvard University Press, 1939), p. 325.

[28] A. Cleveland Coxe (ed.), *The Second Apology of Justin*, ch. 7, in *ANF*, vol.1, p. 190.

of Deucalion. '[T]hey speak … of a deluge,' he wrote, 'and of a monstrous ark, having within it all things [i.e. all living things], and of a dove and a crow as messengers, falsifying and recklessly altering the story of Deucalion; not expecting, I suppose, that these things would come to light, but imagining that they were inventing stories merely for young children.'[29]

In the second half of the second century CE, a work entitled *On the Syrian Goddess*, attributed to the Syrian satirist Lucian of Samosata (c.125–c.180 CE), was to tell the story of a universal deluge endured by Deucalion that combined Babylonian and Biblical elements. Unlike the story of Apollodorus, but like Genesis, Lucian attributed the reason for the flood to the wickedness of men and the salvation of Deucalion to his wisdom and piety. Unlike Apollodorus, there is no mention of Deucalion's wife Pyrrha, although, like Genesis, Deucalion took along a number of others, specifically his wives and children. Like other flood heroes, he embarked into a great ark. Unlike Apollodorus, but like Genesis, there arrived swine, horses, lions, snakes, and everything else that lived on the earth, all in couples, for Deucalion to take with him. They did Deucalion no harm, and the god Zeus imposed concord between the animals. There they all remained until the flood subsided.[30] Unlike Apollodorus, where the earth was re-populated as a result of a miracle orchestrated by Hermes, in *On the Syrian Goddess*, as in Genesis, the re-

---

[29] *Contra Celsum (Origen)*, bk. 4, ch. 41. Available at www.newadvent.org/fathers/04164.htm.

[30] See H. A. Strong (trans.) and John Garstang (ed.), *Lucian's* On the Syrian Goddess, 12 (Oxford, OH: Faenum Publishing, 2013), p. 45.

population of the world is made possible, we can assume, through those that Deucalion took along with him.

The story of Deucalion and Pyrrha was transmitted from the Greeks to the Romans. Thus, at the beginning of the first century CE, the *Metamorphoses* of the Roman poet Ovid (43 BCE–17/18 CE) contained a much more elaborate version of the flood suffered by Deucalion and his wife Pyrrha. In this case, the divine protagonist was Jupiter who wandered the earth to see if human beings were really as wicked as they seemed to be. He concluded that they were when King Lycaon served him a dinner of the boiled and roasted flesh of a human hostage. Jupiter's punishment was to turn the king into a wolf and a determination to destroy humanity. The gods were worried about the state of the world without humans, but they were reassured by Jupiter's promise that there would be a new humanity different from the first and from a wondrous origin.

At first, Jupiter pondered hurling volleys of thunderbolts and destroying the earth by fire. But mindful of the likelihood that this would destroy not only men but everything else, he chose instead 'To overwhelm humanity with an endless deluge / Pouring down from every square inch of sky.'[31] So he cut loose the south wind to pour rain down from the sky, the sea god to roll out huge waves, and the rivers to tumble unbridled down to the sea. Neptune himself struck the earth with his trident until

[31] Stanley Lombardo (trans.), *Ovid: Metamorphoses*, 1.272–3 (Cambridge: Hackett Publishing Company, 2010), p. 13. See also, R. Scott Smith, 'Bundling Myth, Bungling Myth: The Flood Myth in Ancient and Modern Handbooks of Myth,' *Archiv für Religionsgeschichte* 16 (2015), pp. 243–262.

'All was sea, but it was a sea without shores.'[32] All human-kind and most creatures drowned. Those who survived the waters succumbed to slow starvation.

Only the virtuous Deucalion and his pious wife Pyrrha were saved: 'Only one man left, from so many thousands / Only one woman, each innocent, each reverent.'[33] Their boat landed on Mount Parnassus, the only place not covered by water. When Jupiter saw that the whole world was nothing but a stagnant pond, he quietened the storm. He told Triton to blow his conch horn and to signal the waters to withdraw. The world was restored.

Deucalion and Pyrrha visited the shrine of the goddess Themis to inquire of her how the world could be re-populated: 'Tell us, O Themis, how our race can be restored, / And bring aid, O most mild one, to a world overwhelmed.'[34] The goddess told them that they must go with veiled heads and loosened robes and throw their 'great mother's bones' over their shoulders. They were puzzled until Deucalion realised that the bones were stones in the great mother earth. They did as they had been ordered, and the stones thrown by Deucalion became men and those thrown by Pyrrha became women. 'In no time at all,' we read, 'by divine power, the stones / Thrown by the man's hand took the form of men / And from the woman's scattered stones women were born.'[35] The earth itself then spontaneously generated other forms of life: 'So when Mother Earth's diluvian mud / Again grew warm under the rays of the sun, / She brought forth innumerable species, restoring some / Of the

---

[32] *Ibid.*, 1.303, p. 13.  [33] *Ibid.*, 1.338-9, pp. 14-15.
[34] *Ibid.*, 1.392-3, p. 16.  [35] *Ibid.*, 1.428-9, p. 17.

ancient forms, and creating some new and strange.'[36] Thus was life restored to a new world.

As we have seen, stories of a universal flood that destroyed all humanity except for one notable man and a few of those close to him, along with the creation of a new world after the deluge, abounded in the Ancient Near East and in the Greek and Roman worlds. But it was the story of Noah in the book of Genesis, continually retold and reinterpreted over the succeeding centuries, that has remained down to our times as the definitive story of primeval humanity's wickedness and its partial redemption through the survival of Noah.

## The Man of Righteousness

Considering the remarkable role that Noah plays in the primeval history recounted in Genesis 6-9, effectively as the second Adam of a new creation after the flood, it is surprising how little importance is accorded to him in the rest of the Old Testament and later in the New Testament. We catch only glimpses. He is listed in the first book of Chronicles as the tenth in a line of succession that begins with Adam, and is immediately followed by his sons Shem, Ham, and Japheth (1 Chronicles 1.4). The Gospel of Luke (c.85 CE) includes him in a genealogy that begins with Jesus and stretches back via sixty-six persons to Noah, thence via nine more to Adam (Luke 3.23-38). The genealogy from Noah to Adam in Luke mirrors that in the first book of Chronicles.

When he is remembered, it is as an exemplar of righteousness. Thus, for example, the book of Ezekiel has God

[36] *Ibid.*, 1.450-4, p. 18.

declaring that, when the sins of any land are great, he sends sword, famine, wild animals, and pestilence upon it. In each case, it is said that even were those paragons of virtue – Noah, Job, and Daniel – in the land, they alone would be saved 'by their righteousness', and not even their sons and daughters would be spared (Ezekiel 14.12-20). How much more so, God declared, would he send these punishments upon Jerusalem for its sins. A punishment by flood is not mentioned. So, we can assume that the Noah that Ezekiel has in mind is the pious man delivered from the universal flood. We next encounter Noah in the book of Isaiah. God's promise to preserve humankind after the flood is here used as a source for God's enduring commitment to the preservation of Zion: 'This is like the days of Noah to me: Just as I swore that the waters of Noah would never again go over the earth, so I have sworn that I will not be angry with you and will not rebuke you. For the mountains may depart and the hills be removed, but my steadfast love shall not depart from you, and my covenant of peace shall not be destroyed' (Isaiah 54.9-10).[37]

New Testament references to Noah are similarly few. Aside from the mention in the genealogy in the gospel of Luke, we find five others – one in each of the Gospels of Matthew and Luke, one in the Letter to the Hebrews, and one in each of the two Letters of Peter. All of these have an eschatological flavour. That is to say, they indicate that, just as Noah and his contemporaries were living in

---

[37] On possible allusions to the flood elsewhere in the Old Testament, see Jack P. Lewis, *A Study of the Interpretation of Noah and the Flood in Jewish and Christian Literature* (Leiden: Brill, 1978), pp. 8–9.

the last days before the destruction of the world by flood, so too early Christians were living in expectation of the return of Jesus, the end of the world, and the division of all people into the saved and the damned. Thus, for example, the Gospel of Matthew (c.90 CE) has Jesus preaching that the end of the world will come but that no one knows the day or the hour when heaven and earth will pass away. Nevertheless, as in the time of Noah, it will come suddenly: 'For as the days of Noah were, so will be the coming of the Son of Man. For as in those days before the flood they were eating and drinking, marrying and giving in marriage, until the day Noah entered the ark, and they knew nothing until the flood came and swept them all away, so too will be the coming of the Son of Man' (Matthew 24.37-9, see also Luke 17.26-7).

The mention of Noah in the Letter to the Hebrews (c.70 CE) has a similar eschatological edge. Noah is listed as one of the eighteen worthy 'ancients' who acted 'by faith'. Noah is the exemplary person who, warned by God about events yet to come, builds an ark to save himself and his household. By doing so, he condemns the world and becomes 'an heir to the righteousness that is in accordance with faith' (Hebrews 11.7). So the readers of the letter are being warned, like Noah, of an impending cataclysm from which they can only be saved by their faith. As Noah had to respond before the flood began, so the faithful must now act based on a warning about a judgement that is not yet perceptible to the eye.[38]

---

[38] See Craig R. Koester, *Hebrews: A New Translation with Introduction and Commentary* (New York: Doubleday, 2001), p. 483.

The mention of Noah in the First Letter of Peter (c.80 CE) is imbedded within one of the most enigmatic passages in the New Testament.[39] Christ, we are informed,

> was put to death in the flesh, but made alive in the spirit, in which also he went and made a proclamation to the spirits in prison, who in former times did not obey, when God waited patiently in the days of Noah, during the building of the ark, in which a few, that is, eight persons were saved through water. And baptism, which this pre-figured, now saves you – not as a removal of dirt from the body, but as an appeal to God for a good conscience, through the resurrection of Jesus Christ, who has gone into heaven and is at the right hand of God, with angels, authorities, and powers made subject to him.
>
> (1 Peter 3.18-22)

Within the Western tradition, the story of Christ's preaching 'to the spirits in prison' was the Biblical basis for the doctrine of the Harrowing of Hell. According to this doctrine, after his death but before his resurrection, Christ descended into Hell or Hades to give all the dead located there prior to the time of Jesus the chance to hear the teaching of Jesus and to have the opportunity of salvation.[40] In their original context in the First Letter of Peter, however, these verses have a quite different meaning. While going into heaven, Christ confirmed

---

[39] See John H. Elliott, *1 Peter: A New Translation with Introduction and Commentary* (New York: Doubleday, 2000), pp. 644–710. I am indebted to Elliott for this discussion.

[40] See J. L. MacCulloch, *The Harrowing of Hell: A Comparative Study of an Early Christian Doctrine* (Edinburgh: T. & T. Clark, 1930). See also Philip C. Almond, *Afterlife: A History of Life After Death* (Ithaca, NY: Cornell University Press, 2016), ch. 2.

the imprisonment in one of the heavens of the 'sons of God' – the 'angelic spirits' – who mated with the daughters of men. The baptism of believers in the present was prefigured by the flood. Like Noah and his family in the primeval times, the faithful were saved in end times through the waters of baptism, as was Noah and his family through the waters of the flood. Having been 'made alive in the spirit', the resurrected Jesus Christ was at the right hand of God with the cosmic powers in subjection to him.

The imprisonment of the 'sons of God' or 'the angelic spirits' who sinned in the days of Noah is clearer in the Second Letter of Peter (c.90 CE). For there, God did not spare them, 'but cast them into hell and committed them to chains of deepest darkness to be kept until the judgment' (2 Peter 2.4). Nor did God spare the ancient world except for Noah who was 'a herald of righteousness' with seven others 'when he brought a flood on a world of the ungodly' (2 Peter 2.5). There is no mention in Genesis of Noah having attempted to preach repentance to his contemporaries. But the author of the Second Letter of Peter may have been picking up on a common tradition of his time, one which softened God's remorseless destruction of everyone without any opportunity of repentance. The first-century Jewish historian Josephus, for example, reported that Noah was uneasy at the actions of the sons of the angels and tried to persuade them 'to change their dispositions and their acts for the better; but seeing they did not yield to him, but were slaves to their wicked pleasures ... he departed out of that land'.[41]

---

[41]  Whiston (trans.), *The Antiquities of the Jews*, bk. 1, ch. 3, para. 1, p. 31.

Similarly, Book One of the Jewish *Sybilline Oracles* (early first century CE), a collection of prophetic utterances attributed to the ancient Sybil of Babylon, informs us that God told Noah to proclaim repentance to all the peoples so that all might be saved.[42] The Sybilline author then supplied Noah with a long speech in which he exhorted the wicked to change their ways (*Sybilline* 1.175-95). 'Men sated with faithlessness,' Noah declared, 'smitten with a great madness, what you did will not escape the notice of God, for he knows all things ... Be sober, cut off evils, and stop fighting violently with each other, having a bloodthirsty heart, drenching much earth with human blood' (*Sybilline* 1.150-6).[43] Noah's attempt to persuade his contemporaries to change their ways will become a feature of the story in Jewish, Christian, and Muslim literature.

## Noah and 'the Watchers'

If the Old Testament was surprisingly reticent about Noah, Jewish literature after the period of the Old Testament (c.400 BCE–c.100 CE), the so-called inter-testamental or deutero-canonical literature, is filled with stories about him. Thus, for example, the eschatological *First Book of Enoch* (c.200 BCE), traditionally ascribed to Enoch, the great-grandfather of Noah, contains an elaborate account of the 'sons of God', now called 'the

---

[42]  I follow the dating of this section of the *Sybilline Oracles* by James Charlesworth. See James H. Charlesworth, *The Old Testament Pseudepigrapha Volume 1: Apocalyptic Literature and Testaments* (New York: Doubleday, 1983), p. 331.

[43]  *Ibid.*, p. 338.

Watchers'. This landmark elaboration of Jewish demon-
ology is aligned with an expanded account of the story
of Noah.

The disparate account of sons of God, the giants, the
Nephilim, and Noah within Genesis is now woven into a
coherent story. Thus, according to 'The Book of the
Watchers' (chs. 1–36), the mating of the sons of God with
the daughters of men was an act of rebellion against
God that stemmed from their lust and resulted in the
production of 'bastards' and 'half breeds'.[44] Two hundred
Watchers, under the command of their chief Shemihazah,
took wives for themselves from among the daughters of
men and defiled themselves through them. They taught
the women sorcery and charms and revealed to them the
cutting of roots and plants (that is, medicine and magic).
The women bore them giants who begat the Nephilim.
Unlike in Genesis, the giants of Enoch were ruthless.
They devoured the labour of men, killed and ate them,
drank their blood, and ate one another's flesh. The giants
would die in the flood, but the spirits that went forth from
their bodies were evil. Unlike in Genesis, men were the
victims, not the perpetrators of this wickedness, and they
cried out for help to the four archangels – Michael, Sariel,
Raphael, and Gabriel – who relayed the message from
men to God.

The end of the First Book of Enoch contains an
account of the birth of Noah (chs. 106–107). There, the
narrator Enoch tells us that he took a wife for his son

---

[44] George W.E. Nickelsburg, *A Commentary on the Book of 1 Enoch,
Chapters 1–36; 81–108* (Minneapolis, MN: Fortress Press, 2001), 10.9,
p. 215.

Methuselah. She bore a son called Lamech who, in turn, took a wife who bore him a son who would come to be called Noah. Now when the child was born, 'his body was whiter than snow and redder than a rose, his hair was all white and like white wool and curly. Glorious was his face. When he opened his eyes, the house shone like the sun. And he stood up from the hands of the midwife, and he opened his mouth and praised the Lord of eternity.'[45] Believing that Noah was not his son but had been fathered by an angel, Lamech was afraid of him and sent his father Methuselah to Enoch who was living with the angels to find out the truth. Enoch told Methuselah that God was planning a flood of great destruction, but that Noah and his three children would be saved. Noah's physical appearance was not the consequence of having been fathered by an angel but of his righteousness and blamelessness. The story ends with a promise of eventual good things for the earth, for Noah will be the remnant that will survive the flood and renew the earth.

Meanwhile, back at the 'Book of the Watchers', God commissioned Raphael to imprison the watcher Asael (Shemihazeh's second-in-command) under the earth, Gabriel to destroy the giants, Michael to bind Shemihazah and the others who mated with the women and imprison them under the earth, and Sariel to tell Noah that the end is coming and how he might escape it.

Elsewhere in the First Book of Enoch, we find a different account of how Noah heard of the impending destruction, this time narrated by Noah. Terrified by an earthquake, Noah sets out for the ends of the earth to

---

[45] *Ibid.*, 106.2-3, p. 536.

speak to his great-grandfather Enoch. He learns from Enoch that, due to the wickedness of the earth's inhabitants, God is intending to execute a great judgement. He will punish sinful humanity along with the rebellious angels who have taught people forbidden secrets. But Noah will be preserved and established as the first of a righteous and holy humanity. The story ends with Noah having a vision of the angels of punishment who were ready to 'let loose all the power of the water that is beneath the earth, that it might be for the judgment and destruction of all who reside and dwell on the earth'.[46] Then Noah leaves Enoch to return home.

A slightly different tradition follows. Here, Noah reports that the word of the Lord came to him that he was blameless and that 'the angels are making a wooden (vessel)' that God will protect.[47] From it would come the seed of life so that the earth would not remain desolate. God promised not to bring temptation on the face of the earth again and to scatter and make fruitful those who descend from Noah. The eternal punishment of the fallen angels, the kings, and the mighty in a burning valley is then announced by Noah. The story concludes with Noah receiving a book that contains all the secret knowledge and the parables that were given to him by Enoch.

As in the First Book of Enoch, the author of the Book of Jubilees (second century BCE) attempted to create a coherent narrative from the Biblical account, both

---

[46] George W. E. Nickelsburg and James C. Vanderkam, *A Commentary on the Book of 1 Enoch, Chapters 37–82* (Minneapolis, MN: Fortress Press, 2012), 66.1, p. 273.

[47] *Ibid.*, 67.2, p. 273.

creating and omitting details, harmonising the Biblical story, and emphasising the dating of the events. Thus, we hear for the first time that Noah married a woman whose name was Emzara, the daughter of his father's brother (and thus Noah's cousin). The giants were the progeny of the sons of God (the angels) and the daughters of men. The whole earth – people, animals, birds, and creeping things – was corrupted, and wickedness was universal. God determined to obliterate all animate beings, being pleased only with Noah.

The judgement on all animate beings is then connected with the punishment of the angels and their progeny. God ordered that the giants should all kill each other: 'They began to kill each other until all of them fell by the sword and were obliterated from the earth.'[48] Their fathers saw them slaughtering each other. Soon afterwards, they were tied up and imprisoned in the depths of the earth until the great day of judgement. Jubilees then picked up on God's order to Noah to build the ark to save himself from the floodwaters.

Genesis spent little time detailing the life of Noah after the flood. But Jubilees fills in the blanks. After Noah, his family, and the animals disembarked from the ark, Noah offered the sacrifice of a bull, a ram, a sheep, goats, salt, a turtledove, and a dove to God who then made a covenant with Noah never to destroy the earth through a flood again. For their part, Noah and his sons swore an oath not to consume any blood that was in any animate being. The Noah of Jubilees is a priestly Noah, one who adheres

---

[48] James C. Vanderkam, *Jubilees: The Hermenaia Translation* (Minneapolis, MN: Augsburg Fortress Publishers, 2020), 5.9, p. 25.

to the Festival of Weeks and the Festival of First Fruits. In short, we are told, Jewish festivals began with Noah. As in the Genesis account, Noah plants and celebrates his vineyard by becoming drunk. Later, he gives a long speech to his children. Land is allotted to his descendants.

Noah also becomes a physician and an apothecary, a new role built into, surprisingly, a new story about demons. Some fifteen years after Noah apportioned land to his sons, they came to him to report that impure demons were causing disease and death among his grand-children. Despite the earlier passage that seemed to have them all locked up, these were spirits, offspring of the sons of God, who had remained free. Noah prayed to God to shut them up and hold them all captive. But Mastema, the leader of the spirits, appealed to God to leave a tenth of them free to punish wrongdoers, 'because the evil of humanity is great.'[49] God agreed to this but, suspecting that the demons would not operate fairly, told one of them to teach Noah all their medicines 'for their diseases with their deceptions so that he could cure (them) by means of the earth's plants'.[50] Noah wrote all the medi-cines down in a book that he handed on to his favourite son, Shem. Noah was, after all, a man of the soil, and it was not unreasonable that he came to be imagined as the original natural healer. He was a New Age man in more senses than one. And the story showed that Jewish medi-cine had priority, and therefore excellence, over that of other cultures. At any rate, we read, the evil spirits were stopped from pursuing Noah's children.

[49] *Ibid.*, 10.8, p. 43.     [50] *Ibid.*, 10.8, p. 43.

A similar but expanded account of the birth of Noah appears in the so-called Genesis Apocryphon (1QapGen) (first century CE), one of the original Dead Sea Scrolls discovered in 1946 by Bedouin shepherds in a cave near Qumran.[51] The text is fragmentary, but the overall narrative is clear. The birth of Noah in the Genesis Apocryphon is a slightly elaborated account of that in the First Book of Enoch. For when the appearance of Noah leads his father to the belief that Noah is the child of a Watcher, he questions his wife Bitenosh whether she had conceived by one of the sons of heaven. The Watchers did, after all, take wives from among female humans. So, he had some grounds for his suspicions. Weeping passionately, she replied, 'O, my brother, my Lord, remember my voluptuousness [...] in the heat of lovemaking, and my ardent response. I [am telling you] the whol[e] truth.'[52] Lamech was persuaded. But Bitenosh continued, 'O, my lord, my [brother, remember] my pleasure. I swear to you by the great Holy One, by the King of He[aven...] that this seed comes from you, this conception was by you, the planting of [this] fruit is yours [It was] not by any stranger, neither

---

[51] The relationship between the First Book of Enoch, the Book of Jubilees, and the Genesis Apocryphon remains a matter of scholarly dispute. See Daniel A. Machiela, *The Dead Sea Genesis Apocryphon: A New Text and Translation with Introduction and Special Treatment of Columns 13-17* (Leiden: Brill, 2009), pp. 9–17. The relation that is held to obtain between these three texts affects, in turn, the relative dating of each. On the flood story in the Dead Sea Scrolls more generally, see Florentino Garcia Martínez, 'Interpretations of the Flood in the Dead Sea Scrolls,' in Florentino Garcia Martínez and Gerard P. Luttikhuizen (eds.), *Interpretations of the Flood* (Leiden: Brill, 1998), pp. 86–108.

[52] 1QapGen, col.2, in Michael O. Wise, et al. (trans.), *The Dead Sea Scrolls: A New Translation* (San Francisco: Harper, 2005), pp. 91–92. Lamech's wife is named Betenos in Jubilees, 4.28.

by any of the Watchers, nor yet by any of the Sons of Heaven.'[53] Nonetheless Noah seeks reassurance from his father via Enoch.[54]

Noah himself then picks up the story, telling us that he is a righteous man who has been warned of darkness. He marries his cousin Emzara (mother of seed) by whom he had sons and daughters, taking wives for his sons from his brother's daughters and giving his daughters to his brother's sons, 'in accord with the law of the eternal statute'.[55] Like Deucalion and Pyrrha, Noah and Emzara were father and mother to a new humanity.[56] A Watcher now comes to Noah with a warning about a coming flood. Noah survives the flood with his family, the ark coming to rest on the mountains of Ararat. Noah leaves the ark and makes a sacrifice to God. He then explores the land and praises God for its fruitfulness. God then appears to Noah and makes a covenant with Noah and his sons that they should rule the land as long as they do not consume blood. The rainbow is given as a sign of this. Noah and his sons begin to cultivate the land, and Noah plants a vineyard. Many children are born to Noah's sons and daughters.

---

[53] *Ibid.*, col. 2, p. 92.
[54] See Aryeh Amihay and Daniel A. Machiela, 'Traditions of the Birth of Noah,' in Michael E. Stone, Aryeh Amihay, and Vered Hillel (eds.), *Noah and His Book(s)* (Atlanta, GA: Society of Biblical Literature, 2010), pp. 53–70.
[55] Wise, et al. (trans.), *The Dead Sea Scrolls: A New Translation*, col. 6, p. 94.
[56] See Michael E. Stone, 'The Axis of History at Qumran,' in Esther G. Chazon and Michael E. Stone (eds.) with Avital Pinnick, *Pseudepigraphic Perspectives: The Apocrypha and Pseudepigrapha in Light of the Dead Sea Scrolls* (Leiden: Brill, 1999), pp. 133–149.

Four years after planting the vineyard, it produces wine for him, and Noah holds a festival to celebrate and to thank God. There is no mention here of Noah's becoming drunk, nor of his drunken nakedness being seen by his son Ham. Noah is, in this text, a patriarchal hero. Rather than drunkenness and shame, having fallen asleep, Noah has a vision of a cedar tree and an olive tree, along with an interpretation of it. He is the cedar tree who will have many shoots – that is, many descendants. But the majority will be evil, and 'the man coming from the south with a sickle in his hand, and fire with him' will punish those who rebel.[57] A long account of how Noah divides up the land among his sons, and his sons among their sons, brings the story to an end, the hero of the rest of the Genesis Apocryphon now becoming Abraham.[58]

Noah's narration in the Genesis Apocryphon begins with the words, 'The Book of the Words of Noah.'[59] There was a tradition within Jewish literature, after the time of the Old Testament, to ascribe books to important Biblical figures. The key figures in Genesis – Adam and Eve, Moses, Abraham, Shem, Isaac, Enoch, Jacob, Joseph, and so on – all have books ascribed to them. So, might there have been a Book of Noah that is now missing?

[57] Wise, et al. (trans.), *The Dead Sea Scrolls: A New Translation*, col. 15, p. 97.
[58] On the Genesis Apocryphon, see Esther Eshel, 'The Noah Cycle in the Genesis Apocryphon,' in Michael E. Stone, Aryeh Amihay, and Vered Hillel, *Noah and His Book(s)* (Atlanta, GA: Society of Biblical Literature, 2010), pp. 77–96.
[59] Wise, et al. (trans.), *The Dead Sea Scrolls: A New Translation*, col. 5, p. 93. Noah is the narrator in cols. 6-17.

Aside from the Genesis Apocryphon, we find several references to writings by Noah in other texts. Thus, for example, as we noted earlier, in the Book of Jubilees, after Noah is taught the arts of healing by an angel, we read that 'Noah wrote down in a book everything (just) as we had taught him ... and he gave all the books that he had written to his oldest son Shem because he loved him much more than all his sons.'[60] In a later passage in Jubilees, we hear of a number of regulations concerning the eating of sacrificial meat that are 'written in the book of my ancestors, in the words of Enoch and the words of Noah'.[61] Third, in the Dead Sea Scroll text known as the Aramaic Levi Document (early second century BCE), we read, 'For thus my father Abraham commanded me for thus he found in the writing of the book of Noah concerning the blood.'[62] In addition, as in the Genesis Apocryphon (cols. 6-17), so also in the First Book of Enoch (chs. 66–68.1), Noah speaks in the first person.

Was there then a Book of Noah? The uncertainties that surround the textual materials make it difficult to sustain the argument that there was. On the other hand, the references to it, together with the texts where Noah is the narrator, should make us wary of ruling it out. What we can say is that, in the period between the Old and New Testaments, there developed an array of traditions about Noah that were variously incorporated into a number of texts, both in the first and third

[60] Vanderkam, *Jubilees*, 10.13-14, p. 44.   [61] *Ibid.*, 21.10, p. 77.
[62] Jonas C. Greenfield, Michael E. Stone, and Esther Eshel, *The Aramaic Levi Document: Edition, Translation, Commentary* (Leiden: Brill, 2004), 10.10, p. 91.

person – traditions about his birth, his priestly character, his sacrificial instructions, and his role as the father
of Jewish medicine. Most importantly, the Noachic
traditions had a highly developed angelology. It was
one that emphasised that evil was not the result of the
sin of Adam and/or Eve infecting later humanity, but
rather the consequence of angelic (demonic) intervention in the world at the time of Noah, sufficient for God
to begin again with a new humanity based on Noah and
his family. Even then, evil continued due to the remnant
of demons who survived the flood. In sum, the elaboration of the story of Noah and the flood in the Noachic
traditions reflected the increasing importance and significance of Noah from the time after the Old
Testament until that of the New.[63]

Within the Christian tradition, the view that evil was
the result of the fallen angels had only a brief history.
Saint Augustine (354–430 CE) ignored its literal meaning
and gave only an allegorical interpretation in terms of the
heavenly and earthly cities. The mainstream Christian
tradition did accept the tradition that evil angels were
present in the world, creating havoc. But it brought the
fall of the angels to a time before the creation of Adam
and Eve. This enabled the chief of the fallen angels, Satan,
to play a role as the serpent in the Fall of Adam and Eve.
The sin of Adam and Eve, rather than that of the sons of

---

[63] For an argument in favour of a Book of Noah, see Michael E. Stone,
'The Book(s) Attributed to Noah,' in Michael E. Stone, Aryeh Amihay,
and Vered Hillel, *Noah and His Book(s)* (Atlanta, GA: Society of Biblical
Literature, 2010), pp. 7–26.

God before the flood, then came to be read as the event from which human wickedness ensued.[64] That said, it was only from Noah and his family that a new humanity was to arise after the flood.

---

[64] On the Watchers within the Christian tradition, see Philip C. Almond, *The Devil: A New Biography* (Ithaca, NY: Cornell University Press, 2014), pp. 1–15.

## 2

# Building Narrative Arcs

∼

## A Hellenistic Noah

The overall meaning of the story of Noah in the book of Genesis is clear. It is that of a wrathful God determined to punish sinful humankind, cleanse a corrupted world by flood, and make a fresh start through Noah, the only righteous man on earth. 'I have determined,' God said to Noah, 'to make an end of all flesh, for the earth is filled with violence because of them; now I am going to destroy them along with the earth' (Genesis 6.13). Only Noah, his sons, and their wives, along with the creatures that he took into the ark, were to survive. If it were only that simple.

There are many meanings to the story of Noah, only to be found within the history of the attempts to interpret it. The history of the story of Noah since the beginning of the common era, as noted earlier, has been the history of the many attempts to create a coherent narrative from the Biblical story by adding to or subtracting from it, by ironing out its contradictions and incoherencies, and by making its story historically credible, scientifically verifiable, culturally relevant, and theologically acceptable. Learning, piety, and imagination have all been brought to the Biblical text to inform or persuade its readers from an array of religions, societies, and cultures over the past twenty centuries of its truth, its value, and its possible relevance to their lives.

Take the Jewish historian Josephus. He read the story of Noah in accord with the overall theme of his *The Antiquities of the Jews* in the decade after the fall of Jerusalem in 70 CE. According to Josephus, 'men who conform to the will of God, and do not venture to transgress laws that have been excellently laid down, prosper in all things beyond belief, and for their reward are offered by God felicity; whereas, in proportion as they depart from the strict observance of these laws, things (else) practicable become impracticable, and whatever imaginary good thing they strive to do ends in irretrievable disasters'.[1] Josephus was in no doubt that God punished those who did not obey his laws – both the natural laws at the time of creation and the revealed laws later delivered to Moses. According to Josephus, for seven generations after Adam, people remained faithful to God and took virtue for their guide. But eventually, they abandoned the customs of their fathers for a life of depravity: 'They no longer rendered to God His due honours, nor took account of justice towards men, but displayed by their actions a zeal for vice twofold greater than they had formerly shown for virtue, and thereby drew upon themselves the enmity of God.'[2] In addition, the sons of the angels and the women 'were overbearing [ὑβριστάς] and disdainful of every virtue'.[3] Those readers familiar with Greek tragedy would not have missed Josephus' use of the

---

[1]  H. St. J. Thackeray (trans.), *Josephus: Jewish Antiquities, Books i–iv* (Cambridge, MA: Harvard University Press, 1930), vol. 4, bk.1, sec. 14.
[2]  *Ibid.*, vol. 4, bk. 1, secs. 72–73.    [3]  *Ibid.*, vol.4, bk. 1, sec. 73.

word 'hubris' [ὕβρις]. For the overbearing ways of the progeny of the angels were soon to be brought down by a divine nemesis.[4]

Josephus was clearly worried that God appeared to have lost control of his creation. Thus, he has Adam foreshadow the inevitability of the flood. This occurs in the context of an addition to the Genesis story by Josephus about Adam's third son after Cain and Abel, Seth. His descendants, we are informed, discovered the science of the heavenly bodies and their orderly array. Knowing of Adam's prediction that there would be a destruction of the universe, at one time by fire and at another by flood, they erected two pillars, one of brick and the other of stone, inscribing their discoveries on both. Should the pillar of brick disappear in the deluge, 'that of stone would remain to teach men what was graven thereon . . . It exists to this day in the land of Seiris.'[5] Josephus was also concerned that God's virtue should appear questionable for his not giving due warning to the wicked of their impending doom. So, Josephus has Noah urging the wicked to come to repentance. As for Noah's leaving them to it, Josephus invents the idea that Noah, with his family, left the country for fear that he would be murdered.[6]

Josephus' intention in his *The Antiquities of the Jews* was, above all, a teacherly one. As Steve Mason notes, his aim was 'to provide a handbook of Judean law, history and

---

[4] See Louis H. Feldmann, 'Josephus' Portrait of Noah and Its Parallels in Philo, Pseudo-Philo's *Biblical Antiquities*, and Rabbinic Midrashim,' *Proceedings of the American Academy of Jewish Research* 55 (1988), p. 37.
[5] *Ibid.*, vol. 4, bk. 1, sec. 71.    [6] *Ibid.*, vol. 4, bk. 1, sec. 74.

culture for a Gentile audience in Rome that is keenly interested in Jewish matters'.[7] To wade through sixty thousand lines in twenty volumes, you'd want to be. Be that as it may, Josephus *was* committed to demonstrating to his readers that the story of Noah and the flood was an historical one. Thus, for example, he was particularly exercised to justify the chronology of the book of Genesis and that of the flood. In particular, he addressed the probable scepticism of his audience on the longevity of the Biblical heroes. That they lived so long, he suggested, was because God loved them, their vegetarian diet was conducive to it, and they needed that long for their scientific work in astronomy and geometry. Moreover, he declared, 'my words [about patriarchal longevity] are attested by all historians of antiquity'.[8]

As the above passage suggests, the key for Josephus in justifying the historicity of the book of Genesis was aligning it with the accepted histories of the Hellenistic world. Thus, for example, of the deluge, he declared,

> This flood and the ark are mentioned by all who have written histories of the barbarians. Among these is Berosus the Chaldaean, who in his description of the events of the flood writes somewhere as follows: 'It is said, moreover, that a portion of the vessel still survives

---

[7] Steve Mason, '"Should any wish to enquire further" (Ant.1.25): The Aim and Audience of Josephus's *Jewish Antiquities/Life*,' in Steve Mason (ed.), *Understanding Josephus: Seven Perspectives* (Sheffield: Sheffield Academic Press, 1998), p. 101.

[8] Thackeray (trans.), *Josephus: Jewish Antiquities, Books i–iv*, vol. 4, bk. 1, sec. 106. See also, Michael Tuval, 'The Role of Noah and the Flood in *Judean Antiquities* and *Against Apion* by Flavius Josephus,' in Michael E. Stone, Aryeh Amihay, and Vered Hillel (eds.), *Noah and His Book(s)* (Atlanta, GA: Society of Biblical Literature, 2010), pp. 167–181.

in Armenia on the mountain of the Cordyaeans, and that persons carry off pieces of the bitumen, which they use as talismans.' These matters are also mentioned by Hieronymus the Egyptian, author of the ancient history of Phoenicia, by Mnaseas and by many others.[9]

In the book of Genesis, having smelled Noah's burnt offerings on the altar, a gratified God made a covenant with Noah never again to destroy every living creature. But Josephus is writing after the fall of Jerusalem, the destruction of the temple, and the slaughter of those sheltering within by the Romans. The sacrificial rituals of the Jewish religion focused on the temple in Jerusalem had been, of necessity, since the fall of Jerusalem, replaced by the prayers of a dispersed Jewish population. Thus, Josephus underplayed Noah's sacrifice of a clean animal and a clean bird and replaced it with a prayer. And it was in answer to Noah's prayer, and not his sacrifice, that God agreed never to destroy the earth by flood:

> 'Howbeit from henceforth I will cease to exact punishment for crimes with such wrathful indignation; I will cease above all at thy petition. And if ever I send tempests of exceeding fury, fear ye not the violence of the rainfall; for never more shall the water overwhelm the earth ... Moreover I will manifest the truce that ye shall have by displaying my bow.' He meant the rainbow, which in those countries was believed to be God's bow. Having spoken these words and promises God left him.[10]

Within the book of Genesis, there are two accounts of the populating of the world after the flood. In the first of

---

[9] *Ibid.*, vol. 4, bk. 1, secs. 93–94.   [10] *Ibid.*, 1. 101–03, pp. 49–51.

these, the whole earth is populated by the sons of Noah – Shem, Ham, and Japheth (Genesis 9.18-19, 10.32). In the second, the whole earth is populated as a punishment from God for human arrogance in attempting to build a tower in Babel (Babylon) that would reach to the heavens. So, Josephus invented a story to harmonise these two accounts. According to Josephus, on account of the growing population on the plain of Senaar (Shinar) to which the sons of Noah had descended from the ark, God told them to send out colonies to ensure peace, cultivate the earth, and enjoy its fruits. They refused to obey. They were incited to disobedience by Nebrodes (Nimrod), a grandson of Noah. Although there is no suggestion to this effect in Genesis, Josephus has Nebrodes as the instigator of the idea to build a tower 'to have his revenge on God if he wished to inundate the earth again; for he would build a tower higher than the water could reach and avenge the destruction of their forefathers'.[11] To forestall their attempt, God created discord among them by making them speak different languages so that they could not understand each other. He then dispersed them all throughout the whole world. The dispersion occurred after Babel, but readers of Josephus knew the precise connections he was making between the descendants of Noah and the nations of the world. This was, in short, that Noah was the father of all the Gentiles.

Deucalion, we recall, was lauded by Plato for having survived a great flood, along with his wife Pyrrha. Deucalion was mentioned by the Jewish Biblical exegete Philo (c.10 BCE–50 CE), perhaps for the first time, as the

---

[11] *Ibid.*, 1. 114, p. 55.

Greek Noah. Interestingly, this is the only occasion where Philo identified a Biblical character with a non-Biblical one.[12] Now, Philo was writing for a Greek-educated Jewish readership, so he was, no doubt, assuring his audience of the factual nature of events in the Bible. That said, unlike Josephus, his interests were philosophical rather than historical.

The Septuagint, the Greek version of the Hebrew Scriptures, had been translated in Alexandria, Philo's hometown, in the first half of the third century BCE. It was Philo's particular aim to interpret the Septuagint by reference to the philosophies of Platonism and Stoicism. In order to do so, he treated the text literally as well as allegorically on the assumption that, whatever its literal meaning might be, it also contained a hidden meaning. The text had, as it were, both body and soul. In the broadest terms, according to Philo, the hidden meaning of the historical parts of the Pentateuch (the first five books of the Bible) was a 'tale of the human soul and its vicissitudes and ascent'.[13] On the one hand, following the Stoics, it was a portrayal of the ethical progress of the individual through the cultivation of the virtues. On the other, following the Platonists, it was a progress towards

---

[12] See Louis H. Feldman, 'Questions about the Great Flood, as Viewed by Philo, Pseudo-Philo, Josephus, and the Rabbis,' *Zeitschrift für die Alttestamentliche Wissenschaft* 115 (2006), p. 402. I am indebted to Feldman for this discussion. See also Albert C. Geljon, 'Philo's Interpretation of Noah,' in Michael E. Stone, Aryeh Amihay, and Vered Hillel (eds.), *Noah and His Book(s)* (Atlanta, GA: Society of Biblical Literature, 2010), pp. 183–191.

[13] Adam Kamesar, 'Biblical Interpretation in Philo,' in Adam Kamesar (ed.), *The Cambridge Companion to Philo* (Cambridge: Cambridge University Press, 2009), p. 86.

the vision or contemplation of God. This distinction of the literal from the allegorical (or, in Philo's case more generally, the philosophical) was later to become a bedrock of Christian Biblical interpretation. And it was to flow through the history of Christian reading of the Bible until the Protestant Reformation in the sixteenth century and beyond.

On Philo's allegorical understanding, Biblical characters became exempla of the ethical life, indicative of the 'dispositions of the soul'.[14] Thus, Philo's first trio of Biblical heroes – Enosh, Enoch, and Noah – represented hope, repentance and improvement, and justice and restfulness, respectively. 'Just' and 'rest' were particularly apt titles for Noah. For Philo, Noah was a Stoic sage, more excellent than Enosh and Enoch: '"Just" was obviously so, for nothing was better than justice, the chief among the virtues ... But "rest" was appropriate also, since its opposite, unnatural movement, proved to be the cause of turmoil and confusion and factions and wars.'[15] Noah, his soul at rest, had overcome the passions. He was not only just or righteous (δίκαιος) but perfect (τέλειος) in God's eyes. Noah became perfect, we read, 'thereby shewing that he acquired not one virtue but all, and having acquired them continued to exercise each as opportunities allowed'.[16] Moreover, unlike other Biblical characters, Noah had no list of forebears in the male and female line.

<hr>

[14] For an extensive account of Philo's allegorical reading of the Noah story, see Lewis, *A Study of the Interpretation of Noah and the Flood in Jewish and Christian Literature*, pp. 58–74.
[15] Jeffrey Henderson (ed.) and F. H. Colson (trans.), 'On Abraham,' 27-8, *Philo VI* (Cambridge, MA: Harvard University Press, 1935), p. 19.
[16] *Ibid.*, 34, p. 21.

Only his virtues were listed: 'these are the descendants of Noah. Noah was a righteous man, blameless in his generation' (Genesis 6.9). This was 'little less,' wrote Philo, 'than a direct assertion that a sage has no house or kinsfolk or country save virtues and virtuous actions'.[17]

Perfect Noah might have been. But his perfection was only relative to his generation. There were other sages – Abraham, Isaac, and Jacob, for example – whose virtue was 'by nature'. Thus, in the virtue race, considering the times in which he lived, Noah came in only second. Still, the times considered, this was no mean feat: 'That time bore its harvest of iniquities, and every country and nation and city and household and every private individual was filled with evil practices; one and all, as though in a race, engaged in rivalry pre-willed and premeditated for the first places in sinfulness.'[18]

Noah's virtue and his following of right reason were also demonstrated by his having three sons, unlike other men of his generation. Their wickedness was so great that their only children were daughters: 'For since just Noah who follows the right, the perfect and truly masculine reason, begets males, the injustice of the multitude appears as the parent of females only.'[19] It made the daughters easy prey for the evil angels. Allegorically, they were wicked men who rejected reason for the passions: 'But when the light of the understanding is dimmed and clouded, they who are of the fellowship of darkness win

---

[17] *Ibid.* 31, p. 21.   [18] *Ibid.*, 40, p. 23.
[19] Jeffrey Henderson (ed.), F. H. Colson and G. H. Whitaker (trans.), 'On the Giants,' 5, *Philo II* (Cambridge, MA: Harvard University Press, 1929), p. 449.

the day, and mating with the nerveless and emasculated passions, which he [Moses] has called the daughters of men, beget offspring for themselves and not for God. For the offspring of God's parentage are the perfect virtues, but the family of evil are the vices, whose note is discord.'[20] Literally, the family of evil were the giants. Allegorically, they were earth-born men: 'The earth-born are those who take the pleasures of the body for their quarry, who make it their practice to indulge in them and enjoy them and provide the means by which each of them may be promoted.'[21]

On Philo's Platonic presuppositions, God was unchangeable and above all passions. So, Philo struggled to explain how God could be angry that he had made men. His most persuasive answer was that the wickedness of men was so great that, had God been capable of anger (which he wasn't), he would have been provoked and incited to it by men. Philo was worried too by God's having destroyed all the animals, since, lacking freedom of choice, they could not have sinned. He had an answer, if not a particularly persuasive one. In the first place, he argued, just as a king is killed in battle, his military forces are also destroyed, so too, when the human race is killed like a king, other beasts should be destroyed along with it. Second, when the head is cut off, the rest of the body dies, so too when man who is like a ruling head is destroyed, the rest of the living things should perish with him. Third,

---

[20] F. H. Colson and G. H. Whitaker (trans.), 'On the Unchangeableness of God', 3-4, *Philo III* (Cambridge, MA: Harvard University Press, 1938), pp. 11–13.

[21] Henderson (ed.), Colson and Whitaker (trans.), 'On the Giants,' 60, *Philo II* (Cambridge, MA: Harvard University Press, 1929), p. 475.

since the beasts were made to service the needs of men, it was right that, when men were destroyed, the animals were too. Finally, allegorically speaking, when the soul (man) is deluged by such passions that it is metaphorically dead, it is right that the earthly parts of the body (the animals) die with it.[22]

Philo also wanted to explain why, if Noah was the only righteous man, his household were allowed to embark on the ark with him. It was a matter of virtue acquired from Noah. Simply put, just as many soldiers are saved by a good commander, so the righteous man 'acquires virtue not only for himself but also for his household'.[23] Allegorically, as fares the mind, so fares the body. That said, Philo made no mention of Noah's wife. Women in general, like the 'daughters of men', did not rate highly on his list of the virtuous. No Essene Jewish sectary takes a wife, he declared, 'because a wife is a selfish creature, excessively jealous and an adept at beguiling the morals of her husband and seducing him by her continued impostures'.[24] And, he went on to say, their fawning talk is like that of an actress on a stage. They ensnare the sight and hearing and cajole the sovereign mind, sufficiently so for the man to pass from freedom to slavery.

The animals too embarked with Noah, two of every kind according to Philo's *Life of Moses*.[25] This was to

---

[22] Ralph Marcus (trans.), *Philo: Questions and Answers on Genesis* (Cambridge, MA: Harvard University Press, 1953), 2.9, p. 83.

[23] *Ibid.*, 2.11, p. 83.

[24] F. H. Colson (trans.), 'Hypothetica,' 11.14, *Philo: Volume IX* (Cambridge, MA: Harvard University Press, 1954), p. 443.

[25] Philo's *Questions and Answers on Genesis* focuses on the seven pairs of clean beasts and one pair of unclean 'to nourish seed on all the earth'.

preserve seed in expectation of better times to come. The ark was, as a result, 'a miniature of earth in its entirety, comprising the races of living creatures, of which the world had carried before innumerable specimens, and perhaps would carry them again'.[26]

Unlike Josephus, who has Noah urging the wicked to come to repentance, Philo has Noah and his household entering the ark without any warning of impending doom to the wicked. However, noting that the book of Genesis has a seven-day gap between their entry and the beginning of the rain (Genesis 7.10), Philo reads this time period as one of warning: 'The benevolent Saviour grants repentance of sins in order that when they see the ark over against them ... they may have faith in the announcing of the flood; (and that) fearing destruction, they may first of all turn back (from sin), breaking down and destroying all impiety and evil.'[27] The *seven* days was a reminder that, as the earth was created in seven days, it was now to be destroyed at the end of seven days. God decided, we read, 'to fix a time for their destruction equal to that which He had determined for the creation of nature and the first production of living beings'.[28]

The flood represented the passions and desires to which body and soul are prone: '[T]his is truly a great flood when the streams of the mind are opened by folly, madness, insatiable desire, wrongdoing, senselessness,

The seven pairs of birds (Genesis 7.3) are not discussed. See Marcus (trans.), *Philo: Questions and Answers on Genesis*, 2.12, pp. 84–85.

[26] F. H. Colson (trans.), 'On the Life of Moses, Book 2', 62, *Philo Volume VI* (Cambridge, MA: Harvard University Press, 1935), p. 479.

[27] Marcus (trans.), *Philo: Questions and Answers on Genesis* 2.13, pp. 87–89.

[28] *Ibid.*, 2.14, p. 91.

recklessness and impiety; and when the fountains of the body are opened by sensual pleasure, desire drunkenness, gourmandism and licentiousness with kin and sisters and by incurable vices.'[29] Thus, the ark into which Noah and the household entered was a symbol of the body. Philo's allegory of the ark is both exhaustive and exhausting. No detail about the literal ark escaped his allegorising imagination.[30] Thus, for example, the ark was constructed of quadrangular beams, and most parts of the body are like that. Like the ark tarred with bitumen inside and out, the body was united inside and out. The dimensions of the ark were proportionate to those of the human body. The window in the side of the ark symbolised the anus. The three decks in the ark represented the different levels of bodily digestion. Thus, in the skilled constructing of the ark, Noah and his household 'learned more clearly the principle and proportions of the human body. For nothing so enslaved man as the bodily elements of his being, and those things through which passions [or vices] come, and especially wicked passions of pleasure and appetites.'[31]

Ever the righteous one, as Noah had entered the ark at the command of God, so he only left it on the divine command. According to the Septuagint, Noah entered the ark with his sons and his wife and his sons' wives (Genesis 7.7) but left it with his wife and then his sons, and his sons' wives (Genesis 8.18). From this change of word order Philo concluded that there was no sex on the ark. Thus, the Biblical text was indicating 'that those who

---

[29]  *Ibid.*, 2.18, p. 99.    [30]  See *Ibid.*, 2.2-7, pp. 69–81.
[31]  *Ibid.*, 2.7, pp. 79–81.

went in should abstain from intercourse with their wives and that when they went out, they should sow seed in accordance with nature'.[32] The time after the flood was to be a new start for humanity. And, we can presume, Philo did not wish to have any pregnancies before the new creation to come. Noah and his household were to become 'leaders of the regeneration, inaugurators of a second cycle, spared as embers to rekindle mankind, that highest form of life, which has received dominion over everything whatsoever upon earth, born to be the likeness of God's power and image of His nature, the visible of the Invisible, the created of the Eternal'.[33] Noah was now, as far as possible, similar 'to the first earthborn man'.[34] He was almost perfect, although not quite as much so as his predecessor, Adam, or his successors, Abraham and Moses.

Josephus did not deal with the issue of Noah's drunkenness. For Josephus it mattered little, since Noah was not perfect anyway. Bur for Philo, Noah was perfect (or close to it), so his drunkenness was a problem. Following Genesis 9.21 literally, Philo informs us that Noah did not drink *all* of the wine but only a portion of it, as wise men do: 'For there is a twofold and double way of becoming drunken: one is to drink wine to excess. which is a sin peculiar to the vicious and evil man; the other is to partake of wine, which always happens to the wise man.'[35] Elsewhere, Philo seemed willing to give Noah more leeway when dealing at some length with the question,

---

[32] *Ibid.*, 2.49, p. 129.
[33] Colson (trans.), *On the Life of Moses, Book 2*, 62, *Philo Volume VI*, p. 481.
[34] Marcus (trans.), *Philo: Questions and Answers on Genesis*, 2.17, p. 97.
[35] *Ibid.*, 2.68, p. 160.

'Will the wise man get drunk?' Wise readers of this work, fond of a glass or two (or so), will perhaps be comforted by his answer: '[F]or the wise man becomes a more genial person after indulging in wine than when he is sober, and accordingly we should not be wrong in asserting on this ground as well as on those others that he will get drunk.'[36]

Noah's nakedness, while drunk, was another problem for Philo. To excuse it, he read Genesis 9.21 literally. Noah's nakedness was not for all the world to see, having occurred inside his house. But Philo also read it allegorically. Noah's nakedness when drunk meant complete insensibility, foolish talking and raving, insatiable greediness, and cheerfulness and gladness. It was bereft of virtue. But at least Noah did not spread his sin, containing it within himself. All things considered, the soberness of soul and body was to be much preferred: 'In fact, every evil which has drunkenness for its author has its counterpart in some good which is produced by soberness.'[37]

The Genesis text tells us that Ham, having seen Noah's nakedness, told his two brothers outside (Genesis 9.22). According to Philo, he not only reported his father's naked drunkenness to his brothers *and* to all those standing around outside, but he did so derisively and jokingly. Thus did Philo begin the long tradition of Ham's mocking Noah. But why was it that Ham's son Canaan was cursed even though he had done nothing wrong (Genesis 9.25)? Allegorically, Philo suggested, 'Ham' is the name for vice

---

[36] F. H. Colson and G. H. Whitaker (trans.), *Concerning Noah's Work as a Planter*, 166, *Philo Volume III* (Cambridge, MA: Harvard University Press, 1930), p. 299.

[37] Colson and Whitaker (trans.), *On Sobriety*, 1.1, *Philo Volume III*, p. 443.

in principle, but 'Canaan' is the name for vice in practice. There is nothing in Genesis to suggest any of this. So, Philo improvised. In cursing Canaan, Philo declared, '*virtually* he does curse his son Ham . . ., since when Ham has been moved to sin, he himself becomes Canaan, for it is a single subject, wickedness, which is presented in two different aspects, rest and motion'.[38] Similarly, Philo wrote, 'both father and son practised the same wickedness, both being mingled without distinction, as if using one body and one soul'.[39] More prosaically, Philo suggested that Canaan was to blame for having spread the story around while Shem and Japheth kept it quiet.[40]

Philo was writing for his fellow Jews in Alexandria. But he was hopeful that, eventually, all would convert to follow the Mosaic law. Philo was aware that his religious tradition was not faring well. But he remained hopeful for the future. If a fresh start could be made, he wrote, how great a change for the better would be seen: 'I believe that each nation would abandon its peculiar ways, and, throwing overboard their ancestral customs, turn to honouring our laws alone.'[41] This was, as we know, a forlorn hope.

## The Gnostic Noah

Josephus and Philo were both committed to the truth of the Biblical texts, whether as literal history in the case of

---

[38] *Ibid.*, 10.47, p. 469. Emphasis added.

[39] Marcus (trans.), *Philo: Questions and Answers on Genesis*, 2.77, p. 169.

[40] F. H. Colson and G. H. Whitaker (trans), *Allegorical Interpretation of Genesis II, III*, 2.16.62, *Philo Volume I* (Cambridge, MA: Harvard University Press, 1929), p. 263.

[41] Colson (trans.), 'On the Life of Moses,' 2, 44, *Philo Volume VI*, p. 471.

Josephus or allegorical philosophy in that of Philo. But there was another group of interpreters in the second to fourth centuries CE, whom we generally gather under the broad title of 'Gnostics', for whom the story of Noah and the flood was a decisive one. Originating within both Jewish and Christian late first-century sects, the Gnostics demonstrate, as Sergey Minov neatly puts it, 'the considerable exegetical efforts exerted by those ancient readers who tried to find a way out of the conundrum constituted by their alienation from the Biblical tradition and, at the same time, their inability or unwillingness to reject it'.[42]

The solution of the Gnostic writers to this conundrum was to reverse the meaning of the story of Noah and the flood, thus turning a Biblical story into a Gnostic one. They did so as a consequence and by means of their commitment to three key foundational tenets within the Gnostic traditions. The first of these was their belief that, as enlightened persons of 'knowledge' ('gnosis'), they had access to the complete truth about God, the world, and humankind. Second, they viewed the early history of humankind as that of a struggle between the powers of light – the sphere of the fully transcendent God – and the powers of darkness – the domain of the evil, arrogant, and

---

[42]  Sergey Minov, 'Noah and the Flood in Gnosticism,' in Michael E. Stone, Aryeh Amihay, and Vered Hillel (eds.), *Noah and His Book(s)* (Atlanta, GA: Society of Biblical Literature, 2010), pp. 215–216. See also Gerard P. Luttikhuizen, 'Biblical Narrative in Gnostic Revision: The Story of Noah and the Flood in Classic Gnostic Mythology,' in Florentino García Martínez and Gerard P. Luttikhuizen (eds.), *Interpretations of the Flood* (Leiden: Brill, 1998), pp. 109–123. I am indebted to both of these works.

envious creator God (the Platonic demiurge) of the
Biblical story. Third, they held that the existence of those
who were not Gnostics was the result of the influence of
the evil powers upon their forebears, while they themselves were nothing less than the 'seed', 'race', or 'generation' of the highest God and, as a consequence,
essentially divine.

Without putting too fine a point on it, we can picture
the 'spiritual' universe of the Gnostics in the following
way. There is an ultimate, transcendent deity, 'the invisible spirit', out of whom everything, visible and invisible,
has emanated. The first emanation of God is a divine
Mother whose intelligence extends into a multitude of
spiritual entities called aeons, rather like the angels in
Judaism and Christianity. These culminate in the lowest
aeon – the female figure of wisdom, Sophia. She is considered to have fallen away from the divine, thus giving
rise to the material world via the malevolent creator God
named Ialdabaoth (or Sakla[s] or Samael). He is the demiurge and boss of the archons or spiritual rulers of the
world. The archons, rather like the Devil and his demons
within the Christian tradition, are ultimately responsible
for the evil thoughts and actions of humankind. The
Gnostics considered the archons to be the rulers of this
present darkness, the spiritual forces of evil in the highest
places against whom Saint Paul railed (Ephesians 6.12).

On the basis of these tenets, and this worldview, the
story of Noah and the flood in Gnosticism can be found
in five key sources. These are: two texts *against* the
Gnostics written by Christian theologians – *Against
Heresies* by Irenaeus (c.130–c.202 CE) and the *Panarion*
by Epiphanius (c.310–403 CE); and three Gnostic texts

from among the Nag Hammadi texts discovered in Egypt in 1945 – *The Apocryphon (Secret Book) of John*, *The Apocalypse (Revelation) of Adam*, and *The Reality of the Rulers (The Hypostasis of the Archons)*. The Gnostics on Noah is complicated, not least for three reasons: first, because Gnosticism is a broad and somewhat artificial category, under the umbrella of which an array of texts shelter; second, because the texts themselves are complex and occasionally obtuse; and third, because Noah is portrayed as both hero and villain, and on occasion somewhere in between, within them. So, let's begin with Irenaeus and Epiphanius, transition to the three Gnostic texts above, and then circle back to Epiphanius on the Gnostic 'Borborites'.

In his work *Against Heresies*, the Christian bishop Irenaeus informs us of the Gnostic 'Ophites' (or 'Serpentites'). According to them, the flood was caused by the demiurge, the evil creator God, Ialdabaoth. His reason for bringing on the flood was humanity's failure appropriately to worship him. Thus, Ialdabaoth 'sent forth a deluge upon them, that he might at once destroy them all'.[43] The demiurge was, however, opposed by Sophia (the feminine figure of Wisdom) who, as the spirit of the transcendent God, brought light into the creation and was responsible for the element of light that was in humankind. Ialdabaoth was committed to destroying all humankind. But it was Sophia who saved Noah and his household: 'Noah and his family were saved in the ark,' we read, 'by means of the besprinkling of that light which

---

[43]  A. Cleveland Coxe (ed.), *Irenaeus Against Heresies*, 1.30.10, in *ANF*, vol. 1, p. 356.

proceeded from her, and through it the world was again filled with mankind.'[44] The earth was covered in darkness, but Noah and his household, like his Gnostic descendants, were saved by light.

The so-called Sethian branch of Gnosticism placed exceptional importance on its followers being, materially or spiritually, the descendants of Seth.[45] As such, they were a special segment of humanity called variously 'the great generation', 'the living and immoveable race', 'the children of Seth', 'the seed of Seth', and so on. Now, Seth, we recall, was Adam's third son after Cain and Abel. He was so named by Eve because, she said (in the Septuagint), 'God has raised up for me another seed (σπέρμα ἕτερον) instead of Abel, whom Cain slew' (Genesis 4.25). For the Sethians, to be truly human was to be identified as of the lineage of Seth. And the transmission of the lineage of Seth was through Noah and his household (as we will now see – well, almost!)

One account of the Sethians was provided by their most trenchant Christian critic, Bishop Epiphanius of Salamis, in his *Panarion*, a refutation of an array of Christian heretics. According to Epiphanius, the Sethians believed that, with the death of Abel, the divine Mother caused the generation of Seth, planting in him a divine spark or seed as a result of which there would be a new humanity, distinct from the stock of Cain and Abel. However, 'a great deal of intercourse and unruly appetition on the

---

[44] *Ibid.*, 1.30.10, vol. 1, p. 356.
[45] On Sethian Gnosticism, see John D. Turner, 'Sethian Gnostic Speculation,' in Garry W. Trompf, Gunner B. Mikkelsen, and Jay Johnston, *The Gnostic World* (London: Routledge, 2018), pp. 147–155.

part of evil angels and men since the two breeds had come together for intercourse'[46] led the divine Mother to return, bring the flood, and destroy the entire human race with the exception of Noah and seven of his household who were 'of the pure stock that derived from Seth'.[47] However, without the divine Mother's knowledge, the angels slipped Ham, who was of the evil angels' seed, into the ark 'to preserve the wicked stock they had created'.[48] Thus, in spite of the divine Mother's attempt to create a new humanity through Noah, as a consequence of Ham's survival, 'the world reverted to its ancient state of disorder, and was as filled with evils as it had been at the beginning, before the flood'.[49] So, despite what the Gnostics saw as Noah's apparent devotion to the false God Ialdabaoth, Noah and his family, as the seed of Seth, were nevertheless saved. The continuation of human wickedness after the flood was explained by Ham not being of the seed of Seth but descended from Cain and Abel (although with whom Ham might have mated remains unsaid). And it also explained the existence of Gnostics and non-Gnostics in the present world. They were the descendants of the sons of Noah on the one hand (the Jews) and those of Ham on the other (the Gentiles).

In another Gnostic text that has come from the Sethian branch of Gnosticism, namely *The Apocryphon (Secret Book) of John*, Noah is again one of the primeval Gnostics. But here we get a quite different account of

---

[46] Frank Williams (trans.), *The* Panarion *of Epiphanius of Salamis: Book 1 (Sects 1-46)* (Leiden: Brill, 2009), 39.3.1, p. 278.
[47] *Ibid.*, 39.3.1, p. 278.     [48] *Ibid.*, 39.3.2, p. 278.
[49] *Ibid.*, 39.3.4, p. 278.

Noah and the flood. According to this text, Ialdabaoth, the creator of the world, along with his rulers, created Fate to bind humanity in ignorance. Disappointed that he could not prevail over spiritual humanity, he planned to bring a flood upon all humanity to destroy them. However, a female figure, 'the greatness of providence' (Pronoia, πρόνοια), warned Noah about the coming flood. Although he, in turn, warned people of what was to come, they ignored him. Here, the Gnostic text departs from the book of Genesis. For, not only Noah but many other people from the 'immoveable generation' were saved. And they were saved not by being hidden in an ark but by being 'hidden in a luminous cloud'.[50] Illuminated by Pronoia who was with them, they were saved from the flood – that is, from the darkness of ignorance that Ialdebaoth had brought upon the whole earth. Noah knew that he was not under the power of Ialdabaoth. When all humanity was drowned in the darkness of ignorance, Noah and his fellow Gnostics were saved by the light of knowledge. This was the allegorical truth behind the literal story of Noah and the flood.

Granting the destruction of all humanity, except for Noah and his enlightened companions, how did wickedness and other races reemerge in the world? Epiphanius' Sethians above had answered the question through the presence of Ham on the ark and his wicked descendants. But *The Apocryphon of John* answered it by moving the mating of the sons of God with the daughters of men to a

---

[50] Michael Waldstein and Frederik Wisse, *The Apocryphon of John*, 24, *The Gnostic Society Library: The Nag Hammadi Library*. Available at http://gnosis.org/naghamm/apocjn-long.html.

time *after*, rather than *before*, the flood, so that Ialdabaoth and his rulers might create a new humanity: 'And the angels changed their own likenesses into the likeness of each one's mate, filling them with the spirit of darkness, which they mixed with them and with wickedness.'[51] Out of this darkness, non-Gnostic children were born, making possible the birth of children of ignorance and evil.

Yet another variation on these themes is to be found in *The Apocalypse of Adam*. Here, Adam informed his son Seth about events that would happen in the future, one of which was the flood. In this text, it was the ruler of the powers, named Sakla, who caused the flood because of those who continually strove after 'the life of the knowledge which came from me [Adam] and Eve, your mother. For they were strangers to him [Sakla].'[52] Noah, who is here identified with Deucalion, is a non-Gnostic ally of Sakla who, along with his sons, their wives, and the animals and birds, is protected in the ark from destruction, on the condition that Noah and his household will not procreate with the Gnostics. The primeval Gnostics, who are the seed of Seth, however, are saved from the flood by angels of the highest God in a special, spiritual place: 'Afterwards, great angels will come on high clouds, who will bring those men into the place where the spirit of life dwells.'[53] When the seed of Seth reappears after the flood, Noah is accused by Sakla of having reneged on their deal and having created a generation that scorns

[51] *Ibid.*, 25.
[52] George W. Macrae (trans.), *The Apocalypse of Adam*, *The Gnostic Society Library: The Nag Hammadi Library*. Available at http://gnosis.org/naghamm/adam.html.
[53] *Ibid.*, n.p.

him. But Noah denies it saying, 'the generation of these men did not come from me nor from my sons'.[54] The primeval Gnostics then go into a land of their own, where they live for six hundred years, together with the 'angels of the great Light', and Noah divides the earth among his sons.[55]

Now, in this text, *The Apocalypse of Adam*, Noah is an ally of the wicked creator God. But we get a different take on heroes and villains in *The Reality of the Rulers* (or *The Hypostasis of the Archons*). Here, Noah was aligned with the ruler of the forces and the Biblical God Sabaoth, who was on the margin between good and evil. In this text, the rulers of the world (the archons) decided to obliterate all flesh by a deluge. When Sabaoth heard of the decision of the rulers, he told Noah to build an ark and hide in it, 'you and your children and the beasts and birds of heaven from small to large – and set it upon Mount Sir'.[56] The feminine figure Norea comes to Noah wanting to board the ark. Now, Norea was the daughter of Eve, and her descendants were the Gnostics, while the descendants of Seth through Noah were the Jews. When Noah refused her entry to the ark, she destroyed it by fire and Noah had to build it for a second time.

Although Norea was refused entry to the ark, she was nevertheless mysteriously preserved. The rulers of the world intervened and tried to seduce her, telling her that she was the offspring of Eve and the rulers. But Norea

---

[54] *Ibid.*, n.p.   [55] *Ibid.*, n.p.

[56] Willis Barnstone and Marvin Meyer (trans.), *The Reality of the Rulers*, *The Gnostic Society Library: The Nag Hammadi Library*. Available at http://gnosis.org/naghamm/Hypostas-Barnstone.html.

turned to them and said, 'It is you who are the rulers of the darkness; you are accursed. You did not know my mother. Instead it was your own female that you knew. For I am not your descendant. Rather, it is from the world above that I am come.'[57] Unlike the Genesis story in which the sons of God did mate with the daughters of men, here there is a failed attempt by the cosmic rulers to seduce the female ancestor of the Gnostics, a failure that guaranteed that the latter would continue to possess the light.

Norea was then informed by Eleleth, one of the luminaries (angels) of the divine Mother, that 'You, together with your offspring, are from the primeval father. Their souls come from above, out of the incorruptible light. Therefore, the authorities cannot approach them, since the spirit of truth resides in them, and all who have known this way exist deathless in the midst of dying people.'[58] In short, the way to salvation was not by means of the God of Israel but through the knowledge of a divine source beyond him, out of whom all reality has ultimately emanated. Norea's triumph was the triumph of all Gnostics over the forces that opposed them. Thus, there were two groups of people descended from the flood – the Jewish descendants of the misguided Noah and his household, and the Gnostic descendants of Norea who was preserved outside of the ark.

All that said, we can now circle back to Epiphanius and his account of the Gnostic Borborites (Filthy Ones). Now,

---

[57] Barnstone and Meyer (trans.), *The Reality of the Rulers, The Gnostic Society Library: The Nag Hammadi Library*.

[58] *Ibid.*, n.p.

in the Gnostic text, *The Reality of the Rulers*, Norea is the daughter of Eve. But in Epiphanius' account of the Borborites, she is Noah's wife. Nevertheless, it is Norea who is the Gnostic heroine and Noah the Creator archon's villain. Thus, according to Epiphanius, the archon who created the world wanted to destroy Norea in the flood along with everything else. When Noah, in obedience to this archon, would not allow her to enter the ark, she burned it – a first, a second, and then a third time: 'And this is why the building of Noah's own ark took many years – it was burned many times by Noria [Norea].'[59] The archons wished to destroy Norea because of her knowledge of the truth. She 'revealed the powers on high and Barbelo [the divine Mother], the scion of the powers, who was the archon's opponent, as the other powers are. And she let it be known that what has been stolen from the Mother on high by the archon who made the world, and by the other gods, demons and angels with him must be gathered from the power in bodies, through the male and female [sexual] emissions.'[60]

The collecting of physical seed by this means enabled Epiphanius imaginatively to 'report' on the Borborites' related ritual practices – naked worship, offering to God male semen in their hands and eating it, the consuming of female menstrual blood, and of food made from aborted infants. Despite Epiphanius' fertile imagination, it is clear that, regardless of the archons' attempt to seduce her, Norea remained virginally pure, and thus an exemplar

---

[59] Williams (trans.), *The* Panarion *of Epiphanius of Salamis: Book 1 (Sects 1-46)* (Leiden: Brill, 2009), 26.1.8, p. 91.

[60] *Ibid.*, 26.1.9, p. 91.

for Gnostic resistance to the archonic wickedness of the world – in modern terms, an icon of feminist resistance to male domination.[61]

It was perhaps a thousand years later that medieval Judaic magic was to absorb the Norea tradition. This was in a short manuscript of Jewish magic from the Cairo Genizah, a collection of some 400,000 manuscript fragments in the storeroom of a synagogue in old Cairo. But here, we might say, the patriarchy pushed back, and Norea becomes the villain in the piece. Here, Niriyah (Norea) appears in one of three spells as the bride of Noah who invented magic, brought sin into the world, and, more particularly, caused male impotence. Fortunately, God and six angels were able to undo the evil spells originating with Norea. The composer of the spell probably knew of the Norea tradition among the Gnostics and reframed it as a Jewish revenge on the Gnostics. As Reimund Leicht notes, its composer may have been aware of 'the Gnostic method of inverting Biblical myth and he therefore re-inverted their inversion, thus turning the Rulers into helpful angels and the heroine Norea into a wicked witch'.[62]

## Allegories and Prototypes in Early Christian Thought

In contrast to the Gnostics who inverted or subverted the literal or historical meaning of the Biblical text, the early

---

[61] See Anne McGuire, 'Virginity and Subversion: Norea against the Powers in the *Hypostasis of the Archons*, in K. L. King (ed.), *Images of the Feminine in Gnosticism* (Philadelphia: Fortress Press, 1988), p. 258.

[62] Reimund Leicht, 'Gnostic Myth in Jewish Garb,' *Journal of Jewish Studies* 51 (2000), p. 140.

Christians were committed to it, despite their recognition of its often inconsistencies and incoherencies. Thus, for example, even though the Christian Platonist Origen (185–254 CE) was inclined to seek interpretations of a 'spiritual' meaning beyond the literal, he was not averse to spilling much exegetical ink over the literal. Against the argument that the dimensions of the ark were insufficient to house all the animals, he noted that Moses was learned in the wisdom of the Egyptians for whom the dimensions of the ark would have been squared, thereby allowing more than adequate space to house the animals. 'Let these things be said,' he declared, 'against those who endeavour to impugn the Scriptures of the Old Testament as containing certain things which are impossible and irrational.'[63] On this, he was quoted approvingly by Augustine.[64]

That said, early Christian theologians were, nonetheless, committed to appropriating the Jewish Scriptures as Old Testament, now superceded by their own Scriptures in the New. They did so by seeking the 'spirit' behind the 'letter', the deeper spiritual meaning beneath the literal. And although within the Christian tradition itself there is a more nuanced terminology, it is useful for us to distinguish two modes of interpretation of this spiritual meaning – the 'allegorical' and the 'prototypical' or 'prefigural'.[65] The 'allegorical' privileges the 'vertical' relation

[63] Ronald E. Heine (trans.), *Origen: Homilies on Genesis and Exodus* (Washington DC: The Catholic University of America Press, 1981), p. 77.

[64] Marcus Dods (trans.), *St. Augustin's City of God*, 15.27, in *NPNF (First Series)*, vol. 2, p. 307.

[65] I use the terms 'prototypical' and 'prefigural' to steer around the modern debate about the distinction between 'allegory' and 'typology'.

between the earthly texts and the heavenly realities. The 'prototypical', grounded in a 'horizontal' view of Biblical history, rakes through the Jewish Scriptures for proto-types or prefigures of the work of Christ and the church in persons, events, things, and ideas that are mentioned in the Old Testament text.[66]

We recall that Philo allegorically interpreted the ark of Noah in terms of the structure of the human body. Augustine accepted the allegory between the ark and the human body given by Philo. But he found Philo's account of the door in the side of the ark as symbolizing the lower parts of the human body through which efflu-ents passed as unworthy of Scripture. Thus, he reinter-preted Philo's allegory of the opening in the ark, in prototypical terms, as the sacraments of the church flowing from the wound in the side of Christ. According to Augustine, Philo, 'for the sake of saying something, makes this door represent the lower aper-tures of the body. He has the hardihood to put this in words and on paper ... Had he turned to Christ the veil would have been taken away, and he would have found

---

The distinction here between 'allegory' and 'prototype' or 'prefigure' is intended merely as a heuristic device in analysis of the early Christian texts. On the debate over the distinction between allegory and typology in modern scholarship and its application to early Christian interpretation, see Peter W. Martens, 'Revisiting the Allegory/Typology Distinction: The Case of Origen,' *Journal of Early Christian Studies* 16 (2008), p. 285, n. 4.

[66] These two levels of Scripture, the literal and the spiritual, were later elaborated in the medieval West into a fourfold meaning of Scripture – the literal or historical, the allegorical, the moral or tropological, and the anagogical, concerned with the destiny of the soul.

the sacraments of the Church flowing from the side of Christ's human body.'[67]

Augustine nonetheless recognised the value of Philo for Biblical interpretation. He described him as a 'Jew of great learning, whom the Greeks speak of as rivalling Plato in eloquence'.[68] While Philo's Jewish successors ignored him, from around 200 CE, his Christian successors embraced him, mined his writings for clues to interpreting the Old Testament, and, crucially, preserved his works. As David Runia notes, 'The allegorical method of interpreting Scripture in terms of an underlying physical, moral, and spiritual sense was introduced to Christianity through Hellenistic Judaism, and particularly Philo.'[69] In comparison, the prototypical method was distinctively Christian and, as we noted in Chapter 1, it began in the New Testament.

The idea that Noah was an exemplar of righteousness, present in both the Old and New Testaments, was common in the early Christian tradition.[70] For the apologist Justin Martyr (c.100–c.165), it was a key theme in his polemic against Judaism. In particular, Noah provided an argument that, as a righteous man before Moses,

---

[67]  R. Stothert (trans.), *Reply to Faustus the Manichaean*, 12.39, in *NPNF (First Series)* vol. 4, p. 195.

[68]  *Ibid.*, p. 195.

[69]  David T. Runia, 'Philo and the Early Christian Fathers,' in Adam Kamesar (ed.), *The Cambridge Companion to Philo* (Cambridge: Cambridge University Press, 2009), p. 227.

[70]  For the following discussion, I am particularly indebted to Lewis, *A Study of the Interpretation of Noah and the Flood in Jewish and Christian Literature*. See also H. S. Benjamins, 'The Flood in Early Christian Theology,' in Martínez and Luttikhuizen (eds.), *Interpretations of the Flood*, pp. 134–149. Jean Danielou, *From Shadows to Reality: Studies in the Biblical Typology of the Fathers* (London: Burns and Oates, 1960).

observance of the Jewish Law was unnecessary. Thus, it was not necessary for Christians to practice circumcision, adhere to the food laws, or keep the Sabbath, not least because the Law was given to the Jews as a consequence of their inclination to unrighteousness. As Justin informed the Jew Trypho, 'You perceive that God by Moses laid all such ordinances upon you on account of the hardness of your people's hearts, in order that, by the large number of them, you might keep to God continually, and in every action, before your eyes, and never begin to act unjustly or impiously.'[71]

Praise of Noah was common in the early Christian tradition. Justin viewed him and his sons as pleasing to God, despite not being circumcised and not keeping the Sabbath.[72] Ambrose of Milan (c.339–397 CE) was lavish in his praise: 'How wise also was Noah, who built the whole of the ark! . . . How brave he was to overcome the flood! How temperate to endure it! When he had entered the ark, with what moderation he passed the time!'[73] Bishop Cyril of Alexandria (c.375–444 CE) began his discussion of Noah with the words, 'Noah was a good man and a genuine lover of God in the highest degree, putting his own virtuous conduct before all else. Since he was eminent and famous, of very good reputation, highly acclaimed, and much adorned with glorious achievements, he was suitably admired' – the very model of a

---

[71] A. Cleveland Coxe (ed.), *Dialogue of Justin, Philosopher and Martyr, with Trypho, a Jew*, 46, in *ANF* vol. 1, p. 218.

[72] See *ibid.*, 92, vol. 1, p. 245.

[73] H. de Romestin (trans.), *On the Duties of the Clergy*, 1.25, in *NPNF (Second Series)* vol. 10, p. 21.

modern Christian fifth-century bishop, one might say.[74] Augustine was more reserved. Noah's being 'perfect in his generation' (Genesis 6.9), he wrote, meant that, although Noah could not be as perfect as Christians would be when they were immortal like angels, he was as perfect as any could be 'in their sojourn in this world.'[75]

The early Christian interpreters were also heir to the tradition that Noah gave his contemporaries a chance to repent. Thus, for example, the first-century Bishop Clement of Rome (c.35–99 CE) urged his readers to repent to ensure their salvation, declaring that 'Noah preached repentance, and as many as listened to him were saved'.[76] Theophilus of Antioch (d. 180 CE) informs us that Noah, 'when he announced to the men then alive that there was a flood coming prophesied to them saying, Come thither, God calls you to repentance'.[77] Hippolytus of Rome (c.170–c.235 CE) has, intriguingly, Noah placing the body of Adam in the ark and then has God instructing Noah to make a rattle and a hammer of boxwood which he was to strike to attract the attention of the wicked. As soon as he did so, the people came to him, 'and he warned and alarmed them by telling of the immediate approach of the flood, and of the destruction already hasting on and impending. Thus, moreover, was

[74] Nicholas P. Lunn (trans.), *St. Cyril of Alexandria: Glaphyra on the Pentateuch, Volume 1, Genesis*, 2.1 (Washington, DC: The Catholic University of America Press, 2019), p. 81.
[75] Dods (trans.), *St. Augustin's City of God*, 15.26, in *NPNF (First Series)*, vol. 2, p. 306.
[76] Allan Menzies (ed.), *The First Epistle of Clement to the Corinthians*, 7, in *ANF*, vol. 9, p. 231.
[77] Marcus Dods (trans.), *Theophilus to Autolycus*, 19, in *ANF*, vol. 2, p. 116.

the pity of God toward them displayed ... But the sons of Cain did not comply with what Noah proclaimed to them.'[78]

This story of Noah's rattle and hammer is, to the best of my knowledge, unique to Hippolytus. Perhaps also as original is his story of the wife of Ham. To date, in the history of the Noah tradition, we know that the wife of Noah has been given one hundred and three different names, of whom Norea above was one. All of which rather gives the lie to the Mother Goose nursery rhyme, 'Noah of old, and Noah's dame, / I think I never heard her name, / But she went in tho' all the same.' As to the wife of Ham, we know that she has been given some twenty-nine names, Shem's wife thirty, and Japheth's thirty-five.[79] Hippolytus gives us one more for Ham – Zedkat Nabu, another for Shem – Nahalath Mahnuk, and for Japheth – Arathka. And along with that, he gives us a new story. According to this, God had told Noah that whoever first announced the approaching deluge, 'him you shall destroy that very moment.' Zedkat was about to put some bread into the oven when water gushed out, penetrating and ruining the bread. She went to Noah and told him, 'Oh, sir, the word of God is come good.' Noah asked her, 'Is then the flood already come?' to which she replied, 'Thou hast said it.' Noah was about to kill her when God intervened: 'Destroy not the wife of Cham; for from thy mouth is the beginning of destruction – "thou didst first

[78] S. D. F. Salmond (trans.), *Fragments from Commentaries on Various Books of Scriptures*, in *ANF*, vol. 5, p. 197.
[79] See Francis Lee Utley, 'The One Hundred and Three Names of Noah's Wife,' *Speculum* 16 (1941), pp. 426–452.

say, 'The flood is come'" At the voice of Noah, the flood came.'[80]

As the beginning of a new humanity, Noah was also a prototype of Christ. 'For Christ,' declared Justin Martyr, 'being the first-born of every creature became again the chief of another race regenerated by Himself through water, and faith, and wood, containing the mystery of the cross, even as Noah was saved by wood when he rode over the waters with his household.'[81] The Platonist Origen noted that, although the birth of Noah promised rest (Genesis 5.29), this had not happened to those of the generation of the flood. Christ, on the other hand, was the 'spiritual Noah who has given rest to men and has taken away the sins of the world'.[82] For Cyril of Jerusalem, Christ was 'the true Noah,'[83] while for Augustine, 'Christ was represented also in Noah'.[84]

The North African theologian Tertullian (c.155–c.220 CE) was the first to develop the idea of the ark as a prototype of the church. Thus, for example, he argued in his *On Idolatry* that there was no place in the church for worship of idols. In the ark, he declared, there was no animal fashioned to represent an idolater. He concluded this book with the words, 'Let not that be in the Church

---

[80] Salmond (trans.), *Fragments from Commentaries on Various Books of Scriptures*, in *ANF*, vol. 5, p. 196.

[81] Coxe (ed.), *Dialogue of Justin, Philosopher and Martyr, with Trypho, a Jew*, 138, in *ANF* vol. 1, p. 268.

[82] Heine (trans.), *Origen: Homilies on Genesis and Exodus*, p. 80.

[83] Lunn (trans.), *St. Cyril of Alexandria: Glaphyra on the Pentateuch, Volume 1*, 2.5, p. 93.

[84] John Gibb (trans.), *Homilies on the Gospel of John* 9.11, in *NPNF (First Series)*, vol. 7, p. 67.

which was not in the Ark.'[85] And his argument in favour of monogamy in the church looked to that practiced in the ark of Noah. Not only were Noah and his three sons exemplars of monogamy, but so were the animals which, after all, went in two by two, a male and a female.[86]

But it is Origen who sets the pattern of particularly elaborate readings of the ark literally, prototypically, and allegorically.[87] Thus, for example, the decks and rooms in the ark, literally interpreted, enabled the separation of the less active and tame animals from the wild beasts. There were surplus animals to provide food for the carnivores but other provisions stored up for the herbivores.[88] Spiritually, there were no features of the ark that could not be applied to the church or the individuals within it. Thus, for example, those who are saved in the ark, whether men or animals, are those saved in the church: '[T]here are two lower decks and three upper decks and compartments are separated in it to show that also in the Church, although all are contained within the one faith and are washed in the one baptism, progress, however, is not one and the same for all.'[89] The squared planks of the ark that bear all its weight are the teachers and leaders in the church, along with the writings of the prophets and apostles. The clean animals represent memory, learning, and discernment of what we read, the unclean animals the anger and inclination to sin that is in every soul. The pitch

---

[85] S. Thelwall (trans.), *On Idolatry*, 24, in *ANF*, vol. 3, p. 76.
[86] See S. Thelwall (trans.), *On Monogamy* 4, in *ANF*, vol. 4, p. 62.
[87] Formally, Origen distinguishes between literal, spiritual, and moral. See Heine (trans.), *Origen: Homilies on Genesis and Exodus*, p. 85.
[88] See Heine (trans.), *Origen: Homilies on Genesis and Exodus*, p. 74.
[89] *Ibid.*, p. 78.

over the inside and outside of the ark symbolizes the need for Christians to be 'both holy in body without and pure in heart within, on guard on all sides and protected by the power of purity and innocence'.[90] He who hears the Word of God 'is building an ark of salvation within his own heart and is dedicating a library, so to speak, of the divine word within himself. He is erecting faith, hope, and love as its length, breadth, and height.'[91]

Under the influence of Philo, there was also an array of allegorizing of the dimensions (three hundred by fifty by thirty cubits) of the ark. By the time of the Christian philosopher Clement of Alexandria (c.150–c.215), it had become already something of a commonplace. 'Now there are some,' he declared, 'who say that three hundred cubits are the symbol of the Lord's sign [the cross], and fifty, of hope and of the remission given at Pentecost; and thirty, or as in some twelve, they say points out the preaching [of the gospel] because the Lord preached in His thirtieth year; and the apostles were twelve.'[92] Augustine's imaginings were many. The fifty cubits represented the fifty days from Christ's resurrection to the coming of the Holy Spirit. The length of three hundred cubits that make up six times fifty symbolised the six periods in the history of the world during which Christ had never ceased to be preached. The three hundred cubits also made up ten times thirty, representing the ten commandments at the heart of the Jewish law, while Noah himself was the tenth from Adam. The overall

---

[90] *Ibid.*, p. 81.    [91] *Ibid.*, p. 86.
[92] A. Cleveland Coxe (ed.), *The Stromata, or Miscellanies*, 6.11, in *ANF*, vol. 2, p. 500.

proportions of the ark were like those of the human body 'to show that Christ appeared in a human body'.[93] The wood of which the ark was made became a prototype of the wood of the cross. As Ambrose summed it up, 'The wood is that on which the Lord Jesus was fastened when he suffered for us.'[94]

For Augustine, that all kinds of animals were enclosed in the ark pointed to the church containing all nations. But it is clear that the early church was worried about the bad 'animals' within it. Augustine pointed out that there being both clean and unclean animals in the ark pointed to both the good and the bad taking part in the sacraments of the church.[95] Others, like Origen, referred the clean and unclean animals to the good and bad in individuals. The literal meaning of pure and impure animals in the ark, and the dietary laws in Judaism that seemed to go with it, also taxed the minds of early Christian theologians, uncertain whether or not to follow dietary laws and ambivalent about the reasons for so doing.[96] Clement of Alexandria, for example, came up with a dietary reason for not eating swine or fish without scales, namely that they were fat and therefore fattening.[97] John Chrysostom

---

[93] Stothert (trans.), *Reply to Faustus the Manichaean*, 12.14, in *NPNF (First Series)*, vol. 4, p. 188.

[94] Quoted by Lewis, *A Study of the Interpretation of Noah and the Flood in Jewish and Christian Literature*, p. 167.

[95] Stothert (trans.), *Reply to Faustus the Manichaean*, 12.15, in *NPNF (First Series)*, vol. 4, pp. 188–189.

[96] See Moshe Bildstein, 'How Many Pigs Were on Noah's Ark? An Exegetical Encounter on the Nature of Impurity,' *Harvard Theological Review*, 108 (2015), pp. 448–470.

[97] See Coxe (ed.), *The Stromata, or Miscellanies*, 2.20, in *ANF*, vol. 2, p. 370.

(c.347–407) wondered how Noah made the distinction given it predated the law given by Moses (Leviticus 11.1-47). He concluded that the distinction was between animals that should and should not be eaten, partly a matter of cultural preference, partly a matter of nature, instilled in us by God.[98] The Syrian theologian Ephrem (306–373 CE) cut through: 'He [Noah] called the [seven pairs of] gentle animals *clean* and the [two pairs of] vicious ones *unclean*, for even in the beginning, God had multiplied the clean ones.' On the day that Noah was to enter the ark, he continued, 'elephants came from the east, apes and peacocks approached from the south, other animals gathered from the west, and still others hastened to come from the north. Lions came from the jungles and wild beasts arrived from their lairs. Deer and wild asses came from their lands and the mountain beasts gathered from their mountains.'[99] The wicked gathered to watch, not to repent but just to amuse themselves. As a result, Ephrem tells us, God decided there and then to destroy them all.

Following the Biblical story, all were agreed that the flood was, literally, a universal one: '[A]ll the high mountains under the whole heaven were covered ... covering them fifteen cubits deep' (Genesis 7.19-20). But the flood was also read by a large number of commentators as a prototype of baptism by immersion which, from the time of the New Testament, had become the rite of initiation

[98] See Robert C. Hill (trans.), *Saint John Chrysostom: Homilies on Genesis 18-45* (Washington, DC: The Catholic University Press of America, 2010), p. 116.

[99] Edward G. Mathews and Joseph P. Amar (trans.) and Kathleen McVey (ed.), *St. Ephrem the Syrian: Selected Prose Works* (Washington, DC: The Catholic University Press of America, 1994), p. 139.

into Christianity (see 1 Peter 3.18-22). Thus, as Noah and his household were physically saved in the waters of the deluge, so were Christian initiates eternally saved in the waters of baptism. As Cyprian (c.210–258 CE), the bishop of Carthage, put it, quoting the First Epistle of Peter, just as the ark kept Noah and his household safe, '"Thus also shall baptism make you safe."'[100] Similarly, Ambrose of Milan declared that 'in the flood, also, a figure of baptism had preceded ... And thus in that flood all corruption of the flesh perished; only the stock and the kind of the just remained. Is not this a flood, which baptism is, in which all sins are washed away, only the mind and grace of the just are raised up again?'[101] No longer a hostile destructive force that threatened the lives of those in the church, the flood paradoxically also symbolised the saving of the individual soul through the waters of baptism.

But the flood was also a prototype of the end of the world yet to come. God had promised that the world would never again be destroyed *by water*. The flood of Noah, nonetheless, became a prototype of its end by fire. Josephus, we recall, had written of the Jewish tradition of Adam's prediction that there would be a destruction of the universe, at one time by fire and at another by flood. Early Christianity had absorbed this Jewish tradition that the world would end next time by fire. Thus, for example, Justin Martyr, opposing the Stoic belief in the natural and periodic destruction of the world by fire, declared that

[100] Ernest Wallis (trans.), *The Epistles of Cyprian* 74.15, in *ANF*, vol. 5, p. 394.
[101] Roy J. Deferrari (trans.), *Saint Ambrose: Theological and Dogmatic Works* (Washington, DC: The Catholic University of America Press, 1963), p. 279.

God would intervene to end all things once and for all, save those in the church, 'even as formerly the flood left no one but him only with his family who is by us called Noah, and by you Deucalion'.[102] Tertullian declared that, after the flood, the world returned to sin, and thus it was destined to be destroyed by fire. As late as the fourth century, even as expectation of the end of the world was waning, Ephrem could still declare, 'When Christ descended from heaven / Straightway an inextinguishable fire raged everywhere / Before the face of Christ and devoured everything. / And the flood in the time of Noah was the type of this inextinguishable fire. / For just as the Flood covered even the tops of the mountains / So does this fire.'[103] The Spanish bishop Gregory of Elvira (died c.392) put it simply: '[M]an cannot escape the destruction of the whole globe except through the Church, just as also in the cataclysm of the world nobody remained except those whom the ark had shut in.'[104]

The two birds that Noah sent out from the ark – the raven and the dove – were also prototypes of the Christian life. Thus, for the Roman theologian Jerome (c.342–420 CE), for example, the raven was a prototype of baptism in which 'that most unclean bird the Devil is expelled'.[105] According to Gregory of Elvira, the raven signified 'the

---

[102] E. Cleveland Coxe (ed.), *The Second Apology of Justin* 2.7, in *ANF*, vol. 1, p. 190.

[103] Quoted by Danielou, *From Shadows to Reality: Studies in the Biblical Typology of the Fathers*, p. 89.

[104] Luke J. Stephens (trans.), *Gregory of Elvira: On Noah's Ark (De Arca Noe)*, 33. Available at file:///C:/Users/repalmon/Downloads/ Gregory_of_Elvira_On_Noahs_Ark_De_arca_N.pdf.

[105] W. H. Fremantle et al. (trans.), *The Dialogue Against the Luciferians* 22, in *NPNF (Second Series)*, vol. 6, p. 331.

pleasures of the deceitful and impure soul, and the infamy of its black color showed the unrighteous vice of sinners', while its failure to come back to the ark 'showed that the impure pleasures of men must be expelled from the Church and are to return no further'.[106] For Augustine, the raven who did not return was a prototype of men 'defiled by impure desire, and therefore eager for things outside [the church] in the world'.[107]

Of all the creatures in the ark, however, the most significant was the dove. Not only did it tell Noah of dry land, but it was a prototype of the Holy Spirit, not least because it was the Holy Spirit in the form of a dove that descended upon Jesus at the time of his baptism (Mark 1.9). Along with that went the return of the dove with an olive leaf – a prototype of peace. Tertullian seems to have begun the tradition in the second century CE: 'to our flesh – as it emerges from the font, after its old sins, flies the *dove* of the Holy Spirit, bringing us the peace of God, sent out from the heavens, where is the Church, the typified ark'.[108] Ambrose put it simply: Noah 'sent forth a dove which is said to have returned with an olive twig . . . The dove is that in the form of which the Holy Spirit descended, as you have read in the New Testament, Who inspires in you peace of soul and tranquillity of mind.'[109] Augustine took a different tack: The dove of the ark represented the faithful in the church who, like the dove

---

[106] Stephens (trans.), *Gregory of Elvira: On Noah's Ark (De Arca Noe)*, 25.
[107] Stothert (trans.), *Reply to Faustus the Manichaean*, 12.20, in *NPNF (First Series)* vol. 4, p. 190.
[108] S. Thelwall (trans.), *On Baptism*, 8, in *ANF*, vol. 3, p. 673.
[109] H. de Romestin (trans.), *On the Mysteries*, 3.10-11, in *NPNF (Second Series)*, vol. 10, p. 318.

on its first journey, found no peace in the world. The bringing of the olive leaf prefigured those who, baptised outside of the church, might come with the fruit of charity into the one communion. The dove not returning to the ark symbolised the rest of the saints at the end of the world when 'in that unclouded contemplation of unchangeable truth, we shall no longer need natural symbols'.[110]

Noah's drunkenness and nakedness after he left the ark were to stretch interpretative ingenuity. By some, he was denounced. Jerome, for example, was scathing: 'When the body is heated with drink it soon boils over with lust . . . he that drinks himself drunk is not only dead but buried. One hour's debauch makes Noah uncover his nakedness which through sixty years of sobriety he had kept covered.'[111] Elsewhere, Jerome excused him on the grounds that, living in an uncivilised age after the flood, 'perhaps he did not know its power of intoxication'.[112] That said, the drunkenness and nakedness could also be read prototypically. Thus, Augustine declared, opaquely, that 'the planting of the vine by Noah, and his intoxication by its fruit, and his nakedness while he slept, and the other things done at that time, and recorded, are all of them pregnant with prophetic meanings, and veiled in mysteries'.[113]

---

[110] Stothert (trans.), *Reply to Faustus the Manichaean*, 12.20, in *NPNF (First Series)*, vol. 4, p. 190.

[111] W. H. Fremantle et al. (trans.), *Letter LXIX*, 9, in *NPNF (Second Series)*, vol. 6, p. 147.

[112] W. H. Fremantle et al. (trans.), *Letter XXII*, 8, in *NPNF (Second Series)*, vol. 6, p. 25.

[113] Dods (trans.), *St. Augustin's City of God*, 16.1, in *NPNF (First Series)*, vol. 2, p. 309.

Nevertheless, for Augustine, the drunkenness and nakedness of Noah were a prototype of the sufferings of Christ: 'For the mortality of Christ's flesh was uncovered, to the Jews a stumbling block, and to the Greeks foolishness.' Shem and Japheth 'carrying the garment backwards are a figure of the two peoples ... They do not see the nakedness of their father, because they do not consent to Christ's death; and yet they honor it with a covering.'[114] Noah's son Ham was, of course, much criticised for gazing upon his father's nakedness. Although there is no mention of Ham's attitude to his father's nakedness in the Genesis story, Ambrose declared that he 'brought disgrace upon himself; for he laughed when he saw his father naked'.[115] That he was believed to have mocked his father made him a prototype of those who mocked the church. As for Ham, whose name signifies heat, wrote Augustine, 'what does he signify but the tribe of heretics, hot with the spirit, not of patience, but of impatience, with which the breasts of heretics are wont to blaze, and with which they disturb the peace of the saints?'[116]

## A Medieval Moment

The spiritual reading of the ark of Noah was to reach its high point in the twelfth century in Hugh of St. Victor's (1096–1141) *De Arca Noe Morali*, divided into four books

[114] Stothert (trans.), *Reply to Faustus the Manichaean*, 12.23, in *NPNF (First Series)* vol. 4, p. 190.
[115] Romestin (trans.), *On the Duties of the Clergy*, 1.14, in *NPNF (Second Series)* vol. 10, p. 14.
[116] Dods (trans.), *St. Augustin's City of God*, 16.2, in *NPNF (First Series)*, vol. 2, p. 309.

and some seventy chapters. Hugh concluded by emphasising the importance of the ark: 'Into it is woven the story of events, in it are found the mysteries of the sacraments, and there are set out the stages of affections, thoughts, meditations, contemplations, good works, virtues, and rewards. There we are shown what we ought to believe, and do, and hope ... There the sum of things is displayed, and the harmony of its elements explained. There another world is found, over against this passing transitory one.'[117] While Christian interpretation of the Scriptures had recognised the importance of the historical meaning of the text, the historical meaning was often neglected. In contrast to this neglect, it was Hugh's conviction, as Grover Zinn notes, 'that the knowledge of languages and the liberal and mechanical arts ... ought to be utilized in determining the true meaning of the literal sense of Scripture in a much more vigorous manner than had been effected in the past'.[118] For Hugh, only with the correct understanding of the literal sense of the Bible could its spiritual meaning be truly grasped. As he put it, 'All Scripture, if expounded according to its own proper meaning [the literal], will gain in clarity and present itself to the reader's intelligence more easily.'[119]

Only two chapters in Book One of the *De Arca Noe Morali* are devoted to the literal meaning of the ark. They

---

[117] A Religious of C.S.M.V. (trans.), *Hugh of Saint-Victor: Selected Spiritual Writings* (New York and Evanston, IL: Harper and Row, 1962), p. 152.

[118] Grover Zinn, 'Hugh of St. Victor and the Ark of Noah: A New Look,' *Church History* 40 (1971), p. 270. Beryl Smalley, *The Study of the Bible in the Middle Ages* (Oxford: Basil Blackwell, 1952), p. 102.

[119] Quoted by Beryl Smalley, *The Study of the Bible in the Middle Ages* (Oxford: Basil Blackwell, 1952), p. 100.

deal with the shape of the ark in the one and its size in the other.[120] These were the key issues, Hugh suggested, for those who wished to understand the ark according to the letter. On the dimensions of the ark, he followed Augustine and Origen. But on the shape of the ark, he differed not only from Origen's pyramid and Augustine's box but from the whole of the previously existing tradition. The Genesis view on the relative dimensions of the ark was clear – three hundred cubits in length, fifty cubits in width, thirty in height, with a roof finished 'to a cubit above', three decks, and a door in the side (Genesis 6.16). But the Biblical view on the shape of the ark left much to the interpretative imagination.

Until the time of Hugh of St. Victor, although first suggested by Clement of Alexandria, Origen's view on the shape of the ark had become the standard. According to Origen, we should understand the ark 'rising with four angles from the bottom, and the same having been drawn together gradually all the way to the top, it has been brought together in the space of one cubit'.[121] In short, the ark had the form of an asymmetric, quadrangular pyramid, floating on the water (like a raft), and truncated at the top. Hugh clearly has a copy of Origen's work (or an excerpt from it), for he gives us the passage from Origen quoted above. Hugh invited his readers to consider contemporary shipbuilding practices, in the light of which, he believed, the ark à la Origen could not have been stable.

---

[120]  See Book One, chapter 12–13, in A Religious of C.S.M.V. (trans.), *Hugh of Saint-Victor: Selected Spiritual Writings*, pp. 60–63.

[121]  Heine (trans.), *Origen: Homilies on Genesis and Exodus*, p. 73. See also Coxe (ed.), *The Stromata, or Miscellanies*, 6.11, in *ANF*, vol. 2, p. 500.

Simply put, without a hull and without a proper distribution of weight below the surface, top heavy as the ark would have been, it could not have stayed afloat in a storm.

Hugh's ark was significantly different in shape. It was essentially that of a ship's hull with a roof on top, tapering to a single cubit. It had five storeys. There were two below the water line, one containing the animals' dung (four cubits high) and the other their food supplies (five cubits high). The next deck above (six cubits high) contained the wild animals. That took care of the three decks in the Genesis account. Hugh then added two more under the roof. The tame animals were in the fourth (seven cubits high), while humans and birds were in the fifth storey (eight cubits high) at the top. The door in the side of the ark was near the water level, between the second and third stories, to enable ease of entry to the ark. In addition, there was a window in the roof that Noah opened to allow the raven and the dove to search for dry land (Genesis 6.6). And another delightful innovation: on the outer surface of the ark were placed little nests, made specifically for animals that were amphibious, like 'the otter and the seal'.[122]

Despite the Biblical suggestion of only three decks, there was an array of opinions, determined primarily by the need to fit into the ark the variety of animals, birds, reptiles, food, and so on. In opting for five decks, Hugh of Saint Victor was following Origen. Augustine had opted for three.[123] The Christian Sophist Procopius of Gaza

[122] A Religious of C.S.M.V. (trans.), *Hugh of Saint-Victor: Selected Spiritual Writings*, p. 62.
[123] Dods (trans.), *St. Augustin's City of God*, 15.27, in *NPNF (First Series)*, vol. 2, p. 307.

(c.464–528 CE) argued for four – wild beasts, reptiles, domestic animals, and Noah and his household, in ascending order. The English monk, the Venerable Bedc (d. 735 CE), went for three decks, with unclean and then clean animals on the lower two. But he divided the upper deck into three with Noah and his family between tame and carnivorous birds on the third.[124] As we will see in the next chapter, even more variations were offered within the Rabbinic tradition.

Hugh's account of the shape of the ark is more than a matter of arcane (so to say) interest. For his ark – a ship with a roof or a roofed house on top – has become, more or less, the standard depiction of it since that time. Whether Hugh's ark reflected more realistic depictions of the ark that were developing at that time, or whether Hugh's description influenced the depictions, we cannot tell. But both pictures and narrative were reflecting a significant shift in perceptions of Noah and his ark that began at that time.

The pictorial life of Noah had begun around the beginning of the third century.[125] The first representation of which we know occurs on a series of five bronze coins, sponsored by the local Jewish community, the first of

---

[124] See Don Cameron Allen, *The Legend of Noah: Renaissance Rationalism in Art, Science, and Letters* (Urbana: University of Illinois Press, 1963), p. 71.

[125] On the pictorial life of Noah, see Ruth Clements, 'A Shelter Amid the Flood: Noah's Ark in Early Jewish and Christian Art,' in Michael E. Stone, Aryeh Amihay, and Vered Hillel (eds.), *Noah and His Book(s)* (Atlanta, GA: Society of Biblical Literature, 2010), pp. 277–299; Zinn, 'Hugh of St. Victor and the Ark of Noah: A New Look,' pp. 261–272; and John Eric Greenhalgh, 'The Iconography of Noah's Ark,' Master of Arts thesis, Wayne State University, 1982.

which was struck in the reign of the Roman Emperor Septimius Severus (190–211 CE), in the city of Apamea in Phrygia in Asia Minor. It presents two scenes, one of a couple standing on dry land with upraised hands, the other of a couple in a chest floating on water, that is labelled 'Νωε'. Along with the couple in the chest (Noah and his wife), two birds are depicted, presumably a raven perched on the edge and a dove with a branch in its claws. Aside from the birds and Noah and his wife, no other creatures or humans appear. The coin appears to combine the Genesis story of Noah with that of Deucalion and his wife Pyrrha who, we recall, embarked in a 'chest' to escape a flood brought on by Zeus.[126] The image of Noah in a chest (sometimes with chair-like legs) was to last well into the period of the Renaissance. Various thirteenth-century mosaics in St. Mark's Basilica in Venice show Noah pictured with the ark in the form of a large rectangular box (see Plate 8). Michelangelo's painting of the flood in the Sistine Chapel in the early sixteenth century shows the ark as a large rectangular box with a sloping roof.

In keeping with the account of Clement and Origen, the ark was also imagined in a pyramidal form. Thus, for example, the sixth-century Vienna Genesis depicted Noah, his family, and the animals departing from a three-step pyramidal ark. It was an image that was to last until the fifteenth century. The pyramidal ark was to appear on Lorenzo Ghiberti's (1378–1455) doors in the Florence Baptistry. Depictions of the ark also followed

---

[126] See Walter Lowrie, *Monuments of the Early Church* (New York: MacMillan and Company, 1901), p. 237.

the prototype of the ark as the church, begun by Tertullian. A twelfth-century miniature from Regensburg, for example, shows the ark as the hull of a ship upon which rests a Romanesque church.[127] Another ark with a church or cathedral superstructure appears in the twelfth-century Winchester Bible. That said, the new ark that was imagined by Hugh of Saint Victor, essentially that of a ship with a roof or a roofed house on top, also began to appear in depictions of the ark in the twelfth century. Thus, for example, a mosaic from the late twelfth to mid-thirteenth centuries in Monreale Cathedral shows Noah letting the animals out of an ark comprised of a hull surmounted by a roofed house. Similarly, the fifteenth-century Nuremberg Bible depicts Noah looking out for the returning dove from the window of a house on a ship's hull (see Plate 9).

From the minimal description of the dimensions and shape of the ark provided by the Genesis text, Hugh's ark has perhaps no more claim to represent the 'real' shape of the ark intended by the text than the pyramidal or rectangular versions of it. And Hugh's spiritual reading of the ark in *De Arca Noe Morali* outweighed by some sixty-eight chapters the two chapters that he devoted to the literal meaning of its shape, size, and number of decks. Although his spiritual reading of the story of Noah and the ark was the high point in such Christian interpretations, allegorical and prototypical readings of the story were to

---

[127] See Albert Boeckler, *Die Regensburg-Prüfeninger Buchmalerei des XII. und XIII. Jahrhunderts* (München: Reusch, 1924), Plate 27. Available at https://digi.ub.uni-heidelberg.de/diglit/boeckler1924/0167/image, info.

continue until the period of the Reformation in the sixteenth century and beyond. Be that as it may, all the major reformers – Martin Luther, John Calvin, Philipp Melancthon, and Martin Bucer – shared a suspicion of spiritual readings, preferring the literal sense. And Protestant readings of the story from then on were unashamedly focused on the literal sense.

Hugh of Saint Victor was nonetheless in the vanguard of those who, some four centuries before the Reformation, were committed to a religiously motivated quest for knowledge of the world around them, and who used the knowledge thus gained to focus anew on the literal sense of Scripture.[128] Despite the deference paid to the early Christian readings of the Noah story, both literal and spiritual, the period from the twelfth to the sixteenth centuries saw a renewed focus on the literal sense of the story. Biblical interpreters were not only filling in the details absent from the original story, and solving the problems that were ignored in the Genesis account, but they were also using the Biblical story to direct, fashion, and sharpen their own questions about the natural and human worlds.

---

[128] See Peter Harrison, *The Bible, Protestantism, and the Rise of Natural Science* (Cambridge: Cambridge University Press, 1998).

# 3

## Noah and the Flood in Judaism and Islam

~

### Noah and Rabbinic Literature

Two religions arose out of the Hebrew Scriptures in the second half of the first century of the Common Era. Christianity developed into an array of forms as it moved from Israel into the Greco-Roman world. Similarly, Judaism, in various guises, permeated the Greco-Roman world, especially as a result of the destruction of Jerusalem in 70 CE. Of the Judaisms that then arose, Rabbinic Judaism was to become normative and remain predominant.

To the Hebrew Scriptures that it now labelled as The Old Testament, Christianity added its own collection of sacred literature – The New Testament. To the canon of the Hebrew Scriptures (also known as the Mikra or Tanak), Judaism added the Rabbinic writings from the Mishnah (c.200 CE) through to the Talmud of Babylonia (c.600 CE) and beyond. The term 'Rabbinic literature' thus describes the writings 'produced by Jewish teachers ... that became, by the High Middle Ages, the literary patrimony of virtually all of the Jewries of Christian Europe and the Islamic Middle East'.[1]

---

[1] Charlotte Elisheva Fonrobert and Martin S. Jaffee, 'Introduction', in Charlotte Elisheva Fonrobert and Martin S. Jaffee (eds.), *The Cambridge Companion to the Talmud and Rabbinic Literature* (Cambridge: Cambridge University Press, 2007), p. 5.

As the Old Testament was read within Christianity through the prism of the New Testament, the Hebrew Scriptures were read within Judaism through the rabbinic records of the oral teachings of the rabbis. As the New Testament took precedence over the Old Testament, so also the rabbinic interpretations came to take precedence over the Hebrew Scriptures as the rabbis engaged with paganism, Christianity, Gnosticism, and Islam. The rabbis adapted their reading of the Hebrew Scriptures to the cultures that surrounded them as they told and retold the Scriptures, from Bordeaux to Babylon, in the synagogues that had replaced the temple in Jerusalem.[2]

That said, for Rabbinic Judaism, the simple meaning of the Biblical text remained the bedrock of their interpretation. Contradictions were harmonised. Incoherencies were ironed out. Theological problems were resolved. And where the rabbis found gaps in the Biblical narrative, they filled them in. Their interpretations were for the public to hear. They were orators who sought not only to reveal the eternal message of Scripture but to be creative and inventive. They wished not only to educate and to edify but also to entertain their audience. For this discussion, I have chosen the most significant texts that deal with Noah in the rabbinic tradition, covering an eight hundred–year period: from *Genesis Rabbah* in the fifth century, through *The Babylonian Talmud* (sixth century), to *Tanhuma Genesis* (seventh–ninth century), the *Targum Pseudo-Jonathan* (seventh–eighth century),

---

[2]  See Burton L. Visotsky, 'Genesis in Rabbinic Interpretation,' in Craig A. Evans et al. (eds.), *The Book of Genesis: Composition, Reception, and Interpretation* (Leiden: Brill, 2012), pp. 579–606.

*Pirque Rabbi Eliezer* (ninth century), *Abot de Rabbi Nathan* (ninth century), *Sefer haYashar* (at the earliest, tenth century), and the commentary of Rabbi Solomon ben Isaac (also known as Rashi) in the eleventh century.

According to the rabbis, the times were good for the generation of Noah. A single harvest provided food for many years. It was perpetual springtime. The contemporaries of Noah were able to travel from one end of the world to the other in a short time. And they were never troubled by wild animals. Noah had helped. Until 'Noah came,' we are told by Rashi, 'people had no agricultural instruments and he prepared such for them. The earth had brought forth thorns and thistles when they sowed wheat in consequence of the curse imposed upon Adam Harishon: in the days of Noah, however, this ceased.'[3] According to one account, women were pregnant for only three days; according to another, only one. And the children who were born spoke and walked at the time of their birth.[4] The times were so good that the people could ignore God:

> Our Rabbis taught, the generation of the flood waxed haughty only because of the good which the Holy One,

---

[3] M. Rosenbaum and A. M. Silbermann (trans.), 'Rashi on Genesis,' 5.29, in *Pentateuch with Targum Onkelos, Haphtaroth and Prayers for Sabbath and Rashi's Commentary* (London: Shapiro and Vallentine & Co., 1929–1934).

  Available at www.sefaria.org/Rashi_on_Genesis?tab = contents (subsequently referred to as *Rashi*). See also See H. Freedman and Maurice Simon (trans.), *Midrash Rabbah: Genesis in Two Volumes, I* (London: The Soncino Press, 1939), 24.7, p. 202 (subsequently referred to as *Midrash Rabbah: Genesis*).

[4] See *Midrash Rabbah: Genesis*, 36.1, p. 287. J. Israelstam (trans.), *Midrash Rabbah... Leviticus* (London: Soncino Press, 1939), 5.1, p. 60.

blessed be He, lavished upon them. Behold, what is written of them? Their houses are safe from fear, 'neither is the rod of God upon them, it is also written, Their bull gendereth, and faileth not,' their cow calveth, and casteth not her calf; further, They send forth their little ones like a flock, and their children dance; further, They take the timbrel and the harp, and rejoice at the sound of the organ; and it is also written, They spend their days in prosperity, and their years in pleasures; and it is also written, and in a moment go down to the grave. And 'tis that which caused them to say to God, Depart from us; for we desire not the knowledge of thy ways. What is the Almighty, that we should serve him? and what profit should we have, if we pray unto him? They said thus: Do we need Him for aught but the drop of rain?[5]

It was, thus, also the worst of times. It was a time of robbery and violence, idolatry, incest, and murder. Sexual libertinism ran riot. 'The generations of Cain,' said Rabbi Meir, 'went about stark naked, men and women, just like the beasts, and they defiled themselves with all kinds of immorality, a man with his mother or his daughter, or the wife of his brother, or the wife of his neighbour, in public and in the streets, with evil inclination which is in the thought of their heart.'[6] When threatened

5  I. Epstein (ed.), *Sanhedrin Translated into English...*, 108a. Available at https://halakhah.com/sanhedrin/index.html (subsequently referred to as *Sanhedrin*).
6  Gerald Friedlander (trans.), *Pirkei de Rabbi Eliezer: (The Chapters of Rabbi Eliezer the Great)* (London: Kegan Paul, Trench, Trübner & Co. Ltd, 1916), 22, p. 159 (subsequently referred to as *Rabbi Eliezer*). See also, Michael Maher (trans.), *Targum Pseudo-Jonathan: Genesis* (Edinburgh: T. & T. Clark, 1992), 6.2, pp. 37–38. Lewis, *A Study of the Interpretation of Noah and the Flood*, pp. 127–128.

that God would wipe out their children for their wickedness, they refused to have children: 'Behold, we will
restrain ourselves from multiplying and increasing, so as
not to produce the off-spring of the children of men.
What did they do? When they came to their wives they
spilled the issue of their seed upon the earth so as not to
produce offspring of the children of men.'[7] Women
walked around naked, 'with their eyes painted like harlots'
and the angels saw them and took wives from amongst
them'.[8] According to Rabbi Levi, they bore sons 'like a
great reptile', six children at each birth.[9] God regretted
that he had made humanity.

It was not only humans that had become corrupted.
According to Genesis 6.12, 'all flesh had corrupted its
ways upon the earth'. The rabbis agreed. Sex happened
across species: 'Rabbi Johanan said, This teaches that they
caused beasts and animals, animals and beasts, to copulate;
and all of these were brought in connection with man, and
man with them all.'[10] Rabbi Azariah remarked, 'All acted
corruptly in the generation of the Flood : the dog
[copulated]with the wolf, the fowl with the peacock.'[11]
When the flood came, no animals that had sex outside
of their species were allowed on the ark, 'Because the ark
could harbour only pure beings.'[12] Even the earth acted
lewdly: 'wheat was sown and it produced pseudo-wheat

---

[7] *Rabbi Eliezer*, 22, p. 162.    [8] *Rabbi Eliezer*, 22, p. 160.
[9] *Rabbi Eliezer*, 22, p. 161.    [10] *Sanhedrin*, 108a.
[11] *Midrash Rabbah: Genesis*, 28.8., p. 228.
[12] Samuel A. Berman (trans.), *Midrash Tanhuma-Yelammedenu: An English
Translation of Genesis and Exodus...* (Hoboken, NJ: KTAV Publishing
House, 1996), 12, p. 64 (subsequently referred to as *Midrash Tanhuma-
Yelammedenu*).

[rye grass], for the pseudo-wheat we now find came from the age of the deluge'.[13]

About the birth of Noah, the rabbis gave us a fresh reading. The Genesis text said that Noah was born 'blameless' or 'flawless (Genesis 6.9). This was taken to mean that he was among those notables – like Adam, Seth, Shem, Jacob, Joseph, Moses, Samuel, David, Job, Jeremiah, and Zerubbabel (literally, an A-Z of Biblical worthies) – who were born circumcised, and in the image of God. In short, Noah was born in the perfect human shape. Thus, as 'Aboth D'Rabbi Nathan informs us, 'Adam, the first man, also came into the world circumcised, for it is stated, "And God created man in His own image." Seth also was born circumcised, for it is stated "And begot a son in his own likeness, after his image." Noah also was born circumcised for it is stated "In his generations a man righteous and whole-hearted [flawless]."'[14]

There were also many new interpretations of his name. Noah was given his name in Genesis 5.29 where his father prophesied that 'this one shall bring us relief from our work and from the toil of our hands'. Unfortunately, as the rabbis noticed, the root of the Hebrew word 'relief' or 'comfort' and that of the name 'Noah' meaning 'rest' failed to match up. Rabbi Johanan and Rabbi Resh Lakish summed up the problem: 'The name does not correspond to its interpretation nor does the interpretation correspond to the name. Scripture should have written either, "*The*

---

[13] *Midrash Rabbah: Genesis*, 28.8., p. 229.
[14] A. Cohen (trans.), *'Aboth D'Rabbi Nathan*, in *The Minor Tractates of the Talmud... Volume One* (London: The Soncino Press, 1965), 2.5, p. 24. See also *Midrash Tanhuma-Yelammedenu*, 5, p. 51.

*same* yaniḥenu [shall give us rest] "or ... Naḥman ... *the same* ye-naḥamenu [shall comfort us]."[15]

More positively, Noah was said to have brought ease. After Adam but before Noah, declared Rabbi Johanan, neither the cow nor the furrow obeyed the ploughman; but after Noah, they submitted.[16] Resh Lakish noted that, from the time of Adam, the dead were inundated by water in their graves twice daily; but when Noah was born, they had rest.[17] Rabbi Eliezer suggested that Noah was so called because of the scent of the sacrifice that Noah made after the ark rested: '*And the Lord smelled the sweet* (niḥoaḥ) *savour*,'[18] while another rabbi connected his name as 'rest' to the resting of the ark.[19]

But the issue that most exercised the minds of the rabbis was that of Noah's righteousness. Genesis 6.9 said that Noah was a righteous man. Did this mean that he was absolutely righteous or only relatively so? Rashi summed up the opposing views:

> Some of our Rabbis explain it [righteous] to his credit: he was righteous even in his generation; it follows that had he lived in a generation of righteous people he would have been even more righteous owing to the force of good example. Others, however, explain it to his discredit: in comparison with his own generation he was accounted righteous, but had he lived in the generation of Abraham he would have been accounted as of no importance.[20]

[15] *Midrash Rabbah: Genesis*, 25.2., p. 206.
[16] *Midrash Rabbah: Genesis*, 25.2., p. 206.
[17] *Midrash Rabbah: Genesis*, 25.2., p. 206.
[18] *Midrash Rabbah: Genesis*, 25.2., pp. 206–207.
[19] *Midrash Rabbah: Genesis*, 25.2., p. 207.
[20] *Rashi*, 6.9. See also *Midrash Tanhuma-Yelammedenu*, 5, p. 51.
On Noah's righteousness, see Aryeh Amihay, 'Noah in Rabbinic Literature,' in Michael E. Stone, Aryeh Amihay, and Vered Hillel

Rabbi Jeremiah b. Elazar supported the case for absolute righteousness: 'If a man is to be praised to his face only a small part of the praise due him should be given him, but his entire share may be bestowed upon him in his absence, as it is written [Genesis vii. 1]: "For thee I have seen righteous before me in this generation," and [ibid., vi. 9]: "Noah was a just, perfect man in his generations." Thus we see that to his face the Lord merely called Noah righteous, whereas in his absence the verse called him "a just, perfect man."'[21] Similarly, Rabbi Nehemiah declared, 'If he was righteous even in his generation, how much more so [had he lived] in the age of Moses. He might be compared to a tightly closed phial of perfume lying in a graveyard, which nevertheless gave forth a fragrant odour; how much more than if it were outside the graveyard.'[22] Rabbi Ahava not only found Noah righteous but extended righteousness to Noah's sons (but no mention of Noah's wife or of his daughters-in-law), along with the animals, beasts, birds, and creeping things that accompanied him into the ark.[23] At least this explained why others, besides Noah, were considered worthy of being saved.

Noah's claim to absolute righteousness was, of course, tempered by his having succumbed to the delights of alcohol shortly after his exit from the ark. As a result, on

---

(eds.), *Noah and His Book(s)* (Atlanta, GA: Society of Biblical Literature, 2010), pp. 193–214. I am indebted to Amihay for this discussion of Noah's righteousness.

[21] *Tractate Eruvin*, 2. Available at www.jewishvirtuallibrary.org/tractate-eruvin. See also *Sanhedrin*, 108a.

[22] *Midrash Rabbah: Genesis*, 30.9, pp. 237–238.

[23] *Midrash Tanhuma-Yelammedenu*, 5, p. 50.

balance, the overall tendency was to limit his righteousness. Thus, according to Rabbi Judah,

> Only in his generations was he a righteous man [by
> comparison]; had he flourished in the generation of
> Moses or Samuel, he would not have been called right-
> eous: in the street of the totally blind, the one-eyed man
> is called clear-sighted, and the infant is called a scholar.
> It is as if a man who had a wine vault opened one barrel
> and found it vinegar; another and found it vinegar; the
> third, however, he found turning sour. 'It is turning,'
> people said to him. 'Is there any better here?' he
> retorted. Similarly, 'In his generations' he was a right-
> eous man.[24]

On occasion, the view that, compared to his generation,
Noah was righteous was qualified even further. His righteousness was not earned. Rather, it was a matter of the
grace of God and not Noah's works. Thus, for example,
Rabbi Abba b. Kahana suggested that God repented
having made men, *even Noah. He* was saved, he declared,
'not because he deserved it, but because he found grace'.[25]
Even more harsh, Rabbi Ḥanina declared that, because
Noah possessed less than an ounce of merit, he was only
saved through the grace of God.[26] Rabbi Johanan, more
rigid than many, cut Noah little slack. Noah lacked faith,
he declared, and only entered the ark when the water
reached his ankles.[27] Elsewhere, Noah himself declared,
'yet what is the difference between me and them? Only

---

[24] *Midrash Rabbah: Genesis*, 30.9, p. 237.
[25] *Midrash Rabbah: Genesis*, 28.8, p. 229.
[26] See *Midrash Rabbah: Genesis*, 29.1, p. 230.
[27] *Midrash Rabbah: Genesis*, 32.6, p. 252. See also *Rashi*, 7.7.

that Thou showedst love to me and said, "Come thou and all thy house into the ark."[28]

Still, as with the early Christian interpreters, there was a general consensus that Noah had at least preached repentance to his contemporaries and prophesied the approaching doom. 'Noah rebuked them,' declared Rabbi Jose of Caesarea, 'urging, "Repent; for if not, the Holy One, blessed be He, will bring a deluge upon you and cause your bodies to float upon the water like gourds ... Moreover, ye shall be taken as a curse for all future generations."'[29] Genesis 6.3 tells us that, after the sons of God mated with the daughters of men, the days of mortals 'shall be one hundred twenty years'. The rabbis interpreted this period of time as the period of warning that God had given that generation to repent. Thus, for example, Rabbi Huna said, 'The Holy One, blessed be He, forewarned the generation of the flood to repent its misdeeds for one hundred and twenty years.'[30] Similarly, *Midrash Rabbah: Genesis* tells us that, 'For a whole one hundred and twenty years Noah planted cedars and cut them down. On being asked, "Why are you doing this?" he replied: "The Lord of the universe has informed me that He will bring a Flood in the world." Said they [his contemporaries] to him: "If a Flood does come, it will come only upon your father's house!"'[31] According to Rabbi Eliezer, 'Noah said to them: Turn from your ways and evil deeds, so that He bring not upon you the waters of the Flood, and destroy all the seed of the children of

---

[28] *Midrash Rabbah: Genesis*, 32.1, p. 249.     [29] *Sanhedrin*, 108a.
[30] *Midrash Tanhuma-Yelammedenu*, 5, p. 52
[31] *Midrash Rabbah: Genesis*, 30.7, p. 235.

men.'[32] While some rabbis had Noah working hard for many years to build the ark, some were not impressed by his commitment. Rabbi Isaac said that it helped to build itself.[33] Rabbi Johanan, never a fan of Noah, said nothing about his labours.

Like other prophets in the Biblical literature, Noah's warnings were met with contempt. Rabbi Huna put it simply: 'They laughed at him and ridiculed his words ... they continued to mock him.'[34] Rabbi Eliezer graphically reported that the wicked responded, 'If He bring from heaven the waters of the Flood upon us, behold, we are of high stature, and the waters will not reach up to our necks; and if He bring the waters of the depths against us, behold, the soles of our feet can close up all the depths. What did they do? They put forth the soles of their feet, and closed up all the depths. What did the Holy One, blessed be He, do? He heated the waters of the deep, and they arose and burnt their flesh, and peeled off their skin from them.'[35]

The wicked were to get their comeuppance from God. *The Book of Jasher* tells us that, when the flood arrived, around 700,000 people assembled around the ark and cried out in agony, 'Open unto us and let us come into the ark, for why should all of us die?' And they rushed towards the ark to try to find a way in so as to escape the rain, 'which grew terrible all around them.' God ordered the animals and wild beasts that stood near the ark to

---

[32] *Rabbi Eliezer*, 22, pp. 161–162.
[33] See *Midrash Rabbah: Genesis*, 31.11, p. 245.
[34] *Midrash Tanhuma-Yelammedenu*, 5, p. 52
[35] *Rabbi Eliezer*, 22, p. 162. See also *Sanhedrin*, 108b.

attack them and drive them away: 'And the animals and the wild beasts fell over the sons of man, and overpowered them, and drove them away. And the wild beasts killed many of the sons of man, and scattered them all over the earth.'[36] Rabbi Berechiah declared that, when God realised that the flood would not kill all of the wicked, he sent fire upon them from above and 'turned the birds, the wild beasts, and the animals against them to reduce their numbers.'[37]

## Arkan Matters

Generally speaking, the rabbis believed that the deluge had been a universal one, although there was some difference over whether the land of Israel and the Garden of Eden were excluded. At any rate, the world was brought back to how it was before the creation of Adam. Aside from the animals that entered the ark, all were destroyed. As the *Sanhedrin* put it, 'And every living substance was destroyed which was upon the face of the ground.'[38] There was, however, some debate over the fortunes of fish (for whom drowning was not really an option). Genesis 7.22-3 made it clear that everything on the face of the ground was blotted out – and this did seem to exclude fish.[39] 'Some maintain,' *Midrash Rabbah: Genesis* noted, 'that they too were included among those who were to be gathered into [the ark], but they fled to the

---

[36] Edward B. M. Browne (trans.), *The Book Jashar, The Lost Book of the Bible* (New York: United States Publishing Company, 1876), pp. 41–42.

[37] *Midrash Tanhuma-Yelammedenu*, 7, p. 55.     [38] *Sanhedrin, 108a.*

[39] See *Sanhedrin, 108a.*

Ocean [the Mediterranean].'⁴⁰ No need then for any
arkan aquaria.

That said, the destruction of all the animals did seem a
rather gratuitous act of cruelty on God's part. And the
rabbis had to work hard to explain it. Rabbi Judan claimed
that it was the animals that had led man into sin.
He illustrated this by the case of a king who entrusted
his son to a teacher who led him into evil ways, at which
the king became angry with his son and killed the teacher.
'Said the king: "Did any lead my son into evil ways save
this man: my son has perished and this man lives!"
Therefore [God destroyed] "both man and beast."'⁴¹
Perhaps more plausibly, if equally unkindly, it was suggested that, in the absence of men, they were surplus to
requirements: 'This may be compared to a man who set
up a bridal canopy for his son, and prepared a banquet
with every variety [of food]. Subsequently his son died,
whereupon he arose and broke up the feast, saying, "Have
I prepared all this for any but my son? Now that he is
dead, what need have I of the banquet?" Thus the Holy
One, blessed be He, said too, "Did I create the animals
and beasts for aught but man: now that man has sinned,
what need have I of the animals and beasts?"'⁴²

The giants too had tried to get onto the ark. They 'set
their feet on the [opening of the] deep and closed it up,
then each attempted to enter the ark, whereupon his feet
became entangled [in the water].'⁴³ But one of the giants
did survive. This was Og, King of Bashan. The book of

---

⁴⁰ *Midrash Rabbah: Genesis*, 32.11, p. 256.
⁴¹ *Midrash Rabbah: Genesis*, 28.6, p. 227.    ⁴² *Sanhedrin, 108a.*
⁴³ *Midrash Rabbah: Genesis*, 31.12, p. 246.

Genesis had no place for him in the ark, and yet he survived. It led Rabbi Eliezer to an innovative solution: "'And Noah only was left, and they that were with him in the ark" (Genesis 7.23), except for Og, king of Bashan, who sat down on a piece of wood under the gutter of the ark. He swore to Noah and to his sons that he would be their servant for ever. What did Noah do? He bored an aperture in the ark, and he put (through it) his food daily for him, and he also was left, as it is said, "For only Og, king of Bashan, remained of the remnant of the giants" (Deuteronomy 3.11).'[44]

In the meantime, Noah had built the ark according to the specifications that God had laid out for him – three hundred cubits in length, fifty in width, and thirty in height, three decks with rooms inside, a door in the side, a roof (or window) finished to a cubit above (Genesis 6.14-16). This left plenty of scope for disagreement about the details. Rabbi Judah held that the ark had 330 compartments, each ten cubits square, in four rows separated by two corridors each four cubits wide. There was a gangway one cubit in breadth that ran right around the outside of the ark. Rabbi Nehemiah argued for nine hundred compartments, each six cubits square, and three corridors of four cubits in width with the compartments running alongside, leaving two cubits at the outer sides. But there was uncertainty whether the sides were straight or sloping inwards, upwards, and tapering to a cubit.[45]

---

[44] *Rabbi Eliezer*, 23, p. 167.
[45] *Midrash Rabbah: Genesis*, 31.11, pp. 244–245. See also *Rabbi Eliezer*, 23, pp. 164–165; and *Targum Pseudo-Jonathan: Genesis*, 6.14, p. 39.

With the ark all closed up (Genesis 7.16), a source of light had to be found. The 'roof' or 'window' (Genesis 6.16) was understood by Rabbi Meir as 'a light': 'One pearl was suspended in the ark, and shed light upon all the creatures in the ark, like a lamp which gives light inside the house, and like the sun yonder which shines in his might, as it is said, "A light shalt thou make to the ark."'[46] Rabbi Johanan had precious jewels set inside the window to provide light, while Rabbi Phineas imagined a polished gem hung up by Noah so that Noah did not require the light of the sun by day or that of the moon by night.[47]

Where the animals were accommodated was also problematic. For some, the bottom storey was for garbage; the second for Noah, his family, and the clean animals; and the top storey for unclean animals. For others, the unclean animals were on the lowest storey; Noah, his family, and the clean animals in the middle; and the top storey was for the garbage (with Noah shovelling it all through a trapdoor in the side).[48] *Rabbi Eliezer* had all the cattle and animals in the bottom storey, fowl in the next, while reptiles and creeping things were at the top, along with the humans. With 366 kinds of cattle, 366 kinds of fowl, and 366 kinds of reptiles, it was pretty crowded.[49]

The rabbis also wrestled with the question of how all the animals to enter the ark were collected. With the numbers suggested by *Rabbi Eliezer*, little wonder that

[46] *Rabbi Eliezer*, 23, pp. 166–167.
[47] See *Sanhedrin*, 108b; and *Midrash Rabbah: Genesis*, 31.11, p. 244.
[48] *Midrash Rabbah: Genesis*, 31.11, p. 245. See also *Sanhedrin*, 108b where the ascending order is dung, animals, man.
[49] *Rabbi Eliezer*, 23, p. 165.

Noah thought that he lacked the strength to gather all the animals. So, the angels that were appointed over each kind of animal went down and gathered them, along with all their food, to the ark.[50] *The Book of Jasher* had God bring them to Noah who, under instructions from God, determined who would enter the ark and who would be left behind:

> And thou shalt go out and take thy seat by the door of the ark, and all the beasts of the field, the cattle, and the fowls of the heaven, shall assemble and stand before thee, and all those that come around and lie down before thee, thou shalt take and put into the hands of thy sons, and they shall bring them into the ark. But all those that remain standing thou shalt leave alone. And the Lord did accordingly next morning, and great many animals, beasts and fowls came, and all of them surrounded the ark. And Noah went out and seated himself near the door of the ark and all those of all flesh that would lie down before him he gathered into the ark, and those that remained standing he left outside upon the earth.[51]

Other rabbis looked to different selection criteria. On the basis that 'every living thing entered the ark' (Genesis 6.19), Rabbi Hoshaya declared that even spirits who had life but were without bodies entered.[52] According to Rabbi Judah, the re'em or wild ox (or unicorn, according to the King James version of the Bible), a creature reputed to be of enormous height (Job 39.9-12), was not allowed to enter the ark, although its calves were. Rabbi Nehemiah had Noah nonetheless tying it to the ark and

---

[50] *Rabbi Eliezer*, 23, p. 166.    [51] *The Book Jashar*, p. 40.
[52] *Midrash Rabbah: Genesis*, 31.13, p. 247.

ploughing great waves through the water.[53] For rather obscure reasons, *The Book of Jasher* had a lioness rejected but its cubs accepted.[54] On occasion, selection was oddly gendered with God instructing Noah, 'If thou seest a male pursuing a female, accept him; a female pursuing a male, do not accept him.'[55] Rashi, along with Rabbi Samuel ben Nahman, excluded all those animals who had engaged in cross-species sex before the flood.[56] How did Noah know? Rabbi Hisda let the ark decide. He had Noah lead the animals past the ark: '[T]hose which the ark accepted had certainly not been the object of sin; whilst those that it rejected had certainly been the object of it.'[57] On the grounds that cattle were the only species among whom no 'perversion' had been seen before the flood, Rashi had them living separately on the ark.[58]

As we recall, having been assured of their safety, Noah was told by God to embark on the ark with his wife, his three sons, and their wives. The rabbinic tradition paid little attention to the wife of Noah. Nevertheless, *The Book of Jasher* tells us that her name was Naamah, that she was the daughter of Enoch, and that she was 580 old at the time of her marriage. Noah was 498 years of age when he married Naamah, and over 500 old when Shem, Ham, and Japheth were born (Genesis 5.32). Aware of God's intention to wipe out the wicked, Noah had been reluctant to marry and have children. 'Surely,' he said, 'the Lord is about to destroy the sons of man from the

---

[53] *Midrash Rabbah: Genesis*, 31.13, p. 247. The King James version of the Bible, following Jerome's Vulgate, translates this as 'unicorn'.
[54] *The Book Jashar*, p. 40.     [55] *Midrash Rabbah: Genesis*, 31.13, p. 247.
[56] See *Rashi*, 6.22. *Sanhedrin*, 108b.     [57] *Sanhedrin*, 108b.
[58] See *Rashi*, 8.1.

face of the earth, and wherefore should I beget children.'[59] Genesis 4.22 had noted that the sister of
Tubal-cain, a descendant of Adam's son Cain, was called
Naamah. Rabbi Abba b. Kahana identified her as Noah's
wife. She was so called, he said, because her deeds were
pleasing (ne'imim). Others disagreed: '[T]he name
denotes that she sang (man'emeth) to the timbrel in
honour of idolatry.'[60]

Noah had taken enough food onto the ark to last for
twelve months. And God ensured that it would not decay
or rot. But there was some uncertainty about which sort of
food was taken. Some rabbis held that only pressed figs
were on the ark. Rabbi Abba b. Kahana declared that
Noah took in branches for the elephants, plants for the
deer, and grass for the ostriches.[61] Others declared that
each animal was provided with the food it was accustomed
to eat.[62] All that said, life in the ark was tough. Noah's son
Shem was reported as saying,

> [W]e had much trouble in the ark. The animals which are
> usually fed by day we fed by day; and those normally fed
> by night we fed by night. But my father did not know
> what was the food of the chameleon. One day he was
> sitting and cutting up a pomegranate, when a worm
> dropped out of it, which it [the chameleon] consumed.
> From then onward he mashed up bran for it, and when it
> became wormy, it devoured it. The lion was nourished by
> a fever, for Rab said, 'Fever sustains for not less than six
> (days) nor more than thirteen.' As for the phoenix, my

---

[59] *The Book Jashar*, p. 38.     [60] *Midrash Rabbah: Genesis*, 23.3, p. 194.
[61] *Midrash Rabbah: Genesis*, 31.14, p. 247.
[62] *Midrash Tanhuma-Yelammedenu*, 2, p. 41.

father discovered it lying 'in the hold of the ark. "Dost thou require no food?" he asked it. "I saw that thou wast busy," it replied, "so I said to myself, I will give thee no trouble." "May it be (God's) will that thou shouldst not perish," he exclaimed.'[63]

Noah was so constantly occupied with feeding the creatures in his care that he did not sleep for the whole twelve months he was in the ark.[64] He had so much trouble with the cattle and the beasts, Rashi tells us, 'that he was coughing and spitting blood'.[65] Noah was once late in bringing food to a lion, Rashi went on, so it struck him. Others reported that, as Noah was leaving the ark, a lion set on him and maimed him, so that he was not fit to offer a sacrifice to God.[66]

Fear and terror were a constant. The ark rolled in the waters, this way and that. Those in it were continually tossed around. It was as if the ark was likely to be shattered into pieces. All the animals that were in the ark 'were frightened, and the lions were roaring, and the oxen were lowing, and the wolves were howling, and every bird in the ark uttered shrieks after its own language, and the noise re-echoed in the distance'.[67] Noah and his sons cried and wept as if death were imminent. Noah stood and prayed to God: 'Bring me forth from this prison, for my soul is faint, because of the stench of lions. Through me will all the righteous crown Thee with a crown of

---

[63] *Sanhedrin*, 108b.     [64] *Midrash Tanhuma-Yelammedenu*, 2, p. 41.
[65] *Rashi*, 7.23.
[66] *Midrash Rabbah: Genesis*, 30.6, p. 235. See also Israelstam (trans.), *Midrash Rabbah... Leviticus*, 20.1, p. 250.
[67] *The Book Jashar*, p.43.

sovereignty, because Thou hast brought me forth from this prison, as it is said, "Bring my soul out of prison, that I may give thanks unto thy name: for the righteous shall crown me, when thou wilt have dealt bountifully with me [Psalm 142.7]."[68]

Sexual relations for Noah and his household were banned on the ark: 'As soon as Noah entered the ark, cohabitation was forbidden to him, hence it is written, "And thou shalt come into the ark, thou, and thy sons" – apart; "And thy wife, and thy sons' wives" – apart. When he went, He permitted it to him, as it is written, "Go forth from the ark, Thou and thy wife."'[69] Animals were similarly banned from sex for the duration of their time on the ark. According to Rashi, the verse telling Noah to bring all the animals out of the ark that they may 'be fruitful and multiply upon the earth' (Genesis 8.17) 'teaches that cattle and fowls also were separated, male and female, in the ark'.[70] Unlike before the flood, the animals on the ark took it upon themselves to keep to their own species. There were only three who had sex in the ark – the dog, the raven, and Ham: 'The dog was doomed to be tied, the raven expectorates [his seed into his partner's mouth]. And Ham was smitten in his skin.'[71] Only after the exit from the ark were normal relations reassumed. According to Rabbi Judah, Noah was put to shame by Ham finding him naked because, rather than having sex immediately,

---

[68] *Rabbi Eliezer*, 23, p. 169.

[69] *Midrash Rabbah: Genesis*, 34.7, p. 271. See also *Midrash Rabbah: Genesis*, 31.12, p. 246; and *Rashi*, 7.7.

[70] *Rashi*, 8.17. See also *Midrash Rabbah: Genesis*, 34.8, p. 271.

[71] *Sanhedrin*, 108b. Ham's being smitten in his skin refers to the tradition of Ham's descendants being black-skinned. For more, see Chapter 6.

he first planted a vineyard. Rabbi Nehemiah countered that, for exercising self-restraint even after leaving the ark and not having sex straightaway, Noah was esteemed for waiting until God told him and his sons to 'be fruitful and multiply, and fill the earth' (Genesis 9.1).[72]

## The New World

Eventually, God remembered Noah, and the waters subsided, and the ark came to rest on the mountains of Ararat. According to the rabbis, when Noah prepared to send out the raven, it argued back. It accused Noah of hating him, for if he came to grief, there would be no more ravens. He even suggested that Noah desired his mate, the female raven. Noah was furious with him: "'Thou evil one!" he exclaimed; "even that which is [usually] permitted me has [now] been forbidden: how much more so that which is [always] forbidden me!"'[73] Rashi declared that the raven was unconvinced, refused to fly off, and flew in circles around the ark.[74] Eventually it left and, as Rabbi Eliezer reported, 'it went and found a carcase of a man cast upon the summit of a mountain, and it settled thereon for its food, and it did not return with its message to its sender'.[75] Eventually, as we know, the dove too found dry land and did not return.

God had to order Noah to leave the ark for, initially at least, Noah was reluctant to do so, saying, 'Am I to go out and beget children for a curse?'[76] God then swore to

---

[72] See *Midrash Rabbah: Genesis*, 35.1, p. 282.    [73] *Sanhedrin*, 108b.
[74] See *Rashi*, 8.7.    [75] *Rabbi Eliezer*, 23, p. 168.
[76] *Midrash Rabbah: Genesis*, 34.6, p. 270.

Noah that he would not bring another flood upon the world and that Noah could, happily, go forth and multiply. Elsewhere, this slightly rebellious streak in Noah was tempered by his obedience. Thus, when God told him to leave the ark, he went willingly. 'I entered at the bidding of the Holy One, blessed be He,' he declared, 'when He told me, "Come, you and your household into the ark," and I shall not depart except at His bidding. Thereupon God revealed Himself unto Noah, as it is said: "And God spoke to Noah, saying, 'Go forth from the ark'."'[77]

Upon Noah, his family, and the animals leaving the ark, the rabbis took the opportunity to have God give commandments, not for Israel which came into being with the advent of Abraham and received its own commandments, but for *all other* human beings. The children of Noah received seven commandments prohibiting idolatry, incest, murder, blasphemy, fornication, witchcraft, and emasculation.[78] *Targum Pseudo-Jonathan* informs us that Noah built an altar like that of Adam: '[I]t is the altar which Adam built at the time he was banished from the garden of Eden and on which he offered an offering, and upon which Cain and Abel offered their offerings.'[79] Rabbi Eliezer b. Jacob said that it was 'the great altar in Jerusalem'.[80] According to Rabbi Eliezer, the earth was then divided among the sons of Noah. They spread over the whole earth 'as by a huge fish that spawned its eggs

---

[77] *Midrash Tanhuma-Yelammedenu*, 2, p. 56, also p. 60.
[78] *Midrash Rabbah: Genesis*, 34.8, p. 272.
[79] *Targum Pseudo-Jonathan: Genesis*, 8.20, pp. 43–44.
[80] *Midrash Rabbah: Genesis*, 34.8, p. 272.

and filled the earth'.[81] Noah especially blessed 'Shem and his sons, (making them) dark but comely, and he gave them the habitable earth. He blessed Ham and his sons, (making them) dark like the raven, and he gave them as an inheritance the coast of the sea. He blessed Japheth and his sons, (making) them entirely white, and he gave them for an inheritance the desert and its fields.'[82] This is perhaps the earliest example of 'colour-coding' the descendants of Noah.[83]

Be that as it may, for the rabbinic tradition, it was downhill for Noah from the moment he became 'a man of the soil' (Genesis 9.20) and planted a vineyard. There were three that had a passion for agriculture, *Midrash Rabbah: Genesis* tells us, and there was no good in any of them – Cain, Noah, and Uzziah. Noah was a righteous man, suggested the *Targum Neofiti*, until he began to till the soil.[84] 'At first Noah was called a righteous and perfect man,' declared Rabbi Shalum,'but now he is described as a man of the earth.'[85] According to several rabbis, the tree of whose fruit Adam first tasted was a grapevine. Others had God ask Noah, 'shouldst thou not have taken a warning from Adam, whose transgression was caused by wine?'[86] It was 'the demon drink' that got him – literally, according to *Midrash Tanhuma-Yelammedenu:* 'While Noah was planting the vineyard, Satan appeared before

---

[81] *Midrash Rabbah: Genesis*, 36.2, p. 289.

[82] *Rabbi Eliezer*, 23, pp.172–173. See also *Midrash Rabbah: Genesis*, 36.2, p. 289.

[83] See Chapter 6.

[84] See Martin McNamara (trans.), *Targum Neofiti 1: Genesis* (Edinburgh: T. & T. Clark, 1992), 9.20, p. 80.

[85] *Midrash Tanhuma-Yelammedenu*, 2, p. 66.     [86] *Sanhedrin*, 70a.

him and asked: "what are you planting?" He answered: "A vineyard." "What is it?" inquired Satan. "Its fruits are sweet, whether moist or dry," he answered, "and from them one produces a wine that causes the heart of man to rejoice" … Satan suggested: "Come, let us be partners in this vineyard." And Noah replied, "Certainly."[87] Thus did Noah begin to go down the slippery slope, we read, that led him to behave like a lion, then like a pig, and finally like an ape. If the righteous Noah could behave like this, 'how much more so could any other man![88] It all happened quickly: 'He planted it, drank thereof, and was humiliated all in the same day.'[89] The rabbis worried deeply over what was to be done with the drunken former sailor.

According to the Genesis story, drunk and naked, Noah was seen by his son Ham who told his two brothers, Shem and Japheth. When Noah awoke, Noah realised what Ham had done to him. He blessed Shem and Japheth but cursed Ham's youngest son Canaan (Genesis 9.21-7). Noah's realising that Ham had *done something to him* suggested to the rabbis that Ham's sin was more than mere voyeurism on his part. And, in keeping with a tendency among them to see sexual sins as particularly heinous, it was either that Ham had castrated his father or that he had sexually abused him:

> Rab and Samuel [differ,] one maintaining that he castrated him, whilst the other says that he sexually abused him. He who maintains that he castrated him, [reasons

[87] *Midrash Tanhuma-Yelammedenu*, 2, p. 66.
[88] *Midrash Tanhuma-Yelammedenu*, 2, p. 67.
[89] *Midrash Rabbah: Genesis*, 36.4, p. 290. See also *Rabbi Eliezer*, 23, p. 170.

thus;] Since he cursed him by his fourth son [Canaan], he must have injured him with respect to a fourth son. But he who says that he sexually abused him, draws an analogy between 'and he saw' written twice. Here it is written, And Ham the father of Canaan saw the nakedness of his father; whilst elsewhere it is written, And when Shechem the son of Hamor saw her [he took her and lay with her and defiled her]. Now, on the view that he emasculated him, it is right that he cursed him by his fourth son; but on the view that he abused him, why did he curse his fourth son; he should have cursed him himself? – *Both indignities were perpetrated.*[90]

The idea that Noah cursed Canaan, the fourth son of Ham, because Ham had ruined Noah's own chances of a fourth son cleverly explained why Canaan bore the punishment that ought to have been Ham's. As *Midrash Rabbah: Genesis* had Noah declare to Ham, 'You have prevented me from begetting a fourth son, therefore I curse *your* fourth son.'[91] More simply, Rabbi Judah held that, since God had already blessed Noah and his sons

[90] *Sanhedrin*, 70a (my italics). See also, Judah J. Slotki (trans.), *Midrash Rabbah: Numbers* (London: Soncino Press, 1939), p. 348; *Rashi*, 9.23; *Rabbi Eliezer*, 23, p. 170; *Targum Pseudo-Jonathan: Genesis*, 9.24, p. 46 where Noah is told in a dream what has happened. *Midrash Tanhuma-Yelammedenu* sees it only an instance of voyeurism; 2, p. 66.
Interestingly, the Christian Theophilus of Antioch seems to know of a tradition of Noah's castration when he remarks that some have named Noah 'Eunuchus'. See Dods (trans.), *Theophilus to Autolycus*, 19, in *ANF*, vol. 2, p. 117. For modern readings of the sin of Ham, see John Sietze Bergsma and Scott Walker Hahn, 'Noah's Nakedness and the Curse on Canaan (Genesis 9:20-27,' *Journal of Biblical Literature* 124 (2005), pp. 25–40). This article raises the question of whether it was a case of maternal incest.
[91] *Midrash Rabbah: Genesis*, 36.7, p. 293 (my italics).

(Genesis 9.1), Ham could not be punished, although his son could be.[92] The other alternative to explain the curse of Canaan was to invent a new story altogether: Canaan castrated his grandfather before Ham entered and saw what his son Canaan had done. Thus, per Rabbi Eliezer,

> Canaan entered and saw the nakedness of Noah and he bound thread (where the mark of the Covenant was), and emasculated him. He went forth and told his brethren. Ham entered and saw his nakedness. He [Ham] did not take to heart the duty of honouring (one's father). But he told his two brothers in the market, making sport of his father. His two brothers rebuked him. What did they do? They took the curtain of the east with them, and they went backwards and covered the nakedness of their father.'[93]

This was an explanation that sheeted home blame both to Canaan and Ham, the one for castrating his grandfather, the other for gossiping about it and bringing disrepute upon the family patriarch.

For early Christianity, as we have seen, Noah was a prototype of Christ. But there is no sense in the rabbinic tradition of pushing back against the Christian understanding of Noah. Rather, there was a diversity of opinions. On the one hand, Noah was a model of righteousness – pious, obedient, and courageous. On the

---

[92] *Midrash Rabbah: Genesis*, 36.7, p. 293. See also *Midrash Tanhuma-Yelammedenu*, 2, p. 71.
[93] *Rabbi Eliezer*, 23, pp. 170–171. See also *Midrash Rabbah: Genesis*, 36.7, p. 293. Here Rabbi Nehemiah holds that Canaan saw Noah's nakedness first, and therefore the curse attached to him. See also *Midrash Tanhuma-Yelammedenu*, 2, p. 71 where Rabbi Nehemiah's opinion is also reported.

other hand, he was at times a reluctant hero – defiant, querulous, even sinful. And they found it hard to forgive his drunkenness. That said, overall, the rabbis viewed him positively, weaving together, not always completely coherently, the virtues and vices of Noah's character that they perceived within the Biblical text into a positive assessment. They couldn't be too negative. After all, God had chosen him as the only person worthy of being saved from the deluge and the founder of a new humanity to replace the one begun by Adam.

Not as tied to the Biblical Noah as the early Christian fathers or the Judaic rabbis, Islam was more free to create a Noah who, rather like Muhammad the prophet, called his people away from the veneration of idols to the worship of the one true God.

## Noah in the Islamic Tradition

For believing Muslims, the Qur'an is considered to be a literal transcript of the words of God as these were revealed to the prophet Muhammad (c.570–632 CE) from around 610 CE until his death in 632 CE in Medina. According to the Qur'an, Muhammad is the heir of the prophets of Israel in a line that reaches back through Jesus to Abraham to Noah (Nūḥ) and thence to Adam. According to the Qur'an, what God revealed to Muhammad is a recapitulation of what earlier prophets revealed to the people of Israel: 'Surely We have inspired you [Muhammad] as We inspired Noah and the prophets after him, and as We inspired Abraham, and Ishmael, and Isaac, and Jacob, and the tribes, and Jesus, and Job, and Jonah and Aaron and Solomon, and we gave David [the

Psalms]' (Qur'an 4.163).[94] Unfortunately, according to
the Qur'an, both Jews and Christians failed to adhere to
the covenants they had with God and, as a consequence,
needed to repent and to follow the path laid out by
Muhammad (Qur'an 5.12-14). Muhammad is therefore
the last and the greatest of the prophets.

Thus, a central place in the Qur'an belongs to the
prophets who preceded Muhammad. Their role was to
bring an awareness to their own people of their sinful
ways and to call them to repentance. The Qur'an names
twenty-five of them from Adam through to Muhammad.
Except for five of them, all have a counterpart in the
Bible. Six of the chapters (suras) in the Qur'an are named
after prophets – Jonah, Hūd, Joseph, Abraham,
Muhammad, and Noah. Only two of these, Joseph and
Noah, are exclusively devoted to those whose names they
bear. With 131 references to him in the Qur'an, Noah is
the third most popular of the prophets, with Moses (502)
and Abraham (235) coming before and Jesus (93) immediately after.[95] The story of Noah appears in the Qur'an
in an extended form in eight places and is mentioned in
five others.[96] Thus, unlike the story of Noah in the book
of Genesis that forms a continuous story, we need to

[94] Quotations from the Qur'an are taken from A. J. Droge, *The Qur'ān: A New Annotated Translation* (Sheffield: Equinox, 2014).
[95] See Anthony H. Johns, 'Prophets and Personalities of the Qur'an,' in Mustafa Shah and Muhammad Abdel Haleem (eds.), *The Oxford Handbook of Qur'anic Studies* (Oxford: Oxford University Press, 2020), pp. 488–501.
[96] For extended, see Qur'an 7.59-64, 10.71-74, 11.25-49, 23.23-31, 26.105-22, 37.75-82, 54.9-17, 71.1-25. For mentions, see 17.17, 21.76-77, 29.14-15, 51.46, 53.52.

construct the story of Noah from the various references to him across the Qur'an as a whole.

As in the Christian and Judaic traditions, the story of Noah and the flood in the Islamic tradition is also the story of the Muslim interpreters of it. And just as the Christian and Judaic interpretations of Noah and the flood drew upon the story in the book of Genesis, so too did the Qur'anic Noah remain the bedrock of Islamic readings. And where the Islamic commentators found gaps in the Qur'anic account, they filled them in. Where there were difficulties, they clarified them, sometimes by drawing from the details in the Genesis story and in the rabbinic tradition. And they embellished and elaborated on the Qur'anic story of Noah with legends that were told on street corners and in mosques within the earliest Islamic communities, as Islamic interpreters constructed narrative frameworks within which to locate Noah and the other Qur'anic prophets. For this account, I have drawn upon the seminal early Muslim universal histories that chronicle the time from creation via the prophets along with the key early texts in the Muslim literary genre 'Stories of the Prophets'. Within these, Noah functioned, as the Persian commentator al-Tha'labī (d.1035/6) put it, as 'the first of the prophets of the Divine Law and the first summoner sent from God.'[97]

Within the Qur'an, the prophets function as prototypes of Muhammad. The Qur'an constructs the figure of the prophets in ways that are useful for the mission of

---

[97] William M. Brinner (trans.), '*Arā'is al-Majālis fī Qiṣaṣ al-Anbiyā'* or '*Lives of the Prophets*' as recounted by ... al-Tha'labī (Leiden: Brill, 2002), pp. 102–103.

Muhammad. Essentially, the prophets are the subject of persecution stories in which the plot is generally the same: A prophet is sent to a particular people; he delivers his message but is rejected by them; and God destroys the people for their failure to believe the messenger. Noah is the first of these prophets followed by Abraham, Lot, Moses, Hūd, Ṣāliḥ, and Shuʿayb. So, the emphasis in the Qur'an is on the confrontation between Noah and his wicked generation rather than on the details of the ark, the flood, and its aftermath.

Thus, as a prototype of Muhammad, the Qur'an gives us minimal personal details about Noah. The Qur'an, like the Genesis account (Genesis 9.29), tells us only that 'We sent Noah to his people, and he stayed among them thousand years, minus fifty years' (Qur'an 29.14). The Islamic commentators filled in some chronological details. Thus, for example, Muhammad's cousin Ibn ʿAbbās (d. 687) declared that 'God sent Noah to his people when he was 480 years old. Then he called them to God during his prophethood for 120 years. He rode on the boat when he was 600 years old, and then lived after that for another 350 years.'[98] The historian Ibn Isḥāq (704–767), the first to write a collection of stories of the prophets, has Noah's death at the age of 950 years.[99] Following Genesis 7.6, he has the flood beginning in the six hundredth year of Noah's life. Similarly, the historian al-Yaʿqūbī (d.897), following Genesis, has Noah living for 360 years after

---

[98] Quoted by Brannon M. Wheeler (trans.), *Prophets in the Quran: An Introduction to the Quran and Muslim Exegesis* (London: Continuum, 2002), pp. 53–54.

[99] See Gordon Darnell Newby, *The Making of the Last Prophet* (Columbia: University of South Carolina Press, 1989), p. 47.

disembarking from the ark.[100] Al-Tha'labī's *Lives of the Prophets* reported that, after the flood, Noah lived 'for three hundred and fifty years, and his whole life numbered nine hundred and fifty years'.[101] Al-Ṭabarī (829–923) has one calculation, as I read it, at 1,300 or even at 1,650 years.[102]

But we do get one imaginary description of Noah's features in a late twelfth-century text, namely Al-Kisā'ī's *Tales of the Prophets*: He 'was possessed of reason, knowledge and a beautiful voice. He was tall and stout and resembled Adam. He had a broad forehead, an oval face, beautiful eyes, a stout neck, a lank belly, fleshy thighs and calves, an erect stature and graceful feet. He pastured his people's sheep for a period and also learned carpentry, so he led an easy existence.'[103] But Al-Kisā'ī also tells us of his birth. His mother's name was Cainush, daughter of Rakel, in the lineage of Cain. Afraid of the then king, she bore Noah in a cave. Desiring to move freely again, Noah miraculously spoke to her: 'Have no fear on my account, mother; for He who created me will watch over me.'[104] She left Noah in the cave for forty days, after which 'the angels took Noah, adorned and painted with kohl, to his

---

[100] See Matthew S. Gordon et al. (eds.), *The History (Ta'rīkh): Adam to Pre-Islamic Arabia in The Works of Ibn Wāḍiḥ al-Ya'q ūbī: An English Translation, Volume 2* (Leiden: Brill, 2018), p. 271.

[101] Brinner (trans.), *'Arā'is al-Majālis fī Qiṣaṣ al-Anbiyā'*, p. 102.

[102] Franz Rosenthal (trans.), *The History of al-Ṭabarī: Volume 1* (Albany: State University of New York Press, 1989), p. 355.

[103] Wheeler M. Thackston Jr. (trans.), *Tales of the Prophets (Qiṣaṣ al-anbiyā': Muḥammad ibn 'Abd Allāh al-Kisā'ī)* (Chicago: Great Books of the Islamic World, 1997), pp. 92–93.

[104] *Ibid.*, p. 92.

mother, who rejoiced over him and undertook his upbringing until he reached maturity'.[105]

The Genesis story declared that Noah only had sons after he was five hundred years old, and that they were called Shem, Ham, and Japheth (Genesis 5.32). The Qur'an makes no mention of them, although it does intimate in several places that his family were with him on the ark. Nevertheless, the scholars filled in the gap from the Genesis text. Thus, for example, al-Ya'qūbī tells us that 'Children were born to Noah after he was five hundred years old.'[106] Ibn Ishāq names them as Shem, Ham, and Japheth as does the historian al-Ṭabarī (839–923).[107]

The Qur'an is virtually silent on Noah's wife. She remains anonymous. We are only told that 'the wife of Noah and the wife of Lot ... were under two of Our righteous servants [Noah and Lot], but they both betrayed them' (Qur'an 66.10). The commentators filled in the details again. Thus, for example, al-Ya'qūbī tells us that, after Noah began his mission, he remained unmarried for five hundred years. Then, just before God ordered him to build the ark, 'God sent him a revelation to marry Haykal, the daughter of Nāmūsā, the son of Enoch.'[108] For this information, al-Ya'qūbī was drawing

---

[105]  *Ibid.*, p. 92.
[106]  Gordon et al. (eds.), *The History (Ta'rīkh): Adam to Pre-Islamic Arabia* in *The Works of Ibn Wāḍiḥ al-Ya'qūbī*, p. 269.
[107]  See Newby, *The Making of the Last Prophet*, p. 46 and William M. Brinner (trans.), *The History of al-Ṭabarī, Volume II: Prophets and Patriarchs* (Albany: State University of New York Press, 1987), p.10.
[108]  Gordon et al. (eds.), *The History (Ta'rīkh): Adam to Pre-Islamic Arabia* in *The Works of Ibn Wāḍiḥ al-Ya'qūbī*, p. 269.

on the Arabic translation of a sixth-century Christian text in the Syriac language titled *The Book of the Cave of Treasures*. There we read that, when Noah saw the wickedness of his generation, he 'preserved himself in virginity for five hundred years. Then, God spake unto him and said unto him, "Take unto thee to wife Haykêl the daughter of Namûs (or Haykêl Namûs), the daughter of Enoch, the brother of Methuselah."'[109] Al-Ṭabarī attributed to ibn ʿAbbās the claim that 'Noah married a woman [unnamed] of the children of Cain and she bore him a son whom he named Būnāẓir.'[110] Al-Kisāʾī tells us that Noah had two wives – Amorah who bore him three sons (Shem, Ham, and Japheth) and three daughters (Hasura, Mayshura, and Mahbuda), and Walia bint-Mahwil who bore him two sons (Japheth and Canaan).[111] Elsewhere, Canaan is called Yām and Japheth is known as Eber. The latter was said to have died before the flood.[112]

Granting that, according to the Qur'an, Noah's wife had betrayed him, the occasional commentator took the opportunity to construct reasons to have her, as one of the wicked, out of the picture before the flood. Thus, for example, Ibn Isḥāq has Noah, Shem, Ham, and Japheth on board, along with their wives. But there is no mention of Noah's wife on board with them.[113] Al-Kisāʾī remarked that the treachery of Noah's wife was that she 'told her

---

[109] E. A. Wallis Budge (trans.), *The Book of the Cave of Treasures* (London: The Religious Tract Society, 1927), pp. 98–99.

[110] Brinner (trans.), *The History of al-Ṭabarī, Volume 2*, p. 18.

[111] See Thackston Jr. (trans.), *Tales of the Prophets (Qiṣaṣ al-anbiyāʾ: Muḥammad ibn ʿAbd Allāh al-Kisāʾi)*, p. 95.

[112] See Rosenthal (trans.), *The History of al-Ṭabarī: Volume 1*, p. 368.

[113] See Newby, *The Making of the Last Prophet*, p. 46.

people not to strike him because he was mad'.[114] The simple solution to the Quranic account of her betrayal was to have her not enter the ark. Thus, the historian ibn Kathīr (1300–1073) tells us that 'Noah's wife was not a believer with him so she did not join him.'[115] Al-Kisā'ī hints that it was Noah's second wife, Walia bint-Mahwil, who was left behind: She was a hypocrite 'and reverted to her old religion' of polytheistic idolatry.[116]

The fate of Noah's wife was to become entwined with that of one of her sons. For ibn Kathīr went on to say that one of Noah's sons also did not enter the ark because he was 'secretly a disbeliever but had pretended faith in front of Noah'.[117] Ibn Kathīr was drawing here on Qur'an 11.42-47. In this chapter, one of Noah's sons refuses to get on the ark, believing that he can save himself from the flood. 'I shall take refuge on a mountain,' he declared, '[that] will protect me from the water' (Qur'an 11.43). Noah replied that there was no one who would be safe from the edict of Allah. Then, 'the waves came between them, and he was among the drowned' (Qur'an 11.43).[118] But the Noah of the Qur'an was a compassionate man, more so perhaps than the rabbinic Noah. He argued with God for the salvation of his son, but God chastised him,

[114] Thackston Jr. (trans.), *Tales of the Prophets (Qiṣaṣ al-anbiyā': Muḥammad ibn 'Abd Allāh al-Kisā'ī)*, p.157.

[115] Ibn Kathīr, *Stories of the Prophets* (Kindle edition), p. 35.

[116] Thackston Jr. (trans.), *Tales of the Prophets (Qiṣaṣ al-anbiyā': Muḥammad ibn 'Abd Allāh al-Kisā'ī)*, p. 95.

[117] *Ibid.*, p. 35.

[118] See Gabriel Said Reynolds, 'Noah's Lost Son in the Qur'ān,' *Arabica*, 64 (2017), pp. 129–148.

telling him that 'he was not one of your family' and should not have been saved (Qur'an 11.45).

Who was this lost son? The early Islamic commentators were familiar with the Genesis account and with the rabbinic readings of it. But within both Jewish and Christian sources, there is no mention of any sons of Noah other than the three that we are familiar with – Ham, Shem, and Japheth. So, the Qur'anic story of the lost son is unique. The commentators elaborated on the Qur'an. Ibn Isḥāq tells us that Noah 'left behind his son Yam, who was an unbeliever'.[119] Al-Kisā'ī called him 'Canaan', the son of Noah's second wife Walia bint-Mahwil.[120] Al-Thaʿlabī paraphrased the Qur'anic account naming the son 'Canaan'.[121] And he went on give a poignant account, putatively from Muhammad, of the death of both Canaan and his mother:

> If God had pitied anyone of the people of Noah, He would have pitied the woman, the mother of the lad (Canaan), who feared that the waters would reach him, for she loved him greatly. She went with him to the mountain until she reached its peak, and when the water reached her she went out and stood erect on the mountain and carried the boy. When it reached her neck she raised the boy in her hands until the water carried them both

---

[119] Newby, *The Making of the Last Prophet*, p. 46. See also p. 47 where ibn Isḥāq paraphrases the Qur'anic account.

[120] Thackston Jr. (trans.), *Tales of the Prophets (Qiṣaṣ al-anbiyāʾ: Muḥammad ibn ʿAbd Allāh al-Kisāʾī)*, p. 95.

[121] See Brinner (trans.), *'Arāʾis al-Majālis fī Qiṣaṣ al-Anbiyāʾ' or 'Lives of the Prophets'* as recounted by ... al-Thaʿlabī, p. 98.

away. If God had pitied any one of them, He would have pitied this (woman).[122]

That said, the stories of the lost son, and of the disloyal wife left behind, tragic as they were, made clear to Muslims that all unbelievers, even the closest family members, were to be left behind.[123]

It was the wickedness of the generation of Noah that brought about the flood. In the Qur'an, polytheism and the idolatry that went with it were the key sins. When Noah preached to the people, their leaders said, 'Do not forsake your gods, and do not forsake Wadd, nor Suwā, nor Yaghūth, and Ya'ūq, and Nasr' (Qur'an 71.23). Muhammad saw idolatry as the greatest sin of Noah's generation, like that of his own. Thus, one hadith (discourse) from al-Bukhari (810–870) records Muhammad saying, 'All the idols which were worshiped by the people of Noah were worshipped by the Arabs later on ... The names (of the idols) formerly belonged to some pious men of the people of Noah, and when they died Satan inspired their people to prepare and place idols at the places where they used to sit, and to call those idols by their names.'[124]

According to Al-Kisā'ī, King Darmosel, a descendant of Cain, increased the number of idols of the five gods

---

[122] *Ibid.*, p. 99.

[123] See Gordon D. Newby, 'The Drowned Son: Midrash and Midrash Making in the Quran and *Tafsir,*' in Stephen David Ricks (ed.), *Studies in Islamic and Judaic Traditions: Papers Presented at the Institute for Islamic-Judaic Studies, University of Denver* (Atlanta, GA: Scholars Press, 1986), vol. 2, pp. 19–32.

[124] *Sahih al-Bukhari*, 4920. Available at https://sunnah.com/search? q = noah. *Sahih al-Bukhari* is the most important collection of hadith in Sunni Islam.

named in the Qur'an to a total of 1,700. When Noah saw all that, he withdrew into the wilderness.[125] It was then that God sent the angel Gabriel to Noah to tell him of his prophethood and apostleship to his people: "'I am Gabriel. I bear your Lord's greetings and tidings that He has made you a prophet to your people." Drawing near, he clothed Noah with the garb of God's warriors, bound his head with the Turban of Victory, girt him with the Sword of Splendour and said, "Go to Darmasel ... and his people and call them to worship God."'[126]

That God commissioned Noah as a prophet to give his people the warning that, should they not turn to Allah, they would be punished, is the Quran's central message about Noah. Thus, the chapter called 'Noah' begins, 'Surely, we sent Noah to his people: "warn your people before a painful punishment comes upon them." He said, "My people! I am a clear warner for you. Serve God, and guard (yourselves) against Him, and obey me! He will forgive you your sins, and spare you until an appointed time. Surely the time of God, when it comes, cannot be postponed"' (Quran 71.1-4).[127] The Qur'an goes on to report that the people argued with Noah, refusing to heed his message.[128] They thought that he was possessed. A later hadith has Noah warning them about the Dajjall

---

[125] See Thackston Jr. (trans.), *Tales of the Prophets (Qiṣaṣ al-anbiyāʾ: Muḥammad ibn ʿAbd Allāh al-Kisāʾi)*, p. 93. See also ibn Kathīr, *Stories of the Prophets* (Kindle edition), pp. 25–27.

[126] Thackston Jr. (trans.), *Tales of the Prophets (Qiṣaṣ al-anbiyāʾ: Muḥammad ibn ʿAbd Allāh al-Kisāʾi)*, pp. 93–94.

[127] See also Qur'an 7.59; 10.71-2; 11.25-6; 23.23; 26. 106-15.

[128] See Qur'an 7.64; 10.73; 11.27-32; 23.24-5; 26.106-16; 54.9; 71.7-23.

[an Antichrist figure] to come: 'Allah's Apostle [Muhammad] said, "Shall I not tell you about the Dajjall ... The Dajjall is one-eyed and will bring with him what will resemble Hell and Paradise, and what he will call Paradise will be actually Hell; so I warn you against him as Noah warned his nation against him."'[129]

Ibn Isḥāq reported a tradition that the people used not only to argue but to attack Noah: 'and they would choke him until he would pass out'.[130] Al-Thaʿlabī reported that, according to ibn ʿAbbās, 'Noah would be beaten, then wrapped in felt and thrown into his house, and they thought that he had died. But then he would come out and call to them, until he despaired of his people (ever) believing.'[131] He was even beaten up by a boy with a staff.[132] Al-Kisāʾī declared that the people thought that he was mad and would come out of their houses every day and 'beat him until he swooned. Then they would drag him by the feet and throw him on the refuse heaps. When he came to, he would go back and be treated the same way. This continued for three centuries ... with Noah constantly struggling against them and calling them to worship God.'[133]

[129]  *Sahih al-Bukhari*, 3338. On the Antichrist in Islam, see Philip C. Almond, *The Antichrist: A New Biography* (Cambridge: Cambridge University Press, 2020), pp. 133–139.
[130]  Newby, *The Making of the Last Prophet*, p. 45.
[131]  Brinner (trans.), *ʿArāʾis al-Majālis fī Qiṣaṣ al-Anbiyāʾ* or *'Lives of the Prophets'* as recounted by ... al-Thaʿlabī, p. 93.
[132]  See *ibid.*, p. 93.
[133]  Thackston Jr. (trans.), *Tales of the Prophets (Qiṣaṣ al-anbiyāʾ: Muḥammad ibn ʿAbd Allāh al-Kisāʾī)*, p. 95. See also ibn Kathīr, *Stories of the Prophets* (Kindle edition), pp. 27–32.

## The Islamic Ark

Noah's patience eventually wore out and he complained to God about the people's refusal to listen. 'My Lord,' he said, 'surely my people have called me a liar, so disclose (the truth) decisively between me and them, and rescue me and those of the believers who are with me' (Qur'an 26.117-18).[134] Al- Kisā'ī tells us that the earth, the birds, and the beasts also cried out to God to complain of the people's 'haughtiness, disbelief and tyranny'.[135] God too had had enough: 'Do not address Me concerning those who have done evil. Surely they are going to be drowned' (Qur'an 23.27).[136] He told Noah to build an ark.[137] Still, even as he built it, 'whenever the assembly of his people passed by, they ridiculed him' (Quran 11.38). Despite their ridicule, al-Ya'qubi tells us that, having finished the ark, 'he invited them to board it. He informed them that God was going to send the deluge over the whole earth, to cleanse it of disobedient people, but not one of them responded to him.'[138] According to al-Kisā'ī, always fond of a miracle or two, while Noah was building the ark, the people would come by night and set fire to it. But it remained unharmed. Having completed it, Noah went on a pilgrimage. While he was away, the people decided

---

[134] See also Qur'an 23.26; 54.10; 71.5-21.

[135] Thackston Jr. (trans.), *Tales of the Prophets (Qiṣaṣ al-anbiyā': Muḥammad ibn 'Abd Allāh al-Kisā'i)*, p. 97.

[136] See also Brinner (trans.), *'Arā'is al-Majālis fī Qiṣaṣ al-Anbiyā' or 'Lives of the Prophets' as recounted by . . . al-Tha'labī*, pp. 94–95.

[137] I have used 'ark' for the sake of continuity. The Arabic words used in the Qur'an translate as 'ship' or 'boat'.

[138] Gordon et al. (eds.), *The History (Ta'rīkh): Adam to Pre-Islamic Arabia* in *The Works of Ibn Wāḍiḥ al-Ya'qūbī*, p. 269.

again to burn the ark. But God 'commanded the angels to bear it up into the sky, where it stayed, suspended between heaven and earth, with the people still looking up at it but unable to do anything to it'.[139]

Unlike Genesis, the Qur'an was silent on the dimensions of the ark. But al-Ya'qūbī followed the three hundred by fifty by thirty cubits listed in Genesis, along with a lower, a middle, and an upper deck. He reserved the bottom deck for animals (tame, wild, and predators), the middle for birds, and the top deck for Noah and his family, along with food and water.[140] Al-Tha'labī followed suit but had God ordering a much more elaborate ark: 'Make it curved, in three (parts); its head like the head of a cock; its middle like the belly of a bird; and its tail inclining like the tail of a bird. Make it symmetrical and place doors in both its sides'[141] (see Plate 10). Al-Kisā'ī's ark was enormous – one thousand cubits long, five hundred wide, and three hundred high. And he added other decorations: 'its head like a peacock, its neck like an eagle, its face like a dove, its tiller like a cock's tale, its beak like that of a falcon, and its wings like a hawk's. On every feather of the wings he hung multi-coloured jewels, and to the tiller he attached a great mirror.'[142] On each of the planks from which it was made was the

---

[139] Thackston Jr. (trans.), *Tales of the Prophets (Qiṣaṣ al-anbiyā': Muḥammad ibn 'Abd Allāh al-Kisā'i)*, p. 99.

[140] See Gordon et al. (eds.), *The History (Ta'rīkh): Adam to Pre-Islamic Arabia* in *The Works of Ibn Wāḍiḥ al-Ya'qūbī*, p. 269.

[141] Brinner (trans.), *'Arā'is al-Majālis fī Qiṣaṣ al-Anbiyā' or 'Lives of the Prophets'* as recounted by ... *al-Tha'labī*, p. 94. Elsewhere, al-Tha'labī has different dimensions for the ark. See pp. 95, 100.

[142] Thackston Jr. (trans.), *Tales of the Prophets (Qiṣaṣ al-anbiyā': Muḥammad ibn 'Abd Allāh al-Kisā'i)*, p. 99.

name of one of the prophets that shone like stars, except for that of Muhammad that shone as brightly as the sun and moon together. This ark had seven stories, each with a door. Little wonder Noah needed help, not only from his children and his faithful followers, but also from Og, the giant.[143]

Like Genesis, the Qur'an has Noah place two of every kind of animal on the ark (Qur'an 11.40-1, 23.27). According to some of the commentators, Iblis (Satan) made it in as well. Thus, ibn 'Abbās said that the first animal that Noah took into the ship was the ant and the last the ass. 'When the ass entered and got its breast in,' we are told,

> Iblis, may God curse him, grabbed on to its tail, and it could not pick up its feet. Noah began to say, Woe unto you, enter, even if the Devil is with you. The words slipped from his tongue. When Noah said it, the Devil let the ass go on its way, and it entered, and the Devil entered with it. Noah said to him, What caused you to come on board with me, O Enemy of God? He said, Did you not say Enter, even if the Devil is with you? He said, Depart from me, O Enemy of God. The Devil said, There is no way out for you but to carry me, and he was, according to what they assert, in the back of the boat.[144]

Al-Tha'labī recounts the story of the serpent and the scorpion, neither of whom Noah wished to allow on

---

[143] See *ibid.*, pp. 98, 99.
[144] Newby, *The Making of the Last Prophet*, p. 46. See also Brinner (trans.), *'Arā'is al-Majālis fī Qiṣaṣ al-Anbiyā'* or *'Lives of the Prophets'* as recounted by ... al-Tha'labī, p. 96. Here the ant is replaced by a cow.

board. But he relented when each of them promised not to harm anyone who mentioned Noah's name.[145] Worried that some of the other animals would attack each other, Noah asked God what to do: 'God said to him, "Who set enmity between them?" He answered: "You, O Lord." He said, "So shall I reconcile them so that they will not cause harm to one another?"'[146] In the end, there was a mix of animals on the two lower stories. The humans were on the top story although, for reasons that are mysterious, Al-Tha'labī has Noah place 'the parrot with him on the upper level out of solicitude, lest anything evil kill it'.[147] The isolation of the parrot is puzzling. But it may well go the tradition of the language of the birds, lost after the Fall of Man but vestiges of which remain with the parrot. In Qur'an 27.16, Solomon declares that God gave him 'the speech of birds'.

The Genesis account, we recall, had eight people on the ark – Noah and his wife, his three sons, and their wives. But the Qur'an was ambiguous about who was on the ark with Noah. As we have seen, one of his sons wasn't. And the Qur'an does suggest, although doesn't explicitly say so, that his wife was left behind. Noah and his family were on the ark and, we can say, 'whoever has believed. But only a few had believed with him' (Qur'an 11.40). This left plenty of scope for the commentators. Ibn Ishāq, following the Qur'an, included some believers, but he is confusing on whether, besides Noah, his sons,

---

[145] See Brinner (trans.), 'Arā'is al-Majālis fī Qiṣaṣ al-Anbiyā' or 'Lives of the Prophets' as recounted by ... al-Tha'labī, pp. 96–97.
[146] Ibid., p. 97.    [147] Ibid.

and their wives, there were four or six others.[148] Al-Tha'labī cited Qatādah who, following the Biblical account, limited the numbers to eight, including Noah's wife. He cited a further source that had the numbers as seven, leaving out Noah's wife, another that had seventy over and above the Biblical eight, and yet another that held that they were eighty in total.[149]

Within the Islamic tradition, the ark had one unusual traveller – Adam, or at least his body. The scholar al-'Yaqūbī (d. 897/8) tells us that, before Noah brought the animals onto the ark, he and his sons 'went up to the Cave of Treasure. They carried down the body of Adam and put it in the middle of the upper deck of the boat on Friday the seventeenth of Ādhār.'[150] Elsewhere al-Tha'labī reports that the body of Adam was put 'on display as a barrier between the men and the women'.[151] Upon his deathbed, al-'Yaqūbī tells us, Noah ordered his son Shem to go into the ark and retrieve the body of Adam. With his grandson Melchizedek, Shem was to follow an angel to the middle of the earth (Jerusalem) and place the body of Adam where the angel showed him. Melchizedek was commanded to stay there and

---

[148] See Newby, *The Making of the Last Prophet*, p. 46. Al-Tha'labī has different similarly confusing numbers for ibn Ishaq, namely a total of ten, aside from their wives. See Brinner (trans.), *'Arā'is al-Majālis fī Qiṣaṣ al-Anbiyā' or 'Lives of the Prophets' as recounted by ... al-Tha'labī*, p. 98.

[149] See Brinner (trans.), *'Arā'is al-Majālis fī Qiṣaṣ al-Anbiyā' or 'Lives of the Prophets' as recounted by ... al-Tha'labī*, p. 98. See also Newby, *The Making of the Last Prophet*, p. 35.

[150] Gordon et al. (eds.), *The History (Ta'rīkh): Adam to Pre-Islamic Arabia* in *The Works of Ibn Wāḍiḥ al-Ya'qūbī*, p. 269.

[151] Brinner (trans.), *'Arā'is al-Majālis fī Qiṣaṣ al-Anbiyā' or 'Lives of the Prophets' as recounted by ... al-Tha'labī*, p. 98.

'not to marry any woman, or build any building, or shed any blood, or dress in any garment except the skins of wild animals, or cut his hair or nails. Let him sit alone and constantly praise God.'[152]

Again, the Islamic tradition appears to be relying here on the Christian text, the *Cave of Treasures,* for there we read that Noah and his sons retrieved the body of Adam from the cave; that later, Shem and Melchizedek took the body of Adam and placed it in Golgotha in Jerusalem, the centre of the earth; and that Melchizedek remained there for the remainder of his life as a celibate ascetic. And the *Cave of Treasures* illuminates the reason why the body of Adam was placed in the middle of the ark, between the men and the women. For, according to the *Cave of Treasures,* Methuselah, Noah's grandfather (Genesis 5.21-7), ordered Noah to place the body of Adam between the women in the eastern part of the ark and the men in the western part to keep them from having *anything* to do with each other: '[T]hy wives shall not pass over to you, and ye shall not pass over to them. Ye shall neither eat nor drink with them, and ye shall have no intercourse whatsoever with them until ye go forth from the Ark.'[153]

---

[152] Gordon et al. (eds.), *The History (Taʾrīkh): Adam to Pre-Islamic Arabia* in *The Works of Ibn Wāḍiḥ al-Yaʿqūbī,* p. 272. See also Brinner (trans.), *ʾArāʾis al-Majālis fī Qiṣaṣ al-Anbiyāʾ* or *'Lives of the Prophets'* as recounted by ... al-Thaʿlabī, p. 82 for a variety of places on the final burial site of Adam.

[153] Budge (trans.), *The Book of the Cave of Treasures,* pp. 104–105. The story of Noah retrieving the body of Adam from the Cave of Treasures (Caverna Thesaurorum) also occurred in the writings of the Christian Hippolytus of Rome in the third century. See Chapter 2 for more details.

Unlike in the rabbinic tradition, the Islamic commentators generally did not allow Og the giant on to the ark. But he survived anyway. Ibn ʿAbbas declared,

> Og would seize the clouds for himself, and drink from them, because of his height. He would take the whale from the depths of the sea and fry it in the eye of the Sun. He would lift it up to the Sun, then eat it. He said to Noah: 'Take me with you.' But Noah replied: 'Out with you, enemy of God, I have not been ordered to take you with me.' God spread water on the face of the Earth and the mountains, but it did not even reach the knees of Og son of ʿAnaq.[154]

That said, Al-Ṭabarī, following the rabbis, did find a place for Og on the ark.[155] Except for Noah and those with him on the ark (and perhaps Og), everybody and everything else perished.

According to the Qur'an, after Noah had gathered the animals, his family, Og, and other believers into the ark, the flood came. Like the Genesis story, the Qur'an has the waters coming from above and below: 'So We opened the gates of the sky with water pouring (down), and made the earth gush forth with springs' (Qur'an 11-12). And the commentators faithfully followed the Qur'an on this. But the Qur'an also contains another account of whence the waters came: 'our command came and the oven boiled' (Qur'an 11.40). This reflects the rabbinic tradition that the waters of the flood were boiling. And it is redolent of

---

[154] Brinner (trans.), ʿArāʾis al-Majālis fī Qiṣaṣ al-Anbiyāʾ or 'Lives of the Prophets' as recounted by ... al-Thaʿlabī, pp. 99–100. See also Newby, The Making of the Last Prophet, p. 47.

[155] Rosenthal (trans.), The History of al-Ṭabarī: Volume 1, p. 361.

Hippolytus of Rome and his story of the wife of Ham, Zedkat Nabu, whose bread was ruined as water gushed out of the oven – a sign of the deluge to come.[156] But, that said, what was the oven? Al-Tha'labī reported on the variety of possible meanings among the commentators. Several said that it meant no more than the water gushing forth from the surface of the earth; another that it referred to the tannūr – the noblest and highest spot on earth; another said that it was an oven (tannūr) of stone that belonged to Adam.[157] Al-Ṭabarī mentioned that the oven belonged to Eve.[158] Ibn Kathīr believed that it was the oven at Noah's house.[159] There was also debate about the original location of the oven. Al-Kisā'ī declared that when Noah completed his pilgrimage rites in Mecca, 'he turned and saw Adam's kiln to the right of Noah's house, which was where the mosque of Kufa [in Iraq] now stands,' and where, tradition has it, Noah built the ark.[160] This was perhaps the most common opinion, but others located the oven in Syria or even India.[161]

The Qur'an tells us simply that the ark was 'in (the midst of) wave(s) like mountains' (Qur'an 11.42). But Al-Kisā'ī let his imagination soar:

> God told Gabriel to command the wardens of the waters to send them forth in measureless amounts and to strike

---

[156] See Chapter 2.
[157] See Rosenthal (trans.), *The History of al-Ṭabarī: Volume 1*, pp. 95–96.
[158] Rosenthal (trans.), *The History of al-Ṭabarī: Volume 1*, p. 363
[159] See ibn Kathīr, *Stories of the Prophets* (Kindle edition), p. 35.
[160] Thackston Jr. (trans.), *Tales of the Prophets (Qiṣaṣ al-anbiyā': Muḥammad ibn 'Abd Allāh al-Kisā'i)*, p. 100.
[161] See Brinner (trans.), *'Arā'is al-Majālis fī Qiṣaṣ al-Anbiyā' or 'Lives of the Prophets' as recounted by ... al-Tha'labī*, p. 96.

the waters with the Wing of Wrath. Gabriel struck the waters. And springs and wells gushed up profusely; the kiln boiled over, the sky poured down rain, and the waters met as ordained; the water of the sky was dark and that of the earth light. The waters broke freely, and the waves battered against themselves, with the angels in their midst causing lightning and thunder; and the deluge inundated from all sides and every place, the angels of wrath churning it up with their wings. And God commanded the angels of the earth to hold the world lest it be pulled loose from its moorings.[162]

During the flood, it was difficult to tell night from day, although, enlightened by the rabbinic tradition, al-Kisā'ī remarked there was a 'white bead', the light from which diminished by day and increased by night. Those on the ark were also comforted by a cock that crowed at dawn and cried out, 'Praise be to the Blessed King ... who hath taken night away and brought the dawn of a new creation. To prayer, O Noah! God will have mercy upon thee.'[163] Life on the ark was not always pleasant. Adam's body was intended to preclude men and women from having sex. But Ham, we are told by Qatādah (c.581–c.644), 'had intercourse with his wife, and Noah prayed to his Lord ... and Ham's sperm became altered, and he brought forth black (offspring)'.[164] Al-Tha'labī also reported that Noah had forbidden sex to the animals on

---

[162] Thackston Jr. (trans.), *Tales of the Prophets (Qiṣaṣ al-anbiyā': Muḥammad ibn 'Abd Allāh al-Kisā'i)*, pp. 101–102.

[163] *Ibid.*, p. 103.

[164] Brinner (trans.), *'Arā'is al-Majālis fī Qiṣaṣ al-Anbiyā'* or *'Lives of the Prophets' as recounted by ... al-Tha'labī*, p. 97.

the ark, but 'a dog mounted a bitch and Noah cursed him saying: "O God, bring him unto distress."'[165]

Human and animal waste was a problem: '[W]hen the people's waste offended Noah on the ship, he was commanded to stroke the tail of the elephant. So he stroked it, and two pigs came forth from it, and he was freed from it [because they ate it]. The mouse gave birth on the ship, and when the mice troubled him, he was commanded to order the lion to sneeze, and two cats came forth from the nostrils which ate the mice.'[166] Al-Tha'labī related the same legend, told by Shem, who was resurrected by Jesus for the occasion, although the problem was one of cattle dung rather than human.[167] That the pig was only created on the ark from the rear of an elephant provided a legendary reason for the Muslim distaste for pork.[168] As for Noah, he had no sleep from the time that he boarded the ark until he disembarked.

The Genesis story gives both forty and 150 days for the duration of the flood. But the Qur'an gives us no indication how long the flood lasted, nor how long before Noah disembarked. So, the Islamic commentators were free to be creative, suggesting anywhere from 150 days to six months to just over a year. The Qur'an has Noah praying that God will bring him 'to a blessed landing place' (Qur'an 23.29) before the ark came to rest on al-Jūdī. But there was a general agreement that, before landing there, the ark

---

[165] Ibid., p. 97.  [166] Newby, The Making of the Last Prophet, p. 47.

[167] See Brinner (trans.), 'Arā'is al-Majālis fī Qiṣaṣ al-Anbiyā' or 'Lives of the Prophets' as recounted by . . . al-Tha'labī, p. 100.

[168] See Moshe Bildstein, 'How Many Pigs Were on Noah's Ark? An Exegetical Encounter on the Nature of Purity,' Harvard Theological Review 108 (2015), pp. 448–470.

circumnavigated the Kaaba in Mecca. Thus al-Kisā'ī has the ark visiting Jerusalem, then on to the Kaaba, which it circled seven times,[169] while al-Ya'qūbī has the ark circumambulating for a week.[170] To this, drawing on rabbinic sources, he added the story of the dove and the raven. Four months after the ark came to rest on al-Jūdī, he wrote, Noah sent out the raven, to find out how things stood with the water. It found corpses floating on the water, settled upon them, and did not return. Then he sent out the dove. It brought back an olive leaf, so he knew that the water had gone.[171]

## A New Humanity

The Qur'an tells us that, while on the ark, Noah expressed the hope of coming to land (Qur'an 23.29). It also tells us that God eventually ordered the earth to swallow up the water and the sky to stop the rain (Qur'an 11.44). And Noah was told by God to leave the ark (Qur'an 11.48). Of Noah's life after the flood there is no mention in the Qur'an. But there was a general agreement among the commentators that Noah was saddened by it all, although heartened by God's promise never to flood the earth again. Al-Ya'qūbī declared, 'When Noah emerged from the boat and saw people's bones

---

[169] See Thackston Jr. (trans.), *Tales of the Prophets (Qiṣaṣ al-anbiyā': Muḥammad ibn 'Abd Allāh al-Kisā'ī)*, p. 103.

[170] See Gordon et al. (eds.), *The History (Ta'rīkh): Adam to Pre-Islamic Arabia* in *The Works of Ibn Wāḍiḥ al-Ya'qūbī*, p. 270. See also Rosenthal (trans.), *The History of al-Ṭabarī: Volume 1*, p. 362.

[171] See *Ibid.*, p. 270. See also Brinner (trans.), *'Arā'is al-Majālis fī Qiṣaṣ al-Anbiyā' or 'Lives of the Prophets' as recounted by ... al-Tha'labī*, p. 100–101, where it is the resurrected Shem who reports on the raven and the dove.

glimmering, it grieved him and saddened him. God revealed to him, "I will not send the deluge onto the earth ever again after this."[172] Al-Kisā'ī too told the story of the rainbow: 'Noah,' God said, 'I have known from all time that I should not again torment anyone with flood and drowning until the Day of Resurrection, for I have set my rainbow, which thou seest in the sky, as a guarantee for the people of the earth against deluge.'[173] Following the Biblical account, Ibn Isḥāq spoke of Noah's division of the land among his sons, and followed with a long list of the descendants of Noah, as did al-Ṭabarī, giving an array of descendants from a number of sources.[174] Of those other than Noah and his family who were on the ark, al-Ṭabarī tells us that 'they disappeared and perished, and no descendants of theirs survived'.[175] In short, a new humanity began with Noah. Al-Ṭabarī again: 'In this world today, the children of Adam are the direct offspring of Noah and of no other descendants of Adam, as God says, "And we made his offspring the survivors"' (Qur'an 37.77).[176]

And of Noah's drunkenness? Given the disapproval of alcohol in the Qur'an, the commentators ignored it. They did not follow the rabbinic criticism of Noah for his having drunk too much. Noah was far too important to Islam, as one of God's prophets, to have passed out from

---

[172] Gordon et al. (eds.), *The History (Ta'rīkh): Adam to Pre-Islamic Arabia* in *The Works of Ibn Wāḍiḥ al-Ya'qūbī*, p. 270.

[173] Thackston Jr. (trans.), *Tales of the Prophets (Qiṣaṣ al-anbiyā': Muḥammad ibn 'Abd Allāh al-Kisā'i)*, p. 104.

[174] See Newby, *The Making of the Last Prophet*, pp. 48–49. Brinner (trans.), *The History of al-Ṭabarī, Volume 2*, pp. 10–27.

[175] Rosenthal (trans.), *The History of al-Ṭabarī: Volume 1*, p. 368.

[176] *Ibid.*, p. 368.

too much wine. But they did recount the Biblical story of his nakedness. And like Judaism and Christianity, they too wrestled with the apparent unfairness of Noah's cursing Canaan for what was, after all, the sin of Ham.

Thus, for example, ibn Isḥāq ignored the vineyard and drunkenness but reported on Noah's nakedness being uncovered while he slept, Ham's failure to cover him, and Shem and Japheth's doing so. In this case, Noah cursed Canaan, the son of Ham.[177] Similarly, al-Ṭabarī has Canaan cursed, although he also included Ham as a slave to his two brothers.[178] This may have been because al-Ṭabarī was familiar with the rabbinic story that had Ham having sex on the ark: 'Ham attacked his wife [sexually] in the ark, so Noah prayed that his seed be altered, and he produced the blacks.'[179] Al-Ya'qūbī followed the rabbinic tradition of Ham's laughing at his father's genitals, although he laid the curse upon Canaan and explicitly excluded Ham from the curse.[180]

On the other hand, al-Kisā'ī ignored Canaan altogether and placed the curse on Ham. When Noah awoke, he reported, Noah asked Ham, '"Do you laugh at your father's genitals? ... May God change your complexion and may your face turn black!" And that very instant his face did turn black.'[181] And he went on to ask God to

[177] See Newby, *The Making of the Last Prophet*, p. 48.
[178] See Brinner (trans.), *The History of al-Ṭabarī, Volume* 2, pp. 11–12. Al-Ṭabarī has Noah take a softer attitude to Ham later; see p. 14.
[179] Rosenthal (trans.), *The History of al-Ṭabarī: Volume* 1, p. 365.
[180] See Gordon et al. (eds.), *The History (Ta'rīkh): Adam to Pre-Islamic Arabia* in *The Works of Ibn Wāḍiḥ al-Ya'qūbī*, p. 271.
[181] Thackston Jr. (trans.), *Tales of the Prophets (Qiṣaṣ al-anbiyā': Muḥammad ibn 'Abd Allāh al-Kisā'ī)*, p. 105.

make slaves of Ham's progeny from that time on. As for the 'blackness' of his progeny, al-Kisāʾī told his readers that, after the death of Noah, the wife of Ham bore two black children. Ham declared that they were not his. "'They are yours," said his wife, "for the curse of your father is upon us."'[182] After these two children had grown up, Ham laid with her again and she bore two more black children. Ham knew that they were his, and he left his wife and fled. Among the descendants of Ham, al-Kisāʾī declared, 'are the Nubians, the Negroes, the Berbers, the Sindhis, the Indians and all the blacks'.[183] Al-Ṭabarī, following ibn ʿAbbas, had all the descendants of the sons of Noah colour-coded: 'Born to Noah were Shem, whose descendants were reddish-white; Ham, whose descendants were black with hardly any whiteness; and Japheth, whose descendants were reddish-brown.'[184] Thus, as in Christianity and Judaism so too in Islam, all the people of the earth were part of a common humanity. But on the other hand, as in early modern Christianity and Judaism so too in Islam, the connection between Ham, blackness, and slavery was embedded in the story of Islam.[185]

The common theme in accounts of Noah's death was his exhortation to be faithful to one God only. According to al-Kisāʾī, when Noah's time had come, he called Shem to his deathbed: 'I charge you with two things … One of the two with which I charge you is the Profession of faith,

---

[182] *Ibid.*, p. 107.    [183] *Ibid.*, p. 108.
[184] Rosenthal (trans.), *The History of al-Ṭabarī: Volume 1*, p. 368.
[185] For refutations within Islam of the connection of blackness and slavery, see Haroon Bashir, 'Black Excellence and the Curse of Ham: Debating Race and Slavery in the Islamic Tradition', *ReOrient* 5 (2019), pp. 92–116.

"There is no God but God," for this Profession will render asunder heaven and earth, and nothing can veil it ... The second thing is that you increase saying "Praise be to God," and "Praise Him," for He is the repository of all reward.'[186] Thus, on his deathbed, Noah was repeating the verse in the Qur'an (37.35) that is the first part of the Shahada, the central assertion of Islamic faith, and the first of the five pillars of Islam: 'There is no god but God, and Muhammad is his prophet.'

---

[186]  Thackston Jr. (trans.), *Tales of the Prophets (Qiṣaṣ al-anbiyā':*
   *Muḥammad ibn 'Abd Allāh al-Kisā'i)*, p. 106.

# 4

# The Late Medieval and Early Modern Noah

≈

## An Ark of Biblical Proportions

Within the Judaism of the eleventh century, it was the rabbinic commentator Rabbi Solomon ben Isaac, known as Rashi, who set the pattern of a greater emphasis on the literal meaning of the text, as opposed to its moral, legal, or ritual meaning. And this rabbinic emphasis was to influence the Christian interpreters of the later medieval period. The literal readings of Noah and the flood by the Franciscan teacher Nicholas of Lyra (c.1270–1349) and the Spanish theologian Alfonso Tostado (c.1400–1455) were to set the pattern for the literal exegetes of the late medieval and early modern periods.[1]

Nicholas of Lyra developed a primarily literal reading of the Biblical text that was reliant both on the Hebrew text of the Old Testament and on the rabbinic commentaries, especially Rashi's. It was Nicholas who brought to the attention of the Christian West the Jewish legend of Og of Bashan's escape from the flood, the story of the raven's fear that Noah was having an affair with its mate, and the tradition that Noah had to take fish on the ark because the flood waters were boiling hot. In turn, Alfonso Tostado absorbed the literal reading of

---

[1] See Allen, *The Legend of Noah*, pp. 75–77. Allen's account of the legend of Noah in this work remains the definitive discussion of the late medieval and early modern Noah. I am much indebted to it.

Nicholas and added an imaginative flair to his story of Noah and the flood. And when we read his account of life on the ark, the rabbinical influence on his writing can be clearly discerned:

> And because Noah took care of the animals and gave them food which was kept in the apotheca on the second level, there was a stairway from the habitation of Noah to this place so that he could descend and take up food. So he gave them food, walking between the asps, dragons, unicorns, and elephants, who thanks to God did not harm him but waited for him to give them nourishment at the proper time. The Divine pleasure saw to it that there was a great peace among these animals; the lion did not hurt the unicorn, or the dragon the elephant, or the falcon the dove. There was also a vent in the habitation of the tame animals and another in that of the wild animals through which the dung was conveyed to the sentina [bilge]. Noah and his sons collected the dung and cast it by means of an orifice into the sentina so that the animals would not rot in their own offal. One could also believe that the odour of the dung was miraculously carried off so that the air was not corrupted and men and animals were not slain by the pest. So the men in the Ark labored daily and had no great time for leisure.[2]

The emphasis on the literal meaning of the story of Noah and the ark in Nicholas and Tostado was not all that innovative. As Peter Harrison has pointed out, from the twelfth century onwards, there had been warnings given against the overuse of allegorical readings to the exclusion

---

[2] Quoted by *ibid.*

of the literal.³ That said, the long tradition of allegorical readings within Catholic Christianity nonetheless ensured their continuation. Even the Jesuit Athanasius Kircher (1602–1680), author of a three-volume account of the Noah story, primarily focused on a literal reading. His *Arca Noë* (1675) allegorised the ark as a vessel carrying the human soul and as the church outside of which there was no salvation. And he looked on Noah as a prototype of Christ. Nevertheless, there was an increasingly clear sense within the Catholic tradition that, at the least, the literal meaning had to be discerned before any other meaning could be built upon it. On the other hand, Protestant readings from the sixteenth century onwards, in accord with the Protestant commitment to 'scripture alone', were decisively literal and historical in their orientation.

Most importantly, the production of new 'knowledges' in the secular arts and sciences during the late medieval and early modern periods could not but generate critical reflection on the most important 'knowledge' of all, namely that contained within the Bible. In so doing, the importance of the literal and historical meaning of the Bible, now read through knowledges created outside of it, not only reinforced the importance of the literal meaning but also created radically new literal and historical readings. Eventually, as we will see, the use of the secular arts and sciences to clarify, illuminate, and support the literal and historical reading of the Bible was to create as many problems for the Biblical story as it purported to solve.

---

³ See Harrison, *The Bible, Protestantism, and the Rise of Natural Science*, p. 109.

Catholic or Protestant, there were two principal issues that drove the medieval and early modern accounts of Noah and the ark. The first of these was that of the size and shape of the ark. The second was how the ark could accommodate and feed the variety of animals that it had to. As we saw in Chapter 2, by reference to contemporary shipbuilding practices, Hugh of Saint Victor had imagined the ark as a ship with a roof or a roofed house on top – pretty much as we would imagine it to have been. But the question of the size and the shape was not settled by Hugh in the twelfth century. It was to continue as one of the most disputed and debated questions into the late medieval and early modern periods.

The most influential account of the size and shape of the ark was provided by the Catholic mathematician Johannes Buteo (c.1485–c.1560) in a work entitled *De Arca Noë* (1554) within a larger work, *Opera Geometrica*. Buteo focused solely on the literal meaning of the story of Noah and the ark. For Buteo, the question of the ark was one of conflicting designs, to be settled by geometry. Thus, Buteo followed the Biblical dimensions of the ark, with a cubit equalling eighteen inches. He rejected the view that a Biblical cubit would be nine feet long on the grounds that were it so, Goliath the giant, whose height was six cubits and one hand, would have been over fifty-four feet and his head about nine feet high. This was impossible, 'for how could David have stood before Saul, as it is written [1 Samuel 17.57], holding the head cut off from Goliath in his hand?'[4] Thus Buteo's ark was

---

[4]  Tim Griffith and Natali Miller (trans.), *Johannes Buteo's* The Shape and Capacity of Noah's Ark (Eugene, OR: Wipf & Stock, 2008), p. 22.

450,000 cubic cubits (300 × 50 × 30 cubits), with a further 7,500 cubic cubits in the roof.

Along with these dimensions, Buteo also provided five pictorial designs of the ark ranging from that of Origen, Hugo of St. Victor, 'some teachers',[5] and Cardinal Cajetan to his own – a rectangle with a pitched roof to the height of one cubit running along its length (see Plate 11). He argued for this primarily on the grounds that 'arca' simply meant 'chest' – 'called a parallelepiped rectangle by geometricians'.[6] Thus, he was having nothing to do with Origen's pyramid and he was scathing about Hugh of St. Victor's ark design as 'incompetent'.[7] Placing a large window in the side of the ark near the top made of glass with shutters, sufficient to light the top deck, Buteo rejected the rabbinic tradition of a gemstone in the roof that would light up the whole ark as a 'shameless lie.'[8] In fact, he left the animals without light for the whole time that they were in the ark because, he claimed, they happily lived in darkness.

Following the Biblical text (Genesis 6.16), Buteo's ark had three decks, although he had a bilge four cubits high beneath the bottom deck for animal waste. The quadrupeds and reptiles were housed in stalls on the lowest deck with a door for the animals to enter and exit. Birds and humans lived on the top deck. On this deck, there were

---

[5] Athanasius Kircher replicates the diagrams and attributes this design to Nicholas of Lyra. See Athanasius Kircher, *Arca Noë, in Tres Libros Digesta*... (Amstelodami, 1675), p. 43. Available at https://archive.org/details/athanasiikircherookirc_9/page/n5/mode/2up.

[6] Griffith and Natali Miller (trans.), *Johannes Buteo's* The Shape and Capacity of Noah's Ark, p. 15.

[7] *Ibid.*, p. 44.    [8] *Ibid.*, p. 16.

separate quarters for the men and women. Buteo remarked rather coyly (following the rabbinic tradition) that 'it is the accepted opinion that the men on the ark always slept separately from the women'.[9] There were sufficient supplies on the top deck for humans and birds. The middle deck was reserved for food for the animals below – hay, chaff, leafy branches, acorns, nuts, walnuts, and chestnuts. Carnivores were catered for with the addition of 3,650 sheep housed in the middle deck.

Buteo followed the Genesis account that had Noah taking two of each kind, including seven pairs of all clean animals, seven pairs of birds, and one pair of unclean animals (Genesis 7.2-3). But he divided the animals into three groups – larger herbivores, smaller herbivores, and carnivores – and worked generally from the largest down to the smallest. Among the first there were elephants, wild oxen, one-horned oxen, four kinds of camels, rhinoceroses, bison, buffalo, European bison, oryxes, reindeers, one-horned Indian oxen, ostriches, common cows, deer, antelope, red deer, common horses, wild horses, spotted horses, hippopotamuses, domesticated donkeys, wild donkeys, one-horned Indian donkeys, bears, pigs, and boars.

Among the smaller herbivores he counted varieties of sheep and goats, varieties of apes, hares, and rabbits, badgers, squirrels, dormice, and varieties of mice, hedgehogs, and porcupines. The carnivores included lions, leopards, calae, boas, bulls that live by hunting, panthers, tigers, wolves, dog wolves, deer wolves, cephae, lynxes, hyenas, wild asses, sea otters, beavers, giant otters,

---

[9]  *Ibid.*, p. 25.

common otters, hyenas, African hunting dogs, foxes, cats, Egyptian and common weasels, and sea calves.[10] And he included a large number of 'fabulous' beasts – unicorns, pegasi, leucrocotas, dragons, manticores, hellhounds, sphinxes, satyrs, hydras, and basilisks. He was having nothing to do with Hugo's idea of amphibians nesting on the sides of the ark. Were it necessary for fish to be housed, a fish tank could have easily been built and 'easily filled using a Ctesibian machine or some other sort of water pump'.[11] Additional supplies of fish (beyond the requisite pairs) from this aquarium would meet the needs of any amphibians (like seals) that required a fish diet.

Although Augustine had all the animals on the ark eating a vegetarian diet, Buteo saw that there was no Biblical reason why Noah should not have taken more animals than ordered to by God.[12] So, he included extra animals to feed the carnivores. He calculated that the carnivores amounted to the equivalent of forty pairs of wolves. Ten sheep would have been eaten each day by the equivalent of forty wolves, thus requiring 3,650 sheep on the ark to feed the carnivores. A more complicated calculation was made for the herbivores. According to this, the number of herbivores amounted to the equivalent of

[10] *Ibid.*, pp. 31–32. Reptiles are listed on p. 35. He included mice even though he was aware that they were often thought to be spontaneously and not sexually generated. Augustine had excluded from the ark creatures that generated spontaneously. See Marcus Dods (trans.), *St. Augustin's City of God*, 15.27 in *NPNF (First Series)*, pp. 307–308.

[11] *Ibid.*, p. 35. The Ctesibian machine was a force pump with pistons, cylinders, and valves invented by Heron of Alexandria (c. 10 CE–c. 70 CE).

[12] See Dods (trans.), *St. Augustin's City of God*, 15.27 in *NPNF (First Series)*, p. 308.

400 cows on the ark. Experimentation had demonstrated that one cubic cubit bale of hay would be more than sufficient per day for each cow. A total of 146,000 bales would be required for the year. Further calculations demonstrated that there was more than sufficient space on the ark to store both the feed and the extra animals. Curiously, he declared, dogs would be able to scavenge for food in the kitchen on the third floor, even though their pernicious rabies was a nuisance to themselves and others. Therefore, 'it seems,' Buteo concluded, 'that dogs in the ark were a prototype of heretics' – read Protestants! The Reformation could resonate, even in a work on Noah's ark.

## The Floating Zoo

In the accounts of Noah and his ark that followed that of Buteo, it became increasingly fashionable, although perhaps more tiresome for readers, to name all the animals that had entered it.[13] Thus, for example, in 1592, the Jesuit theologian Benedict Pereira (1536–1610) gave an encyclopaedic list of inhabitants that, by my calculation, ran to some 131 different creatures consisting of reptiles (25), carnivorous animals (35), non-carnivorous larger animals (34), non-carnivorous smaller animals (37). All up, some 260 creatures. Despite these four categories, it was an unsystematic collection generated from Classical (especially Pliny the Elder) and contemporary sources. Thus, for example, amongst the last category were an 'animal in the Japanese islands' and the 'Aiotochelli' that

[13] See Allen, *The Legend of Noah*, p. 80.

the conquistador Pedro de Alvarada saw in 'New Spain'. Pereira excluded the phoenix due to doubts about its existence. And fish were absent from his ark, as were those animals that were the product of different species (like mules), and those that spontaneously arose 'from rotting matter' ('ex putrescens materia'). None of these required an ark to survive. Fish would happily survive in the waters of the flood that, unlike that of the rabbis, were not boiling. Animals produced by the mating of different species would appear after the flood again, as would the rotting matter necessary for those creatures that were generated from it.[14]

The calculations of Buteo on the size of the ark were to become the standard way in the early modern period of ensuring that the ark was of sufficient size to house all the animals, or at least a limited number of them. Sir Walter Raleigh (c.1552–1618), for example, had absorbed the work of Buteo. In his *The Historie of the World*, 'this second Parent of Mankind', as Raleigh called Noah, built his ark in the Caucasus to distance himself from the giants who 'rebelled against God and Nature' to ensure an uninterrupted period of construction.[15] Like Buteo, Raleigh was much exercised by the size of the cubit. Rejecting the Egyptian 'geometricall cubit' of Origen that measured six times that of the common cubit, he followed Buteo and settled on eighteen inches – the distance 'from the sharpe of the elbow to the point of the middle

---

[14] See Benedict Pererius, *Commentarium et Disputationum in Genesim, Tomus Secundus* (Rome, 1592), pp. 137–153.

[15] Walter Raleigh, *The Historie of the World in Five Bookes...* (London, 1621), p. 93.

finger'.[16] Thus, following the Biblical measurements, Noah had some 450,000 cubic cubits, including the 7,500 cubits for the one cubit height of the roof (to make up for space taken up by posts, walls, and other partitions), with which to house the animals. That said, Raleigh held that, because men were larger then than in his day, the cubit too was longer, by some six inches. All of which led Raleigh to an ark of '600. foot in length, and 100. foot in bredth, and 60. foot deepe.'[17] As for 'the foolerie of the *Hebrewes*, who suppose that the *Arke* was lightened [illuminated] by a Carbuncle [precious stone], or had Windows of Crystal to receive in Light, and keepe out Water,' this was 'but to revive the buried vanities of former times'.[18]

Raleigh also thought that the question of amphibians on the ark 'a needlesse curiositie'.[19] But he did exclude fish, along with those of mixed species (such as mules and hyenas). And, regardless of the apparently vast numbers of different animals around the world, he limited the numbers by taking account, not of how they were in *his* time, but how they were in the time of Noah: 'of all Creatures, as they were by God created, or out of the earth by his Ordinance produced'. The ark, he went on to say, on the dimensions provided by the common cubit, 'was sufficiently capacious to contayne of all, according to the number by God appointed'.[20] And he settled, following Buteo, on 280 animals on one deck, their food on a second, and the birds and their feed, along with Noah and his family, on a third.

[16] *Ibid.*, p. 94.   [17] *Ibid.*, p. 95.   [18] *Ibid.*, p. 96.   [19] *Ibid.*
[20] *Ibid.*, p. 95.

As part of his quest for a universal language in his *An Essay towards a Real Character and a Philosophical Language* (1668), the Anglican bishop John Wilkins (1614–1672) attempted to name and describe all the things to which names were to be assigned, dividing them into genuses, 'peculiar differences' within the genuses, and species belonging to each of the genuses listed. Among the forty genuses, four concerned the animal world: exanguious (bloodless), fish, birds, and beasts. He was convinced that the orderly classification of animals would contribute to the clearing of some differences in religious opinion and put to rest the belief, among otherwise knowing and learned men, that there were so many sorts of birds and beasts as to be incalculable. According to Wilkins, some ancient heretics and modern atheistical scoffers had used this to raise objections against the truth and authority of Scriptures, particularly concerning the ark of Noah 'where the dimensions of it are set down to be three hundred cubits in length, fifty in breadth, and thirty in height, which being compared with the things it was to contein, it seemed to them upon a general view, (and they confidently affirmed accordingly) that it was utterly impossible for this Ark to hold so vast a multitude of Animals, with a whole years provision of food for each of them'.[21]

Following Buteo, he rejected the argument that the great number of animals could be accommodated by arguing (à la Origen) for a larger ark based on the Egyptian cubit. He argued that the capacity of the ark

[21] John Wilkins, *An Essay towards a Real Character, and a Philosophical Language* (London, 1668), p. 162.

using the common (or 'civil') cubit was sufficient to house the animals, which his own classification had reduced to less than 'a hundred sorts of Beasts' and not 'two hundred of birds.'[22] Moreover, Wilkins's ark was not, like that of Hugo, a ship, but 'intended only for a kind of *Float* to swim above water, the flatness of its bottom, did render it much more capacious for the reception of those many living Creatures, which were to be conteined in it'.[23] And, like Buteo's ark, Wilkins's ark consisted of three stories, each ten cubits high, with a roof along its breadth and length reaching one cubit high: the lower deck containing all the animals, the middle deck for their food, the upper deck for the birds in one part and Noah and his family in the other.

That said, Wilkins did take exception to Buteo's enumeration of species of animals 'several of which are fabulous, some not distinct species, others that are true species being left out.'[24] Although much reliant on Buteo, the importance of Wilkins's account lies in his systematic allocating of animals to the ark in accord with his overall system of animal classification. According to the table that he constructed, there would be ample room on an ark built on Biblical proportions for the 201 animals that he identified.[25] And, having determined the number of animals, he made reasonably precise calculations of how they would be housed according to their size in stalls

---

[22] *Ibid.*    [23] *Ibid.*, p. 166.    [24] *Ibid.*, p. 163.
[25] See *ibid.*, p. 164. Having the capacity to live in water, amphibians were not on the ark. Snakes, lizards, frogs, and so on were lodged in the bilge beneath the bottom deck. Rats, mice, and insects also did not require special housing. Somewhat puzzlingly, Wilkins lists seventeen different herbivores as having seven of each on the ark.

sufficiently large for them to stand, lie, or turn around in. Assuming that some animals *were* carnivorous before the flood and thus needed meat on the ark, Wilkins adopted a Buteo-style calculation to estimate that, granting there were the equivalent of thirty wolves on the ark and that six wolves would eat a sheep a day, 1,825 sheep would be needed to be housed in stalls in the middle deck to feed the carnivorous beasts.

As for the hay to feed the sheep and other hay-eating animals for the year that the flood lasted, he calculated that there needed to be sufficient hay to feed the equivalent of three hundred cattle and sufficient space to house it on the second deck. Finally, he estimated that there would be no shortage of space on the third level for the birds, their feed, Noah and his family, and their utensils. All of which led Wilkins, bishop *and* natural historian, to conclude, 'From what hath been said it may appear, that the measure and capacity of the *Ark*, which some Atheistical irreligious men make use of, as an argument against the Scripture, ought rather to be esteemed a most rational confirmation of the truth and divine authority of it.'[26]

Samuel Pepys (1633–1703) had been really looking forward to the publication of Wilkins's *An Essay towards a Real Character and a Philosophical Language*. Having read it, Pepys tells us that he enjoyed the book mightily, but he made no other mention of it except for its section on the ark: '[M]ade the boy to read to me out of Dr. Wilkins' his "Real Character" and particularly about Noah's arke, where he do give a very good account thereof, shewing

---

[26]  *Ibid.*, p. 168.

how few the number of the several species of beasts and fowls were that were to be in the arke, and that there was room enough for them and their food and dung, which do please me mightily and is much beyond what ever I heard of the subject, and so to bed.'[27]

As Secretary to the Admiralty, Pepys had more than a merely antiquarian interest in the ark of Noah. Aware of the tradition that the ark was a century in the making, he remarked in his *Naval Minutes*, 'Noah's Ark must needs be made of some extraordinary timber and plank that could remain good after having been an hundred years in building, whereas our thirty new ships are some of them rotten within less than five.'[28] That said, Pepys declared that his friend and naval engineer Henry Shere, who had made his own notes on the ark, determined that six months would have sufficed to have built it. And Pepys wondered, if this were the first ship ever, where Noah found carpenters and caulkers to build it.

That said, he thought it disgraceful that contemporary shipbuilders had not caulked naval ships properly, 'the Ark itself being said to be pitcht within and without'.[29] More importantly, Pepys and Shere wondered how, if the ark were the model for all later ships, a uniformity of design in later ships might have been expected. Rather, ship designs were all quite distinct and variously adapted to local conditions. The design of Noah's ark could hardly have provided a model for others because even the most

---

[27] Quoted by Clark Emery, 'John Wilkins and Noah's Ark,' *Modern Language Quarterly* 9 (1948), p. 287.
[28] J.R. Tanner (ed), *Samuel Pepys's Naval Minutes* (London: The Navy Records Society, 1926), p. 205.
[29] *Ibid.*, p. 208.

ignorant and barbarous societies had the best long and narrow shapes to pass through the water, quite different from 'the form described by Moses of the Ark'.[30] Pepys's was an early sceptical note on the generally accepted assumption that all culture, including shipbuilding, had derived from the diffusion of the Noachic family after the flood.

As we know, in thinking about the relationship between the ark and contemporary shipbuilding practices, Pepys was following in the tradition established by Hugh of St. Victor. He was not alone. In the sixteenth and seventeenth centuries, as the number of books on shipbuilding increased, a discussion of the most important Biblical ship became common.[31] Thus, for example, Pepys had in his library fragments of a manuscript by Tudor shipwright Mathew Baker (c.1530–1613). Baker was a key player in the building or rebuilding of some thirteen ships that tackled the Spanish Armada. And his was the earliest English treatise on ship design. It began with a sketch of Noah's ark, depicted as a three-storey stepped box with a door on the bottom storey and Noah depicted as a draftsman and builder. Below the sketch of the ark was a paraphrase of the Biblical instructions by God to Noah on its dimensions (Genesis 6.14-16)[32] (see Plate 12).

[30] *Ibid.*, p. 207.
[31] See Richard W. Unger, *The Art of Medieval Technology: Images of Noah the Shipbuilder* (New Brunswick, NJ: Rutgers University Press, 1991), p. 133.
[32] See Mathew Baker, *Fragments of English Shipwrightry*, Magdalene College, Cambridge University, Pepys Library, no. 2820. This document was so named by Pepys.

Pepys also had a copy of the carpenter-builder Cornelis van Yk's 1697 treatise on Dutch shipbuilding that began with a discussion of the ark of Noah. van Yk conceded that Noah's ark was not the first ship, but he did view it as the largest. Although he nowhere mentioned Kircher, van Yk had more than likely read his *Arca Noë*. For he provided a sketch of five arks, clearly based on those in Kircher – those of Origen, Hugh of St. Victor, Cardinal Cajetan, and Nicholas of Lyra, along with Kircher's preferred option (that van Yk attributed to a Wilhelm Goree). They were the same five versions that Kircher adapted from Buteo. To these, van Yk added sketches of two more: one that looked like a large punt with a flat-bottomed hull; the other, his preferred option, a seventeenth-century ship with a curved bow and stern and a large house on the open deck.[33]

It is somewhat surprising that, with all the attention given to Noah among shipbuilders, there were apparently few attempts to build an ark. We know of only one. In 1604, a rich merchant from the Dutch town of Hoorn by the name of Peter Janszoon had an ark built. It was of Biblical proportions but smaller. Janszoon noted that, while it was not suitable for long or rapid journeys, it was very useful for cargo. It was calculated that it could carry a third more goods than other vessels without requiring a greater number of hands to manage it.[34]

---

[33] See Cornelis van Yk, *De Nederlandsche Scheeps-Bouw-Konst Open Gestellt* (Amsterdam, 1697), pp. 2–4. See also Nicolaes Witsen, *Architectura Navalis et Regimen Nauticum* (Amsterdam, 1690), pp. 1–2.

[34] See E. Mangenot, 'Arche de Noé,' in F. Vigoroux (ed.), *Dictionnaire De La Bible* (Paris: Letouzey et Ané, 1912), vol. 1, p. 923.

## The *Arca Noë* of Athanasius Kircher

The *Arca Noë* (1675) of the Jesuit Athanasius Kircher was the most elaborate of the seventeenth-century accounts of the ark.[35] The founder of the *Museum Kircherianum* in Rome, Kircher imagined the ark of Noah as the world's first museum of natural history. And Kircher's *Arca Noë*, with its rich illustrations and elaborate descriptions of the animals and birds on the ark, was little short of an encyclopaedia of natural history. This was science in the service of theology – and vice versa. For Noah was, according to Kircher, the chief builder of an ark designed by God who infused Noah with the knowledge and skills necessary, with the help of others, to construct it.[36] 'I shall assist you in everything,' God tells Noah, 'I shall instruct you about the ways and methods of proceeding. I shall send my tutelar and ministering angels to you and they will direct you and protect you from the malign efforts of demons who are plotting against you.'[37] As Olaf Breidbach and Michael Ghiselin neatly put it, this was 'baroque "Intelligent Design" theory'.[38] As such, the ark merited comparison with the seven wonders of the ancient world.[39]

Like his predecessors, Kircher rejected the 'pyramidal cubit' for the common cubit of eighteen inches, allowing

---

[35] For a summary of Kircher's three volumes, see Allen, *The Legend of Noah*, pp. 182–191.

[36] See Kircher, *Arca Noë*, pp. 22–23.

[37] Quoted by Allen, *The Legend of Noah*, p. 184.

[38] Olaf Breidbach and Michael T. Ghiselin, 'Athanasius Kircher (1602–1680) on Noah's Ark: Baroque "Intelligent Design" Theory,' *Proceedings of the California Academy of Sciences* 57 (2006), pp. 991–1002.

[39] See Kircher, *Arca Noë*, p. 1.

for a total capacity of 450,000 in³. For Kircher, the Biblical dimensions of the ark – three hundred by fifty by thirty cubits – had theological significance. For the proportions of the height of a man to his width, as created by God, were reflected in those of the ark. 'Proportio humani corporis ad Arcam comparata'[40] was the heading of a diagram illustrating this. Following Buteo, Kircher provided illustrations of (and rejected) the designs of Origen, Hugo of St. Victor, Cardinal Cajetan, and Nicholas of Lyra (Buteo's 'some teachers').[41] He fixed on a design that was essentially that of Buteo – a rect-angular box, consisting of three levels, covered by a roof with a peak along the middle.[42] Below the bottom deck were bilges for excrement. Like Buteo, he placed the window of the ark, made of crystal or selenite, in the middle of the third floor. A door was placed on the lowest level to allow the animals to enter.[43] Kircher's ark housed the birds in cages, along with separate cabins for Noah and his family, on the top deck. Supplies and equipment were stored on the middle level, along with sufficient birds and animals to feed the carnivores. Noah and his family, too saddened by the flood to even think of having sex, refrained from it while on the ark. However, goats, chickens, deer, and doves continued to reproduce. Problems of overcrowding were avoided by Noah feeding

---

[40] 'Proportion of the human body compared to the Ark.'

[41] See *ibid.*, p. 43.

[42] See *ibid.*, p. 38. Available at https://archive.org/details/athanasiikircherookirc_9/page/n69/mode/2up.

[43] See plate of animals entering the ark between pp. 122 and 123. Available at https://archive.org/details/athanasiikircherookirc_9/page/n177/mode/2up

their progeny to the carnivores. These were gathered, along with the non-carnivores, on the lowest deck in three hundred stalls.[44] All in all, there was ample room to house the 130 species of animals, the 150 kinds of birds, and the 30 kinds of snakes.

Unlike Wilkins, Kircher has no systematic classification of the animals. His list of the terrestrial animals on the ark begins, like Buteo's, from the largest, the elephant (following Pliny the Elder's first-century *Natural History*), and proceeds to the smallest. From the portraits and descriptions of animals provided in the text we can include the following: elephant, camel, bull, rhinoceros, buffalo, elk, horse, tiger, bear, lion, deer, ass, onager, bonasus, wolf, pard, goat, sheep, pig, dog, fox, cat, hare, rabbit, squirrel, weasel, badger, dormouse, hedgehog, porcupine, ape, and monkey. All in all, he had some 130 animal species (or 260 animals) to house.

Among the birds pictured in *Arca Noë* we can name the eagle, vulture, ostrich, falcon, crane, stork, heron, hawk, pelican, goose, peacock, turkey, chicken, duck, raven, crow, dove, pheasant, buzzard, woodcock, godwit, partridge, quail, sparrow, parrot, owl, magpie, hornbill, penguin, woodpecker, mynah, thrush, hoopoe, blackbird, swallow, halcyon, nightingale, lark, flycatcher, robin, finch, hobby, wagtail, and wren. Doubtful of their existence, Kircher did not take the griffon or the phoenix. And he excluded the unicorn on the grounds that the

---

[44]  See *ibid.*, plates between pp. 108 and 109, and 116 and 117. Available at https://archive.org/details/athanasiikircherookirc_9/page/n155/mode/2up.

https://archive.org/details/athanasiikircherookirc_9/page/n167/mode/2up.

rhinoceros had been mistaken for it. But the siren transformed into a half human female/half fish (or mermaid) in
the *Liber Monstorum* in the eighth century made it onto
the ark. Kircher's museum, he informed his readers,
'exhibits the tail and bones of the creature; the bones have
a wondrous power of staunching bleeding'.[45] Among the
snakes we can include the viper, asp, cerastes, dipsas,
ptyas, seps, amphisbaena ('a serpent with two heads on
each end of its body', or a two-headed snake), scytale, and
boa.[46] As a mythical creature, the serpent-like basilisk was
rejected. Along with the snakes went some 'amphibians',
the hippopotamus, crocodile, tortoise, otter, beaver, and
the seal among them.

Since fish would survive in the waters of the flood (no
rabbinic boiling waters here), there was no need to have
them on the ark. And Kircher was able to keep the
numbers of animals on board to a minimum by also
excluding the vast number of hybrids that he thought
were especially present in the New World. In short, he
took onto the ark only the 'pure' and 'perfect' species
created by God (in the moderate climate of Paradise in
the Old World) and not those that had come into existence later. But he did explicitly name the following
hybrids: the mule (horse and ass), camelopard (pard and
camel), tragelaph (deer and goat), hippelaph (horse and
deer), the leopard (lion and pard), allopecopithicum (wolf
and ape), armadillo (hedgehog and tortoise), marmota

[45] See *ibid.*, p. 73.
[46] See *ibid.*, pp. 55–56. See also the illustration between pp. 54 and 55.
Available at https://archive.org/details/athanasiikircherookirc_9/page/
n97/mode/2up. Disappointingly, this features the amphisbaena with
only one head.

(badger and squirrel), and leocrocuto (lion and hyena). The American bison was excluded on the assumption it was, like many other New World animals, a degraded version of a European original, the result of a different climate and environment. This was a Creation–Evolution debate in an early modern register. For Kircher was arguing for a kind of proto-Darwinism. He was suggesting the adaptation of species to their environmental circumstances. That said, it was more a degeneration from God's original handiwork than Darwinian survival of the fittest and strongest.[47]

There remained the issue, for Kircher, of how the animals got to the New World, granting the existence of oceans between their exit from the ark on Mount Ararat and the South and North America (Australia not being on his horizon). The Jesuit theologian Juan Eusebio Nieremberg (1595–1658), author of *Historiae Naturae* (1634/1635), argued that God's angels had brought a number of regional species to the ark before the flood and had flown them back to South America, Africa, and other distant regions afterwards. There, they changed into new variations and new species.[48] Perhaps reliant on Nieremberg, the same argument was made by the Jesuit missionary Bernabé Cobo (1582–1657) in c.1653

---

47 On hybridism in the early modern period, see Karl A. E. Enenkel, 'The Species and Beyond: Classification and the Place of Hybrids in Early Modern Biology,' in Karl A. E. Enenkel and Paul J. Smith (eds.), *Zoology in Early Modern Culture: Intersections of Science, Theology, Philology, and Political and Religious Education* (Leiden: Brill, 2014), pp. 57–148.

48 See Juan Eusebio Nierembergii, *Historia Naturae, Maxime Peregrine* (Antwerp, 1635), book 5, chs. 1, 2, 27.

in his argument against post-diluvial migration. The miracle by which God had the angels bring the animals to the ark before the flood, he declared, continued when the angels returned them whence they came after the flood.[49] Since there was a general agreement that God had brought the animals to the ark, this explanation of how they returned whence they came had, at least, the virtue of consistency. That said, Kircher's 'natural' explanation was perhaps, if not to Nieremberg and Cobo, at least to us, a more feasible one. The animals, he suggested, had reached their post-diluvian locations by swimming from one continent to another, by traversing land bridges or isthmuses, or by hitchhiking on ships.[50]

But what about the insect world? There were those who thought that insects were bred by copulation. Thus, a pair of each kind would have needed to have been on the ark to reproduce after the flood (not that they would have taken up much space). But Kircher was heir to a tradition of spontaneous generation that went back to Aristotle, according to which some creatures, the lowest links in the Great Chain of Being, were not produced by sexual reproduction. That they were, declared Kircher 'is sheer hallucination, because everyone knows that insects arise either from putrefaction or spontaneous generation'.[51]

---

[49] See Francisco Mateos (ed.), *Obras del P. Bernabé Cobo* (Madrid: Atlas, 1964), vol. 2, pp. 38–39.

[50] See Kircher, *Arca Noë*, p. 196.

[51] Quoted by Allen, *The Legend of Noah*, p. 185. On spontaneous generation, see Eric Johink, 'Snakes, Fungi and Insects: Otto Marseus van Schriek, Johannes Swammerdam and the Theory of Spontaneous Generation,' in Karl A. E. Enenkel and Paul J. Smith (eds.), *Zoology in Early Modern Culture: Intersections of Science, Theology, Philology, and Political and Religious Education* (Leiden: Brill, 2014), pp. 197–230.

So, there was no need for Noah to take the likes of wasps, ants, worms, bedbugs, beetles, fleas, flies, and all kinds of other assorted creatures. They could reproduce spontaneously after the flood just as they had before it. Their absence, no doubt, made life on the ark more comfortable all around.

## Abandon Ark!

The determination of Biblical interpreters from Hugo of St. Victor to Kircher to hold firm to the Biblical dimensions of the ark entailed that the number of animals that entered it had to be kept to a reasonable number. Pereira, Buteo, Raleigh, Wilkins, and Kircher had all tried to limit the numbers down to several hundreds. But in the sixteenth and seventeenth centuries, there had been an explosive increase in the knowledge of animals. Information about new animals poured in from North and South America, the Malay Islands, Australia, Africa, India, South-East Asia, and even from Europe. Early mentions of new discoveries in letters, journals, and travel books gradually worked their way into more publicly accessible accounts of the geography, fauna, and flora of the New World.[52]

The sheer volume of animals that was being discovered was making highly problematic the traditional view that all the animals on earth had been gathered into the ark

---

[52] See Wilma George, 'Sources and Background to Discoveries of New Animals in the Sixteenth and Seventeenth Centuries,' *History of Science* 18 (1980), pp. 79–104. See also Miguel de Asúa and Roger French, *A New World of Animals: Early Modern Europeans on the Creatures of Iberian America* (Aldershot: Ashgate, 2005).

and dispersed thence after the flood. Robert Burton realised that there was a problem:

> Why so many thousand strange birds and beasts proper to America alone, as Acosta demands *lib. 4. cap. 36*. [W]ere they created in the six days, or ever in Noah's ark? if there, why are they not dispersed and found in other countries? It is a thing (saith he) hath long held me in suspense; no Greek, Latin, Hebrew ever heard of them before, and yet as differing from our European animals, as an egg and a chestnut: and which is more, kine, horses, sheep, &c., till the Spaniards brought them, were never heard of in those parts?[53]

By the middle of the eighteenth century, the number of animal species had grown far too large for them to be accommodated in an ark of Biblical dimensions, however configured. Noah's ark could no longer serve as a lifeboat. It was impossible for the floating zoo to house two of 'every living thing' (Genesis 6.19). Thus, for example, the Swedish naturalist Carl Linnaeus (1707–1778), the founder of the modern conventions for classifying living organisms, named around 7,700 species of plants and around 4,400 species of animals in the tenth edition of his *Systema Naturae* (1758–1759). Linnaeus could not really ignore the problem of the ark and the number of its passengers. But he did. He rejected the idea that God would have created all the animal species at the time of creation and then destroyed them in a universal flood. 'Is it credible,' he asked, 'that the Deity should have

---

[53] Quoted by Allen, *The Legend of Noah*, p. 130. The reference is to the Spanish Jesuit missionary José de Acosta (c. 1539–1600).

replenished the whole earth with animals to destroy them all in a little time by a flood, except a pair of each species preserved in the ark?'[54]

Linnaeus's solution to the problem was radically (for his time) to rewrite the early chapters of the book of Genesis. Linnaeus claimed that dry land was still appearing as waters receded. That, and the evidence of an infinite number of the shells of sea fish to be found on mountains far removed from the sea, justified the conclusion that, at the time of creation, there was a single, small island raised above the primeval waters 'in which, as in a compendium, all things were collected together which our gracious Creator had destined to the use of man'.[55]

Upon this island, there was one individual of each species of plant, one sexual pair of every species of animals created at the beginning, and one pair of humans: 'Thus the garden of Paradise is rendered the most beautiful imagination can conceive, and the infinite glory of the Creator exalted, not depressed.'[56] All of these species, Linnaeus declared, are still present on the earth, descended from these original pairs.[57]

Moreover, the survival of all the original pairs of animals necessitated that they were not all created upon

[54] (Carl) Linnaeus, 'Dissertation II, On the Increase of the Habitable Earth,' in F. J. Brand (trans.), *Select Dissertations from the Amoenitates Academicae, a Supplement to Mr Stillingfleet's Tracts relating to Natural History* (London, 1781), vol. 2, p. 81. See also, Janet Browne, *The Secular Ark: Studies in the History of Biogeography* (New Haven, CT: Yale University Press, 1983).
[55] *Ibid.*, p. 89.     [56] *Ibid.*, pp. 114–115.
[57] See James Edward Smith (trans.), *Reflections on the Study of Nature: Translated from the Latin of the Celebrated Linnaeus* (London, 1785), p. 18.

the same 'natural day' as the Biblical text suggested. Rather, the Biblical term 'day' signified 'some determinate space of time, not what we now limit it to'.[58] Thus, herbivorous animals were created first and multiplied considerably before the carnivores were created else 'the carnivorous animals ... must have destroyed their proper prey (the future founders of specific family) one day, and starved the next'.[59]

It was an island, Linnaeus suggested, that was situated under the equator. There was a high mountain upon it, with snow on its summit (not coincidentally perhaps, like that of the 'mountain of Ararat in Armenia').[60] It was upon this island that Adam dwelt and, rather like Linnaeus himself, named all the animals (Genesis 2.20).[61] The limited size of the island made it possible for Adam to have discovered all the animals so as to give them their names. To suppose that the land originally created was of the same size as it is at present, Linnaeus declared, 'equally full of herbs and trees, equally inhabited by animals, and only two of the human species placed in a single corner of it' is absurd.[62] This was a complete world in miniature, with suitable soil for every plant, suitable plants for every insect, and suitable food and climate for every animal. Animals were thus created, from the sea level to the mountain top, in different environments particularly suited to them.

---

[58] Linnaeus, 'Dissertation II, On the Increase of the Habitable Earth', p. 120.

[59] *Ibid.*, p. 119.      [60] *Ibid.*, p. 90.

[61] See Peter Harrison, 'Linnaeus as a Second Adam? Taxonomy and the Religious Vocation,' *Zygon* 44 (2009), pp. 879–893.

[62] Linnaeus, 'Dissertation II, On the Increase of the Habitable Earth,' p. 81.

When the habitable earth was gradually revealed as the primeval ocean receded, the animals were ready-made to disperse from their Edenic island to environments identical to those on the idyllic island upon which they had been originally created. It was a solution that had its problems, as Thomas Browne (1605–1682) pointed out in his *Religio Medici*,

> How *America* abounded with Beasts of prey, and noxious Animals, yet contained not in it that necessary Creature, a Horse, is very strange. By what passage those, not only Birds, but dangerous and unwelcome Beasts, came over: How there be Creatures there (which are not found in this Triple Continent); all which must needs be strange unto us, that hold but one Ark, and that the Creatures began their progress from the Mountains of *Ararat*.[63]

That said, Linnaeus's story had many features in common with the Biblical account. He had an earth immersed in water (except for a small island), he had a mountain (like that of Ararat), and he had animal pairs dispersing from a single location, as the waters of the primeval ocean receded. However, in this revised version of the origin of species upon the earth, Noah and his ark were no longer necessary. It was an early sign that the new 'natural history' was in the process of relegating the story of Noah from history to myth.

Linnaeus's new reading of the book of Genesis had one great asset. He had shown how, at the time of creation, every animal had been created suitable for the various

---

[63] Charles Sayle (ed.), *Religio Medici in The Works of Sir Thomas Browne, Volume 1* (London: Grant Richards, 1904), p. 36.

environments of the Edenic island. This avoided the need to explain how animals adapted to the new environments in which they arrived after they had dispersed from the island. It was also its great weakness. For, granting the fit between animals and environments, the simpler hypothesis was that the animals had originated, not on an environmentally various Edenic isle from which they had slowly dispersed, but rather in the location where they could now be found.

This was the argument for origins endorsed by the French naturalist Georges-Louis Leclerc, Comte de Buffon (1707–1768). Buffon found no need to square his natural history with a theology derived from the book of Genesis. Simply put, species arose in those places that they currently occupied. Buffon, however, went a step further. Linnaeus's account entailed that the species were fixed at the time of their creation. But Buffon argued in 1766 that when, by force of circumstances, animals moved from their native environment, they adapted to their new environments, undergoing alterations 'so large and so profound, that it is not recognizable at first glance'.[64] In short, species were not fixed but evolved over time by force of external circumstances.

## The New Adam

It was not only animals that spread out from the location where the ark landed. All humanity was the consequence

---

[64] Quoted by Gareth Nelson, 'From Candolle to Croizat: Comments on the History of Biogeography,' *Journal of the History of Biology* 11 (1978), p. 278.

of the sons of Noah – Shem, Ham, and Japheth – dispersing from the ark after the deluge: 'These three were the sons of Noah; and from them the whole earth was peopled' (Genesis 9.19). The book of Genesis then went on to list all the descendants of Noah's sons, 'and from these the nations spread abroad on the earth after the flood' (Genesis 10.32). The book of Genesis had indicated those lands of the Middle East that had been inhabited by the immediate descendants of Noah. As we shall explore in more detail in Chapter 6, the story of the spread of humanity from the three sons of Noah affirmed the unity of all humankind. For the moment, however, we note that the problem for early modern scholars was that Genesis had failed to inform them about the forebears of the nations of Western Europe.

This was a gap that the Dominican friar Annius of Viterbo (1432–1502) attempted to fill in his *Commentaries on Various Authors Discussing Antiquities* (1498). It was a work that contained original sources from genuine Greek authors, along with content from imaginary Greek and Roman authors written by Annius himself. These texts, along with detailed commentary by Annius, gave a comprehensive history of the world, from Adam to the flood to the foundation of Etruria, land of the Etruscans, weaving Biblical history, ancient myths, and medieval Trojan legends into a single story.[65] As Nicholas Popper neatly sums it up, the *Antiquities* 'was a

---

[65] See Anthony Grafton, '1. Inventio of Traditions and Traditions of Invention in Renaissance Europe: The Strange Case of Annius of Viterbo,' in Ann Blair and Anthony Grafton (eds.), *The Transmission of Culture in Early Modern Europe* (Philadelphia: University of Pennsylvania Press, 2010), p. 12. See also, Walter Stephens, 'Complex

vertiginous, self-supporting labyrinth of citation that was proof that Etruria had been the capital of a proto-Christian civilization that had been inherited by Christian Rome and was more glorious and ancient than the Hebrew, pagan Roman, or Greek traditions it subsumed'.[66]

Annius's major forgery in *Antiquities* was the *Defloratio Caldaica*, putatively written by Berosus the Chaldean, the curator of the library of Babylon in the time of Alexander the Great. We met him earlier in Chapter 1. Having been quoted by Josephus, Eusebius, and other ancient worthies, he was well known to the contemporaries of Annius. According to Annius, Berosus, like Moses, had access to the records of the Biblical patriarchs from Adam onwards. Whereas Moses condensed them, Berosus provided a much fuller account of them than Moses had done. He had constructed a history from a mosaic (so to say) of ancient texts, the key one of which was Adamic in origin and, we might say, pre-Mosaic. Annius's story was intended to restore the truths of universal history distorted by the Greeks, to provide possible illustrious pasts for European rulers, and simultaneously to demonstrate that the older pagan gods were no more than divinised versions of Noah and his family. It was one in which the story of Noah served as the key moment at the very beginning of world history.

Pseudonymity: Annius of Viterbo's Multiple Persona Disorder,' *MLN* 126 (2011), pp. 689–708.

[66] Nicholas Popper, *Walter Ralegh's History of the World and the Historical Culture of the Late Renaissance* (Chicago: University of Chicago Press, 2012), p. 40.

As we know, according to Genesis 6.4, there were giants on the earth in those days. According to Annius, Noah was one of them. The only righteous person among the giants was Noah. He lived with his wife Tytea, his three sons Shem, Japheth, and Ham, and their wives Pandora, Noela, and Noegia. Noah built a ship in the form of a covered box, and when the flood came, only he and his seven family members survived. The ship came to rest on Mount Gordieus in Armenia. In addition to his three firstborn sons, Noah had many other giant children after the flood. All the kings of Europe, Chaldea, and Egypt were their descendants. Noah taught his children theology, sacred ritual, natural magic, astronomy and astrology, geography, agriculture, and, fatally, how to make wine. When Noah had passed out drunk, Ham, who hated his father for favouring his latest-born children more, took hold of his father's penis and bewitched him, rendering him impotent.

Armenia became quickly overcrowded and it was necessary to depart from there. Noah and his children eventually weighed anchor and sailed around the Mediterranean Sea. Shem received Asia, Ham received Africa, and Japheth Europe. Noah established his capital in Italy, on the left bank of the Tiber, founding the town of Janiculum (later becoming the god Janus of the Etruscans) and the Vatican (becoming the first Pope). Thus, Noah was the founder of the papacy, long before Peter, the disciple of Jesus. The Borgia Pope Alexander VI was delighted with this genealogy reaching back to Noah that Annius had invented. He rewarded Annius by appointing him papal theologian.

According to Annius, during his time in Italy, Noah completed the business of colonisation, making his favourite grandchildren colonial leaders. Later, he returned to Armenia and reigned there. The leadership of Italy was usurped by Ham who proceeded to bring the vices of the pre-diluvian giants with him. Noah returned there and drove Ham and his followers out of Italy. Noah took over the governing of the Etruscans and moved his capital to Vetulon, now known as Viterbo, the birthplace of Annius.[67]

The authenticity of Annius's *Antiquities* was much disputed from the time of its first publication. Despite that, eighteen editions appeared between 1548 and 1612. There were many defenders and imitators. The desire of early modern European rulers to claim Noah as their forebear was a strong one. After all, he was, in one sense, the original world ruler. Annius's masterful mimicry of contemporary historical method gave intellectual credibility to those imperial desires.[68] It was a story that early modern Europe willed to believe – a heritage that went back to the New Adam more feasibly than to the first Adam. As Don Allen remarks, 'It was not long until almost any man of the Renaissance could tell the story of Noah's wanderings and his plantation of Europe.'[69]

---

[67] For this account of the story of Noah according to Annius I am indebted to Walter Stephens, 'Berosus Chaldaeus: Counterfeit and Fictive Editors of the Early Sixteenth Century.' PhD thesis, Cornell University, 1979.

[68] See Walter Stephens, 'When Pope Noah Ruled the Etruscans: Annius of Viterbo and His Forged Antiquities,' *MLN* 119 Supplement (2004), pp. S201–S223.

[69] Allen, *The Legend of Noah*, p. 117. On Annius in France, see Marian Rothstein, 'The Reception of Annius of Viterbo's Forgeries: The

Annius had a second project. This was to show that the origin of the pagan gods could be found in Noah and his family. Noah and his wife Tytea were the new Adam and Eve, and they were to become for later generations the creator god and goddess. The Scythians were right, declared Annius, when 'they call Noah the Father of all Gods Great and Minor, and Author of the Human People, and Chaos, and the Seed of the World; and also when they called Tytea *Aretia*, that is, the Earth in which Chaos placed his seed, and from whom as though from the Earth all were brought forth'.[70]

Unlike Annius's claim that Noah ended up as ruler of Italy, this one would not have surprised his readers quite so much. For there was a long tradition of Christian mythography, derived from Classical antiquity, that we know as Euhemerism. Beginning in the second century CE, Christians read the pagan gods as nothing more than divinised versions of ancient human heroes and kings who had done great things.[71] This was a good strategic move on the part of early Christianity. For it left the Christian God as the only true God. To prove his case that the origin of pagan religion lay in the divinisation of Noah

*Antiquities* in Renaissance France,' *Renaissance Quarterly* 71 (2018), pp. 580–609. For England, see Glyn Parry, 'Berosus and the Protestants: Reconstructing Protestant Myth,' *Huntington Library Quarterly* 64 (2001), pp. 1–21.

[70] Quoted by Walter Stephens, *Giants in those Days: Folklore, Ancient History, and Nationalism* (Lincoln: University of Nebraska Press, 1989), p. 33. On Annius, see ch. 3.

[71] See John Daniel Cooke, 'Euhemerism: A Mediaeval Interpretation of Classical Paganism,' *Speculum* 2 (1927), pp. 396–410. The term 'Euhemerism' is derived from the Greek mythographer Euhemerus of Messina (fourth century BCE).

and his family, Annius took the names of various Classical gods and goddesses and retrofitted them to an expanded list of thirty more children of Noah – Macrus, Japetus Junior, Prometheus Piscus, Tuyscon Gigas, Crana, Cranus, Granaeus, Araxa Prisca, Regina, Pandora Junior, Thetis, Oceanus, Typhoeus, and the seventeen Titans.

Sir Walter Raleigh had read his Annius, and he knew that much of it was a forgery. But he was not averse to using Annius when necessary, not wanting the facts to get in the way of a good story.[72] He appears to have accepted Annius's identification of Noah with the god Janus and the Seed of the World, along with a host of other divine versions of the earthly Noah. Thus, for Raleigh, Noah was also Saturn, Prometheus, Chaos, Heaven, the Sun, Triton, Dionysus, and Bacchus. These were divine names that Noah was given in recognition of, amongst other things, his being the father of nations, his knowledge of God and heavenly things, his initiating of religious rites and sacrifice, his founding of agriculture and viticulture, astronomy and astrology, and his living safely on the waters of the flood.[73]

Similarly, the royalist soldier Matthias Prideaux (c.1625–1646) had also read his Annius. He declared him a forger. But like Raleigh, he followed Annius in holding that the gods of Classical antiquity originated with Noah. According to Prideaux, Noah became Prometheus, Saturn, Seed or Seminarie (of the earth), Hercules, and Janus. And it was from the flood of Noah that 'all the *Heathenish* great *Inundations*' were

---

[72]  See Popper, *Walter Ralegh's History of the World*, p. 72.
[73]  See Raleigh, *The Historie of the World in Five Bookes*, pp. 91–92.

derived.[74] The Oxford alchemist Edmund Dickinson (1624–1707) aligned Noah with Janus, the sun god Sol, the sky god Caelus, and Saturn.[75] In a like vein, the French Protestant scholar Samuel Bochart (1599–1667), in his *Geographia Sacra*, argued that the Greek myth of Saturn and his sons Jupiter, Neptunus, and Pluto, who divided the world between them, was a transformation of the story of Noah and his three sons who did the same.[76] This was pretty much a standard move for early modern euhemerists and Isaac Newton was among them.

Like many of his contemporaries, Isaac Newton (1642–1726) had his feet firmly planted on euhemerist ground, finding the origin of pagan 'idolatry' in the divinisation of Noah and his family. And he took a leaf directly out of the *Geographia Sacra* of Bochart. 'Bochart,' Newton declared, 'has abundantly proved that Saturn is Noah. The same is to be understood of Janus, the most ancient God of the Italians . . . As Noah was the first Farmer, planted a vineyard and got drunk, so Saturn was the first to teach agriculture . . . and was the patron of drunkenness . . . Moreover Saturn is said to have forbidden by legislation that anyone should view Gods naked without being punished for it. This

---

[74] Mathias Prideaux, *Introduction for Reading all Sorts of Histories* (Oxford, 1655), p. 5.

[75] See Edmund Dickenson, 'Diatriba de Noae in Italiam Adventu,' appendix to *Delphi Phoenicizantes* (Oxford, 1655), pp. 4–32.

[76] See Guy G. Stroumsa, 'Noah's Sons and the Religious Conquest of the Earth: Samuel Bochart and his Followers,' in Martin Mulsow and Jan Assman, *Sintflut und Gedächtnis* (Munich: Fink, 2006), pp. 307–318.

relates to the impiety of Cham, who looked upon his naked father.'[77]

We find Newton's account of the Noachic origins of the gods of antiquity most fully developed in a manuscript entitled 'The Original of Religions' in the early 1690s.[78] Newton imagined the most primitive religion to be 'that of the Prytanea or Vestal Temples. This was spread over all nations until the first memory of things.' And he found the worship of sacred fire in central hearths (prytanea) throughout the ancient world, from Egypt to China, from Scandinavia to Stonehenge. Prytanea were used in the cities of Canaan and Syria before the time of Moses. Wherever altars were mentioned in the Scriptures, they 'were of the same nature with the Prytanea of other nations'.[79]

The universality of fire worship was proof of its antiquity:

> So then this religion of conserving a sacred fire for the use of Sacrifices seems to have been as well the most universal as the most ancient of all religions & to have spread into all nations before other religions took place. There are many instances of nations receiving other religions after this but none (that I know) of any nations receiving this

---

[77] Isaac Newton, 'Miscellaneous Portions of "Theologiae Gentilis Origines Philosophicae,"' Yahuda Ms. 16.2, fol. 12r. Available at www .newtonproject.ox.ac.uk/view/translation/TRAN00010.

[78] See Isaac Newton, 'Draft Chapters of a Treatise on the Origin of Religion and its Corruption,' Yahuda Ms. 41, National Library of Israel, Jerusalem, Israel. Available at www.newtonproject.ox.ac.uk/ view/texts/normalized/THEM00077.

[79] Newton, 'Draft Chapters of a Treatise on the Origin of Religion and its Corruption,' fol. 2r.

after any other Nor [sic] did any other religion which
sprang up later become so general as this.[80]

This original religion was at the same time the home of
a natural philosophy (science), for it was 'one designe of
the first institution of the true religion to propose to
mankind by the frame of the ancient Temples, the study
of the frame of the world as the true Temple of the great
God they worshipped'.[81]

Now this was the religion of Noah. For as soon as
Noah came out of the ark, he built an altar and, with the
sacred fire that he had taken with him onto the ark, made
burnt offerings of every clean beast and bird to God.
Thus, this religion pre-dated Noah as the religion insti-
tuted by God in the beginning. The sacrificing of clean
birds and beasts by a consecrated fire in a consecrated
place was, according to Newton, the original and true
religion that began with Adam. From Noah, it spread to
Egypt and thence into all nations as the earth was re-
populated after the flood. It was also the religion of the
Old Testament that Moses taught the Jews. For Moses
had retained the original Egyptian religion of worship of
the true God. Thus, declared Newton, 'the old religion of
the Egyptians was the true religion tho corrupted before
the age of Moses by the mixture of worship of fals Gods
with that of the true one: & by consequence the religion
of the Iews was no other then that of Noah propagated
down in Egypt till the age of Moses'.[82] Natural philosophy, like the original natural religion, was similarly corrupted in Egypt.

---

[80]  *Ibid.*, fol. 2v.     [81]  *Ibid.*, fol. 5v.     [82]  *Ibid.*, fol. 5r.

But how did the religion of Noah first reach Egypt? According to Newton, after the deluge, Noah stayed in Mesopotamia until after the destruction of the Tower of Babel, some 101 years later (see Plate 13). Then he and his family moved from Babylon to the land of Shinar where he divided the world between his three sons. Shem stayed with Noah, but Ham was sent to Egypt and Japheth to Asia Minor. There the original religion was established. But it was also in Egypt that idolatry began with the worship of the sun, moon, and stars as the visible homes of divinity. Worse was to follow. For the souls of the dead were translated into the stars and the stars 'by virtue of the souls were endued with the qualities of the men & according to those qualities governed the world'.[83] And the souls of the dead then migrated into animals, plants, unshaped rocks, and eventually into statues and graven images of all kinds. From Egypt, the corrupt form of the original religion spread into Greece and other countries through commerce and colonisation.

For his account of how idolatry spread through the nations, Newton relied upon an argument from a text entitled *De Equivocis Temporum*. In theory, it was penned by the Greek philosopher Xenophon, but it was really one of the forgeries of Annius in his *Antiquities*:

> The most ancient members of the families of the noble kings who founded cities are called Saturns. Their first-born children are Jupiters and Junos. And their strongest grandsons are Herculeses. The fathers of the Saturns are the Heavens, their wives are Rheas, and the wives of the Heavens are Vestas. Therefore, there are just as many

[83] *Ibid.*, fol. 9v.

heavens, Vestas, Rheas, Junos, and Herculeses as there are Saturns. Also, the same man who is Hercules to some peoples is Jupiter to others. For Ninus, who was Hercules for the Chaldeans, was Jupiter to the Assyrians.[84]

Thus, according to Newton, following Annius, every nation that deified its kings applied the name of Jupiter to him whom they held most in honour, and the name Saturn to his father. In Egypt, Noah became Saturn, Ham became Jupiter Hammon, and Chus (Ham's son) Hercules. The Chaldeans, 'placing the gods one age lower than the Egyptians', gave the name of Saturn to Ham, Jupiter to Chus (Ham's son), and Hercules to Nimrod (Ham's grandson). Not omitting Noah, they called him the sky god Coelus or Uranus. The Assyrians, placing their gods one age lower than the Chaldeans, gave the name of Coelus to Ham, Saturn to Chus, Jupiter to Nimrod, and Hercules to the son of Nimrod. Noah they called Hypsuranius and Eliun, father of Uranus, 'that is the most High'.[85] Newton was more than pleased with all this:

> Now this difference between the theologies of the three nations is notably confirmed by the light it gives to many difficulties & seeming contrarieties in history. So when we are told in one author that Venus was born of the genitals of Coelus cut off & cast into the sea by his son Saturn, in another that she was born of the genitals of

---

[84] Quoted by Mordechai Feingold and Jed Z. Buchwald, *Newton and the Origin of Civilization* (Princeton, NJ: Princeton University Press, 2013), p. 150.

[85] Newton, 'Draft Chapters of a Treatise on the Origin of Religion and its Corruption,' fol. 14r.

Saturn cut off & cast into the sea by his son Iupiter, in a third that she was the daughter of Iupiter & Iuno: we are to understand the first according to the Assyrian Theology, the second according to the Chaldaean & the third according to the Egyptian. When we are told in an ancient Egyptian monument that Isis was the daughter of Saturn the youngest God, we are to understand the older Saturn to be Noah & the younger to be Ham the Saturn of the Arabians who sometimes reigned in the lower Egypt.[86]

## Noachides and the New World

That the inhabitants of the Old World were the descendants of Noah was almost universally accepted. The land routes were known and the sea voyages short. But how did the descendants of Noah get to America? The English jurist Sir Matthew Hale (1609–1676) put the problem precisely in 1642:

> [T]he late Discovery of the vast Continent of America and Islands adjacent, which appears to be as populous with Men, and as well stored with Cattel almost as any part of *Europe*, *Asia*, or *Africa*, hath occasioned some difficulty and dispute touching the Traduction [Transmission] of all Mankind from the two common Parents supposed of all Mankind, namely Adam and Eve; but principally concerning the storing of the World with Men and Cattel from those that the Sacred history tells us were preserved in the ark.[87]

---

[86] *Ibid.*, fol. 14r.
[87] Matthew Hale, *The Primitive Origination of Mankind, Considered and Examined according to the Light of Nature* (London, 1677), p. 182.

The simplest, if most improbable, solution, accepting
that the Indians of America were human, was that they
were the direct descendants of Noah who, after the
deluge, travelled to the New World. This was the solution
of the French traveller Marc Lescarbot (c.1570–1641) in
his *History of New France* (1611). Noah was, after all, a
great workman and sailor. He could have made another
ship, the ark being stuck fast on Ararat. 'For what hinders
us,' Lescarbot asked, 'from believing that Noah during his
life of 350 years after the Flood did not himself see to it,
and take pains to people, or rather to repeople, these
lands? Is it believable that he remained so long a space
of time without engaging upon and carrying out many
great and lofty enterprises?'[88] Noah had 'knowledge of a
thousand things which we have not' handed down to him
from Adam.[89] Lescarbot too had read his Annius. Having
been especially chosen by God to renew the earth, Noah
had, by report at least, knowledge of these lands, 'to which
he would have no more difficulty in setting sail, after
peopling Italy, than in coming from the end of the
Mediterranean to the Tiber, to found his Janiculum, if
the profane historians are correct, as a thousand reasons
would lead one to believe'.[90]

Lescarbot was the first – and almost the last – to suggest
that Noah had travelled to the New World. It was hinted
at by the Spanish priest Fernando de Montesinos (fl. early
to mid-sixteenth century) in his history of Peru (c.1644).
He reinvented Ophir, the great-great-great-grandson of

---

[88] Marc Lescarbot, *History of New France, Volume 1* (Toronto: The
Champlain Society, 1907), p. 47.
[89] *Ibid.*, p. 47.    [90] *Ibid.*, p. 48.

Noah (Genesis 10.29), as Noah's grandson, enabling Ophir to settle in America 340 years after the flood, and thus in Noah's lifetime. According to Fernando, by 150 years after the flood, the population of Armenia had become so great that Noah commanded his sons and grandsons to go in search of lands to settle. Fernando declared that there was no lack of authorities who had suggested that Noah himself travelled around the whole earth discovering and allotting the lands to his descendants. It would not be difficult, Montesinos concluded, 'to believe that Noah himself had been in Peru'.[91]

The question of which descendants of Noah inhabited the New World was as confused as the problem of which of them inhabited Europe. It was exemplified in 1607 in the *Origen de los Indios de el Nuevo Mundo, e Indias Occidentales* of the Dominican priest Gregorio Garcia (d.1627). He was convinced that Noah had given Asia to Shem, Egypt and Africa to Ham, and Europe to Japheth, and that the people of the Indies had come from one of these three parts. Within these criteria he identified the major contemporary opinions on the origins of the American Indians. We can distinguish these into particular and general theories. Among the former, he examined those accounts that had the origins of the Indians with the Carthaginians, the Spaniards, the Greeks, the Phoenicians, the East Asians (Chinese, Tatars, Scythians), migrants from Atlantis before it was swallowed by the sea, and the ten lost tribes of Israel.

[91] Philip Ainsworth Means (trans.), *Memorias Antiguas Historiales del Peru by Fernando Montesinos* (London: Hakluyt Society, 1920), p. 3.

More generally, first, he considered their possible arrival by sea because of their navigational skills passed on to them by Noah. Second, he thought it possible that they might have arrived by chance as the result of a storm. Third, he considered that they might have arrived by a no longer existing land route. His conclusion? He rejected all and accepted all. The Indians proceeded, he wrote, 'neither from one Nation or people, nor went to those parts from one [part] of the Old World [Mundo Viego]. Nor did the settlers all walk or sail by the same road or voyage at the same time, nor in the same manner. But actually they proceeded from various nations, from which some came by sea, forced and driven by storms; others by art of navigation looking for those lands, of which they had heard. Some came by land.'[92]

The three general solutions offered by Garcia were derived from the Spanish Jesuit missionary José de Acosta's (c.1539–1600) acclaimed *Historia natural y moral de las Indias* (1590). His aim was to find historical arguments that linked the New World populations with those of the Old. Despite Saint Augustine's belief that the immensity of the ocean ruled out crossing to the New World, the presence of humanity there and the Biblical teaching that all men derived from a first man meant they must have done just that. 'Certainly,' he humorously remarked, 'we are not to think that there was a second

---

[92] Quoted by Lee Eldridge Huddleston, *Origins of the American Indians: European Concepts, 1492–1729* (Austin: University of Texas Press, 1967), ch. 2, p. 40 (Kobo Edition). See also Gregorio Garcia, *Origen de los Indios de el Nuevo Mundo, e Indias Occidental* (Madrid, 1729), p. 315. Available at www.digitale-sammlungen.de/en/view/bsb10211329? page = 5.

Noah's Ark in which men were brought to the Indies, nor much less that some angel brought the first inhabitants of this world holding them by the hair, as did an angel with the prophet Habakkuk.'[93]

So, aside from being flown through the air by an eagle or a winged horse, or using fish or mermaids to travel by sea, there were only three possibilities he was willing to entertain. The first of these was that they came deliberately by navigational and sailing skills. It was a solution he could not accept, since the technologies enabling transoceanic travel (like the compass) were too recent to have been used by ancient travellers, nor was there any mention of such technologies among the ancients. Second, he admitted that it was also possible that the original inhabitants of the Indies had been cast upon unknown shores accidentally as the result of violent storms. But this failed to explain how the varieties of animals in the New World had reached there after the flood, for the same explanation must work for animals as well as men. Acosta conceded that some animals that were useful to men may have been on board and shipwrecked along with them. But this failed to explain the presence in the New World of 'wolves and foxes and other such vile and worthless animals'.[94] It is unreasonable,

---

[93] Jane E. Mangan (ed.), *Natural and Moral History of the Indies: José de Acosta* (Durham, NC: Duke University Press, 2002), p. 51. On Acosta, see Andrés I. Prieto, 'Reading the Book of Genesis in the New World: José de Acosta and Bernabé Cobo on the Origins of the American Indians,' *Hispanófila* 158 (Enero 2010), pp. 1–19. The reference to flying prophets is that of Habakkuk's being transported by the hair with food for a hungry Daniel in the lion's den. The story appears in apocryphal additions to the book of Daniel 14.33-42.

[94] *Ibid.*, p. 62.

he declared, to think that such animals might have swum the distance to the Indies.

His third and preferred solution was to postulate a land bridge between Asia and America, somewhere near the northern or the southern end of the American continent. If so, he declared,

> there is an easy answer for the difficult problem that we propounded, how the first dwellers in the Indies crossed over to them, for then we would have to say that they crossed not by sailing on the sea but by walking on land. And they followed this way quite unthinkingly, changing places and lands little by little, with some of them settling in the lands already discovered and others seeking new ones, so that in the course of time they arrived and swelled the lands of the Indies with many nations and peoples and languages.[95]

And it was a solution that simultaneously also explained the fauna of the New World that had similarly travelled overland from Asia to America.

The Garcian tradition predominated in Spain for the remainder of the seventeenth century, while Northern Europe was dominated by the Acostan solution. But there were two more solutions in the seventeenth century that vied for public attention in Northern Europe. The first of these was the Jewish origin of the Indians. Acosta had argued that the belief that the Indians came from the Jews was a false one.[96] But there was a resurgence of this tradition in Holland and England in the mid-seventeenth century. It was stimulated by the first Jewish contribution

---

[95] *Ibid.*, pp. 63–64.    [96] See *ibid.*, pp. 69–71.

to the question of the origin of the American Indians – *The Hope of Israel* (1650) by the Portuguese Jew Menasseh ben Israel (1604–1657).

Manasseh's account chimed in perfectly with contemporary English concerns about the re-admission of the Jews to England as a necessary prelude to the conversion of the Jews and the return of Christ. As the English Puritan Thomas Thorowgood (d. c.1669) put it in his *Iewes in America* (1650), 'From the Jews our faith began, / To the Gentiles then it ran, / To the Jews return it shall, / Before the dreadful end of all.'[97] In sum, Manasseh argued that the West Indies were anciently inhabited by a part of the ten tribes of Israel who arrived there from Tartary via the Strait of Anian in the northwest of America. To his own day, he believed, they kept the Jewish religion. Eventually, in the not-too-distant future, along with members of other lost Jewish tribes elsewhere, they would return to Jerusalem. There and then, all twelve of the tribes of Israel would be reunited under the rule of the Davidic Messiah, never to be driven from their homeland again.[98] This was not an argument for the Jewish origin of the Indians so much as one for a separate tradition of ancient Mosaic observance in America, one that existed still alongside other non-Jewish Americans.

This was a different argument from that of Thomas Thorowgood whose *Iewes in America* was the first sustained argument by an English author for the Jewish

---

[97] Thomas Thorowgood, *Iewes in America, or, Probabilities that the Americans are of that Race...* (London, 1650), p. 24.

[98] Menasseh ben Israel, *The Hope of Israel* (London, 1650), pp. 83–84.

origin of *all* Americans.[99] For Thorowgood it was at least probable that the Americans were the descendants of the lost tribes who had degenerated into paganism. Following Acosta, he thought it likely that they had come to America from Asia at the point where the two land masses were most close – the land or strait of Anian.[100] There were six 'conjectures' why Thorowgood thought that the Americans were Jews. First, the myths of the Indians were suggestive of a Jewish origin; second, their profane fashions, ceremonies, opinions, and sacred rites were comparable; third, their words and manners of speech were consonant; fourth, their cannibalism was prophesied in the Bible; fifth, like the Jews, they would be the last to know Christ; and finally, the calamities suffered by the Indians were predicted for the Jews in the Bible.[101]

Thorowgood had given the English theologian Sir Hamon L'Estrange (1605–1660) a copy of his *Iewes in America* in 1650. L'Estrange was underwhelmed. He took aim at Thomas Thorowgood's *Iewes in America* (along with Manasseh's book) in his *Americans no Iewes* (1651/2), conjecture by conjecture, arguing that the similarities in beliefs, practices, and languages to which Thorowgood had drawn attention were unpersuasive and that the Indians often lived in violation of the precepts of the Mosaic law. Rather belying his title, L'Estrange offered an alternative account of the Jewish origin of American Indians. Simply put, L'Estrange

---

[99] See Richard W. Cogley, 'The Ancestry of the American Indians: Thomas Thorowgood's *Iewes in America* (1650) and *Jews in America* (1660),' *English Literary Renaissance* 35 (2005), pp. 304–330.
[100] Thorowgood, *Iewes in America*, pp. 41–44.     [101] *Ibid.*, pp. 3–35.

argued that America was first populated only 300 years after the flood, some 1,200 years before the ten tribes of Israel became lost. It was Noah's peaceful son Shem and his children, he declared, who, under threat from the warlike progeny of Ham or Japheth, 'removed still more East, and soon after planted and peopled the nearest, and more parts of America'.[102] More of the dispersion of the sons of Noah anon, when, just over a century later, it was incorporated into the beginnings of the European science of race.

[102]  Hamon L'Estrange, *Americans no Iewes, or Improbabilities that the Americans are of that Race* (London, 1651/2), p. 9.

# 5
## Noah and the New Science

~

### Moments, Chronologic and Demographic

'Upon the entrance of the night', on Saturday, 22 October in the year 4004 BCE, God created the universe. Thus did the erudite and scholarly Irish archbishop of Armagh, James Ussher (1581–1656), calculate the date of the creation of the world in his *Annales Veteris Testamenti* (1650), otherwise known as *The Annals of the World*.[1] Ussher's *Annals of the World* was intended to provide a complete account of all historical knowledge, Biblical and Classical, from the creation of the world down to just after the fall of Jerusalem to the Romans in 70 CE. For Ussher, as for many others, the date of creation was a crucial date because the beginning of the world provided the anchor for the rest of human history, both sacred and profane. And the attempts to calculate the beginning of the world, of which Ussher's was a particularly impressive and influential one, were also intended to put to rest a debate that had begun among philosophers in Classical times and had persisted into the seventeenth century. This was a debate about whether the world was created at some time or was uncreated and eternal.

The initial problem to be overcome was the choice of the text – that of the Masoretic version (the Hebrew

---

[1]  See James Ussher, *The Annals of the World...* (London, 1658), p. 1.

version of the Old Testament) or of the Septuagint (the Greek version). Judaism, following the Hebrew version, had set the date of creation at 3760 BCE or 1,656 years before the flood of Noah. The Septuagint differed from the Hebrew version by setting the year of creation 2,242 years before the flood. This was the result of the Septuagint's adding approximately one hundred years to the ages of each of the early Biblical patriarchs in the genealogies in the book of Genesis. Thus, the chronology in the Septuagint had the year of creation around 5500 BCE. This dating had the virtue for its translators of proving the antiquity of the Jews and their history against those who suggested that the Jews had come late into world history.[2]

Within Reformation Europe, this mattered. Roman Catholicism was committed to the Greek Septuagint as the best version of the Old Testament. However, Martin Luther's translation of the Old Testament was based upon the so-called Masoretic (Hebrew) text, produced by a group of Jewish scholars known as the 'Masoretes' between the seventh and tenth centuries CE. This was the text used by the Protestant translators of the Old Testament in the King James version of the Bible in 1611. Thus, within Protestantism, the Hebrew figures for ancient chronology were almost universally followed.

The acceptance of the Hebrew dating in the early modern period was also influenced by the tradition of the earth lasting for 6,000 years, 4,000 of which consisted

---

[2]   See James Barr, 'Why the World Was Created in 4004 B.C.: Archbishop Ussher and Biblical Chronology,' *Bulletin of the John Rylands University Library of Manchester* 67 (1984–1985), p. 582.

of the period between creation and the coming of Christ. In the third century, for example, Julius Africanus (c. 160–240 CE), the first Christian historian to produce a universal chronology, combined the six days of creation with the Biblical notion that a day for God is 1,000 years (Psalm 90.4 and 2 Peter 3.8) to generate the six millennia of world history. Lactantius, Augustine, Isidore of Seville, and Bede also divided the world into six ages to last six thousand years – from Adam to Noah, to Abraham, to David, to the Babylonian captivity, to Christ, to the Last Judgement.[3]

No doubt, the tendency to settle on the year of creation as a century either side of 4000 BCE was a consequence of the belief in the 6,000 years of world history, with estimates ranging from 4103 to 3928 BCE.[4] That there was such variation is hardly surprising. For while it was feasible in the history of Israel to identify Biblical events with extra-Biblical data, the Bible itself does not give us a chronology, and where it does so, it is anything but clear. As Hugh Trevor-Roper neatly puts it,

> The period of the Kings of Israel, from Solomon to the last King Hezekiah, was of particular obscurity, with joint reigns, overlapping reigns, regencies, interregna, all imperfectly defined ... But if the chronologer could

---

[3] See Dennis R. Dean, 'The Age of the Earth Controversy: Beginnings to Hutton,' *Annals of Science* 38 (1981), pp. 437–439. See also Francis C. Haber, *The Age of the World: Moses to Darwin* (Baltimore: Johns Hopkins University Press, 1959).

[4] C. A. Patrides, 'Renaissance Estimates of the Year of Creation,' *Huntington Library Quarterly* 26 (1963), pp. 315–322. This range of dates is derived from 108 sources surveyed by Patrides. For Thomas Browne on the debate, see Robin Robbins (ed.), *Sir Thomas Browne's Pseudodoxia Epidemica* (Oxford: Clarendon, 1981), vol. 1, pp. 440–452.

thread his way through that Serbonian bog, the going gradually improved, and ultimately, as he waded ashore, on the far side of Noah's flood, he would be cheered by the beckoning of the long-lived pre-diluvian Patriarchs whose regularly recorded ages and generations provided accurate milestones back to the creation.[5]

Thus, on a reckoning based on the Hebrew Scriptures, the time between the creation and the flood, when Noah was 600 years of age, was 1,656 years.

Amongst all the various calculation for the date of creation, Ussher's was to become the most widely accepted. Early in the next century, Humphrey Prideaux (1648–1724) was to describe the *Annals* as 'the exactest and most perfect work of chronology that has been published'.[6] The success of its chronology was assured by its inclusion in the margins of Bishop William Lloyd's Bible in 1701. Despite the array of linguistic, mathematical, scientific, astronomical, and exegetical skills that Ussher brought to his task, he was undoubtedly ideologically driven. For there can be little doubt that *all* his effort was determined by his acceptance of the six ages and the desire to locate the creation exactly 4,000 before the birth of Christ.

The four years that remained out of the 4004 BCE were the consequence of the work of the French chronologer Joseph Scaliger (1540–1609). He had shown that if the account of the slaughter of the innocents by Herod the Great were true (Matthew 2.1-28), Christ could not have

---

[5] Hugh Trevor-Roper, *Catholics, Anglicans, and Puritans: Seventeenth Century Essays* (Chicago: University of Chicago Press, 1988), p. 157.

[6] Quoted by *ibid.*, p. 161.

been born in the year traditionally assigned. For Herod the Great, who had ordered the slaughter, had died in 4 BCE, and therefore Christ must have been born in that or the preceding year. On these calculations, it was the year 4004 BCE that was, according to Ussher, 4,000 years before the birth of Christ. This meant that the flood took place 1,656 years after creation, that is, in the year 2349 BCE: 'In the 600 year of the life of *Noah*, upon the 17 day of the second month, answering to the 7 of our *Decemb*, upon a Sunday, when he with his children, and living creatures of all sorts, were entered into the Ark, God sent a rain upon the earth forty days, and forty nights; and the waters continued upon the earth 150 days.'[7] In the left margin of his text, Ussher had written '1656' and in the right margin '2349'.

This all meant that the population of the world, as it was, in the middle of the seventeenth century, had grown to its then number in the 4,000 years or so since God had said to Noah and his sons, 'Be fruitful and multiply, and fill the earth' (Genesis 9.1). That there was rapid population growth soon after the flood was looked upon as little short of miraculous. The English clergyman Andrew Willet (1562–1621) noted that the increase in mankind was so great that 'within three hundred years, *Ninus* King of the Assyrians, had an army of seventeene hundred thousand footmen.'[8]

It was perhaps inevitable that a mathematics of population growth would begin in the seventeenth century.

[7]  Ussher, *The Annals of the World...*, p. 3.
[8]  Andrew Willet, *Hexapla in Genesin & Exodum...* (London, 1633), p. 86. For this discussion on population growth I am indebted to Feingold and Buchwald, *Newton and the Origin of Civilization*, ch 5.

Thus, for example, the French Protestant jurist Jean du Temps (Joannes Temporarius, 1555–?) pioneered the tradition of mathematically calculating growth in population in his *Chronologicarum Demonstrationum* (1596). Du Temps declared that Noah's three sons produced twins annually, a male and a female. They, in turn, began having twins each year after their twentieth year, and so on. By the time of Peleg, some four generations after Noah (Genesis 10.25), and just before the building of the Tower of Babel, the population numbered 1,554,420. In his *Turris Babel* (1679), Athanasius Kircher adopted Temporarius's assumption that each of Noah's sons begat twins each year after the age of thirty. Thus, according to Kircher's calculation, the world numbered 360 people thirty years after the flood, 21,600 after sixty years, and 1,994,000 after ninety years. By the time the Tower of Babel was built, 120 years after the flood, the world population had reached '23,328,000,000' (although this is probably a slip of the quill by Kircher for '233,280,000').[9]

Sir Thomas Browne in the 1640s was to base his calculation of population growth after the flood on considerations of the growth of people before it. Unlike those who believed the earth to have been only slenderly populated before the deluge, Browne argued that there was a 'populous and ample habitation of the earth before the flood'.[10]

---

[9] See Athanasius Kircher, *Turris Babel...* (Amsterdam, 1679), p. 9. Available at https://archive.org/details/turrisbabelsiveaookirc/page/n5/mode/2up. See also Feingold and Buchwald, *Newton and the Origin of Civilization*, p. 168.

[10] Charles Sayle (ed.), *Pseudodoxia Epidemica*, book 6, chapter 6, in *The Works of Sir Thomas Browne, Volume 2* (London: Grant Richards, 1904), p. 322.

His criteria were twofold: first, the long duration of lives in the period before the flood, beyond seven hundred, eight hundred, and nine hundred years, that 'conduceth unto populosity'; second, the large extent of time from the creation to the flood. For his first calculation, Browne assumed a life span of seven hundred years for a man, allowed two or three centuries after creation for enough 'women fit for marriage', estimated that a woman would beget children at the age of sixty, and calculated for having twenty children over a period of forty years. On these estimates, the earth would have a population of 1,347,368,420 souls at least some nine hundred years before the flood. Adjusting for longevity after the flood compared to before it, Browne went on to estimate 'from probabilities, and several testimonies of Scripture and humane Authors', that the world would have been as populous in 1,300 years after the flood as it was in the 1,650 years before it.[11]

## 'The Multiplication of Mankind'

The developing science of demography in the seventeenth century was grounded in the more general issue of 'the multiplication of mankind', and that issue had to do overall with population growth from the time of the flood until the end of the world. Thus, for example, William Petty's (1623–1687) essay on population growth in the City of London was set within the broader context of the growth of population since the time of the flood. Petty's overall aim was to show that the population of

[11] *Ibid.*, pp. 324, 328, 330.

London doubled every 40 years, and that of England every 360 years.

But his interest in global population growth was aroused by a 'worthy Divine' writing against sceptics 'who would have baffled our belief of the Resurrection, by saying, that the whole Globe of the Earth could not furnish Matter enough for all the Bodies that must Rise at the last Day, much less would the surface of the Earth furnish footing for so vast a Number'.[12] On this matter, Petty estimated that the some 20 billion people had died from the creation to the year 1682 with 320 million still alive. Thus, reckoning 4 million graves per square mile, 'the Total of the Quick and the Dead, will amount but unto one fifth part of the Graves, which the surface of *Ireland* will afford, without ever putting two Bodies into any one Grave'.[13] The task that Petty set himself was arithmetically to work out how a population of eight after the flood had reached his estimate of 320 million living people in 1682 some 4,000 years (by his account) after the flood (in 2318 BCE).[14]

His calculation, Petty believed, needed to align with what was known about 'the *Scriptures* and all other good *Histories* concerning the *Number* of the People in Ancient Time'.[15] He realised that, on the evidence provided in

---

[12] William Petty, *Another Essay in Political Arithmetic, Concerning the Growth of the City of London* (London, 1683), p. 23.

[13] *Ibid.*, p. 46.

[14] If we assume that Petty accepted the generally agreed period of 1,656 years from creation to flood, then his date for creation would have been 3974 BCE. This was the date proposed by the Swiss Reformer Heinrich Bullinger (1504–1575). See Patrides, 'Renaissance Estimates of the Year of Creation,' p. 317.

[15] Petty, *Another Essay in Political Arithmetic*, p. 18.

these sources, doubling the population every 150 years would never generate the population that was known, from the Biblical account, to be in the time of Moses (1,000 years after the flood) or in the time of David (1,400 years after the flood). On the other hand, doubling the population every 100 years would have 'over-peopled' the world by 1000 CE. His solution was to propose 'a different Number of Years for the time of doubling the People *in the several Ages of the World*'.[16] Petty's method of progressively reducing rates of doubling had the population at some 8,000 within 100 years after the flood, at over 1,000,000 by 350 years after, and at 16,000,000 in the time of Moses, some 1,000 years after the flood, until it reached 128,000,000 at the time of Christ, 256,000,000 at 1000 CE, and 320,000,000 by 1682. Petty also believed (in proto-Malthusian mode) that, in the next four hundred years, the world would become overpopulated, that there would then be 'great Wars and Slaughters, and that the Strong must then destroy the weake, or the World must come (of necessity) to an end'.[17]

Such arguments as those of Petty proceeded on the assumption that the Scripture contained a true account of the destruction of all living things, and that the flood was a universal one. So, Petty saw himself as offering 'a brave argument against Scripture Scoffers and Prae-Adamites'.[18] No doubt he was thinking of that most eminent of Pre-Adamites, Isaac La Peyrère (1596–1676).

---

[16]  *Ibid.*, p. 25 (emphasis added).
[17]  The Marquis of Lansdowne, *The Petty-Southwell Correspondence 1676–1687* (New York: Augustus M. Kelley, 1967), p. 93.
[18]  *Ibid.*, p. 92.

1 'The Lord saw that the wickedness of humankind was great in the earth' (Genesis 6.5).

**2** 'Make yourself an ark of cypress wood; make rooms in the ark, and cover it inside and out with pitch' (Genesis 6.14).

**3** 'And of every living thing, of all flesh, you shall bring two of every kind into the ark, to keep them alive with you' (Genesis 6.19).

**4** 'For in seven days I will send rain on the earth for forty days and forty nights; and every living thing that I have made I will blot out from the face of the ground' (Genesis 7.4)

**5** 'And the dove came back to him in the evening, and there in its beak was a freshly plucked olive leaf' (Genesis 8.11).

Cõmt noel apõ le deluge annua a tout et nult tous le trtail et fift facrifice et plauta la bigue

**6** 'And every animal, every creeping thing, and every bird, everything that moves on the earth, went out of the ark by families' (Genesis 8.19).

7  At the bidding of Zeus, Deucalion picked up stones, threw them over his head and they became men. The stones that Pyrrha threw became women.

8 'This is how you are to make the ark: the length of the ark three hundred cubits, its width fifty, and its height thirty cubits' (Genesis 6.15).

9 'Make a roof for the ark, and finish it to a cubit above; and put the door of the ark in its side' (Genesis 6.16).

10 'Make it curved, in three (parts); its head like the head of a cock; its middle like the belly of a bird; and its tail inclining like the tail of a bird' (al-Thaʿlabī).

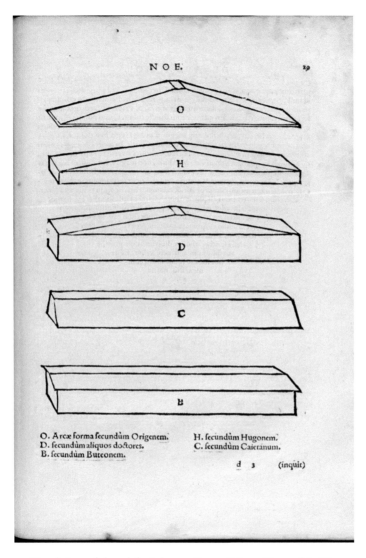

O. Arcæ forma fecundùm Origenem.
D. fecundùm aliquos doctores.
B. fecundùm Buteonem.

H. fecundùm Hugonem.
C. fecundùm Caietanum.

d    3        (inquit)

11 Five designs of the ark by Johannes Buteo: Origen, Hugo of St. Victor, 'some teachers', Cardinal Cajetan, Buteo.

12 Mathew Baker, an Elizabethan shipwright, imagines the ark.

Conte on edifia la tour de babiloine. et le languege fute mue en. lx.xij. Langueges. et les anges la despererint.

**13** 'Come, let us build ourselves a city, and a tower with its top on the heavens' (Genesis 11.4).

F I N I S.

**14** William Blake's engraving of Jacob Bryant's 'moon-ark'.

**15** *A Map of Earth and how after the Flood it was divided among the Sons of Noah*, by Joseph Moxon, hydrographer to King Charles II.

**16** The three continents divided between Shem, Ham, and Japheth – the sons of Noah.

**17** 'And Ham, the father of Canaan, saw the nakedness of his father, and told his two brothers outside' (Genesis 9.22).

**18** 'Cursed be Canaan; lowest of slaves shall he be to his brothers' (Genesis 9.25). But Ham was eventually to take all the blame for uncovering his father's nakedness.

**19** *Shem's Wife Ar'yel in the Kitchen of the Ark*, according to the Ark Encounter, Kentucky.

Peyrère had not only argued for the existence of men before Adam but had also raised doubts about the Mosaic authorship of the first five books of the Bible and the universality of the flood. The deluge came only upon the land of the Jews, he declared, because of 'the sins of the Jews'.[19] Aware that many cultures – Greek, Egyptian, Chinese, and American – all had flood stories, 'why should we not grant to *Palestine* their particular deluge?' he asked.[20] And he seriously doubted that the whole world could be re-populated by the few survivors that the Bible reported had survived the flood. Could it be possible, he inquired, that within five generations after the flood, 'they could inhabit *China*, *America*, the *Southland*, and *Greenland*, and whatsoever land lies betwixt them?'[21]

Putting an end to all attempts to develop a universal chronology from the date of the creation of the world, Peyrère had also advanced the theory that the world was eternal and had no date of creation, or if it had, it was unknown. The foundations of the world, he declared, 'were laid from eternal times, or from eternity, in regard of us, or from times and ages to us unknown, or from that beginning, of which there is no certain knowledge'.[22] All this rather put paid to the grand scheme of history embedded within Christianity – Creation, Fall, Deluge, Redemption, Last Things. Little wonder that the jurist Sir Matthew Hale (1609–1676) in his *The Primitive Origination of Mankind* declared that, were Peyrère's account true, it 'would necessarily not only weaken but overthrow the Authority and Infallibility of the Sacred

---

[19]  Isaac La Peyrère, *Men before Adam...* (London, 1656), p. 243.
[20]  *Ibid.*, p. 255.    [21]  *Ibid.*, p. 250.    [22]  *Ibid.*, p. 261.

Scriptures'.[23] Simply put, the universality of the flood and the re-population of the earth from the survivors of it were crucial to the credibility of Christianity.

As we will shortly see, Matthew Hale used fossil evidence as an argument for the universality of the flood. But it was only on the assumption of its *universality* that he could develop his argument about population growth from Noah and his family. Hale began with some general calculations about population growth. He took the average life span to be sixty years and each male and female to have two children by the age of thirty. Allowing each of these children to have two children before the death of their father, he was able to conclude that, within one generation, 'They become increased in a quadruple proportion, and all coexisting.'[24] If men and women began reproducing at the age of seventeen or eighteen, and men lived until sixty-five years of age, 'the increase would be very much greater'.[25] Increase the longevity and fertility to that of those who lived after the flood, and 'within the compass of 215 Years after the Flood the Sons of *Noah* and their Descendents [sic] might without a Miracle increase to prodigious and incredible multitudes'.[26] Hale was not averse to following the estimate of the French Jesuit Dionysius Petavius (1583–1652) that, within 215 years after the flood, the population may have been 1,219,133,512, all descended from one of the sons of Noah. The numbers based on the Septuagint would be significantly greater, he declared. But even on the Hebrew

[23] Matthew Hale, *The Primitive Origination of Mankind*, p. 185.
[24] *Ibid.*, p. 205.   [25] *Ibid.*   [26] *Ibid.*

reckoning, the increase would be credible 'without the help of a Miracle'.[27]

Peleg was the first person to die some 340 years after the flood (Genesis 11.16-19). His death provided a good point up to which the number of persons alive at that precise time could be calculated. Thus, for example, during the 1690s, Richard Cumberland (1631–1718), the Bishop of Peterborough, on the basis of the death of Peleg, postulated that the average age of the first three generations after the flood was four hundred years. Ignoring the possibility that Noah might have had more children after the flood, he postulated that each of Noah's sons produced a similar number of children and that each produced a child for every twenty years after the flood, male and female equally. When each of these children reached twenty years of age, the cycle resumed at the same rate and recurred every forty years. At the time of Peleg's death, Cumberland calculated the total human population to be 3,333,333,333 couples.[28] He considered his calculation to be a modest one. Nevertheless, his calculation (and the table that he produced to demonstrate it) was sufficient, he believed, to 'stop the mouth of those bold pretenders that say it was impossible that in this time men enough could be begotten to plant those kingdoms; concerning which we have good records'.[29]

---

[27] *Ibid.*
[28] See Richard Cumberland, *Origenes Gentium Antiquissimae; or Attempts for Discovering the Times of the first Planting of Nations in Several Tracts* (London, 1724), p. 150. Available at https://babel.hathitrust.org/cgi/pt?id=uc2.ark:/13960/t4zg6xn3t&seq=194.
[29] *Ibid.*, p. 151.

Petty, Hale, and Cumberland assumed the universality of the flood, and thus the destruction of all people except those upon the ark. This enabled them to calculate the growth in population from the eight survivors of the flood. But conversely, the enormous growth in population before the flood, from Adam to Noah as it were, was also used to demonstrate the universality of the flood. Only a universal flood could thus have destroyed all the people who had spread by that time throughout the whole world. Thus, for example, Thomas Burnet (c.1635–1715), theological geologist or geological theologian (indistinguishable in practice), was focused, above all, on the universality of the flood, but he used population growth from creation to deluge as an important argument for it.

In his *The Theory of the Earth*, Burnet noted that, in the 1,600 or 1,700 years after the flood, when the world was renewed by only eight persons, people had rapidly filled Asia, Europe, and Africa. How much more so, he asked, would the population have increased in the same period, between creation and the flood, when people lived from six hundred to nine hundred years each and were more fruitful? The 'longevity of the first Inhabitants of the Earth seems to have been providentially design'd,' he suggested, 'for the quicker multiplication and propagation of mankind.'[30] In fact, the number of people would have been so great by the time of the flood that there would have been more difficulty caused by the abundance of them than by their scarcity. Burnet proposed that, at the end of the first century, the first couple would have left 'ten pair of Breeders'. Within 1,500 years, there would

---

[30] Thomas Burnet, *The Theory of the Earth...* (London, 1684), p. 21.

have arisen a greater number of people than the earth was capable of sustaining, 'allowing every pair to multiply in the same decuple [tenfold] proportion [as] the first pair did'.[31] So Burnet lowered his estimate of fruitfulness to a quadruple for humankind's rate of population growth, reaching over 10 billion couples by the time of the deluge. He thought this to be a reasonable and moderate figure, and one not excessively high when compared with the present (for him) number of people over the whole earth, commonly estimated to be between 300 million and 400 million. Thus, granting the contemporary population compared to that before the flood, 'it seems to me to be a very groundless and forc'd conceit to imagine that *Judea* only, and some Countries about it in *Asia* were stor'd with people when the Deluge was brought upon the whole world'.[32] Moreover, why would Noah have bothered to build an ark to save himself and his family 'if he might have sav'd himself and them by only retiring into some neighbouring Country'.[33]

Complicating these matters further, there was another chronology in play alongside the Masoretic and the Septuagint versions of the Old Testament. This was contained within the Samaritan version of the Pentateuch (the first five books of the Bible), written in Hebrew but in a different script to that of the Masoretic version. This Samaritan version became known to the West in the early seventeenth century. It added an extra layer to Catholic–Protestant polemics around the Greek and Hebrew versions of the Old Testament. Protestants were worried, with good reason, that the Samaritan would challenge

[31] *Ibid.*, p. 23.    [32] *Ibid.*, p. 24.    [33] *Ibid.*

the Masoretic version, thus strengthening the Catholic preference for the Septuagint. For, as early as 1631, the Catholic scholar Jean Morin (1591–1659) was using the Samaritan version to argue that it was superior to the Masoretic version favoured among most Protestants. As a Protestant, Thomas Browne favoured the Hebrew over the Greek version. But he did notice the difference in chronology between the Samaritan and Masoretic versions – according to him, 1,302 years between creation and deluge in the Samaritan version, compared to 1,656 in the Masoretic. He thought that the Samaritans 'preserved the Text with far more integrity then [sic] the Jews'.[34]

Without putting too fine a point on it, the Samaritan version has different lengths of life for some of the patriarchs compared to those of the Masoretic text, significantly altering the chronologies both before the flood (in Genesis 5) and after the flood up to the time of the death of Terah, Abraham's father (in Genesis 11). By my calculations, the Samaritan version has the patriarchs before the flood living some 488 years less than the Masoretic version. But it has them surviving after the flood some 650 years longer than the Masoretic version.

During the 1620s and 1630s, Archbishop Ussher had acquired a total of six of the Samaritan versions. For his own chronological calculations, Ussher stayed doggedly

---

[34] Robbins (ed.), *Sir Thomas Browne's* Pseudodoxia Epidemica, vol. 1, p. 444. Browne should have said 1,307 years. He had forgotten to add 5 years after Lamech's death 1,302 years after the creation and 5 years before the beginning of the deluge. On the Samaritan Pentateuch, see Robert T. Anderson and Terry Giles, *The Samaritan Pentateuch: An Introduction to its Origin, History, and Significance for Biblical Studies* (Atlanta: Society of Biblical Literature, 2012).

with the Masoretic text, ignoring the Samaritan variations. But on 22 May 1628, his scholarly colleague Joseph Mede (1586–1639) wrote excitedly to the Archbishop that he had come across 'the chronology of your Samaritan Pentateuch, published to the view of the whole world'.[35] He noted correctly that the Samaritan chronology 'much more exceeded the Jewish in the genealogy of the patriarchs after the flood, than it came short in those before it'.[36] So, assuming the end of the world to be 6,000 years after its creation, taking Scaliger's date of the creation of the world as 3949 BCE based on the Masoretic text, and adding in the extra years of the Samaritan over the Masoretic chronologies, Mede calculated that the world would end in 1736, much earlier than would have been expected under the Masoretic chronology. That said, Mede did wonder, perhaps a little tongue in cheek, if the differences in the accounts of the years of the world that the different chronologies produced 'were not ordered by a special disposition of Providence, to frustrate our curiosity in searching for the time of the day of judgement'.[37]

Still and all, Mede remained curious. In a brief essay on the day of judgement coming six thousand years after the creation of the world, we see that Mede was inclining

---

[35] Charles Richard Elrington (ed.), *The Whole Works of the Most Rev. James Ussher, D.D.* (Dublin: Hodges, Smith, and Co., 1864), vol. 15, p. 406. Elsewhere, Mede indicated that Ussher had provided him with a copy of the Samaritan Pentateuch. See Joseph Mede, *The Works of the Pious and Profoundly-Learned Joseph Mede, B.D.* (London, 1777), p. 895.

[36] *Ibid.*, vol. 15, p. 407. Although Mede added in only 311 years for the difference between the Masoretic and Samaritan versions.

[37] *Ibid.*, vol. 15, p. 408.

towards the truth of the Samaritan chronology. He wondered whether 'the computation of the years of the world before the Promise made to *Abraham* were or could be certainly known or not.'[38] For if it were possible, he thought, to add 350 or 360 years (as in the Samaritan and the Septuagint chronologies) more than is counted in the Masoretic version, then that 'Tradition of the Seventh Thousand year to be the Day of Judgment and of the glorious Reign of Christ, will ... have good probability of Truth: Otherwise, I cannot see how possibly it can be admitted.'[39]

According to Mede, after the flood, Noah and his family moved to the land of Shinar, where God had, at the beginning, placed Adam and Eve. Even though their numbers grew, they were reluctant to leave that place. So, God decided to make them speak with many languages (Genesis 11.7) to disrupt the unity of their society: 'God in his wisdom saw that *Plurality of Languages* was the best means to force mankind into a *Plurality of Societies*.'[40] By confusing their languages, they were forced to disperse from the place of Paradise all over the earth. Now, Mede was aware that the chronologists were troubled that the one hundred years from the flood to the time of the building of the Tower of Babel seemed 'too small a time for eight persons to multiply unto such a number as may be presumed to have been at the building of the Tower of *Babel*, and at their dispersion thence'.[41] In fact, even

---

[38] Mede, *The Works*, pp. 894–895.
[39] *Ibid.*, p. 896. On Mede's millenarianism, see Jeffrey K. Jue, *Heaven upon Earth: Joseph Mede (1586–1638) and the Legacy of Millenarianism* (Dordrecht: Springer, 2006).
[40] *Ibid.*, p. 271.    [41] *Ibid.*, p. 896.

though the increased time between the flood and the birth of Abraham better fitted his calculation of the end of the world, he did not use this extra time to endorse significant population growth after the flood. On the contrary, at the time of the dispersal, he believed that the population was small. When this division was made, after the people had established a city and built the tower, he declared, '[T]he number of mankind was small; for besides women and children, their number in all could not be above seven thousand.'[42]

Only a few argued, like Mede, for *limited* population growth after the flood. One of them was the eccentric English antiquary Aylett Sammes (c.1636–c.1679) in his *Britannia Antiqua Illustrata* (1676). The overall thrust of his 600-page work was to demonstrate that the antiquities of Britain were derived from the Phoenicians. And he began this project by examining 'the increase of Mankind in the Primitive Ages of the World'.[43] Concerning the supposed enormous increase of humankind after the flood, he wrote, the Scriptures make no mention of it. Noah had but three sons, he declared, Japheth seven, Shem five, and Ham four. Nor, he believed, did the polygamy of the patriarchs make any noticeable difference. Even in the 192 years from the flood to Abraham, the land of Armenia where the ark had landed was not fully populated. A hundred years later, Simeon and Levi, without any assistance, destroyed a whole city, or at least the men within it (Genesis 34.25). Even three hundred

---

[42] *Ibid.*, p. 275.

[43] Aylett Sammes, *Britannia Antiqua Illustrata: or the Antiquities of Ancient Britain derived from the Phœnicians* (London, 1727), p. 7.

years after Jacob went into Egypt, his 600,350 male descendants outnumbered the Egyptians (Exodus 12.37-8) – at most, only two-thirds of the present inhabitants of London and Paris.

It was unlikely, therefore, that a Britain emptied of people by the flood was populated early by the sons of Japheth. Rather, every generation added one step to the spread of population, so that 'by long time, and short journeys', people gradually diffused.[44] For Sammes, the key to the settlement of Britain was the development of shipping among the Phoenicians some 1,270 years after the flood. Having escaped the persecution by Joshua and the Israelites when they lived in Canaan, 'they were driven up into a slender Nook of Earth, too narrow to contain so great and numerous a Body, [and] dispersed themselves into good Shipping, to seek their fortunes in most parts of the World, of whose Company, *Britain* received a considerable share'.[45] Sammes restricted the Phoenicians to the coasts of Britain. Others, like the Celts, he thought, might have beaten the Phoenicians to inland parts. Thus, Britain might have first been populated some 2,560 years after creation and 800 to 900 years after the flood. Rather fancifully, he suggested that the Phoenicians were giants because the time of their arrival in Britain coincided with the age of the giants in the Bible.[46]

---

[44] *Ibid.*, p. 8.    [45] *Ibid.*, p. 73.

[46] Presumably, Sammes was referring to the period of Og, the last of the giants from the age of Noah, who was defeated by the Israelites under the leadership of Moses (Numbers 21.33-5, Deuteronomy 3.11).
On Sammes, see Graham Parry, *The Trophies of Time* (Oxford: Oxford University Press, 2007), pp. 308–331.

Sammes's proposal of the Phoenicians as early settlers in Britain was significantly influenced by the French Protestant scholar Samuel Bochart's (1599–1667) *Geographia Sacra* (1646). Like Sammes, Bochart had identified the Phoenicians with the Canaanites that had been driven out of their land by the Israelites. Importantly, it was Bochart's *Geographia Sacra* that had put the Phoenicians on the intellectual agenda of ancient geography, along with the Greeks and Romans.[47] So, eccentric as he was, Sammes was sailing in respectable intellectual currents. We know that Isaac Newton both owned an extensively dog-eared copy of Bochart's *Geographia Sacra* and had read it. It is more than likely that Newton had also read Sammes's *Britannia Antiqua Illustrata*. And Newton was undoubtedly familiar with the *Works* of Joseph Mede. For he had copies of Sammes and Mede in his library.[48] But Newton was having none of Bochart's and Sammes's derivation of the Phoenicians from the Canaanites who had been driven out of Israel by Joshua. And unlike Mede's and Bochart's penchant for the Samaritan chronology, Newton stayed firmly committed to that of the Masoretic version. But that said, like Sammes and Mede, Newton *did* hold to the idea of limited population growth after the flood. This was because, unlike those primarily interested in population growth, Newton was much more focused on the chronology of ancient kingdoms.

---

[47] See Zur Shalev, *Sacred Words and Worlds* (Leiden: Brill, 2011), pp. 141–203.

[48] See 'Books in Newton's Library,' *The Newton Project*. Available at www .newtonproject.ox.ac.uk/his-library/books-in-newtons-library.

The slow rate of population growth for Newton was the consequence of his making the rise of ancient kingdoms later. He did this to be able to exalt Israelite kingship as amongst the oldest in the world. Simply put, Newton's account of the origin of civilisation was along these lines: from the sons of Noah arose large numbers of families; growing populations led from families to towns; assemblies of 'fathers' produced laws; laws required a judge; towns with courts and judges evolved into cities; judges transformed into kings; and kingdoms slowly grew by conquest or merger. Thus, for Newton, the story of the flood onwards was one of a long road from simplicity to civilisation:

> The first men after the flood lived in caves of the earth & woods & planes well watered by rivers for feeding their heards [sic] & flocks... By degrees they cut down the woods & learnt to build houses & towns of brick in the planes & to live in society under laws & governments. And this gave occasion to the rise of the first cities & kingdoms in the fertile planes of Assyria Babylonia & Egypt. From thence men spread into places less fertile & as they spread erected built towns & erected governments.[49]

William Whiston (1667–1752) was Isaac Newton's successor in the Lucasian Chair of Mathematics at the University of Cambridge. As we will see shortly,

[49] Isaac Newton, 'Chap. 1. Of the Times before the Assyrian Empire.' Ms. 361(2), New College Library, Oxford, UK. Available at www .newtonproject.ox.ac.uk/view/texts/diplomatic/THEM00097. See also Frank E. Manuel, *Isaac Newton Historian* (Cambridge, MA: The Belknap Press, 1963), ch. 8.

Whiston's *A New Theory of the Earth* (1696) was focused on the flood rather than its aftermath. But he found it hard to avoid at least some speculation about the rate of population growth after the deluge. Like Newton, he was committed to the Masoretic chronology, rejecting that of the Septuagint. But he thought the Masoretic chronology more than sufficient to account for the growth of population after the flood. The 427 years from the flood until Abraham went into Canaan, granting the average of 300 years for each man's life, were enough 'to produce the greatest Numbers of Men which in that, or the immediately succeeding Ages, any Authentick Histories of those Ancient Times do require us to suppose'.[50]

Whiston had read William Petty's essay on the multiplication of mankind just as his *A New Theory of the Earth* was at the printer. Six years later, following the pattern if not the detail established by Petty, Whiston had thought his way more thoroughly into the issue. Thus, in his book on Old Testament chronology in 1702, Whiston assumed that the then present population of the earth did not exceed 4 billion. He also accepted that the overall population doubled every 400 years, 'ever since the present Period of Human Life was fix'd in the days of [King] *David*'.[51] Further, he believed it was evident that, from the flood until the days of David, men lived six if not seven times longer than that which had obtained since then. Thus, beginning with the eight survivors of the flood,

---

[50] William Whiston, *A New Theory of the Earth, from its Original, to the Consummation of all Things* (London, 1696), p. 285.

[51] William Whiston, *A Short View of the Chronology of the Old Testament, and of the Harmony of the Four Evangelists* (London, 1702), p. 65.

and doubling in number every 60 years from the flood until David (about 1,300 years), and then doubling every 400 years in the 2,700 years since, we reach the present 4 billion.

The diagram that Whiston devised to demonstrate population growth from the flood to the present demonstrated, he claimed, 'that the number of years according to the *Hebrew* chronology, will very naturally account for the present number of Souls upon the face of the Earth'.[52] To have used either the Septuagint or the Samaritan chronology, he maintained, would have produced up to a thousand times as many as the present population of the earth. What Whiston's diagram also showed, however, was that if he thought that the Tower of Babel and the dispersion of the people occurred around one hundred years after the flood, there was only minimal population growth up to that time. On his reckoning, there would have only been a few thousand to begin building the Tower of Babel – hardly enough to build a tower 'with its top in the heavens' (Genesis 11.4) or to spread 'over the face of all the earth' (Genesis 11.9).

## The Universal Flood

Isaac La Peyrère, we recall, had questioned the universality of the flood. The deluge came only upon the land of the Jews, he declared, because of 'the sins of the Jews'.[53] Aware that many cultures – Greek, Egyptian, Chinese,

---

[52] *Ibid.*, p. 68. See https://babel.hathitrust.org/cgi/pt?id = ia.ark:/13960/t9183dx5z&seq = 85&q1 = noah.

[53] La Peyrère, *Men before Adam...*, p. 243.

and American – all had flood stories, 'why should we not grant to *Palestine* their particular deluge?' he asked.[54] The argument could, of course, cut in exactly the opposite direction. If all these different cultures had accounts of a universal flood, then there must have been one. Thus, for example, John Webb (1611–1672) argued that the reports of the flood in Chinese history were nothing but reports of the universal flood of Noah. Not surprising perhaps, granted that he argued, a little eccentrically even for his time, that Noah himself, 'before and after the Deluge lived in China',[55] and that Chinese was the original language of humankind, both before and after the flood.

Still, floods in Chinese history and elsewhere did seem to endorse the Biblical account of the flood as universal. All nations, declared Bishop Symon Patrick (1626–1707), had heard something of this flood. 'And now it appears,' he continued, 'that the *Americans* have had a tradition of it, (as credible authors, *Acosta*, *Herrera*, and others inform us) which saith, The whole Race of Mankind was destroyed by the Deluge, except some few that escaped. They are the words of *Augustin Corata*, concerning the *Peruvian* Tradition, and *Lupus Gomara* saith the same from those of *Mexico*. And if we can believe *Mart. Martinius*'s History of *China*, there is the like among the People of that Country.'[56]

The flood was universal, but it had also destroyed the perfection of the world as it was when it was created.

[54] *Ibid.*, p. 255.
[55] John Webb, *The Antiquity of China...* (London, 1678), p. 58.
[56] Symon Patrick, *A Commentary upon the Historical Books of the Old Testament* (London, 1732), vol. 1, p. 35.

In the 1691 second edition of his *The Theory of the Earth*, Thomas Burnet wrote to King William III, 'We still have the broken materials of that first World, and walk upon its Ruines; while it stood, there was the Seat of *Paradise*, and the Scenes of the *Golden Age*; when it fell, it made the Deluge; and this unshapen earth we now inhabit, is the Form it was found in when the Waters had retir'd, and the dry Land appear'd.'[57] The purpose of *his* book was to give a *natural* explanation of how all this had come about. It was, in effect, a new scientific version of Paradise lost.

Burnet plunged right into the deep end with the issue of whence had come the vast amounts of water that were needed, not only to cover the whole earth but to do so to a height of fifteen cubits over the tops of the mountains. The story of the flood, he wrote, 'is a short story of the greatest thing that ever yet happened in the world, the greatest revolution and the greatest change in Nature; and if we come to reflect seriously upon it, we shall find it extremely difficult, if not impossible, to give an account of the waters that compos'd this Deluge, whence they came or whither they went.'[58] The waters had to cover the surface of the earth, to above the tops of the highest mountains, 'a prodigious amount of water,' he declared.[59] In all, he reckoned, 'there would be at least eight Oceans requir'd, or a quantity of water eight times as great as the Ocean, to bring an universal Deluge upon the earth, as that Deluge is ordinarily understood and explained'.[60] In short, there was no quantity of water sufficient for a

[57] Thomas Burnet, *The Sacred Theory of the Earth* (London: Centaur Press, 1965), p. 13.
[58] *Ibid.*, p. 28.  [59] *Ibid.*  [60] *Ibid.*, p. 30.

universal deluge, either on, above, or below the earth. Moreover, if the earth had been deluged with such an amount of water, it could never have dissipated in the few months indicated in the Bible.

Still, Burnet was not willing to retreat from the idea of the universality of the flood. Nor would he countenance the idea that God would have specially created *new* waters for the flood and then miraculously removed them afterwards. The only solution was that the earth was radically different before the flood than after it. More specifically, 'That face of the Earth before the Deluge was smooth, regular and uniform; without Mountains, and without a Sea ... An Earth without a Sea, and plain [flat] as the *Elysian* fields; if you travel it all over, you will not meet with a Mountain or a Rock, yet well provided of all things requisite for an habitable World ... and so continu'd for many hundreds of years.'[61] Thus, the amount of water then required to cover a smooth earth would be no more than that now contained in the oceans.

Burnet went on to give a theory of the formation of the earth at its beginning. According to this, there was originally a primordial chaos that consisted of all the materials and ingredients of all bodies, 'but mingled in confusion one with another'.[62] The earth was created when the various parts of the chaos separated out. The heaviest matter formed a solid core at the centre, like the yoke and membrane of an egg. Above this, water formed in a sphere around the central core, like the white of an egg. Surrounding 'the fountains of the deep' (Proverbs

[61] *Ibid.*, p. 53.    [62] *Ibid.*, p. 54.

8.28) was the earth, like the shell of an egg.[63] It was what the Psalmist was referring to, declared Burnet, when he said that God 'spread out the earth on the waters' (Psalm 136.6).

The whole earth then was paradisal with a perfect climate and no disruptions to nature. There was no ice, snow, hail, or thunder. Winds were neither impetuous nor irregular, 'seeing there were neither Mountains nor any other inequalities to obstruct the course of their Vapours'.[64] The earth was always the same distance from the sun, so all the seasons were the same. There was a perpetual spring and equinox over all parts of the earth. The climate perfectly explained the longevity of those who lived before the flood. Burnet was dissatisfied with all the traditional explanations for their longevity. He rejected the idea that it was due to the greater virtue of the fruits, herbs, and plants of those days. Rather, it was the consequence of the perfect weather:

> [A]ll the parts of the year had one and the same tenour, face and temper; there was no Winter or Summer, Seed-time or Harvest, but a continual temperature of the Air and Verdure of the Earth. And this fully answers the first and fundamental character of the Golden Age and of *Paradise*; And what Antiquity, whether Heathen or Christian, hath spoken concerning that perpetual serenity and constant Spring that reign'd there.[65]

This was all to be destroyed in the flood, when the features of the earth as we know it took shape, the earth's

---

[63] See *ibid.*, p. 63, also p. 62, figure 6.    [64] *Ibid.*, p. 164.
[65] *Ibid.*, p. 147.

diurnal rotation began, and the seasons came into being. For Burnet, the loss of Paradise had not occurred after Adam and Eve were thrown out of the Garden of Eden, but after the universal flood of Noah. Sadly, it was the result of the perfect climate that obtained before it. For the continual sun slowly dried out the earth, and cracks, wide and deep, penetrated its depth until great portions of the earth fell into the abyss beneath. The waters were forced upwards and spread over the whole earth. But Noah had been forewarned: 'Providence that ruleth all things and all Ages, after the earth had stood above sixteen hundred years, thought fit to put a period to that world, and accordingly, it was reveal'd to *Noah*, that for the wickedness and degeneracy of men, God would destroy mankind with the *Earth* (*Gen.* 6.13) in a Deluge of Water.'[66] Scientific and theological accounts were thus in accord with each other. 'This seems to me,' declared Burnet, 'the great Art of Divine Providence, so as to adjust the two Worlds, Humane and Natural, Material and Intellectual . . . [that] they should all along correspond and fit one another, and especially in their great Crises and Periods.'[67] As Basil Willey neatly puts it, 'disproportion'd sin chimed punctually with Nature's crash'.[68] And then the full force of the flood came upon the earth. 'And 'tis not easie,' wrote Burnet,

> To represent to ourselves this strange scene of things,
> when the Deluge was in its fury and extremity; when the

---

[66] *Ibid.*, p. 82.    [67] *Ibid.*, p. 89

[68] Basil Willey, *The Eighteenth Century Background: Studies on the Idea of Nature in the Thought of the Period* (London: Chatto & Windus, 1950), p. 33.

Earth was broken and swallow'd up in the Abysse, whose
raging waters rise higher than the Mountains, and fill'd
the Air with broken waves, with an universal mist, and
with thick darkness, so as Nature seem'd to be in a second
Chaos; and upon this Chaos rid the distrest Ark, that bore
the small remains of Mankind. No Sea was ever so tumul-
tuous as this, nor is there any thing in present Nature to
be compar'd with the disorder of these waters ... The Ark
was really carri'd to the tops of the highest Mountains,
and into the places of the Clouds, and thrown down again
into the deepest Gulfs ... It was no doubt an extraordinary and miraculous Providence, that could make a Vessel,
so ill man'd, live upon such a Sea; that kept it from being
dash't against the Hills, or overwhelm'd in the Deeps.
That Abysse which had devour'd and swallow'd up whole
Forests of Woods, Cities, and Provinces, nay the whole
Earth, when it had conquer'd all, and triumph'd over all,
could not destroy this single Ship ... We may ... suppose
the good Angels to have lookt down upon this Ship of
*Noah*'s; and that not out of curiosity, as idle spectators, but
with a passionate concern for its safety and deliverance.
A Ship, whose *Cargo* was no less than a whole World; that
carri'd the fortune and hopes of all posterity, and if this
had perisht, the Earth, for any thing we know, had been
nothing but a Desert, a great ruine, a dead heap of
Rubbish.[69]

Here, there was no appreciation of the beauties of nature,
no inklings of the infinite within the finite, as were to
occur in Romanticism a century later. Mountains were
quite simply blots on the landscape: '[I]f you consider
them singly, they do not consist of any proportion of

---

[69] Burnet, *The Sacred Theory of the Earth*, p. 84.

parts that is referrable to any design, or that hath the least footsteps of Art or Counsel. There is nothing in Nature more shapeless and ill-figur'd than an old Rock or Mountain.'[70] The receding waters of the flood had become the ocean, filling the cracks in the once seamless surface of the world. When Burnet thought of the great trench beneath the oceans, 'emptied of all its waters, naked and gaping at the Sun, stretching its jaws from one end of the Earth to another, it appears to me the most ghastly thing in nature'.[71]

That mountains were not a part of the world as originally created had a long history within Christianity. Their existence was a consequence of the disruption to the earth that had been caused by the sin of Adam and Eve. But others, before Burnet, had also suggested that nature had been further corrupted by the flood. Thus, for example, the Anglican clergyman Godfrey Goodman (1582–1656) had suggested in his *The Fall of Man* (1616) that the deluge had brought about 'the generall confusion of Nature'.[72] The unevenness of the earth – the hills and the vales – were caused by the flood of Noah. It was certain, he declared, 'that all the terrible tokens, and signes of Gods anger and wrath, did accompanie the deluge; and as the waters did swell above measure, so the billowes and waves of the Sea did arise in a wonderful and fearefull manner; and these (surely) might well cause a great inequalitie in the earth'.[73] But Burnet *was* unique

---

[70] *Ibid.*, p. 112.    [71] *Ibid.*, p. 102.
[72] Godfrey Goodman, *The Fall of Man, or the Corruption of Nature...* (London, 1616), p. 280.
[73] *Ibid.*, p. 287.

in asserting the existence of a completely smooth earth without mountains, rivers, lakes, or seas *before* the flood.

Burnet's account provoked many critical responses, both Biblical and scientific.[74] But he had many admirers, not least Isaac Newton. 'Of our present sea, rocks, mountains etc.,' Newton wrote to Burnet, 'I think you have given the most plausible account.'[75] And despite its many critics, *The Theory of the Earth* remained much admired. As one of its most trenchant critics, John Keill (1671–1721), put it, '[p]erhaps many of his Readers will be sorry to be undeceived, for as I believe, never any Book was fuller of Errors and Mistakes in Philosophy, so none ever abounded with more beautiful Scenes and surprising Images of Nature; but I write only to those who might perhaps expect to find a true Philosophy in it. They who read it as an Ingenious Romance will still be pleased with their Entertainment.'[76]

## Floods and Comets

For William Whiston, Thomas Burnet had gone way too far. To Whiston, it seemed that Burnet had reduced the Genesis account of the creation of the world from an historical account of how the world came to be to 'a meer Popular, Parabolick, or Mythological relation; in which

---

[74] See Thomas Rossetter, 'The Theorist: Thomas Burnet and His Sacred History of the Earth', Doctor of Philosophy thesis, Durham University, 2019, pp. 195–199.

[75] Quoted by Cohn, *Noah's Flood*, p. 61.

[76] Rossetter, 'The Theorist: Thomas Burnet and His Sacred History of the Earth,' p. 333.

the plain Letter is no more to be accounted for or believ'd, than the fabulous representations of *Aesop*'.[77] In addition, Whiston believed that Burnet's scientific account of the beginnings of the world was seriously wrong. Thus, Whiston's aim was both to get the science right *and* to demonstrate how the truths of science were in the greatest harmony with the truths of the Bible, however much Moses may have adapted his account to a 'vulgar' audience. As a professional astronomer, the key for Whiston to the harmony of science and scripture lay in cometology – the science of comets.

According to Whiston, the earth, in its original primeval state ('a formless void'), was the atmosphere of a comet. Consequently, the description in the book of Genesis of the first six days of creation describes the process by which, over six years (for a day equalled a year during the six 'days' of creation), the earth developed from its original 'cometic' state in a natural way without requiring any supernatural intervention. The only miraculous event during the six 'days' of creation was the creation of man: 'Tho 'tis granted that all the other Days Works mention'd by *Moses* were brought to pass in a natural way by proper and suitable Instruments, and a mechanical Process, as we have seen through the whole Series of the foregoing Creation; yet 'tis evident . . . That an immediate and miraculous Power was exercis'd in the

---

[77] Whiston, 'A Discourse Concerning the Nature, Stile, and Extent of the Mosaic History of The Creation,' *A New Theory of the Earth*, p. 2.
On William Whiston, see especially James E. Force, *William Whiston: Honest Newtonian* (Cambridge: Cambridge University Press, 2002).
I am indebted to Force for his account of Whiston.

formation of the Body, and Infusion of the Soul of Man.'[78]

The primeval earth was perfectly spherical, and the 'Central Heat', being equally distant from all parts of the surface of the earth, affected all parts of the globe equally. As a result, the earth was more equally habitable all over and more fertile than at present, capable of sustaining more inhabitants than currently. The seasons were only slightly distinguishable from each other, and the air was ideal, without winds and storms.[79] Unlike Burnet's primeval world, however, there were mountains, valleys, and plains. But the mountains, far from being eyesores, were as fruitful as the plains and valleys and able to sustain more animals than the plains. All this was to end when Adam and Eve sinned. However, God's punishment of Adam and Eve occurred without any disturbance of the settled course of Nature. For the loss of Paradise aligned with the impact of a comet 'hitting obliquely upon the Earth along some parts of its present equator'.[80] The impact of the comet tilted the axis of the earth and produced the earth's rotation around it. The shape of the earth then degenerated to that of an oblate spheroid. Seasons came into being.[81] Still, between the Fall and the flood, things were not too bad. Only gentle mists fell upon the earth, the absence of heavy rain precluding rainbows. Men and animals continued to live remarkably

[78] Whiston, *A New Theory of the Earth*, p. 253. The preliminary 'Discourse' and *A New Theory of the Earth* are separately paginated.
[79] See *ibid.*, pp. 277–279.
[80] William Whiston, *A New Theory of the Earth, from its Original, to the Consummation of all Things* (London, 1708), second edition, p. 111.
[81] See *ibid.*, pp. 111, 345–346.

long lives, not least because of the purity of the air. The vegetables were more nutritious, and men and animals were vegetarian. Nor was there such an enormous division of the earth into oceans and continents as in the present.

The flood of Noah was to change all this. As with the Fall, divine punishment aligned with the natural order of things, more particularly in this case the passing by of a comet. 'The precise time of the passing of the Comet,' declared Whiston, 'and thereby of destroying the World, is, in the most peculiar manner, and highest degree, the result of the Divine Providence. That exactly at a time which was fit and proper, and in an Age that justly deserv'd so great a Judgement, the Comet should come by, and over-whelm the World, is very remarkably and extraordinarily the Finger of God himself.'[82] On this occasion, the comet narrowly missed the earth. The earth only passed through its tail and atmosphere. '[I]f we consider that a comet,' declared Whiston, 'is capable of passing so close by the Body of the Earth as to involve it in its *Atmosphere* and *Tail* a considerable time, and leave prodigious quantities of the same Condensed and Expanded Vapours upon its Surface; we shall easily see that a Deluge of Waters is by no means an impossible thing.'[83] This was the opening of 'the windows of the heaven' (Genesis 7.11). Moreover, the rainfall broke the surface of the crust of the earth allowing the 'fountains of the great deep' (Genesis 7.11) to gush forth.

Fortunately, Noah and the ark were some distance from where the downpour of the rain from the heavens

---

[82] Whiston, *A New Theory of the Earth*, pp. 358–359.  [83] *Ibid.*, p. 301.

and the eruption of the waters from the deep coincided. Thus, Whiston explained, 'tho' the breaking up of the Fountains of the great Deep, and the Fall of the Waters, were coincident, and upon the same day with the Entry into the Ark, as the Text most expressly asserts; yet the place where the Ark was, escap'd the effects of the same till the Evening; and while the rest of the Earth was abiding the fury of the same, enjoy'd so calm, fair and undisturb'd a day, as permitted their regular and orderly going into the Ark before the Waters overtook them.'[84]

Whiston was in no doubt that the flood was universal. The waters at their highest were some fifteen cubits above the highest mountains and three miles above the surface of the plains and seas. Fortuitously, the ark came to rest upon Caucasus, the highest mountain in the world, so that it would be safe immediately upon the end of the rains.[85] This place remained as habitable and as fruitful as the whole earth had been before the flood, capable of sustaining all those in the ark, until, with the receding of the waters, the rest of the earth became habitable again: 'To this spot therefore, by such a wonderful adjustment of all the requisite Circumstances of the Deluge, preserv'd and distinguish'd from all the rest of the World, the Divine Providence did conduct the Ark.'[86] That said, the earth

---

[84] *Ibid.*, p. 313.

[85] Whiston has to work overtime to explain why the ark landed on Mount Caucasus (or Paropamisus) rather the Biblical Ararat (Genesis 8.4). See *ibid.*, pp. 119–123.

[86] *Ibid.*, p. 342.

was never to return to its state of fertility before the flood. Both diet and climate after the flood progressively reduced human longevity. The vegetables after the flood were less nutritious and the air more polluted. Crucially, the polluted air after the flood reduced the longevity of the generations after it such that, within 800 or 900 years after the flood, length of life was reduced to that of the present day.

Whiston was not the first to look to a comet as the cause of the flood of Noah. The astronomer Edmond Halley (1656–1742) delivered a lecture to the Royal Society on 12 December 1694, some two years before the publication of Whiston's *A New Theory of the Earth*, on the cause of the universal deluge. Like Thomas Burnet, Halley was much exercised by the question of whence had come sufficient water to cover the whole earth and over the highest mountains. On both scientific and theological grounds, he was having nothing of Burnet's solution of an earth without mountains and valleys. But he was not convinced that the Biblical account of rain for forty days and forty nights and the ocean rising onto the land were sufficient to explain a universal deluge. Rather, he suggested, the current world was the consequence of the shock ('choc') to it caused by the impact of a comet radically changing its nature – creating mountains from (what we would call) tsunamis sloshing back and forth, changing the length of the day and year, altering the axis of the globe, increasing the depths of the great lakes, and causing the extremes of climates. The difficulty, he suggested, would be in showing how Noah and the animals could ever have survived such a cataclysmic event. 'That some such thing has happened,' he declared, 'may be guess'd, for that the Earth seems as if it were new made out of the Ruins of an old World.'[87]

Halley delivered 'Some farther Thoughts upon the same Subject' a week later. And he did go 'farther'. For now he suggested that such collisions of comets with the earth were perhaps regular occurrences necessary for the well-being of the future world when it could no longer sustain life. It might be thought harsh, he reflected, that the whole race should be destroyed for the benefit of those who were to come later. But then, 'if we consider Death simply, and how that the Life of each Individual is but of a very small duration, it will be found that as to those who die, it is indifferent whether they die in a Pestilence out of 100000 *per Ann.* or ordinarily out of 25000 in this great City, the Pestilence only appearing terrible to those that survive to contemplate the Danger they have escaped.'[88] It was probably from Halley that Whiston had the idea of the periodic interaction of comets and the earth, an idea that led him to build comets into his accounts of creation, the Fall, the flood, and the final conflagration at the end of the world. It was the comet that appeared in 1680, subsequently named after Halley, that Whiston believed had brought about the deluge that, he calculated, began on 29 November, 1,656 years after the creation and 2349 BCE: 'Indeed,' declared Whiston in 1717,

---

[87] Edmond Halley, 'Some Considerations about the Cause of the Universal Deluge, Laid before the Royal Society, on the 12th of December 1694,' *Philosophical Transactions* 33 (1724), p. 122.

[88] Edmond Halley, 'Some farther Thoughts upon the same Subject delivered on the 19th of the same Month,' *Philosophical Transactions* 33 (1724), p. 124.

the Solution of this most remarkable Phaenomenon of an *Universal Deluge*, with its most numerous and eminent Circumstances, as described in the *Mosaick* History, which till this Age could no way be solved in a Natural way, nay seem'd utterly uncapable of any Philosophical [scientific] solution at all; is now, I think, become so plain, evident, and certain, from the Phaenomena of Comets, with their Atmospheres and Tails, now fully discovered; especially from the particular Circumstances, and Periods of the last most famous Comet of 1680, which appears to have been the Physical Cause of the same Deluge.[89]

## Fossils and the Flood

Cometologist Edmond Halley was convinced of the universal nature of the flood, not least because of the presence of marine fossils 'found far from and above the Sea'.[90] It was evident, he thought, 'that those Parts have been once under Water: or, either that the Sea has risen to them, or they have been raised from the Sea'.[91] That marine fossils were evidence of a universal flood was an ancient tradition. Thus, for example, the second-century theologian Tertullian reminded his readers that there was a time when the whole earth changed, overrun by waters. Even to this day, he wrote, 'marine conches and tritons'

[89] William Whiston, *Astronomical Principles of Religion, Natural and Reveal'd* (London, 1717), pp. 146–147. For the date of the flood, see Whiston, *A New Theory of the Earth*, p. 123.
[90] Halley, 'Some Considerations about the Cause of the Universal Deluge, Laid before the Royal Society, on the 12th of December 1694,' p. 119.
[91] *Ibid.*, p. 119.

horns sojourn as foreigners on the mountains'.[92] The beginning of the fourteenth century saw an alternative theory develop, namely that they were only rocks moulded into animal or vegetable shapes by the forces of nature.[93]

This question of the nature of fossils was still an open one in the latter part of the seventeenth century as the new science of fossils (palaeontology) was emerging. The founder of the science of shells in England (conchology), Martin Lister (1639–1712), declared to the Royal Society in 1671 that seashell fossils were '*Lapides sui generis* [*stones constituting a unique class*], and never any part of an Animal ... it is most certain, that our English Quarry-shells (to continue that abusive name) have no parts of a different Texture from the rock or quarry they are taken, that is, that there is no such thing as *shell* in these resemblances of shells.'[94] Lister's was the majority opinion. When the letter was

---

[92] S. Threllwall (trans.), 'On the Pallium,' in *ANF*, vol. 4, p. 6.

[93] In 1740, the Italian geologist Anton Moro (c.1517–1577) divided opinion on the origin of fossils into two groups – those who affirmed the oceanic origin of marine-mountainous bodies and those who sought elsewhere for their origin. He listed seven variations of the former group and five of the latter, of which their origin from stones was one. See Paolo Rossi, *Dark Abyss of Time: The History of the Earth and the History of Nations from Hooke to Vico* (Chicago: The University of Chicago Press, 1984), pp. 5–6. On the history of fossils, see Martin J. S. Rudwick, *The Meaning of Fossils: Episodes in the History of Palaeontology* (London and New York: Macdonald and American Elsevier Inc., 1972).

[94] Martin Lister, 'A Letter of Mr. *Martin Lister*, written at York *August 25 1671,*'*Philosophical Transactions* 6 (1671), pp. 2282–2283. See also Cindy Hodoba Eric, 'Metamorphoses: Seventeenth-Century Ideas on Fossils and Earth History.' Doctor of Philosophy thesis, The University of Sydney, 2023.

read to a meeting of The Royal Society, it was noted that some applauded Mr. Lister's notion of it. But the eminent biologist Robert Hooke (1635–1703), who was present at the meeting, pushed back 'endeavouring to maintain his own opinion, that all those shells are the *exuviae* [shells] of animals'.[95]

The controversy continued. In 1677, the naturalist Robert Plot (1640–1696) asked himself 'the great *Question* now so much controverted in the World. Whether the stones we find in the forms of *Shell-fish*, be *Lapides sui generis*, naturally produced by some extraordinary *plastic virtue* latent in the Earth or Quarries where they are found? Or whether they rather owe their form and figuration to the shells of the *Fishes* they represent, brought to the places where they are now found by a *Deluge, Earth-quake*, or some other such means, and... turned into stones?'[96] It was the physician and amateur fossil hunter John Woodward (1665–1728) who was to propose that marine fossils pointed inexorably to the universal flood described in the book of Genesis.

In 1695, Woodward published the book that was to become the most influential work on the history of the earth in eighteenth-century Europe – *An Essay toward a Natural History of the Earth and Terrestrial Bodies, especially Minerals*. It began the 'scientific' tradition of diluvianism – that the earth had been formed in its present state by an

---

[95] Thomas Birch, *The History of the Royal Society of London...* (London, 1756), vol. 2, p. 487.

[96] Roberst Plot, *The Natural History of Oxford-shire, Being an Essay toward the Natural History of England* (Oxford, 1677), p. 111.

ancient universal flood.[97] According to Woodward, there-fore, of the world before the flood, no trace remained:

> Here was, we see, a mighty Revolution: and *that* attended
> with Accidents very strange and amazing: the most hor-
> rible and portentous Catastrophe that Nature ever yet
> saw: an elegant, orderly, and habitable Earth quite
> unhinged, shattered all to pieces, and turned into an heap
> of ruins: Convulsions so exorbitant and unruly: a Change
> so exceeding great and violent, that the very
> Representation alone is enough to startle and shock a
> Man. In truth the thing, at first, appeared so wonderful
> and surprizing to me, that I must confess I was for some
> time at a stand [in a state of perplexity].[98]

The key evidence for this global catastrophe was the fossil record. Woodward made two crucial moves in the argument. First, as we noted earlier, at the time of his writing, the issue of whether fossils had an organic or inorganic origin was still an open one. Woodward's first task was to demonstrate that shells and other marine bodies found on land 'were originally generated and formed at Sea: that they are the real spoils [remains] of once living Animals: and not Stones, or natural Fossils, as some late Learned Men have thought'.[99] Second, having determined that they were the remains of once living creatures, his task was then to explain how these marine creatures had been transferred from the seas, to be found

---

[97] For an excellent survey of 'diluvianism', see Kaspar von Greyerz, *European Physico-Theology (1650–c.1750) in Context* (Oxford: Oxford University Press, 2022), ch. 7.

[98] John Woodward, *An Essay toward a Natural History of the Earth and Terrestrial Bodies, especially Minerals...* (London, 1695), p. 82.

[99] *Ibid.*, p. 15.

'in all Parts of the known World, as well in *Europe*, *Africa*, and *America*, as in *Asia*, and this even to the very tops of the highest Mountains'.[100] Woodward began by surveying eight different theories on the origin of marine fossils before concluding that they were 'imaginary and groundless'. He then proposed that 'these Marine Bodies were born forth of the Sea by the Universal Deluge: and that, upon the return of the Water back again from off the Earth, they were left behind at Land'.[101]

How, then, did the deluge occur? Woodward believed that, beneath the crust of the earth, there was 'the great Deep' or 'Abyss' enclosed within the bowels of the earth, composed of a huge orb of water. The ocean on the surface was connected to this orb of water by chasms reaching down to the orb. The waters of the abyss, rising through these chasms, were more than sufficient, he believed, 'if brought out upon the Surface of the Earth, to cover the whole globe to the height assigned by *Moses*; which is, fifteen Cubits above the Tops of the highest Mountains [Genesis 7.20]'.[102] So, before the flood, the waters under the surface of the earth were held in check by the strata of earth lying upon them. But at the time of the flood, those strata were ruptured, and the waters of the abyss broke through to the surface, flooding the whole world. Consequently, the 'whole Terrestrial Globe was taken all to pieces and dissolved at the Deluge' into a thick, earthy soup. The present earth 'was formed out of that promiscuous Mass of Sand, Earth, Shells, and the rest, falling down again' as the water subsided and

---

[100] *Ibid.*, Preface.    [101] *Ibid.*, pp. 46, 72.    [102] *Ibid.*, p. 163.

returned into the abyss.[103] The marine bodies, stranded on dry land as the waters receded, became lodged in different layers of earth, depending upon their relative density, 'those which are heaviest lying deepest in the Earth, and the lighter sorts ... shallower or nearer to the surface'.[104]

Woodward was later to provide an answer as to how this dissolution had happened. Simply put, it was down to gravity. Taking a leaf out of Isaac Newton's account of gravity in his *Principia Mathematica* (1687), Woodward held that solid bodies were held together by the force of gravity. Thus, were gravity to be suspended, everything would dissolve. Thus, 'the supreme Governor of the Universe' almost completely suspended gravity to allow the waters of the abyss to ascend and everything to dissolve into them before later restoring gravity thus enabling everything to be 'formed anew'.[105]

For Woodward, rather than the sin of Adam, the flood reported in the book of Genesis was *the crucial event in the history of humankind*. This was true for the new science generally, not least because the flood was more amenable to the methods of the new science than events in the garden of Eden. Nevertheless, the flood *was* made necessary by human wickedness when, as Woodward put it, the world had become 'little better than a common fold of Phrenticks and Bedlams'.[106] So, God supernaturally intervened 'to reclaim and retrieve the World out of this

---

[103] *Ibid.*, Preface.   [104] *Ibid.*, Preface.
[105] John Woodward, *A Supplement and Continuation of the Essay towards a Natural History of the Earth* (London, 1726), pp. 163, 145.
[106] Woodward, *An Essay toward a Natural History of the* Earth, p. 88.

wretched and forlorn state, the common Father and Benefactor of Mankind seasonably interposed his hand: and rescued miserable Man out of the gross Stupidity and Sensuality whereinto he was thus unfortunately plunged'.[107] Mere punishment of humankind was not sufficient. Only a complete destruction followed by a radical re-creation of an earth less perfect than its original would be effective in rescuing humanity from its excesses of wickedness and 'give it a Constitution more nearly accommodated to the present Frailties of its Inhabitants'.[108] The universal deluge was not only an exercise in the divine punishment of the generation before the flood but also an act of divine compassion for the generations to come:

> That therefore as much Harshness and Cruelty as this great Destruction of Mankind seemingly carries along with it: as wild and extravagant a thing as that Dissolution of the primitive Earth appeared at first sight, yet all the Severity lay in the Punishment of that Generation, (which yet was no more than what was highly just, yea and necessary too:) and the *whole* of the Tragedy terminated there. For the *Destruction* of the *Earth* was not only an Act of the profoundest Wisdom and Forecast, but the most monumental proof that could ever possibly have been, of Goodness, Compassion, and Tenderness in the Author of our *Being*; and *this* so liberal too and extensive, as to reach all the succeeding Ages of Mankind: all the Posterity of *Noah*: all that should dwell upon the thus renewed Earth to the End of the World; by this means

---

[107]  *Ibid.*, p. 88.
[108]  *Ibid.*, p. 84. We would, for example, live less long and have to work harder to survive, the earth being less fruitful than before the flood.

removing the old Charm: the Bait that had so long bewildered and deluded unhappy Man: setting him once more upon his Legs: reducing him from the most abject and stupid Ferrity [brutishness], to his Senses, and to sober Reason: from the most deplorable Misery and Slavery, to a Capacity of being happy.[109]

Woodward's *Essay* was much criticised. Despite that, it was translated into French, German, and Italian. An avid convert to Woodward's cause, the Swiss naturalist Jakob Scheuchzer (1672–1733) produced a Latin translation in 1704. And four years later, Scheuchzer produced his *Complaints and Claims of the Fishes*, a pamphlet in which the fish made their claim to eternal fame: 'We, the swimmers, voiceless though we are, herewith lay our claim before the throne of Truth. We would reclaim what is rightly ours ... Our claim is for the glory springing from the death of our ancestors ... That race [of fish] which lived and was carried on the waves before the Flood ... Moreover, we are defending an even greater cause: we bear irrefutable witness to the universal inundation.'[110]

But more was to come – the discovery by Scheuchzer of what appeared (at least to him and many others) to be a fossilised human skeleton in a limestone quarry in Oeningen, Germany. Scheuchzer believed it to be the remains of one of the wicked who had been destroyed in the flood of Noah. He called it *Homo diluvia testis – Man, a witness of the Deluge*. On the face of it, this was the first

---

[109] *Ibid.*, pp. 93–4.
[110] Translated and quoted by Cohn, *Noah's Flood*, p. 88. See Johanne Jacobo Scheuchzero, *Piscium Querelae et Vindiciae* (Zürich, 1708), pp. 3–4.

fossil of human remains to be discovered. It wasn't quite like discovering Noah's ark, but it was close to it. Little wonder then that it provoked a sensation. It is certain, Scheuchzer wrote in his *Physica Sacra* (1731), that this rock 'is the half, or nearly so, of the skeleton of a man: that the substance even of the bones, and, what is more, of the flesh and of parts softer than the flesh, are there incorporated in the stone: in a word it is one of the rarest relics which we have of that cursed race which was buried under the waters'.[111]

Why were such sacred relics of the flood so rare? Well, Scheuchzer had a deft answer. 'Up to the present time,' he wrote, 'very few remains of human beings drowned in the Flood have been discovered. It may be that the reminders of blameless creatures such as plants, molluscs, fishes, even insects are more numerous because they deserved to be remembered better than the human beings – for all these latter, save for a few of Noah's relatives ... richly deserved to be condemned to eternal oblivion.'[112] Doubts were eventually to be raised. In 1758, Scheuchzer's student Johannes Gessner (1709–1790) suggested it was only the bones of a large fish. Almost thirty years later, the Dutch anatomist Petrus Camper (1722–1789) thought it to be the bones of a large lizard. Still, for many, Scheuchzer's *Homo diluvia testis* remained, for many, empirical confirmation of the Biblical account of the flood of Noah. Unfortunately for Scheuchzer, in 1811, the fossil was examined by the French naturalist Georges

[111] Quoted by Cohn, *Noah's Flood*, pp. 91–92. See also Jacobi Scheuchzeri, *Physica Sacra* (Augsburg and Ulm, 1731), table 49, facing p. 49.
[112] Quoted by *ibid.*, p. 92.

Cuvier (1769–1832). He concluded that it was in fact a giant salamander belonging to the genus *Andrias*. Cuvier's judgement was harsh: '[N]othing less than total blindness on the scientific level can explain how a man of Scheuchzer's rank, a man who was a physician and must have seen human skeletons, could embrace such a gross self-deception. For this fragment, which he propagated so sententiously, and which has been sustained for so long on the prestige of his word, cannot withstand the most cursory examination.'[113] It would have been perhaps little compensation to Scheuchzer, fervent believer in the Biblical story of Noah that he was, that he had, in fact, discovered a new fossil and that, in 1831, it was named *Andreas scheuchzeri* in his honour.

## The Age of the Earth

The credibility of diluvianism depended not only on the fossil evidence for a universal flood but also on a traditional Biblical chronology that believed that the earth had been created some 4,000 years BCE and destroyed by a universal flood some 1,656 years later. By the beginning of the nineteenth century, doubts about the date of the creation of the earth and thus the date of the flood of Noah were creeping in.[114] In his poem, 'The Task', the English poet William Cowper (1731–1800) reflected

[113] Quoted by James L. Hayward, 'Fossil Proboscidians and Myths of Giant Men,' *Transactions of the Nebraska Academy of Sciences and Affiliated Societies*, 12 (1984), p. 95.
[114] On the rise of the earth sciences and the eventual collapse of Biblical chronology, see Cohn, *Noah's Flood*, chs. 8–9; Haber, *The Age of the World*, ch. 4; and Stephen Toulmin and June Goodfield, *The Discovery*

disapprovingly in 1785 on the developing conflict between science and religion about the age of the earth:

> Some write a narrative of wars, and feats
> Of heroes little known; and call the rant
> An history: ... Some drill and bore
> The solid earth, and from the strata there
> Extract a register, by which we learn
> That he who made it, and reveal'd its date
> To Moses, was mistaken in its age.
> Some, more acute, and more industrious still,
> Contrive creation; travel nature up
> To the sharp peak of her sublimest height,
> And tell us whence the stars; why some are fix'd
> And planetary some; what gave them first
> Rotation, from what fountain flow'd their light.
> Great contest follows, and much learned dust
> Involves the combatants; each claiming truth
> And truth disclaiming both. And thus they spend
> The little wick of life's poor shallow lamp,
> In playing tricks with nature, giving laws
> To distant worlds, and trifling in their own.[115]

Doubts about the age of the earth had been raised when the new science first began in the late seventeenth century. Thomas Burnet, William Whiston, and Isaac Newton had all flirted with the idea that the 'days' of creation were actually long periods of time. In 1693, the naturalist John Beaumont (c.1650–1731), in his response to Thomas Burnet's *The Theory of the Earth*, declared that, were it possible to abandon the Biblical dating, he would

---

of Time (Chicago: The University of Chicago Press, 1965). I am indebted especially to Toulmin and Goodfield for this discussion.

[115] Quoted by Toulmin and Goodfield, *The Discovery of Time*, p. 160.

be more inclined to think that the world was eternal, or at least that its origin was so indefinite as to be unknowable.[116] Edmond Halley accepted that the formation of man some 6,000 years (or 7,000 years, following the Septuagint) previously was the last act of creation. But he was uncertain how long the five days that preceded it may have been, since 'we are elsewhere told [in the Bible], that in respect of the Almighty a thousand years is as one Day'.[117] The Baron de Montesquieu (1689–1755) in his *Persian Letters* (1721) appeared to agree with those philosophers in the Aristotelian tradition who denied any original 'big bang', who did not 'believe that matter and created things have been in existence only six thousand years', and who opted for the eternity of the world.[118]

It was, however, another French aristocrat, Georges-Louis Leclerc, Comte de Buffon (1707–1788), who, in his *Epoques de la Nature* (1778), reinterpreted the Biblical seven days of creation in terms of seven epochs, ranging in length from 3,000 to 35,000 years and totalling 75,000 years or so since the beginning of the earth (although in private he estimated from 3 million to 10 million years). Buffon claimed to be a harmoniser of earth science and religion who reminded his readers that 'Because all reason, all truth, comes equally from God, there is no difference between the truths that He has revealed [in

[116] See John Beaumont, *Considerations on a Book, entituled* The Theory of the Earth (London, 1693), p. 19.

[117] Edmond Halley, 'A short Account of the Cause of the Saltness of the Ocean, and of the several Lakes that emit no Rivers...,' *Philosophical Transactions* 29 (1714), p. 296. See also Psalm 90.4 and 2 Peter 3.8.

[118] John Davidson (trans.), 'Letter 114,' *Montesquieu: Persian Letters* (London: George Routledge & Sons Ltd., 1891), p. 254.

scripture], and the truth that we are allowed to discover by our observations and our researches.'[119] But we can perhaps take this as a rhetorical subterfuge, intended to protect him from the guardians of religious orthodoxy in the college of Sorbonne. As a *philosoph* of the European Enlightenment, where reason and Scripture conflicted, Scripture had to give way. So, at the beginning of his *Epochs*, he made it clear that the book of Genesis was written for the vulgar in terms comprehensible by them: 'Everything in the story of Moses is placed within the limits of the intelligence of the people ... to whom it would not do to demonstrate the true system of the Earth.'[120] Nevertheless, on the date of man's creation, Buffon resisted going too far. Despite the long tradition that the earth was created some 4,000 years BCE, Buffon pushed it out to 'no more than six or eight thousand years ago.' That said, Buffon's earth science was nonetheless a radical rewrite of the early chapters of Genesis. All the great deluges, he maintained, had occurred in early epochs. The fossil evidence, far from being evidence of a universal Biblical flood, was only a relic of these earlier floods.

Moreover, it was no Edenic paradise into which primitive humanity was born at the beginning of the seventh epoch. There was no original fall from an original perfection, nor an expulsion from Paradise. It was always 'Nature, red in tooth and claw', as Alfred Lord

---

[119] Jan Zalasiewicz, Anne-Sophie Milon, and Mateusz Zalasiewicz (eds. and trans.), *The Epochs of Nature* (Chicago: University of Chicago Press, 2018), 'First Discourse,' p. 16 (Rakuten Kobo edition).
[120] *Ibid.*, p. 17.

Tennyson was to put it seventy years later. For Buffon, the earliest humans were

> witnesses of convulsive movements of the Earth, then still recent and very frequent, having only mountains as refuges against inundations, often chased from these same refuges by the fires of volcanoes, trembling on an Earth that was trembling under their feet, naked in spirit and in body, exposed to the curses of all the elements, victims of the fury of ferocious animals, of which they could not avoid being the prey; all equally penetrated by a common feeling of baleful terror.[121]

Thus were local inundations transformed into universal catastrophes by the terror they created in those who were the victims of them. The ravages of floods, the chasms opened by earthquakes, the respect for certain mountains where people were saved from floods, along with the horror of those mountains that launched volcanic fires, created a durable and almost eternal memory of these misfortunes of the earth. 'All of these feelings founded upon terror,' Buffon declared, 'have from then on taken possession forever of the heart and mind of man.'[122]

We look in vain in Buffon's *Epochs* for specific reference to the flood of Noah. Perhaps he believed that to deny the universality of the Biblical deluge directly would be to open the floodgates, so to say, to accusations of his unorthodoxy. Whatever his reasons, in the history of the readings of Noah's flood, Buffon's is a turning point. For Buffon ignored the question of the universality of the

---

[121] Zalasiewicz, Anne-Sophie Milon, and Mateusz Zalasiewicz (eds. and trans.), *The Epochs of Nature*, 'Seventh and Last Epoch,' p. 1.
[122] *Ibid.*, p. 2.

flood of Noah that had dominated discussions of the history of the earth for over a century. He demonstrated that a complete theory of the earth could be developed without specifically placing Noah and the flood within it, and without relating a theory of the earth to divine Providence. Within the grand historical drama of the epochs of the earth penned by Buffon, Noah was no longer a key player. As Norman Cohn neatly puts it, '[S]et in such a context, the Biblical Flood was reduced to the status of a minor episode, a mishap too commonplace to be singled out for special mention.'[123]

The Irish geologist James Hutton (1726–1797) was moving in the same direction as Buffon in his *Theory of the Earth* in 1788 – heading back into what Buffon called 'the dark abyss of time'. 'The result, therefore, of our present enquiry,' Hutton concluded, 'is that we find no vestige of a beginning, – no prospect of an end.'[124] So, the world revealed no sign of any original creation, even if it nonetheless showed 'an order, not unworthy of Divine wisdom in a subject which, in another view, has appeared as the work of chance, or as absolute disorder and confusion'.[125] The fossil record, far from being evidence of a recent universal inundation, revealed vast periods of past time. Hutton's earth worked like a Newtonian mechanical system in a law-bound and purposeful process of time rather than space. Of Mosaic history in general or the universal flood of Noah in particular there was no mention.

---

[123] Cohn, *Noah's Flood*, p. 101.
[124] James Hutton, 'Theory of the Earth,' *Transactions of the Royal Society of Edinburgh* 1 (1788), p. 304.
[125] *Ibid.* pp. 210–211.

Opponents of Buffon and Hutton were faced with two alternatives. The first was to assert the literal truth of Mosaic history against the antiquity of the earth proposed by the earth scientists. This was the approach adopted by the Irish geologist and chemist Richard Kirwan (1733–1812) in his *Geological Essays* (1799). For the true account of the flood, it was Moses that mattered. 'Passing over the systems of Burnet, Woodward, and Whiston,' he wrote, 'I recur to the account of this great revolution given by Moses himself, taken in its plain literal sense, as the only one that appears perfectly consistent, with all the new phenomena now known.'[126] It was, therefore, Moses that Kirwan took as his guide 'in tracing the circumstances of the most horrible catastrophe to which the human and all animal species, and even the terraqueous globe itself, had at any period since its origin been exposed'.[127] And Moses ascribed it to a supernatural cause, namely 'the express intention of God to punish mankind for their crimes'.[128]

Like earlier proponents of a universal flood, Kirwan argued that fossilised shells at high elevations indicated a universal deluge, as did the bones of elephants and rhinoceroses, brought to the lower parts of Siberia 'by an inundation from warmer and very distant climates, betwixt which and Siberia mountains above nine thousand feet intervene'.[129] According to Kirwan, the flood began in the southern ocean that reached from India and South America to the South Pole. Noah resided on the borders

[126] Richard Kirwan, *Geological Essays* (London, 1799), pp. 65–66; see also pp. 2–3, 54.
[127] *Ibid.*, p. 54.    [128] *Ibid.*, p. 66.    [129] *Ibid.*, p. 55.

of this ocean, whence the ark was driven north-west to the mountains of Armenia. The deluge began, as Moses indicated, with continual rain for forty days, was augmented by the waters of the great abyss, and swept northwards, eventually reaching the mountains of Sweden. Mosaic devotee that he was, surprisingly, on the animals in the ark, Kirwan gave ground. 'It does not however appear to me necessary to suppose that any others were collected in the ark but those most necessary for the use of man, and those only of the graminivorous [grass eating] or granivorous [seed eating] classes, the others were most probably of subsequent creation.'[130] Carnivorous creatures were created after the flood 'when the graminivorous had multiplied to such an extent that their carcases would have caused infection.'[131] The creation of carnivores after the flood explained the existence of animals 'peculiar to America and the torrid and rigid zones'.[132]

That aside, for Kirwan, any compromise on the literal truth of Genesis was the thin end of the civilisational wedge. He, like many others, was no doubt shaken to his core by the French Revolution that was just coming to an end as he was writing in 1799. According to Kirwan, Buffon, Hutton, and others of their ilk were agents of atheism. '[R]ecent experience has shown,' he wrote, 'that the obscurity in which the philosophical knowledge of this [original] state [of the earth] has hitherto been involved, has proved too favourable to the structure of various systems of atheism or infidelity, as these have been in their turn to turbulence and immorality.'[133] Geology,

---

[130] *Ibid.*, p. 84.   [131] *Ibid.*, p. 85.   [132] *Ibid.*   [133] *Ibid.*, pp. 2–3.

properly done, however, 'ripens, or (to use a mineralogical expression) *graduates* into religion, as this does into morality'.[134] In short, the role of geology was to be the handmaiden of theology, and theology was to be the housemaid of morality.

The second alternative was to acquiesce in the antiquity of the earth but argue nonetheless for the universal flood as described in the Bible. This was the position of William Buckland (1784–1856), Anglican clergyman, Oxford University's first professor of geology, and most avid of diluvians. Thus, Buckland happily endorsed the view that the six days of creation in the book of Genesis were not to be understood as implying the same length of time that is currently occupied by a single revolution of the earth. Moses, he declared, was not so interested in those times not connected with the history of humanity. His only concern was to show that the world was not eternal and self-existent but rather 'was originally created by the power of the Almighty'.[135]

Despite the antiquity of the earth, Buckland believed that, with reference to the presence of humanity on it, the facts established by geology led to the conclusion that '*the existence of mankind* can on no account be supposed to have taken its beginning before that time which is assigned to it in the Mosaic writings'.[136] For its part,

---

[134] *Ibid.*, p. 3.
[135] William Buckland, *Vindiciae Geologicae; or the Connexion of Geology with Religion Explained, in an inaugural Lecture... May 15, 1819* (Oxford: Oxford University Press, 1820), p. 32.
[136] *Ibid.*, p. 23.

geology affirmed the event of a universal flood after the creation of humanity at the time that the book of Genesis suggested:

> Again, the grand fact of an universal deluge at no very remote period is proved on grounds so decisive and incontrovertible, that, had we never heard of such an event from Scripture, or any other authority, geology of itself must have called in the assistance of some such catastrophe, to explain the phenomena of diluvian action which are universally presented to us, and which are unintelligible without recourse to a deluge exerting its ravages at a period not more ancient than that announced in the Book of Genesis.[137]

In short, according to Buckland, the Mosaic account was in perfect harmony with the discoveries of modern science – if the days of creation could be stretched to vast eons of time.

There was, however, a major problem for the supporters of Buckland in the 1820s, a period that came to be known as the 'diluvian decade'. It was one that Jakob Scheuchzer had recognised a century earlier. If the flood had wiped out all humanity except Noah and his family, why had the geologists not discovered human remains? In 1831, the same year that the supposed human fossil that Scheuchzer had called *Homo diluvia testis* – *Man, a witness of the Deluge* was renamed as the salamander *Andreas scheuchzeri* after him, Buckland's disciple Adam Sedgwick (1785–1873), also both clergyman and professor of geology, gave his last address as president of the

[137] *Ibid.*, pp. 23–24.

Geological Society. He recanted his belief in the universal flood of Noah:

> Having been myself a believer [in the Noachian deluge], and, to the best of my power, propagator of what I now regard as a philosophic heresy [diluvianism] ... I think it right, as one of my last acts before I quit this Chair, thus publicly to read my recantation. We ought, indeed, to have paused before we first adopted the diluvian theory, and referred all our old superficial gravel [lying atop the stratified formations beneath them] to the action of the Mosaic flood. For of man, and the works of his hands, we have not yet found a single trace among the remnants of a former world entombed in these ancient deposits.[138]

By 1836, William Buckland too had retreated from his earlier belief in the flood of Noah, although not with such a noticeable splash as Sedgwick. In his *Geology and Mineralogy considered with Reference to Natural Theology*, Buckland moved away from any precise identification of eras in geology with the six days of creation in Genesis, a theory that later came to be known as the 'day age' theory. He settled on what was later called 'the gap' theory. This was the idea that 'millions of years may have occupied the indefinite interval, between the beginning in which God created the heaven and the earth, and the evening or commencement of the first day of the Mosaic narrative'.[139] Buckland had come to the modern realisation

---

[138] Adam Sedgwick, 'Address to the Geological Society, delivered on the Evening of the 18th of February 1831...,' *Proceedings of the Geological Society of London* 1 (1834), p. 313.

[139] William Buckland, *Geology and Mineralogy considered with Reference to Natural Theology* (London: William Pickering, 1836), vol. 1, pp. 21–22.

that the interval between the origin of the earth and recorded human history was boundless. We need to read between the lines of this work to conclude that he no longer believed that the evidence of geology supported a universal deluge of the Biblical kind. But in fact, he *had*, very quietly, let it go. He managed to maintain the harmony between geology and Genesis – if only just. But it was at the expense of the universal flood of Noah.[140] Within the domain of earth science, the Biblical story of Noah and the universal flood had moved from the realm of history to the realm of myth.

[140]  See *ibid.*, p. 16.

# 6

## Noah, Myth, and History

*~*

### Noah and the Druids

Two traditions of writing about the Druids came down from Classical antiquity and were available to the antiquarians of the eighteenth century – the Posidonian and the Alexandrian.[1] The former of these derived from the second-century BCE histories of Posidonius and were used by Strabo, Diodorus Siculus, Athenaeus, and Julius Caesar from between 50 BCE and 200 CE. This tradition provided details about the philosophy and activities of the Druids, in both their benign and malevolent aspects. Here, the Druids were not only teachers, judges, pacifists, moral and natural philosophers, and astronomers but also murderous diviners and sacrificers of humans and animals by knife, fire, and arrows. On the other hand, the Druids of the Alexandrian tradition, consisting of Greek texts from scholars educated in the School of Alexandria from the first century CE onwards, were much more 'idealised' and cleansed of their more barbarous aspects. In the writings of Dio Chrysostom, Clement, Origen, and Diogenes Laertius, 'idealism takes over to build up a romantic image

---

[1] See Stuart Piggott, *The Druids* (London: Thames & Hudson, 1996), pp. 96–99. See also Philip C. Almond, 'Druids, Patriarchs, and the Primordial Religion,' *Journal of Contemporary Religion* 15 (2000), pp. 379–394.

of barbarian philosophers, and we move from Druids-as-known to Druids-as-wished-for'.[2]

Central to the construction of the Druids-as-wished-for in eighteenth-century England was their location in Biblical antiquity. Thus, for example, for the antiquary Henry Rowlands (1655–1723), in his *Mona Antiqua Restaurata* (1723), the Druids were 'our first Masters of Knowledge' who had settled on the island of Mona some centuries after the universal deluge.[3] The most ancient people who first came to Mona were, he believed, 'by the Calculation of the Encrease of Mankind after the Flood within four or five Descents at furthest, to *Noah* or one of his sons'.[4] They brought with them the pure religion that had existed before the flood and had been preserved by Noah and his sons. 'I may presume to affirm,' he declared, 'that some of the first Planters of this Island, being so near in descent, to the Fountains of true Religion and Worship, as to have one of *Noah*'s for Grandsire or Greatgrandsire, may well be imagin'd to have carried and convey'd here some of the Rites and Usages of that true Religion, pure and untainted, in their first propagating of them.'[5]

It was an internal religion that had been inherited from Noah, one that was seated in the heart; was directed only at the one, true, supreme God; and exerted itself 'in very few external Rites and Performances'.[6] That said, the Druids took up the custom of worshipping in oak groves

[2]  *Ibid.*, p. 99.
[3]  Henry Rowlands, *Mona Antiqua Restaurata: An Archaeological Discourse on the Antiquities Natural and Historical of the Isle of Anglesey, the Antient Seat of the British Druids* (Dublin, 1723), p. 55.
[4]  *Ibid.*, p. 45.     [5]  *Ibid.*     [6]  *Ibid.*, p. 46.

from practices before the flood. And it was among the oak groves that, like Noah, they built altars of stone to offer sacrifices to God. 'To which Acts and Devotions,' Rowlands went on to say, 'it seems they wanted [lacked] not Rules and Precepts for those Performances, inculcated and communicated to them from *Noah* himself, that great Preacher of Righteousness ... who no sooner was out of the Ark, but his first Work was to erect an Altar, and offer Sacrifice unto the Lord.'[7] It was both the example of Noah and his exhortations that prevailed on many of his descendants as they re-populated the earth to erect altars in every country into which they went in order to offer to God 'their Adorations and most solemn and grateful Acknowledgements of his goodness unto, and of his Sovereignty over, the Sons of Men'.[8]

William Stukeley (1687–1765), antiquarian and Anglican priest, held similar, if slightly quirkier, views. For Stukeley, there was only one difference between Druidism and Christianity, namely that Druids believed in a messiah that was to come while Christians believed that he already had. Druids, he believed, were a colony of Phoenicians, descendants of Noah, who were the first people to arrive in Britain 'soon after Noah's flood'.[9] Thus, to all intents and purposes, Christianity in its Druidic form had arrived in the earliest times. And the physical evidence for this, according to Stukeley, was all over Britain, and most notably in the stone circles at Stonehenge and Avebury. The religion of the stone

---

[7] *Ibid.*    [8] *Ibid.*

[9] William Stukeley, *Stonehenge: A Temple Restored to the British Druids* (London, 1740), p. 4.

circles, he declared, 'was the first, simple, patriarchal religion'.[10]

This linking of patriarchal religion to the stone circles was virtually Stukeley's invention. It was an appealing idea for, with one stroke of the pen, the patriarchal Druids of the time before the flood were physically linked to the land. Thus, the English landscape bore the imprint of the religion of Noah and the antediluvians. The groves of oaks had gone, but the circles of stone remained. Stukeley's fanciful construction of Stonehenge and Avebury as embodying the Christian doctrine of the Trinity was treated with the scepticism it deserved. But his conviction that Stonehenge, Avebury, and other stone circles were Druidic was to win the day, at least in popular culture. As the antiquarian Francis Grose (c.1731–1791) summed it up in 1773 in his remarks on Stonehenge, 'DOCTOR STUKELEY has at length, by a number of irrefragable arguments, clearly proved this to be a British temple, in which their priests called Druids, officiated.'[11]

Similar themes were to occur in the *Galic Antiquities* (1780) of the Scottish antiquarian John Smith (1747–1807). The patriarchal religion, he declared, remained in its pristine purity among the Druids for several ages after the flood. Its beliefs and practices were sufficiently simple to allow the priests to turn their minds to the study of natural philosophy. Like the traditions of the Magi of Persia, the Brahmans of India, and the Chaldeans of Babylon and Assyria, Smith declared,

[10]  *Ibid.*, Preface.
[11]  Francis Grose, 'Stonehenge, Wiltshire,' *The Antiquities of England and Wales* (London, 1773–1787), vol. 4, n.p.

Druidism arose from the same root – the religion of Noah and the antediluvians via Noah's son Japheth: 'Wherever the Celtic tribes, or posterity of Japhet[h], migrated, they carried this religion along with them.'[12] As a religion derived from Noah, he suggested, we should expect to find the simplicity that distinguished patriarchal religion – 'One God, no temple, no image, an altar of either turf or stone, an offering from the increase of the fold or of the field, accompanied with a pure heart and clean hands.'[13]

John Smith's enthusiasm for the Druids was almost matched by that of the Welsh antiquarian, the Reverend Edward Davies (1756–1831). He denied that the original state of man was that of brutes and savages. Rather, he wrote, 'it was a state of immediate mental exertion, and of rapid progress in civilization, and the acquisition of useful arts, – a picture which *true philosophy* might have presented of rational beings, as formed and disposed by the hand of a good and wise Creator'.[14] Men like Methuselah, he suggested, as a consequence of their longevity, could well have brought their inventions to a higher degree of perfection than such short-lived creatures as ourselves.[15] Thus, by the time of the flood, the wisdom of 1,650 years

---

[12] John Smith, *Galic Antiquities: Consisting of the History of the Druids…* (Edinburgh: T. Cadell and C. Elliot, 1780), p. 3.

[13] *Ibid.*, p. 12.

[14] Edward Davies, *Celtic Researches, on the Origin, Traditions & Language of the Ancient Britons* (London, 1804), p. 10.

[15] That the longevity of the patriarchs enabled a rapid increase in knowledge of both the arts and sciences, and that this occurred for the 1,650 or so years from the creation to the deluge, were common arguments in the seventeenth and eighteenth centuries. See Philip C. Almond, *Adam and Eve in Seventeenth-Century Thought* (Cambridge: Cambridge University Press, 1999), pp. 19–27.

had accumulated, ready to be employed. It is evident, he suggested, 'that Noah and his sons preserved, not only the general history of the primitive world, but as much of its acquired knowledge as could be useful to themselves and their posterity. This *they had ample opportunity of doing*; for the flood, in regard to Noah, was no sudden and unforeseen event. *And it was done*; for Moses records the antediluvian inventors of many arts which had been preserved to his own time.'[16] It was the preservation of the patriarchal religion among the Druids via Noah and his family that, most of all, cemented their position as the ultimate noble savages:

> Their studies embraced those elevated objects which had engaged the attention of the world in its primitive age – The Nature of the Deity – of the Human Soul – of the future State – of the heavenly bodies – of the terrestrial globe, and of its various productions ... Perhaps there was no order of men amongst the heathens, who preserved the history and opinions of mankind, in its early state, with more simplicity, and with more integrity.[17]

For the second half of the eighteenth century, the Druids played a crucial role in the establishment of British national identity, as heirs of the patriarchs Noah and Abraham, and as representatives of the primordial religion. But by 1809, Edward Davies's enthusiasm for the Druids as the heirs of this primeval wisdom had waned somewhat. Like others for whom *all* mythologies were corrupt idolatrous versions of an ancient Noachic tradition, he had come to believe that Druidism arose from

---

[16] Davies, *Celtic Researches*, pp. 10–11.    [17] *Ibid.*, p. 119.

the gradual or accidental corruption of the patriarchal religion:

> The mythology and rites of the Druids have a reference to the history of the Deluge, combined with Sabian idolatry: that this people had preserved many heathen traditions respecting the deluge; that they recognise the character of the patriarch Noah, whom they worshipped as a God, in conjunction with the sun; that this Helio-arkite deity was their chief god, appropriating the attributes of most of the principal gods of the Gentiles, but more particularly corresponding in character with Bacchus... that the worship of this god was connected with that of a goddess, who represented the ark; and that all this corresponds, as history requires it should correspond, with the general superstition of other nations, and is therefore derived from the same source.[18]

The supporters of the patriarchal and Noachic origin of the Druids were themselves supported by those for whom the Celts were the most ancient people in the world, and their language and culture redolent of Noah and the antediluvians. As early as 1706, readers of the Jesuit Paul-Yves Pezron (1639–1706) were familiar with speculation that the language 'of the *Celtae* that fixed in Gaul, was from the first Ages of the *postdiluvian* World, the language of the *Gomerians* and therefore that of Gomer [the grandson of Noah]'[19] In short, the line of descent was clear: from Noah to Japheth to Gomer to the Celts or Britons. In a similar

---

[18]  Edward Davies, *The Mythology and Rites of the British Druids* (London: J. Booth, 1809), p. 180.

[19]  Paul-Yves Pezron, *The Antiquities of Nations; More particularly of the Celtae or Gauls* (London, 1706), p. 144.

vein, the Welsh lawyer and philologist Rowland Jones (1722–1774) located his Celtic research within the context of a search for the natural or Adamic language. It was Celtic, he believed, that best preserved the original language of humankind. Transmitted to the Celts by Ashkenaz, the eldest son of Gomer (Genesis 10.3), it received 'no alteration at Babel'.[20] According to Jones, Noah, Japheth, and Gomer were all Druids. As for the religion and government of the ancient Celts, 'they are best guessed at from the practice of the first patriarchs and Druids, Japhet[h] himself being a Druid, and probably the same as the Jupiter of the Heathens'.[21]

The romantic Druids, successors of the patriarchs and descendants of Noah, were not to survive the middle of the nineteenth century. The patriarchal and primordial origins of Druidism could make sense when it was believed that all of humanity could be traced back to an original diffusion from the survivors in the Ark merely some 2,500 years before the birth of Christ. But, like the ark to which they fondly looked back, they were left historically high and dry as faith in the historical truth of the Genesis tradition faded. The gap between patriarchal and primordial religion widened immeasurably as the primordial became the prehistoric.

## Noah and the Speculative Mythographers

With Jones's conjecturing that Japheth was 'the Jupiter of the Heathens' and Davies speaking of 'Sabian idolatry', a

---

[20] Rowland Jones, *The Origin of Language and Nations...* (London, 1764), Preface.
[21] *Ibid.*

'Helio-arkite deity', and a goddess 'who represented the ark', we are entering the realms of the 'speculative mythographers' of the late eighteenth and early nineteenth centuries. The essence of speculative mythography lay in its attempt to trace the mythology of all nations back to early Hebrew history, and notably to Noah and his descendants. Its most celebrated practitioner dwells in the realms of fiction. In George Eliot's novel *Middlemarch* (1871), we find the unworldly Reverend Edward Casaubon working assiduously on his manuscript 'The Key to All Mythologies'. For Mr. Casaubon

> had undertaken to show (what indeed had been attempted before, but not with that thoroughness, justice of comparison, and effectiveness of arrangement at which Mr. Casaubon aimed) that all the mythical systems or erratic mythical fragments in the world were corruptions of a tradition originally revealed. Having once mastered the true position and taken a firm footing there, the vast field of mythical constructions became intelligible, nay, luminous, with the reflected light of correspondences.[22]

Behind the figure of Casaubon lay a long tradition of Christian mythography, primarily concerned with mapping both 'heathen' traditions and Classical mythologies onto the first religion – that of Noah and the antediluvians. In being shown to derive from the Biblical story, they clearly demonstrated the truth of the primordial

---

[22] George Eliot, *Middlemarch: A Study of Provincial Life*, vol. 1 (Edinburgh and London: William Blackwood and Sons, 1871), p. 32. See Colin Kidd, *The World of Mr Casaubon: Britain's Wars of Mythography, 1700–1870* (Cambridge: Cambridge University Press, 2016), p. 3. I am indebted to Kidd for this discussion of the mythographers.

Biblical history. As Colin Kidd notes, 'Once one had identified within paganism a core of Creation myths, myths of golden ages and falls, serpent myths, flood myths and so forth, the resemblances to the book of Genesis were obvious and overwhelming.'[23] The many different traditions of a universal flood, for example, pointed to the historical veracity of the Biblical flood. As Patrick Delany (1686–1768), Dean of Down in the Anglican Church of Ireland, reported, the tradition of the deluge 'was found as familiar among the *Banians* of *Cambay*, upon the discovery of the *East-Indies*, as it was from time immemorial among the ancient *Persians* and *Chinese*; and that some imperfect memory both of *Noah* and his ark, seems to subsist even among the *Hottentots*. They say, their first parents came into their country through a window; that the name of the man was *Nôh*, and the woman *Hingnoh*.'[24]

The major prototype for Edward Casaubon was the English mythographer Jacob Bryant (1715–1804). His three-volume *A New System, or, An Analysis of Antient Mythology* (1774–1776) was exactly the key to all mythologies which the fictional Mr. Casaubon was to aspire to complete. It was a work that, for its enormous ambition and inventive etymology, was destined to be drowned in a deluge of criticism. The mid-twentieth-century scholar Edward Hungerford said of Bryant that 'he devoted a very long life to scholarship, during the nine decades of which he came to not a single correct conclusion.

[23] Kidd, *The World of Mr Casaubon*, p. 46.
[24] Patrick Delany, *Revelation Examined with Candour...* (London, 1735, third edition), vol. 1, p. 255.

His erudition was equalled only by his capacity to misuse it ... At last, as if Learning could no longer endure the outrage, a book fell on him while he was at work in his study, and he died from the injury.'[25]

But, even among his contemporaries, he was something of a figure of fun. Thus, for example, the antiquary John Landseer, with arkite metaphors abounding, complained of Bryant's reliance on spurious linguistic comparisons. Bryant cannot proceed, he declared, 'through a single page – hardly through a sentence – without trusting to these slippery stepping-stones, whether his purpose be to cross a brook, or surmount a deluge ... erudition is brought to an anchor on the heights of his etymological Ararat'.[26] Nevertheless, by 1807, *A New System* had gone into a third edition (in six volumes), not least because, as Colin Kidd makes clear, Bryant's mythography offered a solution to a central problem of the eighteenth-century Protestant Enlightenment: 'how to construct a global anthropology of pagan otherness which would bolster the unique claims of Judaeo-Christian truth set out in Scripture'.[27]

Bryant will never be accused of clarity. But his work did comprise a grand narrative of the origin of all religions that is derived from the history of humankind after the flood. The destruction of all living things in the flood and the deliverance of only eight persons was such an extraordinary event that the particulars would be gratefully commemorated by Noah himself, and transmitted to every

[25] Edward B. Hungerford, *The Shores of Darkness* (New York: Columbia University Press, 1941), p. 20.
[26] Quoted by Kidd, *The World of Mr Casaubon*, p. 113.   [27] *Ibid.*, p. 117.

member of his family.[28] Bryant intended to demonstrate that 'the history of the deluge was religiously preserved in the first ages: That every circumstance of it is to be met with among the historians and mythologists of different countries: and traces of it are to be particularly found in the sacred rites of Egypt and of Greece.'[29] For these nations, the flood was 'the grand epocha ... the highest point to which they could ascend ... the renewal of the world; the new birth of mankind; and the ultimate of Gentile [pagan] history'.[30] Bryant's linguistic method was to trace all sacred pagan words back to the basic elements of the 'original' (completely unknown) Amonian language that, he said, was established after the flood among the descendants of Ham.

Thus, according to Bryant, there was after the flood a season of great happiness under the mild rule of Noah. However, population growth eventually forced the dispersal of most of humanity. The dispersal of most happened after the flood but before the tower of Babel – Shem to Asia, Japheth to Europe, Ham to Africa. However, the branch of the family related to Chus, the son of Ham and grandson of Noah, stubbornly remained in Asia, their king Nimrod becoming King of Babel. It was he who built the tower of Babel, after which the descendants of Cush (or Chus) were scattered for their idolatry (hence the ultimate unity of *all* mythology). The Cuthites, Cuseans, or Amonians established themselves in Egypt, Syria, Phoenicia, and

---

[28] See Jacob Bryant, *A New System; or, an Analysis of Antient Mythology* (London, 1807), vol. 3, p. 6.
[29] *Ibid.*, vol. 3, p. 7.    [30] *Ibid.*, vol. 1, p. xxxvii.

Canaan, playing the crucial role in the establishing of gentile-pagan cities and the creation of the pagan gods. Traditionally, the Greeks and the Romans were regarded as descendants of Japheth. But Bryant broke new theoretical ground with his claim that the Greeks and the Romans were Hamians, more specifically Cuthites or descendants of Chus.

Bryant argued for a version of euhemerism, according to which the gods were nothing but deified humans. Thus, in Bryant's story, rather like that of Berosus whose writings Bryant knew, all the gods were related to and ultimately derived from the eight survivors of the ark. Thus, for example, the Egyptians called Ham Amon and, 'having in process of time raised him to a divinity, they worshiped him as the Sun: and from this worship they were styled Amonians'.[31] Noah himself was so esteemed by his descendants that 'he would be one of the first among men, to whom divine honours would be paid'.[32] And they honoured him with many titles: 'They styled him Prometheus, Deucalion, Atlas, Theuth, Zuth, Xuthus, Inachus, Osiris. When there began to be a tendency towards idolatry; and the adoration of the Sun was introduced by the posterity of Ham; the title of Helius [Sun] among others was conferred on him. They called him also Μην, and Μαν, which is the Moon.'[33] Noah was the original Zeus, along with Dionysus. Remarkably, Noah was also the Buddha. '[U]nder the character of Buddha,' declared Bryant, 'we may trace innumerable

---

[31] *Ibid.*, vol. 1, p. xxx.    [32] *Ibid.*, vol. 3, p. 6.
[33] *Ibid.*, vol. 3, p. 7; see also vol. 1, p. 2.

memorials of the ark; and of the person [Noah] preserved in it.'[34]

The ark and the moon in its form as a crescent were also synonymous. For the Egyptians, according to Bryant, the ark as the moon was the mother of all beings. And Arkite worship was, as a result, central to all ancient mythologies. The poet William Blake (1757–1827) was a devotee of Bryant: 'The antiquities of every Nation under Heaven, is no less sacred than that of the Jews, They are the same thing, as Jacob Bryant and all antiquaries have proved.'[35] And the final volume of the first edition of *A New System* (1775–1776) ended with an engraving depicting the dove with olive branch beneath the rainbow returning to the moon-ark (see Plate 14). This engraving was probably designed and engraved by Blake while serving as an apprentice to the engraver James Brasire from 1771–1778. The moon-ark, tossed on stormy waters, reappeared in an illustration to Blake's *Jerusalem*.[36] For Blake, taking a leaf out of the work of William Stukeley, Adam and Noah, along with the latter's son Shem, were Druids 'as the Druid Temples (which are the Patriarchal Pillars & Oak Groves) over the whole Earth witness to this day'.[37]

[34] *Ibid.*, vol. 3, p. 586. On the Buddha and comparative mythography, see Philip C. Almond, *The Buddha: Life and Afterlife between East and West* (Cambridge: Cambridge University Press, 2024), ch. 6.

[35] Quoted by Ruthven Todd, *Tracks in the Snow: Studies in English Science and Art* (London: The Grey Walls Press, 1946), p. 37.

[36] See https://upload.wikimedia.org/wikipedia/commons/9/9e/Blake_Jerusalem_Plate_24_copy_E.jpg.

[37] Geoffrey Keynes (ed.), 'Jerusalem,' 1.27, in *Poetry and Prose of William Blake* (Bloomsbury: The Nonesuch Press, 1923), p. 597.

In sum, for Bryant and his supporters such as Blake, the key to the mythology of all nations was comprised of two elements: memories of the ark, the flood, and its survivors; and worship of the sun as an idolatrous form of the primordial worship of the one God. It was a theory that *The Edinburgh Review* in 1804 labelled insightfully, if a little unkindly, 'the Helio-arkite superstition'.[38]

Despite his critics, Bryant's influence was a far-reaching one. His creative imaginings were, for example, to find a place in the developing discipline of Indology. Thus, for example, the philologist and Indologist William Jones (1746–1794) did not follow his friend Bryant in believing that there was a key to *all* mythologies. But he was not averse to the idea of inferring 'a general union or affinity between the most distinguished inhabitants of the primitive world, and the time when they deviated, as they did too early deviate, from a rational adoration of the only true God'.[39] He was, in a sense, Bryant in a minor key. Thus, for example, he declared, that while he could not believe like Bryant that

> all the heathen divinities are only different attributes and representations of the Sun or of deceased progenitors . . . yet I cannot but agree, that one great spring of and fountain of all idolatry in the four quarters of the globe was the veneration paid by men to the vast body of fire [the sun] . . . and another, the immoderate respect shown to the memory of powerful or virtuous ancestors,

---

[38] Anon., review of George Stanley Faber, *A Dissertation on the Mysteries of the Cabiri. . .*, *The Edinburgh Review* 3 (1804), pp. 314–315.

[39] William Jones, 'On the Gods of Greece, Italy, and India. . .', *Asiatic Researches*, 1 (1788), p. 221.

especially the founders of kingdoms, legislators, and warriors, of whom the *Sun* or the *Moon* were wildly supposed to be the parents.[40]

Elsewhere he declared that it proved beyond controversy that the Hindus 'were the adorers of those very deities, who were worshipped under different names in old *Greece* and *Italy*'.[41]

It was on 2 February 1786 that William Jones delivered 'The Third Anniversary Discourse' to the Asiatic Society of Bengal in what was then called Calcutta. The lecture is remembered for his announcing that Sanskrit, Greek, and Latin all had a common Proto-Indo-European source, a view still held among linguists today. No philologist could examine all three, he declared, 'without believing them to have sprung from some common source, which, perhaps, no longer exists'.[42] So he was strongly rejecting any suggestion that Bryant's Amonian was the primitive language of Noah or derived from it. The language of Noah, he believed, was lost irretrievably. But he was declaring the common linguistic roots of all three languages, and was thus endorsing the view that the sacred words embedded in these languages were intimately connected.

Jones's philological insight about an original source of Sanskrit, Greek, and Latin, along with Gothic, Celtic, and Old Persian, was based, nonetheless, on his acceptance of the Biblical story of Noah and the re-population after the flood by Noah's descendants. But rather than associating the origin of the Indo-European languages with Japheth,

---

[40] William Jones, *The Works of Sir William Jones* (London, 1799), vol. 1, p. 30.
[41] *Ibid.*, vol. 1, p. 28.  [42] *Ibid.*, vol. 1, p. 26.

as was commonplace, Jones followed Bryant in aligning them with Ham.

It was in Jones's 'The Ninth Anniversary Discourse' in 1792 that he delivered his account of the three original 'races' that descended from the three sons of Noah after the ark landed in Iran. In this lecture, Jones tells us that a deluge destroyed the whole race of man except for Noah and his wife, his three sons, and their wives. The universal flood was an event that he also found reported in Sanskrit literature. In an earlier essay, Jones had concluded that 'the *Mosaick* and *Indian* chronologies are perfectly consistent; that Menu [i.e. Manu], son of Brahmá, was the *Ádima*, or *first*, created mortal, and consequently our Adam; that Menu, child of the Sun, was preserved with *seven* others, in a *bahitra* or capacious ark, from an universal deluge, and must, therefore, be our Noah'.[43]

According to Jones, the descendants of Japheth became the Tartarian race, the descendants of Shem the Arabians, and the descendants of Ham, 'the most powerful and adventurous of whom were the progeny of Cush, Mist, and Rama (names remaining unchanged in *Sanscrit*, and highly revered by the *Hindus*)', became the Indians, along with the Egyptians, the Greeks, and Italians, the Chinese, the Japanese, and even perhaps the Mexicans and Peruvians.[44] Thus, as he put it, he had arrived at the same conclusion as Jacob Bryant, albeit by a different route. It is absolutely certain, he concluded, 'if Moses then was endued [sic] with supernatural knowledge ... that the

---

[43] *Ibid.*, vol. 1, p. 326.
[44] *Ibid.*, vol. 1, pp. 135–136. See also Jones, 'On the Gods of Greece, Italy, and India. . .', p. 268.

whole race of man proceeded from *Iràn*, as from a centre, whence they migrated at first in three great colonies; and that those three branches grew from a common stock, which had been miraculously preserved in a general convulsion and inundation of this globe'.[45] In short, the recently discovered new world of Sanskrit literature was being absorbed into, and appropriated by, a global history, one that was dependent upon the Biblical account of the flood of Noah and the subsequent dispersal of his descendants.

## Noah and the Rise of Race Science

In seeing Europeans as the descendants of Ham, Bryant and Jones were outliers. Nevertheless, each was in agreement with the commonplace tradition in the seventeenth and eighteenth centuries that Ham, Shem, and Japheth were the progenitors of all humanity after the flood (their wives rarely rating a mention). There was, in short, a unity to all humankind. Any distinction between different peoples was accidental and not essential. The Christian doctrine of salvation required it. It is hard to conceive, wrote Edward Stillingfleet (1635–1699), 'how the effects of Man's fall should extend to all Mankind, unless all Mankind were propagated from *Adam*; so it is inconceivable how the account of things given in Scripture should be true, if there were persons existent in the world long before *Adam* was'.[46] Moreover, our common humanity

---

45 *Ibid.*, vol. 1, p. 137.
46 Edward Stillingfleet, *Origines Sacrae: Or A Rational Account of the Grounds of Natural and Revealed Religion* (Cambridge, 1702), p. 367.

depended on it. Thus, for example, the philosopher Nathanael Carpenter (1589–c.1628) maintained that the lists in the book of Genesis of the many descendants of Adam and Noah were intended so that men might understand themselves to be all descended from the same original, and in itself 'there is no greater means to conciliate and ioyne mens affections for mutuall amitie and conversation'.[47] Some seventy years later, Richard Kidder (1633–1703), bishop of Bath and Wells, suggested that the origin of all people was from one man to ensure that claims of superiority could not arise, that 'men might not boast and vaunt of their extraction and original ... and that they might think themselves under an obligation to love and assist each other as proceeding from the same original and common parent'.[48]

The book of Genesis was explicitly committed to monogenesis – that is, the view that everyone was derived originally from Adam and Eve and, after the flood, from Noah and his wife – rather than polygenesis, the view that there were (a la Peyrère) multiple origins to humankind. After the deluge, the populating of the world began again with Noah and his family. Consequently, there arose the fundamental question: How were all the different peoples of the world derived from Noah and his family?

We recall that, according to Genesis, the drunken Noah had been seen naked by his son Ham and his nakedness covered by his sons Shem and Japheth. After

[47] Nathanael Carpenter, *Geography Delineated Forth in Two Books* (Oxford, 1625), bk. 2, p. 207.
[48] Richard Kidder, *A Commentary on the Five Books of Moses* (London, 1694), p. 6.

awakening from his drunken state, Noah blessed Shem and Japheth but cursed Canaan, the son of Ham: 'Blessed by the Lord my God be Shem; and let Canaan be his slave' (Genesis 9.26). Among early modern commentators within the Western tradition, the descendants of Shem (later to be known as Semites) were considered to have populated the Middle East and Asia, those of Ham Africa, and those of Japheth Europe.

But, alongside the assigning of the three continents to the sons of Noah, the long lists of their direct descendants in the book of Genesis (10.1–11.32) also provided plenty of opportunities for speculation about which of Noah's sons or their descendants founded which people. The sons of Ham were identified as Cush, Egypt, Put, and Canaan. The children of Shem were named as Elam, Asshur, Arpachshad, Lud, and Aram. Genesis listed seven sons of Japheth – Gomer, Magog, Madai, Javan, Tubal, Meshech, and Tiras, along with seven grandsons – Ashkenaz, Riphath, and Togarmah (sons of Gomer) and Elishah, Tarshish, Kittim, and Rodanim (sons of Javan). Each of these could be named as the progenitors of various peoples – Gomer of the Galatians, Magog of the Scythians, Tartars, and Turks, Tubal of the Spanish, Elishah of the Greeks, and so on. Walter Raleigh listed the sons of Shem – Elam, Asshur, Arpachshad, Lud, and Aram (Genesis 10.22) – as the founders of the Elamites, the Assyrians, the Chaldeans, the Lydians, and the Syrians, respectively.[49]

In the early modern period, however, as the father of the Europeans, most interest was shown in the sons and

[49] See Raleigh, *The Historie of the World in Five Bookes*, pp. 144–145.

grandsons of Japheth. From these fourteen, the European nations were variously derived. As Arnold Williams has remarked, 'it would hardly be possible to find, except perhaps in the harmony of the chronology of Genesis with that of the profane historians, a subject in which scholarship is more confused or contradictory'.[50] Thus, for example, the descendants of Gomer were the Galatians in Greece, along with the Welsh. The descendants of Rodanim were clearly the people of the island of Rhodes. The descendants of Magog were variously Scythians, Goths, Germans, and Sarmatians. Those of Elishah were the Aeolian Greeks and the Italians, although the Romans were often assigned to Kittim. The descendants of Tubal, the fourth son of Japheth, were the Spaniards. Ashkenaz was the ancestor of the Phrygians. Both Ashkenaz and Togarmah were proposed as the ancestors of the Germans (hence 'Ashkenazi Jews'), but Tuisco, a fourth son of Noah invented by Annius, was also said to be the ancestor of the Germans. In short, the derivation of all peoples from Noah and his wife and their three sons, Shem, Ham, and Japheth, could be endlessly fine-tuned – and endlessly confused. Noachic geography was anything but simple.

Take, for example, Joseph Moxon (1627–1691), hydrographer to King Charles II. He showed the dispersion of the families of the sons of Noah in his 'A map of all the Earth and how after the flood it was divided among the sons of Noah' (1681) (see Plate 15). His was one of the

---

[50] Arnold Williams, *The Common Expositor: An Account of the Commentaries on Genesis 1527–1633* (Chapel Hill: The University of North Carolina Press, 1948), p. 156.

many fanciful reconstructions of the final destinations of the descendants of Noah that generated plenty of heat but very little light.[51] Thus, deciphering his map with not some little difficulty, we find in Europe Ashkenaz and Ripath (the sons of Gomer), along with Kittim, Elishah, Rodanim, and Tiras (the sons of Javan). In Africa, there is mention of Mishraim (or Egypt, son of Ham), of Lehabim and Anamim (the sons of Egypt), and Put (the son of Ham). In the Middle East, there is Canaan (the son of Ham), Lud, Ashur, Elam, Arpachshad, and Aram (the sons of Shem), Tarshish (the son of Javan), Gether and Uz (the sons of Aram), Seba and Sabtah (the sons of Cush), and finally Tubal (the son of Japheth).[52]

Heber is also mentioned on the Middle Eastern portion of the map, not only because he was the great grandson of Shem but also because it was after him that the Hebrews were named (Genesis 10.21-4) and among whom, it was believed, the original language of Adam and Noah had been preserved. Augustine and Isidore of Seville (c.560–636) had held that the original Adamic language was Hebrew. This remained the most commonly held opinion throughout the medieval and early modern periods. The Protestant advocacy of the Hebrew Scriptures was, at least in part, the result of the belief that this was the language that God had imparted to Adam, that it had been the language of all peoples until the confusion of languages at the time of the tower of Babel, and that it had been preserved by Heber and his

---

[51] See *ibid.*, pp. 154–160.
[52] I have modernised the names that appear on Moxon's map in line with the New Revised Standard Version of the Bible.

descendants.[53] The family of Heber also preserved their belief in the one true God, a legacy that was passed on to Heber's descendant Abraham, thus avoiding the polytheism and idolatry of other peoples.

The Eastern region of Joseph Moxon's map had Japheth's son Magog getting as far East as Tartary. But no one, according to his map, had reached China.[54] When Moxon drew his map, however, there was already a tradition emerging that Chinese, rather than Hebrew, was the language spoken by Noah. It originated in the quest for the patriarchal language from Adam to Noah – a language, it was believed, that had a 'real relation' between the written sign and the thing signified by it, as Chinese characters appeared to (and alphabetic languages failed to). Thus, as John Webb wrote in 1669, 'In vain do we search for the PRIMITIVE Language to remain with those Nations whose Languages consist in Alphabets.'[55] Rather, it was probable, as the title of his work indicated, 'that the Language of the Empire of China is the Primitive Language'. Thus, although he knew not a character of Chinese, he declared in his 'Epistle Dedicatory',

> Scripture teacheth, that the whole Earth was of one language until the Conspiracy at BABEL; History informs that CHINA was peopled, whilst the Earth was so of one

---

[53] See Almond, *Adam and Eve in Seventeenth-Century Thought*, pp. 126–136.

[54] The eastern coast of Australia, then known as New Holland, was yet to be filled in. The first mapping of the east coast was by James Cook some ninety years later in 1770.

[55] John Webb, *An Historical Essay Endeavoring a Probability that the Language of the Empire of China is the Primitive Language* (London, 1669), p. 151.

Language, and before that Conspiracy. Scripture teacheth that the Judgment of Confusion of Tongues fell upon those only that were at BABEL: History informs, that the CHINOIS being fully setled before, were not there [at Babel].[56]

According to Webb, Chinese was the primitive language that Noah spoke and took with him into the ark. Webb stretched the landing place of the ark eastwards so that it could be said to have come to rest close to China, whence Noah could return to the place that he had once visited before the deluge. In sum, wrote Webb, Noah 'presented all things as vertue required, with such a natural aptness, as if goodness had been born with him ... whereby [as the legendary Emperor Yao] he filled *China* with his just and pious deeds, and all Ages with his memory; for he lived a reputed Saint amongst them at this day'.[57]

Webb's speculations on Noah were pretty much forgotten until they resurfaced some sixty years later in the English antiquarian Samuel Shuckford's (c.1693–1754) *Sacred and Prophane History of the World.* 'There is indeed another Language in the World,' declared Shuckford, 'which seems to have some Marks of its being the first original Language of Mankind, it is the Chinese ... *Noah,* as has been observed, very probably settled in these parts; and if the great Father and Restorer of Mankind came out

---

[56] *Ibid.,* sigs. A3r-v. I have removed several italics from this passage.

[57] *Ibid.,* p. 67. On Webb, see J. D. Frodsham, 'Chinese and the Primitive Language: John Webb's Contribution to 17th Century Sinology,' *Asian Studies* 2 (1964), pp. 389–390. On the search for the Adamic language, see Umberto Eco, *The Search for the Perfect Language* (Oxford: Blackwell, 1995).

of the Ark and settled there, 'tis very probable that he left here the one universal Language of the World.'[58] Shuckford wanted to rebut emerging claims that Chinese history was older than the Biblical story, in line with his overall aim of squeezing all global history into the confines of a Biblical chronology inspired by Archbishop Ussher. The history of the Chinese, he claimed, reached no further back than Noah. In fact, the legend of the first Chinese emperor Fohi was none other than a corrupted version of the story of Noah. Both lived about the same time, and both lived near where the ark rested in North-West China. Fohi was fatherless and Noah, analogously, 'the first Man in the Postdiluvian World'.[59] Fohi's mother conceived him surrounded by a rainbow, 'a Conceit very probably arising from the Rainbow's first appearing to Noah'.[60] And there was more than a dash of Bryant, and a hint of Casaubon, as Shuckford found Noah replicated in the mythologies of the world – in Janus (as did Webb) and in Bacchus.[61]

The Chinese Noah aside, Joseph Moxon's allocation of the sons and grandsons of Noah to locations all over most of the then known world points more generally to the fluidity and instability in the allocation of the descendants of Noah to various places. Intriguingly, perhaps as a sign of the growing importance of the Americas, Japheth is named not on the European section of the map but on its

[58] Samuel Shuckford, *The Sacred and Prophane History of the World Connected...* (London, 1731), vol. 1, pp. 122–123.
[59] *Ibid.*, p. 102.   [60] *Ibid.*
[61] On Shuckford, see R. J. Arnold, '"Learned Lumber": The Unlikely Survival of Sacred History in the Eighteenth Century,' *The English Historical Review* 125 (2010), pp. 1139–1172.

North American part. Ham and Shem receive no mention at all. Moreover, Moxon identified seventy-eight particular places on the map. But surprisingly, despite Africa, Asia, and Europe having been recognised as continents (as we would understand them) since the beginning of the seventeenth century, Moxon makes no mention of them. In fact, Moxon appears to be ignoring what by the middle of the century was the generally accepted position – that the descendants of Japheth, Shem, and Ham had populated Europe, Asia, and Africa, respectively.

This was a tradition that, more or less, reached back to the first-century Jewish historian Josephus. According to Josephus, Ham occupied parts of Africa and Asia, Japheth parts of Europe and Asia, and Shem Asia (although eastwards no further than Afghanistan).[62] Early Christian commentators, Jerome and Isidore of Seville, were to follow Josephus. But it was Alcuin of York (c.735–804), a scholar at the court of Charlemagne, who created the three sons–three continents view. Despite Isidore's more complicated view, it was Alcuin's account of three sons aligned with three continents that received pictorial representation in the first printed edition of Isidore's *Etymologiae* in 1472 (see Plate 16).[63] These Biblical classifications – Hamitic, Shemitic, and Japhetic – were to

---

[62]  See H. St. J. Thackeray (trans.), *Josephus: Jewish Antiquities, Books i–iv* (Cambridge, MA: Harvard University Press, 1930), vol. 4, bk. 1, secs. 109–150.

[63]  See Benjamin Braude, 'The Sons of Noah and the Construction of Ethnic and Geographical Identities in the Medieval and Early Modern Periods,' *The William and Mary Quarterly* 54 (1997), pp. 103–142; and Colin Kidd, *The Forging of Races: Race and Scripture in the Protestant Atlantic World, 1600–2000* (Cambridge: Cambridge University Press, 2006).

continue from the sixteenth well into the nineteenth centuries. But over the period, they shifted register – from geography to ethnology, from places to races. No longer tied to matters of peoples or nations but to races, the same classifications reinforced the emergence of the idea of racial superiority, and with it the birth of modern racism.

It is in 1771 that we find the first classification of peoples into Hamitic, Semitic, and Japhitic in the Göttingen historian Johann Gatterer's (1727–1799) *Einleitung in die synchronistische Universal-historie* (*Introduction to a synchronistic Universal History*). In keeping with the Noachide (and the monogenist) tradition, he saw the three groups as having spread from 'the region of the mountains of Ararat or Parapamisus, that is, in the northwest of India or around Bactria'.[64] Broadly speaking, he found the Semites at the time of Moses stretching from the west of India to the Middle East; the Hamites living in the Middle East, across Northern Africa, and perhaps later in Abyssinia or Ethiopia; and the Japhetites from Bactria in the east to Greece and Italy in the west and north to the 'Riphean Mountains', the northern boundary of the known world. And there is a hint of the superiority of the Japhetites. 'It is not to be forgotten,' he declared, 'what Gen. IX, 25-7 states, that the Japhetites ..., having been promised by Noah a large expansion, came also into Semitic countries as a result of one of their victories and that the Canaanites, like the Semites, should serve them.'[65]

[64] Johann Christoph Gatterer, *Einleitung in die synchronistische Universalhistorie* (Göttingen: Verlag der Wittwe Vandenhoek, 1771), p. 68.
[65] *Ibid.*, p. 68.

This early classification of peoples led to an identical classification of languages. Thus, the Göttingen historian August Ludwig Schlözer used the same terms to identify closely related groups of languages:

> When the world was young (up to the time of Cyrus), there were not yet many languages, and so not many peoples yet, or vice versa.
>
> From the Mediterranean Ocean to the Euphrates, and from Mesopotamia down through Arabia, only one language dominated, as is well known. So, the Syrians, Babylonians, Hebrews, and Arabs, were one people. Also, the Phoenicians (Hamites) spoke this language, which I would like to call Semitic; they had, however, only learnt it at their borders. Now northwards, – and eastwards behind this Semitic linguistic and ethnic space, a second begins: With Moses and Leibniz, I want to call this the Jafetic.[66]

Schlözer's account clearly still moves within a Biblical space. Even the connecting of language with peoples and places is Biblical: 'These are the descendants of Shem, by their families, their languages, their lands, and their nations' (Genesis 10.31). This was Enlightenment thinking; but it was still determined by the monogenesis of the Biblical story.

This is the case even with another Göttingen naturalist Johann Friedrich Blumenbach (1752–1840), who is often viewed as precipitating the turn away from the theological and towards the secular in the origins of the modern idea of race. In the third edition in 1795 of his *On the Natural*

---

[66] August Ludwig Schlözer, 'Von den Chaldäern,' *Repertorium für Biblische und Morgenländische Litteratur* 8 (1781), p. 161.

*History of Mankind*, Blumenbach outlined his now-famous
scheme of the five principal races (Hauptrassen) of
humankind – the Caucasian, Mongolian, Ethiopian,
American, and Malay. The Caucasian occupied the middle
position between the two extremes of the Ethiopian and
the Mongolian. The Caucasian, he declared, 'diverges in
both directions into two, most remote and very different
from each other; on the one side, namely, into the
Ethiopian, and on the other into the Mongolian. The
remaining two occupy the intermediate positions between
that primeval one [the Caucasian] and these two extreme
varieties; that is, the American between the Caucasian and
Mongolian; the Malay between the Caucasian and
Ethiopian.'[67] In effect, the overall classification still
reflected that of the three sons of Noah and their location
in Europe, Africa, and Asia. This becomes evident when
we see that to the Caucasians belong the inhabitants of
Europe and those of Eastern Asia (east to the Ganges and
south to North Africa), to the Mongolian belong the
remaining inhabitants of Asia and the 'Esquimaux' diffused
over North America, and to the Ethiopian belong all the
Africans except those of the north. The classifications of
Malay and American, covering the people of America
(except for the Esquimaux), the inhabitants of South-East
Asia, and the islanders of the Pacific Ocean, were added in,
as sub-varieties, to cover the discoveries of the Americas
and the Pacific while still retaining the earlier essential
tripartite distinction.

[67] Thomas Bendyshe (trans. and ed.), *On the Natural Variety of Mankind in
The Anthropological Treatises of Johann Friedrich Blumenbach* (London:
Longman, Green, Longman, Roberts, & Green, 1865), pp. 264–265.

The book of Genesis was vague about the specific landing place of the ark, declaring that 'the ark came to rest on the mountains of Ararat' (Genesis 8.4). But the history of the interpretation of this verse tended towards locating the landing place somewhere in west Asia, reading the mountains of Ararat as in the Caucasus. In line with this tradition, Blumenbach declared that he took the name 'Caucasian' from Mount Caucasus: '[I]n that region, if anywhere, it seems we ought with the greatest probability to place the autochthones [originals] of mankind.'[68] Blumenbach's reasoning was, however, aesthetic rather than Biblical. The region around Mount Caucasus 'produces the most beautiful race of men' from which the others diverge by easy gradations to the extremes of the Mongolian and the Ethiopian.[69] Moreover, the Caucasian race 'is white in colour, which we may fairly assume to have been the primitive colour of mankind, since . . . it is very easy for that to degenerate into brown, but very much more difficult for dark to become white'.[70] In short, white was the ideal colour, Noah and Adam were white, and the variations from it were to be explained as the consequence of different climates.

It would be easy to conclude, based on all other varieties as degradations of the Caucasian, that Blumenbach was asserting the racial inferiority of the non-European 'other'. But Blumenbach was a monogenist and committed to the *equal* humanity of all races. His monogenist position was a bulwark against the development of an ideological assertion of essential and fundamental differences between races. That said, in opening the door to an

---

[68] *Ibid.*, p. 269.   [69] *Ibid.*   [70] *Ibid.*

aesthetically based hierarchical ordering of people as a
falling away from a white original, along with a colour-
coded racial hierarchy, he was providing grounds for
more pernicious readings of the *essential* differences
between various peoples. As Bruce Baum notes,
'Whereas Blumenbach used the notion of a Caucasian
race to designate one of the five principal varieties of
human beings that "run into each other by insensible
degrees," the "Caucasian race" category was now widely
adapted to more explicitly racist – specifically, "white"
supremacist – modes of racial classification.'[71]

Like Blumenbach, the French naturalist Georges
Cuvier (1769–1832) was a monogenist. He accepted that
all humans were derived from Adam. And he maintained
that the three major races – the Caucasian, the
Mongolian, and the Ethiopian – had 'escaped in different
directions after the last catastrophe [the Biblical flood],
some five thousand years before, and had developed in
geographical isolation from each other'.[72] I can find no
explicit reference in Cuvier to the three sons of Noah. But
the use of the term 'Caucasian' and the determination of
three races located primarily in Europe, Asia, and Africa
strongly suggest that Biblical categories still resonated
with him. In short, after the flood of Noah, the
Japhethites had become Caucasians, the Hamites
Ethiopians, and the Shemites Mongolians.

That said, Cuvier's monogenism was as close to
polygenism – and, as a result, as near to a strong assertion

---

[71] Bruce Baum, *The Rise and Fall of the Caucasian Race: A Political History of
Racial Identity* (New York: New York University Press, 2006), p. 95.
[72] Quoted by *ibid.*, p. 103.

of racial superiority – as to make no difference. This was, not least, because Cuvier had turned away from environmental accounts of racial variations 'to an emphasis on internal, physiological causes that led some races to stagnate and others to flourish'.[73] Thus, for example, the Caucasian, he declared in his *Le Règne Animal* (1817), was distinguished by the beauty of the oval head; and it is this 'which has given rise to the most civilized nations, – to those which have generally held the rest in subjection'.[74] The name has been affixed, he wrote, 'to the race from which we descend' that originated in the Caucasian mountains, the people of which were still considered the most handsome on earth.[75] The Mongolian, known by his projecting cheekbones, flat visage, narrow and oblique eyebrows, scanty beard, and olive complexion, has established great empires in China and Japan, although 'its civilization has always remained stationary'.[76] The Ethiopian is black, with crisped hair, compressed cranium, and flattened nose. The projecting muzzle and thick lips 'evidently approximate it to the Apes'.[77] The 'hordes of which it is composed,' he concluded, 'have always continued barbarous'.[78]

By the middle of the nineteenth century, the commitment to monogenesis was coming to be more honoured in the breach than in the full-blown observance of it. In fact, the monogenist paradigm was on the edge of collapse. The Biblical chronology that supported it was

[73] *Ibid.*, p. 100.
[74] George Cuvier, *Cuvier's Animal Kingdom...* (London: Wm. S. Orr and Co., 1840), p. 50.
[75] *Ibid.*    [76] *Ibid.*    [77] *Ibid.*    [78] *Ibid.*

disappearing. The idea of the universal flood reported in Genesis was on the wane. The question of the origins of humankind was shifting from the diffusion of humankind after the flood to its evolution. A biology of racial diversity was on the way to replacing a theology of human unity. Moreover, the monogenist explanation for differences in terms of the external environment was losing ground. As John Jackson and Nadine Weidman note, 'As doubts accrued about the efficacy of the environment to alter physical or mental traits in any lasting way, the reigning monogenist consensus was weakened, and polygenists solved the problem by arguing that racial differences were primordial and permanent.'[79]

It was to become what we would call 'a culture war' – a conflict between religion and science. In 1857, the Egyptologist George Gliddons (1809–1857) coined the two terms (that we still use) to describe the combatants – monogenists and polygenists. For him, monogenesis was tainted with 'the religious dogma of mankind's *Unity* of origin'.[80] It was a worthless religious myth. To the idea of 'the unity of the human species,' he declared, 'trembling orthodoxy clutches like sinking mariners their last plank.'[81] Although supporters of polygenesis generally agreed that the dark races were inferior to the white, without a Biblical framework to draw upon, they disagreed scientifically on the identification and the number

---

[79] John P. Jackson Jr. and Nadine M. Weidman, *Race, Racism, and Science: Social Impact and Interaction* (Santa Barbara, CA: ABC-CLIO, 2004), p. 56.

[80] J. C. Nott and G. R. Gliddon, *Indigenous Races of the Earth* (Philadelphia and London: F.B. Lippincott & Co. and Trübner & Co., 1857), p. 428.

[81] *Ibid.*, p. 510.

of races. As Charles Darwin (1809–1882) pointed out, 'Man has been studied more carefully than any other organic being, and yet there is the greatest possible diversity amongst capable judges whether he should be classified as a single species or race, or as two (Virey), as three (Jacquinot), as four (Kant), five (Blumenbach), six (Buffon), seven (Hunter), eight (Agassiz), eleven (Pickering), fifteen (Bory St. Vincent), sixteen (Dumoulins), twenty-two (Morton), sixty (Crawfurd), or as sixty-three, according to Burke.'[82] However, despite their disagreements, polygenists did give the appearance of 'hard science' rather than the monogenists of 'soft theology'. Reinforced by the developing quantitative sciences, the polygenists collected, categorised, classified, and measured their way to dominance. As Gliddons summarily declared, 'Natural history teaches us that the white and black races, for example are distinct species.'[83]

Ironically, it was biology in the form of the theory of evolution that was to put monogenesis, albeit without a religious flavour, back into the territory of science. Charles Darwin was a believer in the original unity of humankind. For him, the similarities between different peoples suggested more their unity than their racial plurality. Whether one species or many, the races, he wrote, 'graduate into each other, and ... it is hardly possible to discover clear distinctive characters between them'.[84]

[82] Charles Darwin, *The Descent of Man* (Princeton, NJ: Princeton University Press, 2008), p. 226. Darwin drew this statement primarily from Hudson Tuttle, *The Origin and Antiquity of Physical Man Scientifically Considered...* (Boston: W. White & Company, 1866), p. 35.

[83] Nott and Gliddon, *Indigenous Races of the Earth*, p. 360.

[84] Charles Darwin, *The Descent of Man*, p. 226.

Thus, Darwin saw no impossibility in the varieties of humans having sprung from a single pair of progenitors. 'Finally,' he declared in 1871, 'we may conclude that when the principles of evolution are generally accepted, as they surely will be before long, the dispute between the monogenists and the polygenists will die a silent and unobserved death.'[85] By 1871, of course, as a result of Darwin's *On the Origin of Species* in 1859, the conflict between religion and science had shifted from the question of religion and race to that of religion and evolution. It was no longer a question of the *unity* of humankind, but of the *uniqueness* of humankind (regardless of its varieties or otherwise), compared to the rest of creation. Darwin had given whites and blacks a common humanity, but for many of his critics this was tainted by his finding that both had a common ancestor in the apes.

## The Curse of Ham

When Noah awoke from his drunken stupor, he knew that his son Ham had seen his nakedness and had told his brothers, Shem and Japheth (see Plate 17). Noah cursed Ham's son Canaan, declaring that he would be 'the lowest of slaves' to his brothers, Cush, Egypt, and Put (Genesis 9.25). Why was the curse pronounced upon Canaan (or one or more of his brothers) and not Ham? The simplest explanation is that this text was written at a time, around 1000 BCE, when the Hebrew people were looking to explain their defeat of the people of Canaan when they

---

[85] *Ibid.*, p. 235.

invaded that land.[86] It retrospectively justified the take-over of the promised land and the enslavement of the people who were already there.

Canaan played little role in the Western interpretation of Noah's curse. By the third and fourth centuries CE, the curse laid upon him had been transformed into the curse of Ham (see Plate 18). And by the end of the sixteenth century, Canaan had disappeared from the narrative altogether. Thus, for example, in the first commentary in English on the book of Genesis, the bishop of Worcester, Gervase Babington (c.1549–1610), repeated the tradition that Ham, having seen his father's naked-ness, went 'mockingly' and told his brothers of it. Ham played so lewd a part that 'he procureth a curse and not a blessing'.[87] He was the true pattern 'of all such wilde spirites, as joye in the publishing of other men's wants, whom yet for many graces they ought to reverence'.[88] As for Canaan, Babington failed to mention him at all.

As Canaan was written out of the story, Ham was written into the Western story to explain why he should have been the recipient of Noah's curse. So, as the trad-ition developed, he was thought to have done far more than merely gaze upon his father's nakedness and joke about it. Although sceptical of the tradition, The Dutch

---

[86] See Gerhard von Rad, *Genesis: A Commentary* (Philadelphia: Westminster Press, 1972), p. 137.

[87] Gervase Babington, *Certaine Plaine, Briefe, and Comfortable Notes upon everie Chapter of Genesis* (London, 1592), fol. 38v. On the disappearance of Canaan, see David M. Whitford, *The Curse of Ham in the Early Modern Era: The Bible and the Justifications for Slavery* (Farnham, Surrey: Ashgate, 2009), ch. 4. I am indebted to Whitford for this discussion.

[88] *Ibid.*, fol. 38r.

philosopher Pierre Bayle (1647–1706), in his *Dictionary Historical and Critical* around the late 1600s, provided a useful summary of the curse of Ham as it had developed over the centuries:

> It has been believed that since Ham had displayed such indiscretion toward his father, he was a cursed soul who had committed all sorts of abominations. He is said to be the Inventor of Magic and many things are told about this. It is claimed that he gave an example of unchastity not very edifying, that is to say that he made his wife pregnant in the ark itself. Some say that the offense which he committed against his father is infinitely more atrocious than the way in which it is represented in the Holy Scripture. Some believe that he castrated him; others say that he made him impotent thanks to some magical spells; others claim that he wallowed in incest with Noah's wife.[89]

If the causes of the curse of Ham were various, its results were clear. Noah established slavery as a result of the sin of Ham, and his descendants were to be in subjection to others. The earliest analysis of the curse of Ham came in the late fourth century in the writings of Ambrosiaster. In his commentary on Paul's first letter to the Corinthians, Ambrosiaster declared that sin created slaves 'as Ham, the son of Noah, was made a slave because of his sin and lack of prudence'.[90] For Ambrosiaster, Ham

---

[89] Quoted by Stephen R. Haynes, *Noah's Curse: The Biblical Justification of American Slavery* (Oxford: Oxford University Press, 2002), p. 38.

[90] Gerald L. Bray (trans. and ed.), *Commentaries on Romans and 1-2 Corinthians: Ambrosiaster* (Downers Grove, IL: IVP Academic, 2009), p. 153.

mocked the father to whom he owed reverence. 'Slaves are made by sin,' he declared, 'like Ham, the son of Noah, who was the first to receive the name of slave by merit.'[91]

As Classical slavery evolved into medieval serfdom, a new interpretation of the curse of Ham arose. It was initiated by Honorius of Autun (c.1080–c.1140) in his encyclopaedic *Imago Mundi*. In his discussion of the 'Second Age' – the age after the flood – Honorius declared that it was during the time of Noah that the 'species of man' ('genus humanum') was divided into three groups of people: 'Freemen from Shem, soldiers from Japheth, slaves from Ham'.[92] In effect, according to Honorius, the division of people at the time of Noah mirrored the medieval structure of society into the free-man, the noble, and the serf.

As feudalism declined in the late medieval period, so did the threefold identification of the sons of Noah with freemen, nobles, and serfs. This decline provided another intellectual space for the identification of the descendants of Ham. A fresh Western reading of the curse of Ham arose as a result of the rising trade in sub-Saharan African slaves in the course of the fifteenth to the seventeenth centuries. Thus, in the late sixteenth and early seventeenth centuries, the curse of Ham became both *the slavery and the blackness of his African descendants*. In the collection of travel stories *Purchas His Pilgrimes* (1625) of Samuel Purchas (c.1577–1626), we read George Sandy's

---

[91] *PL* 17. 432.
[92] 'Liberi de Sem, milites de Iapheth, servi de Cham'. Nicholas Ryan Foster, 'The *Imago Mundi* of Honorius Augustodunensis,' Master of Arts thesis, Portland State University, 2008, p. 266.

description of a caravan of African slaves that he encountered: 'These ["Negros"] are descended of *Chus*, the Sonne of cursed *Cham*; as are all of that complexion, Not so by reason of their Seed, nor heat of the Climate; nor of the Soyle, as some have supposed; for neither haply will other Races in that Soyle proove black, nor that Race in other Soyles grow to better complexion; but rather from the Curse of *Noe* upon *Cham* in the Posterities of *Chus*.' And in the margins of the text, we find '*Chams* curse continuing still' and 'black colour whence'.[93]

With Ham connected to slavery, blackness, and Africa, it was only a small step to read the curse of Ham as involving both slavery and blackness. The turning point for connecting the curse of Ham with the enslavement of black Africans came in the entry to 'Cham' in the 1728 supplement to the French Benedictine monk Augustin Calmet's (1672–1757) *Dictionnaire historique et critique*. 'The author of the Tharik-Thabari [al-Ṭabarī]', Calmet informed us, 'teaches that Noah directed his curse to Ham and Canaan. The effect of this curse was not only that their posterity was enslaved to their brothers, and thus born into slavery, but also that suddenly the colour of their skin became black.'[94] Despite occasional dissenting voices, the curse of Ham continued to serve as the

[93] George Sandys, 'Journey begun 1610,' in *Purchas His Pilgrimes in Five Bookes* (London, 1625), bk. 6, ch. 8, sec. 3, p. 913.

[94] Quoted by Benjamin Braude, 'Cham et Noé: Race, Esclavage et Exégèse entre Islam, Judaïsme et Christianisme,' *Annales: Histoire, Sciences Sociales* 57 (2002), p. 96 (my translation). I am indebted to Benjamin Braude for directing me to his article. On Al-Ṭabarī and the curse of Ham, see Chapter 3. At the time of Al-Ṭabarī (ninth–tenth centuries CE), Canaan was still included in the curse in Islam. On the curse of Ham and blackness in Judaism, see also Chapter 3.

justification for black slavery in Europe and America through the eighteenth and into the nineteenth century.

It was, of course, difficult to combine a justification of slavery with a commitment to the Biblical view of the monogenetic unity of humankind. But those who defended the institution of American slavery in the nineteenth century were not averse to squaring that particular circle, attempting to align the unity of humankind embedded in the story of Adam and Eve with the essential divisions that resulted from the curse of Ham. Thus, for example, on the eve of the American Civil War, the American Methodist Samuel Davies Baldwin (1810–1866) defended, in Biblical terms, the racial distinctions that underpinned slavery. According to Baldwin, there was a unity of humankind before the flood. Since then, however, it has been divided into a trinity of types, God reorganising 'the framework of nature so as to preserve these types from amalgamation'.[95] These three types were scattered over the earth: the one fair in complexion, active in mind, and superior in morals; another brown, gentle in mind, and medium in virtue; the last black, low in intellect, and, as he put it, 'grovelling in principles and passions'.[96]

Since the flood, Baldwin wrote, the earth has been under the law of Noah, a law that denies political equality as a right to all men. Rather, it makes one race servile to the others. This is seen everywhere since the flood but 'most sublimely in America'. It is obvious, Baldwin

95 Samuel Davies Baldwin, *Dominion: Or, the Unity and Trinity of the Human Race* (Nashville, TN: Southern Methodist Publishing House, 1858), p. 409.
96 *Ibid.*, p. 412.

continued, 'in a universal and permanent trinity of races; in their political inequality of condition; in the Christianization of all the Japhetic nations, and of no others; in the occupation of the Shemitic wilderness of America by Japheth; and in the service of Ham to Japheth in the Southern States, in the islands, and in South America'.[97] And Baldwin had a clear message for his abolitionist compatriots: slavery was part of the divine plan. 'God's plan,' he declared,

> is through the *humility of bondage*. And this being his plan, it is the only really feasible and benevolent one. To interrupt it, or to attempt its removal or modification before it has run its needful and natural and appointed course, is to injure the very persons we purpose thereby to assist... *Colonisation in Africa* and *Hamitic bondage in America* are God's plan for ameliorating the condition of the Hamites.[98]

With the end of the Civil War, slavery ended. And with the end of slavery, references to the story of Noah's drunkenness and the curse that resulted from it (Genesis 9.20-27) also disappeared. It was not, of course, the end of a belief in the superiority of whites and the inferiority of blacks. As Stephen Haynes notes, 'Precisely because Genesis 9: 20-27 was considered so germane to the question of American slavery, it did not seem applicable to race relations in a free society. Thus, confident references to Genesis 9 so common in the antebellum [prewar] period became conspicuously absent, as proponents of white supremacy looked elsewhere to support their arguments.'[99]

[97] *Ibid.*, p. 17.     [98] *Ibid.*, pp. 24–25.
[99] Haynes, *Noah's Curse*, p. 103.

# 7

# Legends of Noah and the Ark

~

## The Sources of the Flood Story

By the middle of the nineteenth century, the veracity of the story of Noah was assailed by criticisms *external* to it. But later in that same century, historical criticism of the book of Genesis was beginning to question the *internal* consistency, coherency, and originality of the story of Noah. In 1878, the German Biblical scholar Julius Wellhausen (1844–1918) published his *Geschichte Israels* (*History of Israel*).[1] In this work, Wellhausen argued that the book of Genesis, and the account of Noah and the flood within it, was not a unified account of the early ages of the world, but rather a work compiled from a number of different sources, arising in different times, and intended for a variety of theological purposes.

For the century following Wellhausen's work, the overwhelming scholarly consensus was that the story of the flood combined two literary strands: the Yahwist or J source dating from the tenth or ninth century BCE, and the Priestly or P source dating from the Exilic or early post-Exilic period some four centuries later, with the Yahwist as a source for the later Priestly strand. Without putting too fine a point on it, there was a number

---

[1] The book was republished in 1883 as *Prolegomena zur Geschichte Israels*. The 1885 English translation, *Prolegomena to the History of Israel*, was a translation of this edition.

of significant apparent differences between the P and non-P sources within the story that led to the questioning of the unity of the text.[2] Thus for example, the text alternates between two names for God – Yahweh (or Jahweh) (YHWH) and Elohim. God sees the evil of humanity twice (Genesis 6.5, 11-12). Noah appears to enter the ark twice (Genesis 7.7, 13). Some passages speak of a flood that lasted forty days and forty nights (Genesis 7.4, 12, 17); others suggest a cosmic deluge that continued for 150 days (Genesis 7.11, 24). One passage tells Noah to bring two of every kind of animal into the ark (Genesis 6.19-20), while another has God tell Noah to take seven pairs of clean animals and a pair of unclean animals (Genesis 7.2-3).

Historical criticism treated the Bible like any other ancient text, thus threatening its privileged status. That said, as liberal Christians had come to terms with geology and evolution, they soon came to terms with historical criticism. The book of Genesis became sacred legend rather than sacred history. The Biblical story of the flood became just one of the many ancient accounts of universal floods, one whose immediate origins were to be found in *The Epic of Gilgamesh* and parallels to it in the Classical world. The source hypothesis came under strain under the weight of its own scholarly refinements over the last 140 years. And the study of the first five books of the Bible moved beyond asking 'Did it happen?' to 'What does it mean?' That said, historical criticism is still viewed as

---

[2] To avoid continual complications in the narrative of Noah and the ark up to this point in this book, I have put these variations as far aside as possible.

enabling access to the historical contexts in which the texts were created.[3] Crucially, the view that the Biblical story of Noah and the flood consisted of Hebrew versions of traditions of the flood that pre-existed it and that were variously incorporated into it still holds.

Another discovery was to transform all future understandings of Noah and the ark. Assyriologist George Smith (1840–1876) was sorting and classifying fragments of cuneiform tablets from the library of the Assyrian King Ashurbanipal (reigned from 669–c.631 BCE) in the British Museum. Smith noticed that some of the fragments told of a flood. And then, he later wrote, 'my eye caught the statement that the ship rested on the mountains of Nazir, followed by the account of the sending forth of the dove, and its finding no resting-place and returning. I saw at once that I had here discovered a portion at least of the Chaldaean account of the Deluge.'[4] Smith had, in fact, discovered the source of the Biblical story of Noah – the eleventh tablet of *The Epic of Gilgamesh* and the flood story of its hero Uta-napishti.[5] On 3 December 1872, he read his account of the Gilgamesh flood to the Society of Biblical Archaeology.[6] It was then realised that not only did the Biblical story of Noah and the flood consist of stories that pre-existed it, but also that these stories were

---

[3] For an excellent summary of the history of research into the sources in Genesis, see Joseph Blenkinsopp, 'The Documentary Hypothesis is in Trouble,' *Bible Review* 1 (1985), n.p. Available at https://library .Biblicalarchaeology.org/article/the-documentary-hypothesis-in-trouble.

[4] Quoted by Cohn, *Noah's Flood*, p. 20.    [5] See Chapter 1.

[6] See George Smith, 'The Chaldean Account of the Deluge,' *Transactions of the Society of Biblical Archaeology* 2 (1873), pp. 213–234.

themselves drawn from an earlier Mesopotamian narrative of a universal flood. This meant that the Biblical story, like all the stories that were later to be based upon it, was itself a retelling and a re-imagining of an earlier legend contained within *The Epic of Gilgamesh*.

For conservative believers, however, historical criticism of the Bible was seen not only as undermining its authority, inspiration, and infallibility but also, in the case of the first five books of the Bible, as sabotaging the traditional attribution of their authorship to Moses. It was the thin end of a wedge that led to unbelief and atheism. As the conservative American theologian Franklin Johnson (1836–1916) put it in 1910, 'The natural [historical] view of the Scriptures is a sea which has been rising higher for three-quarters of a century. Many Christians bid it welcome to pour lightly over the walls which the faith of the church has always set up against it, in the expectation that it will provide a healthful and helpful stream. It is already a cataract, uprooting, destroying, and slaying.'[7] Almost, one might say, like a Biblical deluge!

## The Flood and the Young Earth

Those who believed in the historical accuracy and inerrancy of the Bible would always do battle (and still do) with

---

[7] Franklin Johnson, 'Fallacies of the Higher Criticism,' in [Lyman Stewart and Milton Stewart] (eds.), *The Fundamentals* (Chicago: Testimony Publishing Company, 1910), vol. 2, p. 68. This was the third essay in the second volume of the twelve volumes of ninety essays titled *The Fundamentals: A Testimony to the Truth* (1910–1915). These twelve volumes are the foundation documents of the Christian movement that became known as 'Fundamentalism'.

the historical criticism of the Bible. That said, by the end of the nineteenth century, even conservative defenders of Christianity accepted that the Bible allowed for an ancient earth in accord with the science of geology. As Ronald Numbers notes,

> With few exceptions, they accommodated the findings of historical geology either by interpreting the days of Genesis 1 to represent vast ages in the history of the earth (the so-called day-age theory) or by separating a creation "in the beginning" from a much later Edenic creation in six literal days (the gap theory). Either way, they could defend the accuracy of the Bible while simultaneously embracing the latest geological and paleontological discoveries.[8]

In short, the creation story of the Bible was harmonised with geology and palaeontology.

But in the early twentieth century, a 'young earth' movement arose from the writings of the Seventh-Day Adventist George McReady Price (1870–1963). And creation was dated at some 6,000 (following Usher's chronology) to 10,000 years ago (allowing for gaps of time in the Biblical genealogies). It was to lead in the 1960s to the advent of 'creation science'. With the rise of this movement, the flood of Noah was to reassume its place at the centre of the debate between science and ultra-conservative evangelical Christianity. 'The Genesis Flood,' declared the text *Scientific Creationism* in 1974, 'is the real crux of the conflict between the evolutionist and

---

[8] Ronald L. Numbers, *The Creationists: From Scientific Creationism to Intelligent Design* (Cambridge, MA: Harvard University Press, 2006), p. 7.

creationist cosmologies.'[9] And if the earth was no older than 6,000 to 10,000 years, the historical and scientific veracity of the Bible, against both geology and Darwinian evolutionary biology, was vindicated.

Like Ellen White (1827–1915), the co-founder of his Seventh-Day Adventist Church, George McReady Price was deeply committed to an uncompromising literal reading of Genesis. The book of Genesis taught unambiguously, he believed, that 'life has been on our globe only some six or seven thousand years; and that the earth as we know it ... was brought into existence in six literal days'.[10] Fossils, rather than being evidence of successive ages, pointed rather to the creatures whose remains they were as having lived at the same time and to all having been destroyed 'by one overwhelming world disaster', namely the flood of Noah.[11] 'The one simple postulate,' Price wrote, 'that there was a universal Flood clears up beautifully every major problem in the supposed conflict between modern science and modern Christianity.'[12] The scientific evidence for a universal flood, he believed, was 'as firmly established as a real historical event as the reign of Hammurabi or the wars of Attila'.[13]

Price gave little attention to how such a universal flood was caused. But he had no doubt that there was sufficient

---

[9] Quoted by *ibid.*, p. 8.    [10] Quoted by *ibid.*, p. 92.
[11] George McReady Price, *The Modern Flood Theory of Geology* (New York: Fleming H. Revell Company, 1935), p. 7.
[12] *Ibid.*, p. 6.
[13] George McReady Price, *The New Geology: A Textbook for Colleges, Normal Schools, and Training Schools; and for the General Reader* (Mountain View, CA: Pacific Press Publishing Association, 1923), p. 687.

water on the earth to cover all of it to a depth of a mile and a half. The only astronomical cause of a universal deluge, he surmised, 'would be something of the nature of *a jar or shock from the outside*, which would produce an abnormal tidal action, resulting in great tidal waves sweeping twice daily around the earth from east to west, this wave travelling at 1,000 miles an hour at the equator'.[14]

After the flood, the large variety of new species arose, not so much from Darwinian evolution as from divine intervention. We may be very sure, Price wrote, 'that the great superintending Power which is over nature, adapted these men and these animals and plants [after the deluge] to their strange world'.[15] As for the varieties of human-kind, Price looked to divine intervention after the Tower of Babel. Before then, all of humankind were of one speech and one race. God again intervened, scattering people across the earth. And, 'just as artificial barriers of language were interposed to keep them from again blending into one world-embracing despotism, so we may well suppose that the barriers of race and colour were also interposed at this same time, these racial barriers assisting in segregating the people of the world off into self-contained groups.'[16] In short, the Bible record of the dispersal of mankind soon after the flood provided 'by far the most believable explanation of the facts as we now know them through archaeology and philology'.[17]

---

[14] *Ibid.*, p. 642.
[15] George McReady Price, *The Phantom of Organic Evolution* (New York: Fleming H. Revell Company, 1924), p. 105.
[16] *Ibid.*, p. 106.    [17] *Ibid.*, p. 107.

## The Flood and Creation Science

Price's flood geology was driven by his unwavering belief in the authority and inerrancy of Scripture. Significantly influenced by the writings of Price, John C. Whitcomb (1924–2020) and Henry M. Morris (1918–2006), the founding fathers of creation science, proceeded in *The Genesis Flood* (1961) 'from the perspective of full belief in the complete divine inspiration and perspicuity of Scripture, believing that a true exegesis thereof yields determinative Truth in all matters with which it deals'.[18] Not much room for harmonising compromises there then! Rather than geology's estimate of the age of the earth at 4.5 billion years, creation science held to somewhere between 6,000 and 10,000 years. 'The decision must then be faced,' declared Morris, 'either the Biblical record of the Flood is false and must be rejected or else the system of historical geology which has seemed to discredit it is wrong and must be changed. The latter alternative would seem to be the only one which a Biblically and scientifically instructed Christian could honestly take, regardless of the "deluge" of scholarly wrath and ridicule that taking such a position brings on him.'[19] Their target was a twofold one – any science that threatened the infallibility of the Bible and any theology that compromised Biblical truth in support of science.

---

[18] John C. Whitcomb and Henry M. Morris, *The Genesis Flood: The Biblical Record and Its Scientific Implications* (Phillipsburg, NJ: P and R Publishing, 1961), p. 6. Whitcomb was primarily responsible for chapters 1–4, Morris for chapters 5–7.

[19] *Ibid.*, p. 118.

For Whitcomb and Morris, it was flood geology that was the key to deciding between creation on the one hand and evolution on the other. If it could be shown that the fossil-bearing strata had not been laid down over long periods of time but rather during the course of a single year at the time of the flood of Noah, 'The last refuge of the case for evolution immediately vanishes away, and the record of the rocks becomes a tremendous witness, not to the operation of a naturalistic process of Godless development and progress but rather to the holiness and justice and power of the living God of Creation.'[20] That said, while science that was in conflict with their flood geology was to be rejected, Whitcomb and Morris continually drew upon modern science to validate the Biblical account of the earth before, during, and after the flood. Wherever possible, science was to be the handmaiden of Biblical truth.[21] Thus, armed with their flood geology and the results of congenial science, the theologian Whitcomb and the hydraulic engineer Morris were able to weave a new (apparently) scientifically supported 'modern' legend of Noah and the flood.

According to *The Genesis Flood*, with the exception of Noah, the wickedness of humanity was such as to require its destruction. A universal flood was necessary because from the time of Adam to Noah, the population of the world had spread across all of it. Moreover, 'the longevity

---

[20]  *Ibid.*, p. 451.

[21]  The footnotes of *The Genesis Flood* demonstrate clearly their 'science as handmaiden' approach. In the early 1970s, Morris repackaged his 'science in service of theology' as 'science' under the titles 'Creation Science' and 'Scientific Creationism', severing it from its Biblical trappings. See Numbers, *The Creationists*, ch. 12.

and fecundity of the antediluvians would allow for a very rapid increase in population, even if only 1,656 years elapsed between Adam and the flood'.[22] Whitcomb and Morris calculated a population of 1 billion people on earth at the time of the deluge. The evidence of human fossils scattered all over the world suggested that humanity had spread before the flood way beyond the Near East.

The opening of the windows of the heavens and the breaking up of the fountains of the deep were supernatural acts of God. But, throughout the entire process, '"the waters which were above the firmament" and "the waters which were under the firmament" *acted according to the known laws of hydrostatics and hydrodynamics.* They churned up, carried away, and deposited sediments according to natural hydraulic processes, moving at velocities and in directions that were perfectly normal.'[23] According to their calculations, the flood lasted just over a year, six weeks to reach maximum height above the mountains, followed by twenty-two weeks before it began to subside, and a further thirty-one weeks for the waters to subside sufficiently to make an exit from the ark possible.

Animals of all kinds lived within the vicinity of the ark. God imparted a 'migratory directional instinct' in the animals that enabled them to reach it.[24] Because there were not then all the varieties of animals present in the world today, the barge-shaped ark only needed to contain at most 35,000 air-breathing vertebrate animals. At their estimate of 1,396,000 cubic feet, 'the Ark had a carrying capacity equal to that of 522 standard stock cars as used by

[22] Whitcomb and Morris, *The Genesis Flood*, p. 34.    [23] *Ibid.*, pp. 76–77.
[24] *Ibid.*, p. 74.

modern railroads or of eight freight trains with sixty-five such cars in each'.[25] Dinosaurs may also have been represented on the ark, 'probably by very young animals, only to die out because of hostile environmental conditions after the Flood', or not represented at all 'for the very reason of their intended extinction'.[26] As to the care of the animals on the ark, they required minimal attention. They hibernated their way through the time of the flood, 'having received from God the power to become more or less dormant'.[27] There remained the problem of explaining the distribution of animals from the ark after it landed on the mountains of Ararat. Rapid dispersion and land bridges provided the main answers. Thus, for example, 'it is quite conceivable that marsupials could have reached Australia by migration waves from Asia, before that continent became separated from the mainland'.[28]

From the time of the six days of creation until the flood, a protective canopy of water vapour over the earth ('the waters above the firmament') ensured the longevity of the antediluvian population. It furnished a warm, pleasant, and healthy environment with no rainfall throughout the world. And it provided 'a shield against the intense radiations impinging upon the earth from space'.[29] After the flood, with the canopy disappearing, variations in climate appeared. The declining life span after the flood was also the consequence of the dissipation of this protective cloud. That said, longevity declined slowly, and the

[25] *Ibid.*, pp. 67–68.　[26] *Ibid.*, p. 69, n. 3.　[27] *Ibid.*, p. 74.
[28] *Ibid.*, p. 87.　[29] *Ibid.*, p. 399.

population growth after the flood was abnormally high, more than sufficient to have produced the current population from the eight survivors of the ark.

Needless to say, the community of non-creation scientists was not buying any of it. Flood geology caused hardly a ripple of regard, more an ocean of disdain. For *The Genesis Flood* of Morris and Whitcomb looked far more like a harmonising product of the science of the seventeenth century than that of the twentieth. The days of Noah and the flood that destroyed the world and all living things within it playing a significant role in secular science were well and truly over.

## Searchers for the Lost Ark

According to the book of Genesis, the ark came to rest 'on the mountains of Ararat' (Genesis 8.4). Within the Old Testament, it is clear that the reference to Ararat is to a mountainous kingdom called 'the land of Ararat' (2 Kings 19.37, Isaiah 37.38) broadly in the region of Armenia in West Asia.[30] As early as the first century CE, the Jewish historian Josephus remarked that 'the ark rested on the top of a certain mountain in Armenia'.[31] Jerome's Latin version of the Bible known as the Vulgate (383–404 CE) translated 'on the mountains of Ararat' as 'super montes Armeniae'. John Chrysostom asked of unbelievers, 'Do not the mountains of Armenia testify to it, where the Ark

---

[30] The modern literature on the location of the ark and the search for it is, to say the least, enormous, complex, almost impenetrable, and mostly driven by the belief in the historicity of the story of the ark.

[31] Whiston (trans.), *The Antiquities of the Jews*, bk. 1, ch. 3, para. 4, p. 32.

rested? And are not the remains of the Ark preserved there to this day very for our admonition?'[32]

That said, the boundaries of 'Armenia' were sufficiently porous for a number of more specific sites to be imagined. The book of Jubilees (second century BCE) had the ark coming to rest on 'the top of Lubar, one of the mountains of Ararat'.[33] Similarly, Epiphanius of Salamis reported that the ark came to rest 'in the mountains of Ararat, in the midst of [or "in between"] the mountains of Armenia and of Kurdistan [Gordyene], on a mountain called Lubar'.[34] Josephus reported that the Babylonian Berossus had told of a part of the ship in Armenia, at the mountains of the Cordyaeans, and that 'some people carry off pieces of the bitumen, which they take away, and use chiefly as amulets for the averting of mischiefs'.[35] The Greek historian Nicolaus of Damascus (64 BCE–4 CE), Josephus added, spoke of 'a great mountain in Armenia, over Minyas, called Baris, upon which it is reported that many who fled at the time of the Deluge were saved; and that one who was carried in an ark came on shore upon the top of it; and that the remains of the timber were a great while preserved. This might be the man about whom Moses the legislator of the Jews wrote.'[36]

---

[32] John Warwick Montgomery, *The Quest for Noah's Ark: A Treasury of Documented Accounts from Ancient Times to the Present Day of the Ark...* (Minneapolis, MN: Bethany Fellowship, Inc., 1972), p. 73. I am indebted to Montgomery for this collection of primary sources.

[33] Lloyd R. Bailey, *Noah: The Person and the Story in History and Tradition* (Columbia: University of South Carolina Press, 1989), p. 79.

[34] *Ibid.*, p. 79.

[35] Whiston (trans.), *The Antiquities of the Jews*, bk. 1, ch. 3, para. 6, p. 33.

[36] *Ibid.* On Berossus, see Chapter 1.

A specific 'Mount Ararat' soon appeared as part of a legend that was to have many variations throughout the medieval period. The fifth-century Armenian historian Faustus of Byzantium tells us of St. Jacob of Nisibis who travelled to the mountains of Armenia, 'that is to say, to Mount Ararat in the principality of Ararat', and, nearing the summit, received from an angel a piece of wood from the ark. Upon his descent, he gave the wood to the people of the city, 'and it is preserved to this day among them as the visible sign of the Ark of the patriarch Noah'.[37] In the sixth century, Isidore of Seville remarked that 'Ararat is a mountain in Armenia, where the historians testify that the Ark came to rest after the Flood. So even to this day wood remains of it are to be seen there.'[38]

Islamic traditions were also to enter into the issue of the location of the ark. The Qur'an, we recall, has Noah praying that God will bring him 'to a blessed landing place' (Qur'an 23.29) before the ark came to rest on al-Jūdī (or Cudi). In the period after the founding of Islam up to the end of the first millennium, there was a general agreement among Muslims, Christians, and Jews that the mountain referred to in the Qur'an was the peak now called Cudi Dag (Mount Cudi), within the borders of ancient Armenia. Thus, for example, the Arab geographer al-Mas'udi (d. 956) had the ark resting on Mount al-Judi at the head waters of the Tigris River. Similarly, the tenth-century Arab traveller ibn Hawqal identified Mount Judi as near Nisibin in the same region (reflecting

---

[37] John Warwick Montgomery, *The Quest for Noah's Ark*, p. 68.
[38] *Ibid.*, pp. 75–76.

the Christian tradition that associated the ark with St. Jacob of Nisibis).

The location of the ark in Armenia was also a commonplace within medieval Christianity. Eutychius (877–940), the Orthodox Patriarch of Alexandria, declared that 'the ark rested on the mountains of Ararat, that is, Jabal Judi near Mosul'.[39] The encyclopedist Vincent of Beauvais (c.1184–1264) knew the story of Jacob of Nisibin or at least a variant of it. He told of a city in Armenia near Mount Ararat, where Noah's ark rests, at the foot of which is the city called Laudume built by Noah. He then recounted the story of the monk who, having finally reached the summit of Ararat, 'brought one of the beams from the Ark back with him. At the foot of the mountain, he then built a monastery in which he faithfully placed this same beam as (so to speak) a holy relic.'[40] The location of the ark in Armenia was a tradition that lasted into the thirteenth century. Thus, for example, the monk Jehan Hayton wrote of a mountain in Armenia by the name of Ararat, the highest in the world, upon which the ark of Noah landed. Because of the quantity of snow all year round, no one could climb it. But at the summit, 'a great black object is always visible, which is said to be the Ark of Noah'.[41]

At least by the thirteenth century, the focus of attention for the location of the ark had moved northwards from

---

[39] Bailey, *Noah*, p. 67.
[40] Montgomery, *The Quest for Noah's Ark*, p. 77.
[41] *Ibid.*, p. 78. On Hayton, see Roubina Shnorhokian, 'Hayton of Korykos and *La Flor des Estoires*: Cilician Armenian Mediation in Crusader-Mongol Politics, c. 1250–1350,' Doctor of Philosophy thesis, Queen's University, 2015.

Mount Cudi or Judi to another 'Mount Ararat' – to the mountain known as Agri Dag (Mount Agri) in Eastern Turkey. The Franciscan traveller William of Rubruck (c.1214–c.1270), on a mission on behalf of Louis IX of France to the Mongol emperor Möngke Khan, was the first European to identify Mount Agri as the site of the ark. Near the city of Naxua, he wrote, 'are mountains in which they say that Noah's ark rests … and there is a town there called Cemamum, which interpreted means "eight", and they say that it was thus called from the eight persons who came out of the ark, and who built it'.[42] William then went on to tell the story of Jacob of Nisibin as Faustus of Byzantium had reported it. Until the nineteenth century, Mount Agri and Mount Cudi would compete as the two likeliest places for the site of the ark. Each mountain has a tradition of the ark, floating northwards, having stopped temporarily elsewhere; each was the site of a monastery connected with the ark story; and each has a grave of Noah nearby.[43]

There were many possible locations of the ark, tales of ascents, accounts of wood retrieved from it, and towns built by the first family nearby. And there was no shortage of mountains to suggest themselves as the site of the ark's coming to rest. Yet, as Lloyd Bailey notes, no one claimed to have seen the ark, to have visited the landing site, or to have spoken directly with someone who had.[44] Thus, for example, early in the eighteenth century, the French traveller Jean Chardin (1643–1713) told his readers, 'Twelves leagues to the east of Erivan [in Armenia] one sees the

[42] Montgomery, *The Quest for Noah's Ark*, p. 82.
[43] Bailey, *Noah*, pp. 78–79.   [44] See *ibid.*, p. 81.

famous mountain where almost everyone agrees that Noah's ark landed – though no one offers solid proof of it.'[45] Perhaps Chardin also heard of the Armenian legend that Noah, while looking in the direction of Erivan, exclaimed 'Yerevats!' ('it appeared!'). Chardin, like others before him, went on to tell the story of Jacob of Nibilis receiving a piece of the ark from an angel.

The variety of locations was, no doubt, due to the *religious* importance of the site of the ark. In the scheme of Christian history, its location was as crucial as that of the garden of Eden. For where the ark landed was the point on earth closest to heaven; it was a cosmic centre from which human civilisation had begun again, and it was a site where relics of the ark were to be discovered, revealed, kept, and treasured. In the nineteenth century, however, the location of the ark became a matter of scientific exploration, and the quest for hard evidence seriously began. The search for the lost ark on Mount Agri (now identified with Mount Ararat) began in earnest, and the first 'eyewitness' accounts began to emerge. The first ascent to the summit was by the German explorer Johann Friedrich Parrott and five others (1791–1841) in 1829. Parrott reported that the summit contained sufficient space for the ark to have landed upon it, 'three hundred ells [cubits] long and fifty wide, would not have occupied a tenth part of the surface of this depression'.[46] However, he reported, while the ark may well have landed there, the snow and ice that began to cover the ark after

---

45  *Ibid.*, p. 101.
46  Friedrich Parrott, *Journey to Ararat* (New York: Harper & Brothers Publishers, 1859), p. 192.

the flood was sufficient to cover it from sight. Before beginning their descent, 'we gladly poured a libation to the Patriarch Noah'.[47]

Later ascents announced greater fortune. In 1876, the intrepid English holiday-maker James Bryce (1838–1922) found a piece of wood some 4,000 feet below the summit, four feet long, five inches thick, and clearly shaped by a tool. While he recognised that its presence there might have another explanation, he did not wish to discredit his own relic. The argument that it was a piece of the ark, he declared, was exceptionally strong: '[T]he Crusaders who found the Holy Lance at Antioch, the archbishop who recognised the Holy Coat at Treves, not to speak of many others, proceeded upon slighter evidence.'[48] Actually, perhaps, that was not really saying very much.

Mount Ararat provided fertile soil for charlatans. John Joseph was 'Prince of Nouri', 'Grand-Archdeacon of Babylon', and 'Episcopal Head of the Nestorian Church of Malabar'. The Christian missionary Frederick G. Coan (1859–1943) reported on his encounter with Joseph in the early twentieth century in Tehran. According to Coan, Joseph had succeeded in reaching the summit of Mount Ararat on his third attempt. There he had seen the ark, wedged in the rocks, and covered with snow and ice. He had made careful measurements that, he claimed, coincided exactly with those in Genesis. Coan was unpersuaded. As he admits, his question to Joseph whether 'he

---

[47] *Ibid.*, p. 198.
[48] James Bryce, *Transcaucasia and Ararat being Notes of a Vacation Tour in the Autumn of 1876* (London: Macmillan and Co., 1896), p. 281.

saw Mrs. Noah's corset hanging up in her bedroom' was rather mean-spirited.[49]

A conspiracy theory, wrapped in 'fake news', on the discovery of the ark appeared in the Los Angeles' *New Eden Magazine* in 1940 under the title "Noah's Ark Found' by a Russian aviator Vladimir Roskovitsky. According to this, Roskovitsky saw the ark on Mount Ararat from the air just before the Russian Revolution. It was a strange craft, he wrote, 'built as though the designer expected the waves to roll over the top most of the time'. He and his co-pilot reported their find on their return. Their captain told them it was Noah's ark, 'sitting up there for nearly five thousand years', and duly reported it to the Russian government. The Czar sent 150 soldiers to investigate. They found the ark and took measurements and photographs of a ship containing hundreds of small rooms, some very large with high ceilings 'as though designed to hold beasts ten times as large as elephants'. Above the ship they found a rough, stone hearth 'like the altars the Hebrews use for sacrifices'. Unfortunately, a few days after this expedition sent its report to the Czar, 'the government was overthrown and godless Bolshevism took over, so that the records were never made public and probably were destroyed in the zeal of the Bolsheviks to discredit all religion and belief in the truth of the Bible'.[50]

This was not the last occasion on which photographic evidence went missing. According to a later account, in

---

[49] Frederick G. Coan, *Yesterdays in Persia and Kurdistan* (Claremont, CA: Saunders Studio Press, 1939), p. 165.

[50] Rene Noorbergen, *The Ark File* (Mountain View, CA: Pacific Press Publishing Association, 1974), pp. 85–87. This work contains a full account of this story; see pp. 82–96.

the late summer of 1952, mining engineer George Jefferson Greene, on an exploration of Ararat, saw a strange object protruding from the ice. '"The Ark!" was Greene's first startled thought.' Back in the United States, on examination of the photographs that he had taken, he became more and more convinced that he had found the ark. Unable to raise an expedition to return to Ararat, he left for British Guyana where, in 1962, he was murdered. None of his possessions, including the ark photographs, were ever recovered. Fortunately, he had shown them to an acquaintance, Fred Drake. And fortunately, Drake remembered the photographs of the ark sufficiently well to draw some sketches of it that he sent to real estate agent and well-known arkeologist Eryl A. Cummings. In the attached letter, he told Cummings that the further discovery of it on Ararat 'will be the most important discovery that the modern world has ever known'.[51] That was true. But nothing more ever came of it.

On one occasion, a hoax became clear. In February 1993, the television special entitled 'The Incredible Discovery of Noah's Ark' was broadcast to 20 million viewers.[52] Without ever saying so, it was undoubtedly sympathetic to the young earth creationist view. In the program, a George Jammal told how he had discovered the snow-covered location of Noah's ark on Mount Ararat. He displayed what he claimed to be a piece of

---

[51] Montgomery, *The Quest for Noah's Ark*, pp. 121–124. The letter appears in a photograph of Drake's drawing on p. 123.

[52] Henning Schellerup, 'The Incredible Discovery of Noah's Ark' (1992). Available at https://archive.org/details/the-incredible-discovery-of-noahs-ark-1992. The Jammal segment has been edited out of this version.

wood from the ark that he had hacked from it. 'This piece of wood is so precious – and a gift from God.' Having entered the ark, he said, 'We got very excited when we saw part of this room was made into pens, like places where you keep animals,' he recalled. 'We knew then that we had found the ark!' In October of the same year, Jammal, an out-of-work actor living in California, admitted that his story was a hoax. The 'sacred wood' from the ark was in fact a piece of California pine that he had hardened by cooking it in a mixture of blueberry and almond wine, iodine, sweet-and-sour barbecue sauce, and teriyaki sauce.[53] He had never been to Turkey, he admitted. 'They should have asked me,' he said in 2007, 'why Noah's ark smelled like teriyaki sauce.'[54]

This story has its own long history. It began on 1 November 1985 when Jammal wrote in jest to Duane Gish, then president of The Institute for Creation Research, telling Gish that, on his third trip to Turkey in search of the ark, he and his companion Vladimir

---

[53] See Daniel Cerone, 'Admitting "Noah's Ark" Hoax: Television: A man who claimed on a CBS special to have located the ark now says it was a set up,' *Los Angeles Times*, 30 October 1993.
  Available at www.latimes.com/archives/la-xpm-1993-10-30-ca-51222-story.html.
  See also Jim Lippard, 'Sun goes down in Flames: The Jammal Ark Hoax,' *Skeptic* 2 (1993). Available at www.talkorigins.org/faqs/ark-hoax/jammal.html, and Leon Jaroff, 'Phony Arkaeology,' *Time*, 5 July 1993.
  Available at https://content.time.com/time/subscriber/article/0,33009,978812-1,00.html.
[54] George Jammal, 'Hoaxing the Hoaxers: or, The incredible (phony) Discovery of Noah's Ark,' *Atheist Alliance*, 11 September 2007. Available at https://web.archive.org/web/20070911024306/http://atheistalliance.org/library/jammal-hoaxing.php.

crawled into an ice cave which proved to be the ark. Each chipped off a piece of wood to prove what they had found. Unfortunately, Jammal's companion fell into a crevasse, along with his piece of wood and photographic proof, and was killed. On 10 June 1986, creation scientist John D. Morris (1946–2023), son of Henry Morris, interviewed Jammal who had, by then, read up on the search for the lost ark, on Mount Ararat and surrounding regions, and had watched the videotape of the precursor to 'The Incredible Discovery of Noah's Ark' – the 1976 production 'In Search of Noah's Ark'. Jammal failed to show Morris his piece of the ark, and Morris was uncertain about the truth of it all.

However, in 1992, Morris gave Jammal's name to Sun International Pictures, the producers of these ark programs. By this time, Jammal had become acquainted with the Religious Studies scholar Gerald Larue (1916–2014) from the University of Southern California. Believing that he had been badly treated in an earlier Sun production, Larue came in on the hoax. Sun International Pictures took the bait, and the program went to air with Jammal's fake story included. Jammal's story was part of a program filled, wrote Leon Jaroff of *Time*, 'with a mixture of fact, conjecture, fantasy, and arrant nonsense, while offering no clues as to which was which' – a harsh but fair judgement.[55]

During the twentieth century, for conservative evangelical Christianity, the search for the lost ark became the religious equivalent of the hunt for the Loch Ness monster. For the most part, the sincerity of those involved in

[55] Jaroff, 'Phony Arkaeology.'

the search cannot be doubted. However, without engaging in a finely grained analysis of every supposed 'find', and putting hoaxes aside, the accounts of ark sightings or pieces of wood discovered on Mount Ararat have been unpersuasive, photographic evidence of the ark mysteriously disappearing has been questionable, and aerial or satellite photography of it unconvincing.[56] Thus, with hard evidence still absent, even among those predisposed to believe in the presence of the ark on Mount Ararat, it has become more a matter of faith than of knowledge. And searchers live more in hope than in expectation.

In 1961, after 130 years of ascents to the summit, the founders of creation science, John Whitcomb and Henry Morris, admitted that discoveries of the ark on Mount Ararat have never been confirmed and 'any hope of its preservation for the thousands of years of post-diluvian history is merely wishful thinking'.[57] The Baptist conservative Timothy F. LaHaye (1926–2106) and John D. Morris, in their survey of the history of the search for the ark on Ararat, declared that the discovery of the ark would 'ring the death knell to the already fragile theory of evolution' and lead the world to realise 'that the Bible is true'.[58] But despite the paucity of the evidence, they could do little more in the end than assert their unwavering determination to believe, quite simply because they believed in the inerrancy of the Bible.

---

[56] See Montgomery, *The Quest for Noah's Ark*.

[57] Whitcomb and Morris, *The Genesis Flood*, pp. 87–88, n. 1.

[58] Tim F. LaHaye and John D. Morris, *The Ark on Ararat* (Nashville, TN and New York: Thomas Nelson Inc. Publishers and Creation-Life Publishers, 1976), 4. LaHaye is best known for his ten-volume 'Left Behind' series.

By 2015, John D. Morris had travelled to Ararat over a dozen times. But, he declared unhappily in that same year, 'we never found the Ark'.[59] Creation science now appears to have given up the quest. 'Despite so many supposed sightings and evidences over the years,' concluded Tim Chaffey on 'Answers in Genesis', a creation science website, 'it seems unlikely that Noah's Ark has been found in recent times. And even though we would be ecstatic if the Ark were discovered, we have reason to doubt that it will be found in the future.'[60] Unlike other legends in which a ship carries the hero in search of an object of desire, the quest here was for the ship itself. This quest was an admittedly fruitless and unsuccessful one.

## Creators of the Lost Ark

On 7 July 2016, the 'Ark Encounter' opened in Williamstown, Kentucky. It was a date (seventh day of the seventh month) chosen to correspond to Genesis 7.7: 'And Noah with his sons and his wife, and his sons' wives went into the ark to escape the waters of the flood.' Its showpiece is a 'replica' of the ark of Noah, built (more or less) to Biblical measurements, five hundred and ten feet

[59] John D. Morris, *Noah's Ark: Adventures on Ararat* (Dallas, TX: Institute for Creation Research, 2014), p. 35.
[60] Tim Chaffey, 'Has the Ark been Found?,' *Answers in Genesis* website. Available at https://answersingenesis.org/noahs-ark/noahs-ark-found/has-ark-been-found/?aigcb = 9218. Chaffey gives an excellent summary of five recent supposed sites of the ark, concluding that none of them are persuasive. These five sites are: the Durupinar site; the Ahora Gorge; the Ararat Anomaly; Ararat – NAMI Expedition; and Mount Suleiman. He even goes as far as to reject Mount Agri as the location of the ark.

long, eighty-five feet wide, and fifty-one feet high (based on a 'royal cubit' of 20.4 inches). It is constructed, not of 'cyprus wood' (Genesis 6.14) but of New Zealand pine with uprights of Engelmann spruce. Its base is made of concrete and is not therefore intended to survive another of the divine's watery whimsies. It contains some 132 bays, each about 18 feet high spread over three decks, with a volume of 1.88 million cubic feet, 'enough to contain 450 semi-truck trailers'.[61] The Encounter Ark is an extraordinary feat of modern design and construction and is, at the time of writing, the world's largest free-standing timber frame structure. The building of this ark is both a homage to the Bible's offering of a 'blueprint' of the ark and a making-real of the literal truth of the Genesis text.

But there is another agenda for the Kentucky Ark creators. They want to use the Ark Encounter experience to validate the respectability of young earth creationism by showing how to reconcile fossil evidence and the variety of animal species, among other phenomena, with a Biblical chronology. To this end, the Ark Encounter adopts a 'methodological naturalism' according to which science proceeds *as if* the supernatural does not exist while accepting that it may. They vehemently reject 'metaphysical naturalism' according to which science simply rejects the possible existence of the supernatural. 'Methodological naturalism', on the other hand, enables the Ark Encounter to use carefully selected science to show the validity of the Biblical young earth creation

---

[61] [Tim Chaffey and Mike Belknap], *Ark Signs That Teach a Flood of Answers* (Green Forest, AR: Master Books, 2017), p. 6.

model, leaving the possibility of God's activity in the world in place.

The Ark Encounter is the result of a partnership between the young earth creationist group, 'Answers in Genesis', and the 'Ark Encounter LLC'. Its intention is to 'lend credence to the Biblical account of a catastrophic flood and to dispel doubts that Noah could have fit two of every kind of animal onto a 500-foot-long ark'.[62] While the Ark Encounter recognises over two hundred myths from around the world about a major flood, 'the true account,' it declares, 'was recorded by Moses' in the book of Genesis. The people who dispersed from the Tower of Babel passed on their knowledge of the Biblical flood. Thus, other flood myths are 'retellings of the real event that have been distorted through centuries of passing down information'.[63]

Within the Kentucky ark, through text, music and animal sounds, art, sculptures, interior settings, and interactive animatronics figures, a new legend of Noah is created. This new legend is based on the Biblical account. But the story in Genesis is read through the theology of creation science and its commitment to the young earth, as filtered through the 'Answers in Genesis' organisation. Thus, the Kentucky ark draws on non-Biblical sources to create a back story to the Biblical account.

In particular, the back story to the life of Noah, up to the time of the flood, is provided by the three-volume

---

[62]   Roger Alford, 'Full-scale replica of Noah's Ark planned in Kentucky,' *USA Today*, 3 December 2010.

[63]   Anon., 'Other Flood Traditions.' *Ark Encounter*.
       Available at https://arkencounter.com/noahs-ark/.

fictional account of Noah in the 'The Remnant Trilogy' by Tim Chaffey and K. Marie Adams. This trilogy provides much of the content for many of the exhibits of the pre-flood world in the Ark Encounter. As a result, in creating the exhibits within the Ark Encounter, as its (fortuitously named) founder Ken Ham and its content manager Tim Chaffey admit, much 'arktistic licence' was taken, imaginatively to fill in the gaps in the Biblical story and create their new legend of Noah and the flood.

The new legend of Noah that is reflected in the Ark Encounter begins with the creation of the world in six days, some 6,000 years ago. Initially everything was good.[64] But Adam and Eve rebelled against God and thus brought suffering, disease, bloodshed, and death into the world. As their descendants multiplied, the world became an exceedingly wicked place (pretty much, the Ark Encounter creators suggest, like the world outside of the Ark Encounter today). Pagan worship of a serpentine god resulted in polygamy, child sacrifice, and ritual prostitution. People were sacrificed in the arena to giants and prehistoric animals. Even music and metalworking were used for immoral purposes. It was a culture filled with violence and obsessed with death. Men lived only for pleasure in orgies of 'wine, women, and song', we might

---

[64] This legend is drawn primarily from Tim Chaffey and K. Marie Adams, 'The Remnant Trilogy' (*Noah: Man of Destiny, Noah: Man of Resolve,* and *Noah: Man of God,* [Tim Chaffey and Mike Belknap], *Ark Signs: That Teach a Flood of Answers* (Green Forest, AR: Master Books, 2017), [Tim Chaffey and Mike Belknap] *Journey Through the Ark Encounter* (Green Forest, AR: Master Books, 2017). This last volume records the signs within the Ark Encounter. The *Answers in Genesis* website provided further information.

say. Noah held to the original belief in the one true God, as did his wife, his sons, and their wives. So, God judged the world by destroying it with a global flood but mercifully saved Noah's family and the animals on board the ark.

Filling out the above outline, we find, in the final chapter of the first volume of the trilogy, that Noah and his wife Emzara board the ark in order to flee a demonic serpent God whose idol is revealed 'Coated in shimmering gold from its coiled base to its terrifying face, poised as if ready to strike, the towering statue of the Great Deceiver dominated the massive stage.'[65] A version of the serpent idol is shown in the following exhibits: 'The Pre-Flood World' (second deck), 'Who was Noah? (second deck), and 'Flood Geology' (third deck).

In chapter twenty-three of volume two, Naamah, the daughter of Cainite King Lamech of Kalneh, announces the institution of sacred prostitution as a feature of the pre-flood world.[66] 'We've learned,' declares Naamah to the crowd, 'that Nachash [the serpent god] is pleased when one of his followers engages in an act of sacred union with one of his priestesses.' Emzara leans close to Noah. 'I think I'm going to be sick.' Noah nods.[67] 'The

---

[65] Tim Chaffey and K. Marie Adams, *Noah: Man of Destiny* (Green Forest, AR: Master Books, 2016), p. 261. 'Emzara' is the name of Noah's wife in the Book of Jubilees. See Chapter 1.

[66] 'Naamah' is mentioned in Genesis as a descendant of Cain, the daughter of Lamech, and the sister of Tubal-cain. Interestingly, 'Naamah' is common within Rabbinic Judaism as the wife of Noah. See Utley, 'The One Hundred and Three Names of Noah's Wife,' p. 432.

[67] Tim Chaffey and K. Marie Adams, *Noah: Man of Resolve* (Green Forest, AR: Master Books, 2017), p. 164.

Pre-Flood World' exhibit shows people about to take part in ritual prostitution.

In chapter thirty-three of the same volume, after Noah is arrested for refusing to worship the serpent god, he finds himself facing death in an arena. 'People of Iri Geshem,' he declares, 'Nachash is the Great Deceiver and the old stories are true. Just as he tricked our Greatmother Eve, he has misled the world, and now you, into following him.'[68] Noah is confronted with a 'grendec' (based on a Carnotaurus, a smaller version of a Tyrannosaurus Rex). 'Perched more than eight cubits in the air, the gaping maw displayed dozens of long bony daggers ... Two absurdly small arms dangled from its torso, while brown and gray scales rippled over unbelievably powerful leg muscles ... Noah stared in wonder at the mighty creature, but remained calm. *Almost too calm.*'[69] As we recall, 'The Nephilim [giants] were on the earth in those days' (Genesis 6.4). And, along with the grendec, Noah was confronted in the arena by a giant warrior. 'The Pre-Flood World' exhibit features a large diorama picturing this dinosaur and the giant in the arena of Iri Geshem. Dinosaurs are plentiful in the Ark Encounter. Thus, for example, the starboard side of the lowest deck contains sculpted dinosaurs such as pterosaurs and scutosaurs 'that have gone extinct since the Flood'.[70] And here we begin to see the creators of the Ark Encounter setting out to reconcile the age of the dinosaurs, some 250–66 million years ago, with a

---

[68] *Ibid.*, p. 230.    [69] *Ibid.*
[70] [Chaffey and Belknap], *Journey Through the Ark Encounter*, p. 16. The physical appearance of the giant is based on the designer Tim Chaffey.

Biblical chronology of the world that, according to their estimates, began some 6,000 years ago.

Finally, amongst many more crossovers between 'The Remnant Trilogy' and 'The Ark Encounter', we find, in the last chapter of volume three, the herding of the last of the animals, two giant pigs, into the ark, as Naamah and hundreds, if not thousands, of soldiers arrive as the flood begins. After Noah's and the family's narrow escape into the ark, God miraculously closes the door of the ark with them safely inside. The sounds from outside are dampened – 'An array of animal sounds within the ark overpowered the muffled screams, wind, torrential rain, and thunder.'[71] Noah asks Shem to put the pigs away and then join the rest of the family in prayer in the sitting room. Emzara reminds Noah that it was all as God had told him: 'Still hurting from the heightened awareness that everyone outside the ark would soon be gone, but thankful for God's mercy to him and his family, Noah nods and pulls Emzara close again. "Another reminder that we can always trust the Creator."'[72] And, with those words, 'The Remnant Trilogy' ends. This closing scene in 'The Remnant Trilogy' is depicted at the end of the 'First Floor Show' of the Ark Encounter. For visitors, this is the first encounter with Noah's family.

The legend of the Ark Encounter continues with Noah, his wife Emzara, his sons Shem, Ham, and Japheth, and their three wives on board the ark. The wives of Noah's sons are now named (quite originally), Ar'yel, Kezia, and

---

[71] Tim Chaffey and K. Marie Adams, *Noah: Man of God* (Green Forest, AR: Master Books, 2018), p. 277.

[72] *Ibid.*, p. 278.

Rayneh, respectively.[73] On the ark, as a good wife and mother, we are told, Emzara prioritised family time. But as an animal lover from her youth, she knew more about the animals than anyone else and showed her skills in caring for them and keeping notes on their well-being. Her favourite animal was the keluk, a pre-flood version of the giraffe. Ar'yel, the wife of Shem, was a convert to the true God after hearing Noah speak. She joined the family in building the ark. She loved to have discussions about God with Shem and read accounts of what life was like before the flood when it was filled with wickedness (see Plate 19). Kezia, Ham's wife, grew up around Noah's family as the ark was being built. She is the medical expert in the family, having learned her skills from her mother. When her parents left her to pursue other interests, she grew up among Noah's family. Ham and Kezia grew close as she cared for the wounds he received from an animal attack, leaving his face permanently scarred. Japheth's wife Rayneh also grew up with Noah's family, helping Japheth with his farming. She was the artistic one in the family, making pots and painting intricate designs on them. She worked closely with Emzara, sketching the animals on the ark while studying and recording their habits. In addition, during the construction of the ark, she created many of the clothes and tapestries on board. To its credit, the Ark Encounter gives roles to the wife of Noah and the wives of his sons. They emerge from their

[73] In the history of the Noachic traditions, the sons' wives have been variously named. These three names are new to the tradition.
On earlier traditions of the sons' wives, see Utley, 'The One Hundred and Three Names of Noah's Wife.'

invisibility in the Genesis story, if only to fill 'traditional' female roles on the ark.

According to this legend, we are all descended from Adam, then from Noah, and then from Noah's sons and their wives. On this monogenetic account, we are all members of one human race. Thus, there is no Biblical justification for slavery. Sadly we are told, 'some professing Christians have misused passages from the Bible to spread racist ideas, such as slavery based on a person's skin tone or the notion that "interracial" marriage is sinful'.[74] Noah and his wife had 'middle-brown skin', and their children could genetically have 'exhibited the whole range of skin tones from light to dark' within a few generations.[75] The descendants of Shem and Ar'yel, Ham and Kezia, Japheth and Rayneh were eventually to populate the world.[76]

That said, the descendants of Noah refused to follow God's command to multiply and fill the earth, happy to multiply but not so keen on filling. They gathered on the plain of Shinar (Genesis 11.2) and decided to build a city with a tower that reached to the heavens (Genesis 11.1-4). Because the people refused to disperse as ordered, God confused their language. From the confusion of language at Babel have arisen the ninety language families that have since evolved. Metals that were available before the flood had to be rediscovered and advances in technology reinvented for: '[A]s the various people groups scattered

---

[74] [Chaffey and Belnap], *Ark Signs*, p. 101.  [75] *Ibid.*, p. 101.
[76] There are suggestions in the literature around the Ark Encounter that Africans and Asians were the descendants of Ham. With its strong anti-racist messaging, the Ark Encounter does not specify who came from which son.

from that place, scientific achievements and technological advancements came slowly since most people spent their time struggling to meet their basic needs, such as food and shelter.'[77]

Another aspect of the legend of the Ark Encounter is its appropriation of 'scientific' thinking to explain some difficulties for Biblical inerrancy that science itself might have seemed to produce. One problem is the adequacy of the ark, despite its size, to accommodate all the terrestrial species that we know about today. This is resolved in an interesting way, via a distinction between 'kinds' and 'species', supplemented by a fast-tracked process of evolution after the flood. Thus, according to the Ark Encounter, Noah needed to bring only land-dependent animals onto the ark, fish, insects, and other invertebrates surviving outside of it. And he needed to embark only 'two of every kind' ('min' in Hebrew) along with birds, seven pair of clean animals, and one pair of unclean animals (Genesis 6.19-20). 'Kind' was a much broader category than 'species'. Thus, Noah did not have to fit two of every species on the ark. Only two of each kind or family of animals were necessary. From these would later develop the many modern species of animals that have survived to this day, along with those that have become extinct.[78] Thus, a representative pair of ancestors to all later species were on the ark – the Felid (cat) kind, the Alligator kind, the Pongid (great ape) kind, the Rhinoceros kind (formerly thought to be unicorns), the

---

[77] [Chaffey and Belknap], *Ark Signs*, p. 114.

[78] 'Family' is loosely defined in terms of the ability to breed with each other. Thus, for example, dogs are a kind.

Thylacosmilid kind (now extinct), and so on. So, although there are some 34,000 land-dependent vertebrate species today, Noah then had to care, by Ark Encounter estimates, for 1,398 animal kinds (thus, give or take a few, 2,796 animals) on board.[79]

Crucially, for the sake of a young earth account of creation, the Ark Encounter is willing to build a super-fast version of evolution into its account of biological origins, one in keeping with 'the mercy, creativity, and foresight of the Creator'.[80] In short, a young earth and flood geology matter more than the conservative tradition of opposition to *any accommodation* with the Darwinian account of the evolution of species. All this, however, with the exclusion of one species – the humans – which was a divine creation some 6,000 years ago, 1,500 years before the flood: 'The Bible is clear that God made man from the dust of the ground, and woman was made from his rib. There are no ape-like creatures in our ancestry.'[81]

After the flood, the animals that exited from the ark developed into different species within kinds: Species gave rise to new species, characteristics were modified over time, and the fittest animals survived. Since the flood, therefore, large numbers of species of animals have become extinct. In short, animals developed to the number of species within the world today by natural selection, mutations, and other natural mechanisms. This has happened within the very short period of time since the universal flood. Thus, despite the 150 years of

---

[79] Within Ark Encounter literature, the numbers occasionally differ, from around 2,800 to 6,800.
[80] [Chaffey and Belknap], *Ark Signs*, p. 31.      [81] *Ibid.*, p. 119.

conflict between the Biblical account of creation and the Darwinian theory of evolution, the Ark Encounter accepts evolution and natural selection as the major cause of the multiplication of animal species, along with the extinction of many of them (including the dinosaurs). In short, this is Darwinian evolution but within a young earth chronology – a genuinely original harmonising of evolution and the Bible.

Noah and his family were easily able to look after this number of animals, not least because of the high levels of technology that had developed since the time of Adam: The longer life spans before the flood 'enabled innovators and inventors to collaborate for decades, or even centuries, to produce sophisticated technologies'.[82] The ark contained complex technologies to care for the animals on board – automated smart feeders to allow animals to eat and drink at will, slotted floors with angled trays beneath to allow animal waste to be easily collected at the bottom of the stack, clay pots with water within to enable reptiles and amphibians to be held in a moist environment, and central cribs to house moths that would allow them to climb directly into the clay pots. Fortunately, many animals were not such picky eaters back then – koalas, vampire bats, and anteaters had wider diets than their modern descendants. Wave power was utilised to pump air through the ark, aided by convection currents within. Both oil lamps and light through sky-lights at the top of the ark provided lighting. Clean water was funnelled from the roof into large storage tanks with a

---

[82] *Ibid.*, p. 111.

system of spigots and bamboo (or even copper) pipes to deliver water from these to the ark.[83]

The animals, 85 per cent of which weighed 22 pounds or less, were held in 22 extra-large cages, 186 large, 293 medium, 174 small, 308 cages for birds, and 415 for amphibians. The ark was sufficiently large for many more animals than this. But even for this number of animals, 322,400 gallons of water needed to be stored and captured, while there were 15,000 storage vessels for food. Carnivores on the ark were catered for with preserved meat prepared for them beforehand. Noah and his family were vegetarians until after the flood, so meat, fresh or otherwise, was not a problem for them. The eight persons on board were sufficient to manage ark maintenance – three to clean the cages; two to water and feed the animals; half to shovel waste from pit to pump; one and a half to manage laundry, human waste, maintenance, and animal care; and one to deal with human food and special diets.

After a year, the world before the flood was completely ruined. Land animals were progressively destroyed and buried in the rapidly accumulating layers of sediment on the submerged land masses, which eventually led to their fossilisation. Mountain ranges were forced up from these submerged land masses, which would eventually be filled with fossil remains (and misguided judgements about their age by later old earth geologists). The highest hills were covered by water to a depth of fifteen cubits (greater than twenty-two feet). Eventually, the ark came to rest 'on

[83] These technologies are only presented as possibilities in the Ark Encounter.

one of the newly formed mountains in the region of Ararat' but not on Mount Ararat.[84] The Ark Encounter, like Creation Science more generally, has given up on Mount Ararat (Agri) as the site of the lost ark. Approximately one year after boarding, Noah, his family, and the animals left the ark.

From the one continent before the flood, seven new continents were created. After the flood, with the build-up of snow and ice on land trapping water inland, and with so much water removed from the ocean, sea levels were hundreds of feet lower. This enabled land bridges from one continent to another, across which the animals spread to the new lands. They also reached distant shores by swimming, floating on debris, and with people on boats.

According to the young earth Ark Encounter, all the fossil evidence points to a universal flood some 4,500 years ago, not the millions of years of old earth geology. And it has no interest in harmonising Biblical chronology with old earth geology. 'In a misguided attempt,' we read, 'to blend Biblical teaching with the popular idea that the earth is millions of years old, some Christians have invented imaginative ways to reinterpret the Bible's creation account. However, every concept they have developed, such as the gap theory, progressive creationism, the framework hypothesis, and the day-age theory, is littered with problems.'[85] Only flood geology can make sense of the scientific evidence available.

That said, in repeatedly attempting to demonstrate through scientific evidence the truth of the Biblical

[84] [Chaffey and Belknap], *Ark Signs*, p. 65.    [85] *Ibid.*, p. 81.

account of Noah and the ark, the overall theological purpose of this new legend of Noah becomes clear. In the time of Noah, the world was destroyed by a flood sent by God. The rainbow is a reminder that it will never again be destroyed by a worldwide deluge. Next time, the world will be destroyed by fire. Rescue from the judgement of God at the final end of the world will then only be for those who have found refuge from the world in Jesus Christ.

Thus, despite its commitment to the literal reading of the story of Noah and the flood, the Ark Encounter looks to the deeper meaning of the story of the flood in the Christian allegorical tradition of the interpretation of it. The ultimate purpose of the Ark Encounter is thus a theological one. The door through which Noah, his family, and the animals entered the ark in the Ark Encounter is illuminated by a cross. 'The Ark's door reminds us,' we are told, 'that we need to go through a door to be saved. Jesus Christ is our one door to salvation, the "Ark" is our door to salvation, the "Ark" that saves us from God's judgment for eternity.'[86] For good or ill, for the Ark Encounter, the meaning of the story of Noah and the flood is to be found in the next life rather than in this one.

---

[86] *Ibid.*, p. 57.

# EPILOGUE: A LEGEND FOR OUR TIME

~

For the last two thousand years and more, the story of
Noah and the flood in the book of Genesis has been
thought of as an historical account of what happened
around 2,500 BCE, some 1,500 years after the creation of
the world. For the last several hundred years, for many, as
we have seen, it has become the stuff of myth and legend,
but not of history, as the intellectual foundations upon
which its truth was grounded began to crumble.

But whatever the many imaginings and re-imaginings
of this story as history or myth over the past millennia, its
meaning is, overall, a simple one. The earth and all living
things upon it were once destroyed by a cataclysmic climate event brought about by human wickedness. With
the exception of Noah and his family, humanity then was
unredeemable and not worth saving. It is hard to think of
a legend in Western thought that has greater relevance in
the present moment than that of Noah and the flood. For
once again, the earth is faced with cataclysmic climate
disaster brought about by human wrongdoing.

The environmental disaster that the world currently
faces is the central theme of Darren Aronofsky's film
*Noah* (2014). The world that Noah inhabits in this film
is a highly enchanted one. But its message is for a modern
disenchanted world. For Aronofsky, the original earth was
a paradisal place. In the beginning there was nothing,
declares Noah – 'Nothing but the silence of an infinite

darkness.' But out of nothing, God created the world – 'our beautiful fragile home'.

As the days of the first week of creation passed, and the land emerged from the seas, there was a thick blanket of green stretching across all creation, and the waters teemed with life with vast multitudes of fish. Soon the sky was streaming with birds. And then the whole world became full of living beings. Everything was clean and unspoiled. Aronofsky's is the vision of a world that has an intrinsic spiritual value, beyond any instrumental benefit it may provide to humans.

Until the creation of man and woman, the earth was a paradise. But after Adam and Eve followed the temptation of the serpent, this paradisal world was destroyed by human wickedness. Noah and his family lived in a barren wasteland where the cities were dead, refugees abounded, and violence against women, children, and animals ruled. As Noah explains to his family,

> And all was in balance. It was paradise. A jewel in the Creator's palm. Then the Creator made Man. And by his side, Woman. Father and mother of us all. He gave them a choice. Follow the temptation of darkness or hold on to the blessing of light. But they ate from the forbidden fruit. Their innocence was extinguished. And so, for the ten generations since Adam, sin has walked with us. Brother against brother. Nation against nation. Man against Creation. We murdered each other. We broke the world. We did this. Man did this. Everything that was beautiful, everything that was good, we shattered.

In the story of creation in the first chapter of the Bible, God gave humanity dominion 'over the fish of the sea, and over the birds of the air, and over the cattle, and over all the wild animals of the earth' (Genesis 1.26). For Aronofsky, it was the irresponsible use of this dominion that led to the destruction of the world, except for Noah, his family, and the animals that Noah saved. For Aronofsky's Noah, people – even including himself and his family – were not worth saving. The salvation of the animals was infinitely more important than the salvation of humanity. For the well-being of earth was more likely with the destruction of all humanity rather than with its survival. Noah was thus the first environmentalist, and the first to realise that dominion over all living things meant responsibility for them and the earth they inhabit. With the animals gathered on the ark, Noah tells his son Japheth, 'All of these innocent creatures are now in our care. It's our job to look after them.' At the end of the film, Noah finally realises that humanity too, along with the animals, has been given a new beginning. The film ends with Noah's declaration that the world after the flood will again be in our care.

> The Creator made Adam in his image and placed the world in his care. That birthright was passed down to us. To my father, then to me, and to my sons Shem, Japheth, and Ham. That birthright is now passed to you, our grandchildren. This will be your work, and your responsibility. So, I say to you, be fruitful and multiply, and replenish the earth.'

In Aronofsky's *Noah*, the rainbow that follows Noah's blessing of his grandchildren is the still visible sign of the responsibility that his descendants have for the earth and all living things upon it.

In a world in which God seems no longer to be present, the future of the earth lies in our hands, as it once did in Noah's. This is the meaning of the legend of Noah for our time. Whether we are able to meet that responsibility remains to be seen.

# BIBLIOGRAPHY

Alford, Roger, 'Full-scale replica of Noah's Ark planned in Kentucky,' *USA Today*, 3 December 2010.

Allen, Don Cameron, *The Legend of Noah: Renaissance Rationalism in Art, Science, and Letters* (Urbana: University of Illinois Press, 1963).

Almond, Philip C., *Adam and Eve in Seventeenth-Century Thought* (Cambridge: Cambridge University Press, 1999).

Almond, Philip C., 'Druids, Patriarchs, and the Primordial Religion,' *Journal of Contemporary Religion* 15 (2000), pp. 379–394.

Almond, Philip C., *The Devil: A New Biography* (Ithaca, NY: Cornell University Press, 2014).

Almond, Philip C., *Afterlife: A History of Life after Death* (Ithaca, NY: Cornell University Press, 2016).

Almond, Philip C., *God: A New Biography* (London: I.B. Tauris, 2018).

Almond, Philip C., *The Antichrist: A New Biography* (Cambridge: Cambridge University Press, 2020).

Almond, Philip C., *The Buddha: Life and Afterlife between East and West* (Cambridge: Cambridge University Press, 2024).

Amihay, Aryeh, 'Noah in Rabbinic Literature,' in Michael E. Stone, Aryeh Amihay, and Vered Hillel (eds.), *Noah and His Book(s)* (Atlanta, GA: Society of Biblical Literature, 2010), pp. 193–214.

Amihay, Aryeh, and Daniel A. Machiela, 'Traditions of the Birth of Noah,' in Michael E. Stone, Aryeh Amihay, and Vered Hillel (eds.), *Noah and His Book(s)* (Atlanta, GA: Society of Biblical Literature, 2010), pp. 53–70.

Anderson, Robert T., and Terry Giles, *The Samaritan Pentateuch: An Introduction to Its Origin, History, and Significance for Biblical Studies* (Atlanta, GA: Society of Biblical Literature, 2012).

Anon., 'Other Flood Traditions.' *Ark Encounter*. Available at https://arkencounter.com/noahs-ark/.

Anon., review of George Stanley Faber, *A Dissertation on the Mysteries of the Cabiri...*, *The Edinburgh Review* 3 (1804), pp. 313–320.

Arnold, R. J., '"Learned Lumber": The Unlikely Survival of Sacred History in the Eighteenth Century,' *The English Historical Review* 125 (2010), pp. 1139–1172.

de Asúa, Miguel, and Roger French, *A New World of Animals: Early Modern Europeans on the Creatures of Iberian America* (Aldershot: Ashgate, 2005).

Babington, Gervase, *Certaine Plaine, Briefe, and Comfortable Notes upon everie Chapter of Genesis* (London, 1592).

Bailey, Lloyd R., *Noah: The Person and the Story in History and Tradition* (Columbia: University of South Carolina Press, 1989).

Baker, Mathew, *Fragments of English Shipwrightry*, Magdalene College, Cambridge University, Pepys Library, no. 2820, c.1586.

Baldwin, Samuel Davies, *Dominion: Or, the Unity and Trinity of the Human Race* (Nashville, TN: Southern Methodist Publishing House, 1858).

Barnstone, Willis, and Marvin Meyer (trans.), 'The Reality of the Rulers,' *The Gnostic Society Library: The Nag Hammadi Library*. Available at http://gnosis.org/naghamm/Hypostas-Barnstone.html.

Barr, James, 'Why the World Was Created in 4004 B.C.: Archbishop Ussher and Biblical Chronology,' *Bulletin of the John Rylands University Library of Manchester* 67 (1984–1985), pp. 575–608.

Bashir, Haroon, 'Black Excellence and the Curse of Ham: Debating Race and Slavery in the Islamic Tradition,' *ReOrient* 5 (2019), pp. 92–116.

Baum, Bruce, *The Rise and Fall of the Caucasian Race: A Political History of Racial Identity* (New York: New York University Press, 2006).

Beaumont, John, *Considerations on a Book, entituled The Theory of the Earth* (London, 1693).

Bedrosian, Robert (trans.), *Eusebius' Chronicle: Translated from Classical Armenian.* Available at https://archive.org/details/EusebiusChroniclechronicon/page/n7/mode/2up.

Bendyshe, Thomas (trans. and ed.), *On the Natural Variety of Mankind* in *The Anthropological Treatises of Johann Friedrich Blumenbach* (London: Longman, Green, Longman, Roberts, & Green, 1865).

Bendysche, Thomas, 'The History of Anthropology,' *Memoirs Read before the Anthropological Society of London* 1 (1863–1864), pp. 335–364.

Benjamins, H. S., 'The Flood in Early Christian Theology,' in Florentino Garcia Martínez and Gerard P. Luttikhuizen (eds.), *Interpretations of the Flood* (Leiden: Brill, 1998), pp. 134–149.

Bergsma, John Sietze, and Scott Walker Hahn, 'Noah's Nakedness and the Curse on Canaan (Genesis 9:20–27),' *Journal of Biblical Literature* 124 (2005). pp. 25–40.

Berman, Samuel A. (trans.), *Midrash Tanhuma-Yelammedenu: An English Translation of Genesis and Exodus...* (Hoboken, NJ: KTAV Publishing House, 1996).

Bildstein, Moshe, 'How Many Pigs Were on Noah's Ark? An Exegetical Encounter on the Nature of Impurity,' *Harvard Theological Review*, 108 (2015), pp. 448–470.

Birch, Thomas, *The History of the Royal Society of London...* (London, 1756).

Blenkinsopp, Joseph, 'The Documentary Hypothesis is in Trouble,' *Bible Review* 1 (1985), n.ps. Available at https://library.biblicalarchaeology.org/article/the-documentary-hypothesis-in-trouble.

Blenkinsopp, Joseph, *Creation, Un-creation, Re-creation: A Discursive Commentary on Genesis 1-11* (London: T. & T. Clark International, 2011).

Boeckler, Albert, *Die Regensburg-Prüfeninger Buchmalerei des XII. und XIII. Jahrhunderts* (München: Reusch, 1924).

'Books in Newton's Library,' *The Newton Project*. Available at www.newtonproject.ox.ac.uk/his-library/books-in-newtons-library.

Brakke, David, 'The Seed of Seth at the Flood: Biblical Interpretation and Gnostic Theological Reflection,' in Charles A. Bobertz and David Brakke (eds.), *Reading in Christian Communities: Essays on Interpretation in the Early Church* (Notre Dame, IN: University of Notre Dame Press, 2002), pp. 41–62.

Braude, Benjamin, 'The Sons of Noah and the Construction of Ethnic and Geographical Identities in the Medieval and Early Modern Periods,' *The William and Mary Quarterly* 54 (1997), pp. 103–142.

Braude, Benjamin, 'Cham et Noé: Race, Esclavage et Exégèse entre Islam, Judaïsme et Christianisme,' *Annales: Histoire, Sciences Sociales* 57 (2002), pp. 93–125.

Bray, Gerald L. (trans. and ed.), *Commentaries on Romans and 1-2 Corinthians: Ambrosiaster* (Downers Grove, IL: IVP Academic, 2009).

Breidbach, Olaf, and Michael T. Ghiselin, 'Athanasius Kircher (1602–1680) on Noah's Ark: Baroque "Intelligent Design" Theory,' *Proceedings of the California Academy of Sciences* 57 (2006), pp. 991–1002.

Brinner, William M. (trans.), *The History of al-Ṭabarī, Volume II: Prophets and Patriarchs* (Albany: State University of New York Press, 1987).

Brinner, William M. (trans.), *'Arā'is al-Majālis fī Qiṣaṣ al-Anbiyā'* or *'Lives of the Prophets'* as recounted by ... al-Thaʿlabī (Leiden: Brill, 2002).

Browne, Edward B. M. (trans.), *The Book Jashar, The Lost Book of the Bible* (New York: United States Publishing Company, 1876).

Browne, Janet, *The Secular Ark: Studies in the History of Biogeography* (New Haven, CT: Yale University Press, 1983).

Bryant, Jacob, *A New System; or, an Analysis of Antient Mythology* (London, 1807).

Bryce, James, *Transcaucasia and Ararat Being Notes of a Vacation Tour in the Autumn of 1876* (London: Macmillan and Co., 1896).

Buckland, William, *Vindiciae Geologicae; or the Connexion of Geology with Religion Explained, in an inaugural Lecture... May 15, 1819* (Oxford: Oxford University Press, 1820).

Buckland, William, *Geology and Mineralogy Considered with Reference to Natural Theology* (London: William Pickering, 1836).

Budge, E. A. Wallis (trans.), *The Book of the Cave of Treasures* (London: The Religious Tract Society, 1927).

Burnet, Thomas, *The Theory of the Earth...* (London, 1684).

Burnet, Thomas, *The Sacred Theory of the Earth* (London: Centaur Press, 1965).

Burstein, Stanley Mayer, *The 'Babylonaica' of Berossus* (Malibu, CA: Undena Publications, 1978).

Carpenter, Nathanael, *Geography Delineated Forth in Two Books* (Oxford, 1625).

Cerone, Daniel, 'Admitting "Noah's Ark" Hoax: Television: A man who claimed on a CBS special to have located the ark now says it was a set up,' *Los Angeles Times*, October 30, 1993. Available at www.latimes.com/archives/la-xpm-1993-10-30-ca-51222-story.html.

Chaffey, Tim, 'Has the Ark Been Found?,' *Answers in Genesis*. Available at https://answersingenesis.org/noahs-ark/noahs-ark-found/has-ark-been-found/?aigcb=9218.

Chaffey, Tim, and K. Marie Adams, *Noah: Man of Destiny* (Green Forest, AR: Master Books, 2016).

Chaffey, Tim, and K. Marie Adams, *Noah: Man of Resolve* (Green Forest, AR: Master Books, 2017).

Chaffey, Tim, and K. Marie Adams, *Noah: Man of God* (Green Forest, AR: Master Books, 2018).

Chaffey, Tim, and Mike Belknap, *Ark Signs That Teach a Flood of Answers* (Green Forest, AR: Master Books, 2017).

Chaffey, Tim, and Mike Belknap, *Journey through the Ark Encounter* (Green Forest, AR: New Leaf Publishing, 2017).

Charlesworth, James H., *The Old Testament Pseudepigrapha Volume 1: Apocalyptic Literature and Testaments* (New York: Doubleday, 1983).

Coan, Frederick G., *Yesterdays in Persia and Kurdistan* (Claremont, CA: Saunders Studio Press, 1939).

Cogley, Richard W., 'The Ancestry of the American Indians: Thomas Thorowgood's *Iewes in America* (1650) and *Jews in America* (1660),' *English Literary Renaissance* 35 (2005), pp. 304–30.

Cohen, A. (trans.), '*Aboth D'Rabbi Nathan*, in *The Minor Tractates of the Talmud... Volume One* (London: The Soncino Press, 1965).

Colson, F. H. (trans.), *Philo: Volume VIII* (Cambridge, MA: Harvard University Press, 1939).

Colson, F. H. (trans.), *Philo: Volume IX* (Cambridge, MA: Harvard University Press, 1954).

Colson, F. H., and G. H. Whitaker (trans.), *Philo Volume I* (Cambridge, MA: Harvard University Press, 1929).

Colson F. H., and G. H. Whitaker (trans.), *Philo Volume III* (Cambridge, MA: Harvard University Press, 1930).

*Contra Celsum (Origen)*. Available at www.newadvent.org/fathers/04164.htm.

Cooke, John Daniel, 'Euhemerism: A Mediaeval Interpretation of Classical Paganism,' *Speculum* 2 (1927), pp. 396–410.

Coxe, A. Cleveland (ed.), *Dialogue of Justin, Philosopher and Martyr, with Trypho, a Jew*, in *ANF*, vol. 1.

Coxe, A. Cleveland (ed.), *The Second Apology of Justin*, in *ANF*, vol. 1.

Coxe, A. Cleveland (ed.), *The Stromata, or Miscellanies*, in *ANF*, vol. 2.

Cumberland, Richard, *Origenes Gentium Antiquissimae; or Attempts for Discovering the Times of the first Planting of Nations in Several Tracts* (London, 1724), p. 150. Available

at https://babel.hathitrust.org/cgi/pt?id=uc2.ark:/13960/t4z
g6xn3t&seq=194.

Cutler, Alan, *The Seashell on the Mountaintop: Nicolaus Steno –
The Unsung Genius Who Invented Geology, Turned Science and
Religion Upside-Down, and Forever Changed Human
Understanding* (London: Penguin, 2003).

Cuvier, George, *Cuvier's Animal Kingdom...* (London: Wm.
S. Orr and Co., 1840).

Danielou, Jean, *From Shadows to Reality: Studies in the Biblical
Typology of the Fathers* (London: Burns and Oates, 1960).

Darwin, Charles, *The Descent of Man* (Princeton, NJ: Princeton
University Press, 2008).

Davidson, John (trans.), *Montesquieu: Persian Letters* (London:
George Routledge & Sons Ltd., 1891).

Davies, Edward, *Celtic Researches, on the Origin, Traditions &
Language of the Ancient Britons* (London, 1804).

Davies, Edward, *The Mythology and Rites of the British Druids*
(London: J. Booth, 1809).

Day, John, *From Creation to Babel: Studies in Genesis 1-11*
(London: Bloomsbury, 2013).

Dean, Dennis R., 'The Age of the Earth Controversy:
Beginnings to Hutton,' *Annals of Science* 38 (1981),
pp. 435–456.

Deferrari, Roy J. (trans.), *Saint Ambrose: Theological and
Dogmatic Works* (Washington, DC: The Catholic
University of America Press, 1963).

Delany, Patrick, *Revelation Examined with Candour... third edition* (London, 1735).

Dickenson, Edmund, 'Diatriba de Noae in Italiam Adventu,'
appendix to *Delphi Phoenicizantes* (Oxford, 1655).

Dods, Marcus (trans.), *St. Augustin's City of God*, in *NPNF (First
Series)*, vol. 2.

Dods, Marcus (trans.), *Theophilus to Autolycus*, in *ANF*, vol. 2.

Droge, A. J., *The Qur'ān: A New Annotated Translation*
(Sheffield: Equinox, 2014).

Eco, Umberto, *The Search for the Perfect Language* (Oxford: Blackwell, 1995).

Eliot, George, *Middlemarch: A Study of Provincial Life, vol. 1* (Edinburgh and London: William Blackwood and Sons, 1871).

Elliott, John H., *1 Peter: A New Translation with Introduction and Commentary* (New York: Doubleday, 2000).

Elrington, Charles Richard (ed.), *The Whole Works of the Most Rev. James Ussher, D.D.* (Dublin: Hodges, Smith, and Co., 1864).

Emery, Clark, 'John Wilkins and Noah's Ark,' *Modern Language Quarterly* 9 (1948), pp. 286–291.

Enenkel, Karl A. E., 'The Species and Beyond: Classification and the Place of Hybrids in Early Modern Biology,' in Karl A. E. Enenkel and Paul J. Smith (eds.), *Zoology in Early Modern Culture: Intersections of Science, Theology, Philology, and Political and Religious Education* (Leiden: Brill, 2014), pp. 57–148.

Epstein, I. (ed.), *Sanhedrin Translated into English...* Available at https://halakhah.com/sanhedrin/index.html.

Eshel, Esther, 'The Noah Cycle in the Genesis Apocryphon,' in Michael E. Stone, Aryeh Amihay, and Vered Hillel (eds.), *Noah and His Book(s)* (Atlanta, GA: Society of Biblical Literature, 2010), pp. 77–96.

Feingold, Mordechai, and Jed Z. Buchwald, *Newton and the Origin of Civilization* (Princeton, NJ: Princeton University Press, 2013).

Feldman, Louis H., 'Josephus' Portrait of Noah and Its Parallels in Philo, Pseudo-Philo's *Biblical Antiquities*, and Rabbinic Midrashim,' *Proceedings of the American Academy of Jewish Research* 55 (1988), pp. 31–57.

Feldman, Louis H., 'Questions about the Great Flood, as Viewed by Philo, Pseudo-Philo, Josephus, and the Rabbis,' *Zeitschrift für die Alttestamentliche Wissenschaft* 115 (2006), pp. 401–422.

Fonrobert, Charlotte Elisheva, and Martin S. Jaffee, 'Introduction,' in Charlotte Elisheva Fonrobert and Martin

S. Jaffee (eds.), *The Cambridge Companion to the Talmud and Rabbinic Literature* (Cambridge: Cambridge University Press, 2007), pp. 1–14.

Force, James E., *William Whiston: Honest Newtonian* (Cambridge: Cambridge University Press, 2002).

Foster, Nicholas Ryan, 'The *Imago Mundi* of Honorius Augustodunensis,' Master of Arts thesis, Portland State University, 2008.

Frazer, James George (trans.), *Apollodorus: The Library, Volume 1: Books 1-39* (Cambridge, MA: Harvard University Press, 1921).

Freedman, H., and Maurice Simon (trans.), *Midrash Rabbah: Genesis in Two Volumes, I* (London: The Soncino Press, 1939).

Fremantle, W. H., et al. (trans.), *Letter XXII*, in *NPNF (Second Series)*, vol. 6.

Fremantle, W. H., et al. (trans.), *Letter LXIX*, in *NPNF (Second Series)*, vol. 6.

Fremantle, W. H., et al. (trans.), *The Dialogue Against the Luciferians*, in *NPNF (Second Series)*, vol. 6.

Friedlander, Gerald (trans.), *Pirkei de Rabbi Eliezer: (The Chapters of Rabbi Eliezer the Great)* (London: Kegan Paul, Trench, Trübner & Co. Ltd, 1916).

Frodsham, J. D., 'Chinese and the Primitive Language: John Webb's Contribution to 17th Century Sinology,' *Asian Studies* 2 (1964), pp. 389–390.

Garcia, Gregorio, *Origen de los Indios de el Nuevo Mundo, e Indias Occidental* (Madrid, 1729). Available at www.digitale-sammlungen.de/en/view/bsb10211329?page = 5.

Gatterer, Johann Christoph, *Einleitung in die synchronistische Universalhistorie* (Göttingen: Verlag der Wittwe Vandenhoek, 1771).

Geljon, Albert C., 'Philo's Interpretation of Noah,' in Michael E. Stone, Aryeh Amihay, and Vered Hillel (eds.), *Noah and His Book(s)* (Atlanta, GA: Society of Biblical Literature, 2010), pp. 183–191.

George, Wilma, 'Sources and Background to Discoveries of New Animals in the Sixteenth and Seventeenth Centuries,' *History of Science* 18 (1980), pp. 79–104.

Goodman, Ailene S., 'The Extraordinary Being: Death and the Mermaid in Baroque Culture,' *Journal of Popular Culture* 17 (1983), pp. 32–48.

Goodman, Godfrey, *The Fall of Man, or the Corruption of Nature...* (London, 1616).

Gordon, Matthew S., et al. (eds.), *The History (Taʾrīkh): Adam to Pre-Islamic Arabia* in *The Works of Ibn Wāḍiḥ al-Yaʾqūbī: An English Translation, Volume* 2 (Leiden: Brill, 2018).

Grafton, Anthony, '1. Inventio of Traditions and Traditions of Invention in Renaissance Europe: The Strange Case of Annius of Viterbo,' in Ann Blair and Anthony Grafton (eds.), *The Transmission of Culture in Early Modern Europe* (Philadelphia: University of Pennsylvania Press, 2010), pp. 8–38.

Greenfield, Jonas C., Michael E. Stone, and Esther Eshel, *The Aramaic Levi Document: Edition, Translation, Commentary* (Leiden: Brill, 2004).

Greenhalgh, John Eric, 'The Iconography of Noah's Ark,' Master of Arts thesis, Wayne State University, 1982.

von Greyerz, Kaspar, *European Physico-Theology (1650–c.1750) in Context* (Oxford: Oxford University Press, 2022).

Griffith, Tim, and Natali Miller (trans.), *Johannes Buteo's The Shape and Capacity of Noah's Ark* (Eugene, OR: Wipf & Stock, 2008).

Grose, Francis, 'Stonehenge, Wiltshire,' *The Antiquities of England and Wales* (London, 1773–1787).

Haber, Francis C., *The Age of the World: Moses to Darwin* (Baltimore: Johns Hopkins Press, 1959).

Hale, Matthew, *The Primitive Origination of Mankind, Considered and Examined According to the Light of Nature* (London, 1677).

Haller, Jr., John S., 'The Species Problem: Nineteenth-Century Concepts of Racial Inferiority in the Origin of

Man Controversy,' *American Anthropologist* 72 (1970), pp. 1319–1329.

Halley, Edmond, 'A short Account of the Cause of the Saltness of the Ocean, and of the several Lakes that emit no Rivers...,' *Philosophical Transactions* 29 (1714), pp. 296–300.

Halley, Edmond, 'Some Considerations about the Cause of the Universal Deluge, Laid before the Royal Society, on the 12th of December 1694,' *Philosophical Transactions* 33 (1724), pp. 118–123.

Halley, Edmond, 'Some farther Thoughts upon the same Subject delivered on the 19th of the same Month,' *Philosophical Transactions* 33 (1724), pp. 123–125.

Hamilton, Edith, and Huntington Cairns (eds.), *The Collected Dialogues of Plato* (Princeton, NJ: Princeton University Press, 1961).

Harrison, Peter, *The Bible, Protestantism, and the Rise of Natural Science* (Cambridge: Cambridge University Press, 1998).

Harrison, Peter, 'Linnaeus as a Second Adam? Taxonomy and the Religious Vocation,' *Zygon* 44 (2009), pp. 879–893.

Haynes, Stephen R., *Noah's Curse: The Biblical Justification of American Slavery* (Oxford: Oxford University Press, 2002).

Hays, Christopher B. (ed.), *Hidden Riches: A Sourcebook for the Comparative Study of the Hebrew Bible and Ancient Near East* (Louisville, KY: Westminster John Knox Press, 2014).

Hayward, James L., 'Fossil Proboscidians and Myths of Giant Men,' *Transactions of the Nebraska Academy of Sciences and Affiliated Societies*, 12 (1984), pp. 95–102.

Heine, Ronald E. (trans.), *Origen: Homilies on Genesis and Exodus* (Washington, DC: The Catholic University of America Press, 1981).

Henderson, Jeffrey (ed.), F. H. Colson, and G. H. Whitaker (trans.), 'On the Giants,' *Philo II* (Cambridge, MA: Harvard University Press, 1929).

Henderson, Jeffrey (ed.) and F. H. Colson (trans.), *Philo VI* (Cambridge, MA: Harvard University Press, 1935).

Hill, Robert C. (trans.), *Saint John Chrysostom: Homilies on Genesis 18-45* (Washington, DC: The Catholic University Press of America, 2010).

Hodoba Eric, Cindy, 'Metamorphoses: Seventeenth-Century Ideas on Fossils and Earth History.' Doctor of Philosophy thesis, The University of Sydney, 2023.

Holford-Stevens, Lefranc, 'Sirens in Antiquity and the Middle Ages,' in Inna Naroditskaya and Linda Phyllis Austern (eds.), *Music of the Sirens* (Bloomington: Indiana University Press, 2006), pp. 16–51.

Huddleston, Lee Eldridge, *Origins of the American Indians: European Concepts, 1492–1729, Kobo Edition* (Austin: University of Texas Press, 1967).

Hungerford, Edward B., *The Shores of Darkness* (New York: Columbia University Press, 1941).

Hutton, James, 'Theory of the Earth,' *Transactions of the Royal Society of Edinburgh* 1 (1788), pp. 209–304.

Ibn Kathīr, *Stories of the Prophets* (Kindle edition).

Israel, Menasseh ben, *The Hope of Israel* (London, 1650).

Israelstam, J. (trans.), *Midrash Rabbah... Leviticus* (London: Soncino Press, 1939).

Jackson, Jr., John P., and Nadine M. Weidman, *Race, Racism, and Science: Social Impact and Interaction* (Santa Barbara, CA: ABC-CLIO, 2004).

Jammal, George, 'Hoaxing the Hoaxers: or, The Incredible (phony) Discovery of Noah's Ark,' *Atheist Alliance*, 11 September 2007. Available at https://web.archive.org/web/20070911024306/http://atheistalliance.org/library/jammal-hoaxing.php.

Jaroff, Leon, 'Phony Arkaeology,' *Time*, 5 July 1993. Available at https://content.time.com/time/subscriber/article/0,33009,978812-1,00.html

Johink, Eric, 'Snakes, Fungi and Insects. Otto Marseus van Schriek, Johannes Swammerdam and the Theory of Spontaneous Generation,' in Karl A. E. Enenkel and Paul J. Smith (eds.), *Zoology in Early Modern Culture: Intersections of*

*Science, Theology, Philology, and Political and Religious Education* (Leiden: Brill, 2014), pp. 197–230.

Johns, Anthony H., 'Prophets and Personalities of the Qur'an,' in Mustafa Shah and Muhammad Abdel Haleem (eds.), *The Oxford Handbook of Qur'anic Studies* (Oxford: Oxford University Press, 2020), pp. 488–501.

Johnson, Franklin, 'Fallacies of the Higher Criticism,' in [Lyman Stewart and Milton Stewart] (eds.), *The Fundamentals* (Chicago: Testimony Publishing Company, 1910), pp. 48–68.

Jones, Rowland, *The Origin of Language and Nations...* (London, 1764).

Jones, William, 'On the Gods of Greece, Italy, and India...', *Asiatic Researches*, 1 (1788), pp. 221–275.

Jones, William, *The Works of Sir William Jones* (London, 1799).

Jue, Jeffrey K., *Heaven upon Earth: Joseph Mede (1586–1638) and the Legacy of Millenarianism* (Dordrecht: Springer, 2006).

Kamesar, Adam, 'Biblical Interpretation in Philo,' in Adam Kamesar (ed.), *The Cambridge Companion to Philo* (Cambridge: Cambridge University Press, 2009), pp. 65–91.

Keynes, Geoffrey (ed.), *Poetry and Prose of William Blake* (Bloomsbury, IN: The Nonesuch Press, 1923).

Kidd, Colin, *The Forging of Races: Race and Scripture in the Protestant Atlantic World, 1600–2000* (Cambridge: Cambridge University Press, 2006).

Kidd, Colin, *The World of Mr Casaubon: Britain's Wars of Mythography, 1700–1870* (Cambridge: Cambridge University Press, 2016).

Kidder, Richard, *A Commentary on the Five Books of Moses* (London, 1694).

Kircher, Athanasius, *Arca Noë in Tres Libros Digesta...* (Amstelodami, 1675). Available at https://archive.org/details/athanasiikircherookirc_9/page/n5/mode/2up.

Kircher, Athanasius, *Turris Babel...* (Amsterdam, 1679). Available at https://archive.org/details/turrisbabelsiveaookirc/page/n5/mode/2up.

Kirwan, Richard, *Geological Essays* (London, 1799).

Kocher, Paul H., *Christopher Marlowe: A Study of His Thought, Learning, and Character* (Chapel Hill: University of North Carolina Press, 1946).

Koester, Craig R., *Hebrews: A New Translation with Introduction and Commentary* (New York: Doubleday, 2001).

LaHaye, Tim F., and John D. Morris, *The Ark on Ararat* (Nashville, TN/New York: Thomas Nelson Inc. Publishers and Creation-Life Publishers, 1976).

Lambert W. G., and A. R. Millard, *Atra-hasis: The Babylonian Story of the Flood* (Oxford: Clarendon Press, 1969).

Lang, Bernhard, 'Non-Semitic Deluge Stories and the Book of Genesis: A Bibliographical and Critical Survey,' *Anthropos* 80 (1985), pp. 605–616.

Lansdowne, The Marquis of, *The Petty-Southwell Correspondence 1676–1687* (New York: Augustus M. Kelley, 1967).

La Peyrère, Isaac, *Men before Adam. . .* (London, 1656).

Leicht, Reimund, 'Gnostic Myth in Jewish Garb,' *Journal of Jewish Studies* 51 (2000), pp. 133–140.

Lescarbot, Marc, *History of New France, Vol. 1* (Toronto: The Champlain Society, 1907).

L'Estrange, Hamon, *Americans no Iewes, or Improbabilities that the Americans are of that Race* (London, 1651/2).

Lewis, Jack P., *A Study of the Interpretation of Noah and the Flood in Jewish and Christian Literature* (Leiden: Brill, 1978).

Linnaeus, (Carl), 'Dissertation II, On the Increase of the Habitable Earth,' in F. J. Brand (trans.), *Select Dissertations from the Amoenitates Academicae, a Supplement to Mr Stillingfleet's Tracts relating to Natural History* (London, 1781), vol. 2, pp. 71–127.

Lippard, Jim, 'Sun goes down in Flames: The Jammal Ark Hoax,' *Skeptic* 2 (1993). Available at www.talkorigins.org/faqs/ark-hoax/jammal.html.

Lister, Martin, 'A Letter of Mr. *Martin Lister*, written at York *August 25 1671*,' *Philosophical Transactions* 6 (1671), pp. 2281–2284.

Lombardo, Stanley (trans.), *Ovid: Metamorphoses* (Indianapolis, IN/Cambridge: Hackett Publishing Company, 2010).

Lowrie, Walter, *Monuments of the Early Church* (New York: MacMillan and Company, 1901).

Lunn, Nicholas P. (trans.), *St. Cyril of Alexandria: Glaphyra on the Pentateuch, Volume 1, Genesis* (Washington, DC: The Catholic University of America Press, 2019).

Luttikhuizen, Gerard P., 'Biblical Narrative in Gnostic Revision: The Story of Noah and the Flood in Classic Gnostic Mythology,' in Florentino Garcia Martínez and Gerard P. Luttikhuizen (eds.), *Interpretations of the Flood* (Leiden: Brill, 1998), pp. 109–123.

MacCulloch, J. L., *The Harrowing of Hell: A Comparative Study of an Early Christian Doctrine* (Edinburgh: T. & T. Clark, 1930).

Machiela, Daniel A., *The Dead Sea Genesis Apocryphon: A New Text and Translation with Introduction and Special Treatment of Columns 13-17* (Leiden: Brill, 2009).

Maher, Michael (trans.), *Targum Pseudo-Jonathan: Genesis* (Edinburgh: T. & T. Clark, 1992).

Mangan, Jane E. (ed.), *Natural and Moral History of the Indies: José de Acosta* (Durham, NC: Duke University Press, 2002).

Mangenot, E., 'Arche de Noé,' in F. Vigoroux (ed.), *Dictionnaire De La Bible* (Paris: Letouzey et Ané, 1912).

Manuel, Frank E., *Isaac Newton Historian* (Cambridge, MA: The Belknap Press, 1963).

Marcus, Ralph (trans.), *Philo: Questions and Answers on Genesis* (Cambridge, MA: Harvard University Press, 1953).

Martens, Peter W., 'Revisiting the Allegory/Typology Distinction: The case of Origen,' *Journal of Early Christian Studies* 16 (2008), pp. 283–317.

Martínez, Florentino Garcia, 'Interpretations of the Flood in the Dead Sea Scrolls,' in Florentino Garcia Martínez and Gerard P. Luttikhuizen (eds.), *Interpretations of the Flood* (Leiden: Brill, 1998), pp. 86–108.

Mason, Steve, '"Should any wish to enquire further" (Ant.1.25): The Aim and Audience of Josephus's *Jewish Antiquities/Life*,' in Steve Mason (ed.), *Understanding Josephus: Seven Perspectives* (Sheffield: Sheffield Academic Press, 1998), pp. 64–103.

Mateos, Francisco (ed.), *Obras del P. Bernabé Cobo* (Madrid: Atlas, 1964).

Mathews, Edward G., and Joseph P. Amar (trans.) and Kathleen McVey (ed.), *St. Ephrem the Syrian: Selected Prose Works* (Washington, DC: The Catholic University Press of America, 1994).

McGuire, Anne, 'Virginity and Subversion: Norea against the Powers in the *Hypostasis of the Archons*, in K. L. King (ed.), *Images of the Feminine in Gnosticism* (Philadelphia: Fortress Press, 1988), pp. 239–258.

McNamara, Martin (trans.), *Targum Neofiti 1: Genesis* (Edinburgh: T. & T. Clark, 1992).

Means, Philip Ainsworth (trans.), *Memorias Antiguas Historiales del Peru by Fernando Montesinos* (London: Hakluyt Society, 1920).

Mede, Joseph, *The Works of the Pious and Profoundly-Learned Joseph Mede, B.D.* (London, 1777).

Menzies, Allan (ed.), *The First Epistle of Clement to the Corinthians*, 7, in *ANF*, vol. 9.

Minov, Sergey, 'Noah and the Flood in Gnosticism,' in Michael E. Stone, Aryeh Amihay, and Vered Hillel (eds.), *Noah and His Book(s)* (Atlanta, GA: Society of Biblical Literature, 2010), pp. 215–236.

Montgomery, John Warwick, *The Quest for Noah's Ark: A Treasury of Documented Accounts from Ancient Times to the Present Day of the Ark...* (Minneapolis, MN: Bethany Fellowship, Inc., 1972).

Morris, John D., *Noah's Ark: Adventures on Ararat* (Dallas, TX: Institute for Creation Research, 2014).

Nelson, Gareth, 'From Candolle to Croizat: Comments on the History of Biogeography,' *Journal of the History of Biology* 11 (1978), pp. 269–305.

Newby, Gordon D., 'The Drowned Son: Midrash and Midrash Making in the Quran and *Tafsir*,' in Stephen David Ricks (ed.), *Studies in Islamic and Judaic Traditions: Papers Presented at the Institute for Islamic-Judaic Studies, University of Denver* (Atlanta, GA: Scholars Press, 1986), vol. 2, pp. 19–32.

Newby, Gordon Darnell, *The Making of the Last Prophet* (Columbia: University of South Carolina Press, 1989).

Newton, Isaac, 'Chap. 1. Of the Times before the Assyrian Empire.' Ms. 361(2), New College Library, Oxford, UK. Available at www.newtonproject.ox.ac.uk/view/texts/diplomatic/THEM00097.

Newton, Isaac, 'Draft Chapters of a Treatise on the Origin of Religion and Its Corruption,' Yahuda Ms. 41, National Library of Israel, Jerusalem, Israel. Available at www.newtonproject.ox.ac.uk/view/texts/normalized/THEM00077.

Newton, Isaac, 'Miscellaneous Portions of "Theologiae Gentilis Origines Philosophicae,"' Yahuda Ms. 16.2. Available at www.newtonproject.ox.ac.uk/view/translation/TRAN00010.

Nickelsburg, George W. E., *A Commentary on the Book of 1 Enoch, Chapters 1-36; 81-108* (Minneapolis, MN: Fortress Press, 2001).

Nickelsburg, George W. E., and James C. Vanderkam, *A Commentary on the Book of 1 Enoch, Chapters 37-82* (Minneapolis, MN: Fortress Press, 2012).

Nierembergii, Juan Eusebio, *Historia Naturae, Maxime Peregrine* (Antwerp, 1635).

Noorbergen, Rene, *The Ark File* (Mountain View, CA: Pacific Press Publishing Association, 1974).

Noort, Ed, 'The Stories of the Great Flood: Notes on Genesis 6:5-9:17 in its Context of the Ancient Near East,' in Florentino Garcia Martinez and Gerard P. Luttikhuizen (eds.), *Interpretations of the Flood* (Leiden: Brill, 1998), pp. 1–38.

Nott, J. C., and G. R. Gliddon, *Indigenous Races of the Earth* (Philadelphia and London: F.B. Lippincott & Co. and Trübner & Co., 1857).

Numbers, Ronald L., *The Creationists: From Scientific Creationism to Intelligent Design* (Cambridge, MA: Harvard University Press, 2006).

Parrott, Friedrich, *Journey to Ararat* (New York: Harper & Brothers Publishers, 1859).

Parry, Glyn, 'Berosus and the Protestants: Reconstructing Protestant Myth,' *Huntington Library Quarterly* 64 (2001), pp. 1–21.

Parry, Graham, *The Trophies of Time* (Oxford: Oxford University Press, 2007).

Patrick, Symon, *A Commentary upon the Historical Books of the Old Testament* (London, 1732).

Patrides, C. A., 'Renaissance Estimates of the Year of Creation,' *Huntington Library Quarterly* 26 (1963), pp. 315–322.

Pererius, Benedict, *Commentarium et Disputationum in Genesim, Tomus Secundus* (Rome, 1592).

Petty, William, *Another Essay in Political Arithmetic, Concerning the Growth of the City of London* (London, 1683).

Pezron, Paul-Yves, *The Antiquities of Nations; More particularly of the Celtae or Gauls* (London, 1706).

Piggott, Stuart, *The Druids* (London: Thames & Hudson, 1996).

Plot, Robert, *The Natural History of Oxford-shire, Being an Essay toward the Natural History of England* (Oxford, 1677).

Popper, Nicholas, *Walter Ralegh's History of the World and the Historical Culture of the Late Renaissance* (Chicago: University of Chicago Press, 2012).

Price, George McReady, *The New Geology: A Textbook for Colleges, Normal Schools, and Training Schools; and for the General Reader* (Mountain View, CA: Pacific Press Publishing Association, 1923).

Price, George McReady, *The Phantom of Organic Evolution* (New York: Fleming H. Revell Company, 1924).

Price, George McReady, *The Modern Flood Theory of Geology* (New York: Fleming H. Revell Company, 1935).

Prideaux, Mathias, *Introduction for Reading all Sorts of Histories* (Oxford, 1655).

Prieto, Andrés I., 'Reading the Book of Genesis in the New World: José de Acosta and Bernabé Cobo on the Origins of the American Indians,' *Hispanófila* 158 (Enero 2010), pp. 1–19.

von Rad, Gerhard, *Genesis: A Commentary* (Philadelphia: Westminster Press, 1972).

Raleigh, Walter, *The Historie of the World in Five Bookes...* (London, 1621).

Religious of C.S.M.V., A (trans.), *Hugh of Saint-Victor: Selected Spiritual Writings* (New York and Evanston, IL: Harper and Row, 1962).

Rendsburg, Gary A., 'The Biblical Flood in the Light of the Gilgamesh Flood Account,' in J. Azize and N. Weeks (eds.), *Gilgamesh and the World of Assyria: Proceedings of the Conference Held at Mandelbaum House, The University of Sydney. 21–23 July 2004* (Leuven: Peeters, 2007), pp. 115–127.

Reynolds, Gabriel Said, 'Noah's Lost Son in the Qur'ān,' *Arabica*, 64 (2017), pp. 129–148.

Robbins, Robin (ed.), *Sir Thomas Browne's Pseudodoxia Epidemica* (Oxford: Clarendon, 1981).

de Romestin, H. (trans.), *On the Duties of the Clergy*, in *NPNF (Second Series)*, vol. 10.

de Romestin, H. (trans.), *On the Mysteries*, in *NPNF (Second Series)*, vol. 10.

Rosenbaum, M., and A. M. Silbermann (trans.), 'Rashi on Genesis,' in *Pentateuch with Targum Onkelos, Haphtaroth and Prayers for Sabbath and Rashi's Commentary* (London: Shapiro and Vallentine & Co., 1929–1934). Available at www.sefaria.org/Rashi_on_Genesis?tab = contents.

Rosenthal, Franz (trans.), *The History of al-Ṭabarī: Volume 1* (Albany: State University of New York Press, 1989).

Rossetter, Thomas, 'The Theorist: Thomas Burnet and His Sacred History of the Earth', Doctor of Philosophy thesis, Durham University, 2019.

Rossi, Paolo, *Dark Abyss of Time: The History of the Earth and the History of Nations from Hooke to Vico* (Chicago: The University of Chicago Press, 1984).

Rothstein, Marian, 'The Reception of Annius of Viterbo's Forgeries: The *Antiquities* in Renaissance France,' *Renaissance Quarterly* 71 (2018), pp. 580–609.

Rowlands, Henry, *Mona Antiqua Restaurata: An Archaeological Discourse on the Antiquities Natural and Historical of the Isle of Anglesey, the Antient Seat of the British Druids* (Dublin, 1723).

Rudwick, Martin J. S., *The Meaning of Fossils: Episodes in the History of Palaeontology* (London and New York: Macdonald and American Elsevier Inc., 1972).

Runia, David T., 'Philo and the Early Christian Fathers,' in Adam Kamesar (ed.), *The Cambridge Companion to Philo* (Cambridge: Cambridge University Press, 2009), pp. 210–230.

*Sahih al-Bukhari.* Available at https://sunnah.com/search?q=noah.

Salmond, S. D. F. (trans.), *Fragments from Commentaries on Various Books of Scriptures*, in *ANF*, vol. 5.

Sammes, Aylett, *Britannia Antiqua Illustrata: or the Antiquities of Ancient Britain derived from the Phœnicians* (London, 1727).

Sandys, George, 'Journey begun 1610,' in *Purchas His Pilgrimes in Five Bookes* (London, 1625).

Sayle, Charles (ed.), 'Of Languages,' in *The Works of Sir Thomas Browne, Vol. 1* (London: Grant Richards, 1904).

Sayle, Charles (ed.), *Pseudodoxia Epidemica* in *The Works of Sir Thomas Browne, Vol. 2* (London: Grant Richards, 1904).

Sayle, Charles (ed.), *Religio Medici* in *The Works of Sir Thomas Browne, Vol. 1* (London: Grant Richards, 1904).

Schellerup, Henning, 'The Incredible Discovery of Noah's Ark' (1992). Available at https://archive.org/details/the-incredible-discovery-of-noahs-ark-1992.

Scheuchzeri, Jacobi, *Physica Sacra* (Augsburg and Ulm, 1731).

Scheuchzero, Johanne Jacobo, *Piscium Querelae et Vindiciae* (Zürich, 1708).

Schlözer, August Ludwig, 'Von den Chaldäern,' *Repertorium für Biblische und Morgenländische Litteratur* 8 (1781), pp. 113–176.

Schmidt, Brian B., 'Flood Narratives of Ancient Western Asia,' in Jack M. Sasson et al. (eds.), *Civilizations of the Ancient Near East* (Peabody, MA: Hendrickson, 1995), vol. 4, pp. 2337–2351.

Sedgwick, Adam, 'Address to the Geological Society, delivered on the Evening of the 18th of February 1831. . .,' *Proceedings of the Geological Society of London* 1 (1834), pp. 281–316.

Shalev, Zur, *Sacred Words and Worlds* (Leiden: Brill, 2011).

Shnorhokian, Roubina, 'Hayton of Korykos and *La Flor des Estoires*: Cilician Armenian Mediation in Crusader-Mongol Politics, c. 1250–1350,' Doctor of Philosophy thesis, Queen's University, 2015.

Shuckford, Samuel, *The Sacred and Prophane History of the World Connected. . .* (London, 1731).

Slotki, Judah J. (trans.), *Midrash Rabbah: Numbers* (London: Soncino Press, 1939).

Slotkin, James S. (ed.), *Readings in Early Anthropology* (Chicago: Aldine Publishing Company, 1965).

Smalley, Beryl, *The Study of the Bible in the Middle Ages* (Oxford: Basil Blackwell, 1952).

Smith, George, 'The Chaldean Account of the Deluge,' *Transactions of the Society of Biblical Archaeology* 2 (1873), pp. 213–234.

Smith, James Edward (trans.), *Reflections on the Study of Nature: Translated from the Latin of the Celebrated Linnaeus* (London, 1785).

Smith, John, *Galic Antiquities: Consisting of the History of the Druids. . .* (Edinburgh: T. Cadell and C. Elliot, 1780).

Smith, R. Scott, 'Bundling Myth, Bungling Myth: The Flood Myth in Ancient and Modern Handbooks of Myth,' *Archiv für Religionsgeschichte* 16 (2015), pp. 243–262.

Snyder, Edward D., *The Celtic Revival in English Literature* (Cambridge, MA: Harvard University Press, 1923).

Stephens, Luke J. (trans.), *Gregory of Elvira: On Noah's Ark (De Arca Noe)*, 33. Available at file:///C:/Users/repalmon/Downloads/Gregory_of_Elvira_On_Noahs_Ark_De_arca_N.pdf.

Stephens, Walter, 'Berosus Chaldaeus: Counterfeit and Fictive Editors of the Early Sixteenth Century.' PhD thesis, Cornell University, 1979.

Stephens, Walter, *Giants in Those Days: Folklore, Ancient History, and Nationalism* (Lincoln: University of Nebraska Press, 1989).

Stephens, Walter, 'When Pope Noah Ruled the Etruscans: Annius of Viterbo and His Forged Antiquities,' *MLN* 119 Supplement (2004), pp. S201–S223.

Stephens, Walter, 'Complex Pseudonymity: Annius of Viterbo's Multiple Persona Disorder,' *MLN* 126 (2011), pp. 689–708.

Stillingfleet, Edward, *Origines Sacrae: Or A Rational Account of the Grounds of Natural and Revealed Religion* (Cambridge, 1702).

Stone, Michael E., 'The Axis of History at Qumran,' in Esther G. Chazon and Michael E. Stone with Avital Pinnick, *Pseudepigraphic Perspectives: The Apocrypha and Pseudepigrapha in Light of the Dead Sea Scrolls* (Leiden: Brill, 1999), pp. 133–149.

Stone, Michael E., 'The Book(s) Attributed to Noah,' in Michael E. Stone, Aryeh Amihay, and Vered Hillel (eds.), *Noah and His Book(s)* (Atlanta, GA: Society of Biblical Literature, 2010), pp. 7–26.

Stothert, R. (trans.), *Reply to Faustus the Manichaean*, in *NPNF (First Series)*, vol. 4.

Strong, H. A. (trans.), and John Garstang (ed.), *Lucian's On the Syrian Goddess* (Oxford, OH: Faenum Publishing, 2013).

Stroumsa, Guy G., 'Noah's Sons and the Religious Conquest of the Earth: Samuel Bochart and His Followers,' in Martin

Mulsow and Jan Assman (eds.), *Sintflut und Gedächtnis* (Munich: Fink, 2006), pp. 307–318.

Stukeley, William, *Stonehenge: A Temple Restored to the British Druids* (London, 1740).

Tanner, J. R. (ed), *Samuel Pepys's Naval Minutes* (London: The Navy Records Society, 1926).

Thackeray, H. St. J. (trans.), *Josephus: Jewish Antiquities, Books i-iv* (Cambridge, MA: Harvard University Press, 1930).

Thackston, Wheeler M. Jr. (trans.), *Tales of the Prophets (Qiṣaṣ al-anbiyā': Muḥammad ibn 'Abd Allāh al-Kisā'i)* (Chicago: Great Books of the Islamic World, 1997).

Thelwall, S. (trans.), *On Baptism*, in *ANF*, vol. 3.

Thelwall, S. (trans.), *On Idolatry*, in *ANF*, vol. 3.

Thelwall, S. (trans.), *On Monogamy*, in *ANF*, vol. 4.

Thorowgood, Thomas, *Iewes in America, or, Probabilities that the Americans are of that Race...* (London, 1650).

Todd, Ruthven, *Tracks in the Snow: Studies in English Science and Art* (London: The Grey Walls Press, 1946).

Toulmin, Stephen and June Goodfield, *The Discovery of Time* (Chicago: The University of Chicago Press, 1965).

*Tractate Eruvin*, 2. Available at www.jewishvirtuallibrary.org/tractate-eruvin.

Trevor-Roper, Hugh, *Catholics, Anglicans, and Puritans: Seventeenth Century Essays* (Chicago: University of Chicago Press, 1988).

Turner, John D., 'Sethian Gnostic Speculation,' in Garry W. Trompf, Gunner B. Mikkelsen, and Jay Johnston, *The Gnostic World* (London: Routledge, 2018), pp. 147–155.

Tuttle, Hudson, *The Origin and Antiquity of Physical Man Scientifically Considered...* (Boston: W. White & Company, 1866).

Tuval, Michael, 'The Role of Noah and the Flood in *Judean Antiquities* and *Against Apion* by Flavius Josephus,' in Michael E. Stone, Aryeh Amihay, and Vered Hillel, *Noah and His Book(s)* (Atlanta, GA: Society of Biblical Literature, 2010), pp. 167–181.

Unger, Richard W., *The Art of Medieval Technology: Images of Noah the Shipbuilder* (New Brunswick, NJ: Rutgers University Press, 1991).

Ussher, James, *The Annals of the World…* (London, 1658).

Utley, Francis Lee, 'The One Hundred and Three Names of Noah's Wife,' *Speculum* 16 (1941), pp. 426–452.

Vanderkam, James C., *Jubilees: The Hermenaia Translation* (Minneapolis, MN: Augsburg Fortress Publishers, 2020).

Van Yk, Cornelis, *De Nederlandsche Scheeps-Bouw-Konst Open Gestellt* (Amsterdam, 1697).

Visotsky, Burton L., 'Genesis in Rabbinic Interpretation,' in Craig A. Evans et al. (eds.), *The Book of Genesis: Composition, Reception, and Interpretation* (Leiden: Brill, 2012), pp. 579–606.

Waldstein, Michael, and Frederik Wisse, 'The Apocryphon of John, 24, *The Gnostic Society Library: The Nag Hammadi Library*. Available at http://gnosis.org/naghamm/apocjn-long.html.

Webb, John, *The Antiquity of China…* (London, 1678).

Webb, John, *An Historical Essay Endeavoring a Probability that the Language of the Empire of China is the Primitive Language* (London, 1669).

Wheeler, Brannon M. (trans.), *Prophets in the Quran: An Introduction to the Quran and Muslim Exegesis* (London: Continuum, 2002).

Whiston, William, *A New Theory of the Earth, from its Original, to the Consummation of all Things* (London, 1696).

Whiston, William *A Short View of the Chronology of the Old Testament, and of the Harmony of the Four Evangelists* (London, 1702).

Whiston, William, *A New Theory of the Earth, from its Original, to the Consummation of all Things second ed.* (London, 1708).

Whiston, William, *Astronomical Principles of Religion, Natural and Reveal'd* (London, 1717).

Whiston, William (trans.), *The Antiquities of the Jews*. Available at https://en.wikisource.org/wiki/The_Antiquities_of_the_Jews/Book_I.

Whitcomb, John C., and Henry M. Morris, *The Genesis Flood: The Biblical Record and Its Scientific Implications* (Phillipsburg, NJ: P and R Publishing, 1961).

Whitford, David M., *The Curse of Ham in the Early Modern Era: The Bible and the Justifications for Slavery* (Farnham, Surrey: Ashgate, 2009).

Wilkins, John, *An Essay towards a Real Character, and a Philosophical Language* (London, 1668).

Willet, Andrew, *Hexapla in Genesin & Exodum...* (London, 1633).

Willey, Basil, *The Eighteenth Century Background: Studies on the Idea of Nature in the Thought of the Period* (London: Chatto & Windus, 1950).

Williams, Arnold, *The Common Expositor: An Account of the Commentaries on Genesis 1527–1633* (Chapel Hill: The University of North Carolina Press, 1948).

Williams, Frank (trans.), *The Panarion of Epiphanius of Salamis: Book 1 (Sects 1-46)* (Leiden: Brill, 2009).

Williams, Michael A., 'Sethianism,' in Antti Marjanen and Petri Luomanen (eds.), *A Companion to Second-Century Christian 'Heretics'* (Leiden: Brill, 2005), pp. 32–63.

Wise, Michael O., et al. (trans.), *The Dead Sea Scrolls: A New Translation* (San Francisco: Harper, 2005).

Witsen, Nicolaes, *Architectura Navalis et Regimen Nauticum* (Amsterdam, 1690).

Woodward, John, *An Essay toward a Natural History of the Earth and Terrestrial Bodies, especially Minerals...* (London, 1695).

Woodward, John, *A Supplement and Continuation of the Essay towards a Natural History of the Earth* (London, 1726).

Zalasiewicz, Jan, Anne-Sophie Milon, and Mateusz Zalasiewicz (eds. and trans.), *The Epochs of Nature* (Chicago: University of Chicago Press, 2018) (Rakuten Kobo edition).

Zinn, Grover, 'Hugh of St. Victor and the Ark of Noah: A New Look,' *Church History* 40 (1971), pp. 261–272.

# INDEX